JUDGMENT DIGESTS OF THE INTELLECTUAL PROPERTY COURT OF THE SUPREME PEOPLE'S COURT

最高人民法院知识产权法庭裁判要旨

（2022）

最高人民法院知识产权法庭　编

Edited by the Intellectual Property Court of the Supreme People's Court

人民法院出版社 | People's Court Press

图书在版编目（CIP）数据

最高人民法院知识产权法庭裁判要旨. 2022 / 最高人民法院知识产权法庭编. -- 北京 : 人民法院出版社, 2024.8

ISBN 978-7-5109-4004-0

Ⅰ. ①最… Ⅱ. ①最… Ⅲ. ①知识产权－审判－案例－中国－2022 Ⅳ. ①D923.405

中国国家版本馆CIP数据核字(2024)第012928号

最高人民法院知识产权法庭裁判要旨（2022）

最高人民法院知识产权法庭　编

责任编辑　兰丽专　丁塞峨
封面设计　天平文创视觉设计/王子莹
出版发行　人民法院出版社
地　　址　北京市东城区东交民巷 27 号（100745）
电　　话　（010）67550656（责任编辑）　67550558（发行部查询）
65223677（读者服务部）
客服 QQ　2092078039
网　　址　http://www.courtbook.com.cn
E-mail　courtpress@sohu.com
印　　刷　天津嘉恒印务有限公司
经　　销　新华书店

开　　本　787 毫米×1092 毫米　1/16
字　　数　503 千字
印　　张　29.75
版　　次　2024 年 8 月第 1 版　2024 年 8 月第 1 次印刷
书　　号　ISBN 978-7-5109-4004-0
定　　价　98.00 元

执行编辑

Executive Editors

廖继博　　徐　飞　　孔立明　　耿　希　　高　雪

Liao Jibo　　Xu Fei　　Kong Liming　　Geng Xi　　Gao Xue

翻译支持

Translation Support

中国法院知识产权司法保护国际交流（上海）基地

China Courts International Exchanges Base (Shanghai) for Judicial Protection of Intellectual Property Rights

前 言
PREFACE

为集中展示最高人民法院知识产权法庭在技术类知识产权和垄断案件中的司法理念、审理思路和裁判方法，法庭从 2022 年审结的 3468 件案件中，精选 61 个典型案例，提炼 75 条裁判要旨，形成《最高人民法院知识产权法庭裁判要旨（2022）》，现予发布，供社会各界研究和参考。

The Judgment Digests of the Intellectual Property Court of the Supreme People's Court (2022) (the Digests) is hereby released to the public for research and reference. The Digests includes 75 judgment digests extracted from 61 typical cases selected from a total of 3, 468 cases concluded by the Intellectual Property Court (the IPC) of the Supreme People's Court (the SPC) in 2022, which may collectively demonstrate the judicial philosophy, ideology and methods of the IPC in dealing with technology-related intellectual property cases and anti-monopoly cases.

目　　录

Table of Contents

一、专利行政案件
Ⅰ. Administrative Patent Cases

1. 商业方法的可专利性
Patentability of business methods

【裁判要旨】

[Judgment Digest]

判断一项涉及商业方法的解决方案是否构成专利法意义上的技术方案，应当整体考虑权利要求限定的全部内容，从方案所解决的是否是技术问题、方案是否通过实现特定技术效果来解决问题、方案中手段的集合是依靠自然规律还是人为设定的规则获得足以解决问题的效果等方面综合评估。

To determine whether a solution involving a business method constitutes a technical solution under the Patent Law, the full content of the claims should be taken into account as a whole from such aspects as whether the solution solves a technical problem, whether the solution solves the problem by achieving specific technical effects, and whether the collection of means in the solution is based on laws of nature or artificial rules to obtain sufficient effects to solve the problem.

【关键词】

[Keywords]

专利申请驳回复审　商业方法　专利保护客体　技术方案

Reexamination of rejection of patent application; business method; subject matter of patent protection; technical solution

【案号】

[Case Number]

(2021) 最高法知行终 382 号

(2021) SPC IP Admin. Final 382

【基本案情】

[Case Facts]

在上诉人西门子股份公司（以下简称西门子公司）与被上诉人国家知识产权局发明专利申请驳回复审行政纠纷案中，涉及申请号为 201580083272.5、名称为“针对处理对象的处理步骤的开启”的发明专利 PCT 申请（以下简称本申请）。国家知识产权局认为本申请权利要求 1-16 所要求保护的方案不构成技术方案，不符合专利法第二条第二款的规定，因此不能被授予专利权。西门子公司不服，向北京知识产权法院（以下简称一审法院）提起诉讼。一审法院维持被诉决定。西门子公司不服，向最高人民法院提起上诉。最高人民法院于 2022 年 11 月 10 日判决驳回上诉，维持原判。

In the administrative dispute between the appellant, Siemens AG (hereinafter referred to as “Siemens”), and the appellee, the China National Intellectual Property Administration (hereinafter referred to as the “CNIPA”), over the reexamination of rejection its invention patent application, which involved the PCT application for the invention “Initiating processing steps for an object to be processed” (hereinafter referred to as “the Application”) with application No. 201580083272.5, CNIPA considered that the solutions protec-

ted by Claims 1 – 16 of the Application did not constitute technical solutions nor comply with Paragraph 2, Article 2 of the Patent Law. Therefore, the patent rights could not be granted. Siemens disagreed and filed a lawsuit with the Beijing Intellectual Property Court (hereinafter referred to as the "Court of First Instance"), which upheld the original decision. Then, Siemens appealed to the SPC. On November 10, 2022, the SPC ruled to reject the appeal and affirm the original judgment.

【裁判意见】

[Judge's Opinion]

最高人民法院二审认为，专利法第二条第二款规定，发明，是指对产品、方法或者其改进所提出的新的技术方案。判断一项解决方案是否构成技术方案，应当整体考虑权利要求中记载的全部特征，从其是否解决技术问题，手段集合与所解决的技术问题之间关系如何，是否实现特定的技术效果等方面进行综合评估。如果方案所采用的手段集合与要解决的问题之间体现的是按照人为制定的规则关系，不受自然规律的约束，其解决的并非技术问题，所获得的结果亦并非技术效果，则该解决方案不构成技术方案，不属于专利法第二条第二款规定的授予专利权的客体。

The SPC, in its second-instance trial, held that according to Paragraph 2, Article 2 of the Patent Law, an invention refers to a new technical solution proposed for a product, process, or its improvement. To determine whether a solution constitutes a technical solution, all the features recorded in the Claims should be considered as a whole, including evaluating whether it solves a technical problem, the relationship between the means employed and the problem to be solved, and whether it achieves specific technical effects. If the means employed in the solution demonstrate a relation based on artificially established rules and are not constrained by natural laws, and if the solution does not solve a technical problem or achieve a technical effect, then such a solution does not constitute a technical solution and does not fall within the scope of subject matter eligible for patent protection under Paragraph 2, Article 2 of the Patent Law.

本案中，本申请权利要求 1 请求保护一种用于开启针对具有所分派的存款（B）的处理对象的处理步骤的方法。根据说明书的记载，所要求保护的方案要解决的问题是：提供一种经改善的并且受操纵保护的方法以及装置，能够在生产设施中实现资源配置。其解决方案是利用公知的自动化生产设施和处理器进行资源分配，通过人为制订某一或某些处理步骤中处理对象的预先固定出价进而达到对整体生产资源的控制，其中使用处理对象与控制单元和/或生产单元的接口发送处理步骤询问以达到借助处理器来确定可用性结果。该解决方案虽然涉及处理器、生产单元等硬件设备，也涉及生产步骤授权开启等处理步骤，但本申请的核心在于利用公知的装置来实现一种交易方法。该解决方案提供的方法既没有给处理器、生产单元的内部性能带来改进，也没有给处理器、生产单元的构成或功能带来任何技术上的改变，同时也未对生产流程带来任何技术上的改进。该方法总体上体现的是一种对标的物进行多方竞价拍卖规则的建立和制定，并按照人为设计的规则对出价、报价进行判断并对竞拍成功者扣款，其中存款的分派、减少以及如何比价的规则都是人为的规定，不受自然规律的约束，也无法与自然规律建立关联。也即是，本申请方案所采用的手段集合与要解决的问题之间体现的是按照人为制定的规则关系，其所解决的问题是如何根据拍卖结果管理生产资源，获得的效果仅仅是依据交易结果管理生产线，因此，本申请权利要求 1 的解决方案不构成技术方案。

In this case, Claim 1 of the Application sought protection for a method of initiating processing steps for an assigned deposit (B). According to the specification, the problem to be solved by the claimed solution is to provide an im-

proved and manipulable method and device for resource allocation in a production facility. The solution involves utilizing known automated production facilities and processors for resource allocation, controlling overall production resources by determining pre-fixed bids for processing objects in one or more processing steps established by humans, and sending processing step inquiries via interfaces between the processing objects and control units and/or production units to determine availability results by means of processors. While this solution involves hardware devices such as processors and production units and also includes authorized initiation of production steps, its core lies in the utilization of known devices to implement a transaction method. The method provided by this solution does not bring any improvement to the internal performance, composition, or functionality of the processors or production units, nor does it bring any technological improvement to the production process. The method essentially establishes and formulates rules for multi-party bidding auctions on the subject matter, judges the bids and offers according to artificially designed rules, and deducts payments from successful bidders. Particularly, the rules for the allocation, reduction, and comparison of deposits are all arbitrarily determined and not bound by natural laws nor associated with them. In other words, the means employed in the solution adopted by the Application reflect a relation based on artificially established rules in relation to the problem to be solved, which is how to manage production resources based on auction results. The effect achieved is only the management of the production line based on transaction results. Therefore, the solution in Claim 1 of the present Application did not constitute a technical solution.

2. 专利申请权利要求新增专利申请文件隐含公开内容的修改超范围判断

Determination on whether the amendments of patent claims by adding elements as implied in the original patent application extend the content of the original patent application

【裁判要旨】

[Judgment Digest]

专利授权程序中，申请人修改权利要求时，增加的内容在原专利申请文件中虽未予明确记载，但已为原专利申请文件隐含公开，则该修改不违反专利法第三十三条之规定，应当得到允许。

When the applicant amends the claims in the patent granting procedure, if any addition is not explicitly written in the original patent application but is implicitly disclosed in such application, then such amendment by addition does not violate Article 33 of the Patent Law and should be permitted.

【关键词】

[Keywords]

专利申请　驳回复审　隐含公开　修改超范围

Patent application; reexamination of rejection; implicit disclosure; amendment beyond the scope

【案号】

[Case Number]

(2021) 最高法知行终 440 号

(2021) SPC IP Admin. Final 440

【基本案情】

[Case Facts]

在上诉人国家知识产权局与被上诉人成都植源机械科技有限公司（以下简称植源公司）发明专利申请驳回复审行政纠纷案中，涉及申请号为201611044305.8、名称为“一种高压自紧式法兰”的发明专利申请（以下简称本申请）。国家知识产权局原审查部门经审查认为，本申请权利要求1-6不具备创造性，驳回了植源公司的申请。植源公司在复审程序中修改了权利要求1，增加了“β<α”等内容。国家知识产权局认为，增加“β<α”，超出了原说明书和权利要求书记载的范围，不符合专利法第三十三条的规定，故作出被诉决定维持驳回决定。植源公司认为，该修改没有超出原说明书和权利要求书记载的范围，故向北京知识产权法院（以下简称一审法院）提起诉讼。一审法院认为，植源公司的修改内容可以由原说明书和权利要求书所记载的内容直接地、毫无疑义地确定，该修改符合专利法第三十三条的规定，判决撤销被诉决定，国家知识产权局重新作出决定。国家知识产权局不服，向最高人民法院提起上诉。最高人民法院于2022年7月13日判决驳回上诉，维持原判。

The case involved a dispute between the appellant, CNIPA, and the appellee, Chengdu Zhiyuan Machinery Technology Co., Ltd. (hereinafter referred to as “Zhiyuan”) over the reexamination of rejection of Zhiyuan's invention patent application for a high-pressure self-locking flange (hereinafter referred to as “the Application”) with application No. 201611044305.8. The examining department of CNIPA rejected Zhiyuan's application based on the grounds that Claims 1 - 6 did not contain inventive steps. Zhiyuan amended Claim 1 during the reexamination procedure by adding the requirement that “β<α” and other content. CNIPA believed that the addition of “β<α” exceeded the disclosure of the original specification and claims, and was not in compliance with Article 33 of the Patent Law. Accordingly, it decided to reject the application. Zhiyuan disagreed with this decision and filed a lawsuit with the Beijing Intellectual Property Court (hereinafter referred to as the "Court of First Instance"), arguing that the amendment did not exceed the disclosure of the original specification and claims. The Court of First Instance held that the amendment made by Zhiyuan could be directly and unambiguously determined based on the content recorded in the original specification and claims, and thus was in compliance with Article 33 of the Patent Law. It ruled to revoke the initial decision and ordered the CNIPA to make a new decision. CNIPA filed an appeal with the SPC, which on July 13, 2022, ruled to dismiss the appeal and uphold the original judgement.

【裁判意见】

[Judge's Opinion]

最高人民法院二审认为，专利法第三十三条规定，申请人可以对其专利申请文件进行修改，但是，对发明和实用新型专利申请文件的修改不得超出原说明书和权利要求书记载的范围。对于“原说明书和权利要求书记载的范围”，应该从所属领域技术人员角度出发，以原说明书和权利要求书所公开的技术内容来确定。原说明书和权利要求书记载的范围应该包括如下内容：一是原说明书及其附图和权利要求书以文字或者图形等明确表达的内容；二是所属领域技术人员通过综合原说明书及其附图和权利要求书可以直接、明确地推导出的内容。虽然申请人在权利要求中增加的内容在原专利申请文件中并未明确记载，但是，如果该增加的内容已为原专利申请文件所隐含公开，属于所属领域技术人员通过阅读原专利申请文件，结合发明目的，能够直接、明确地推导出的内容，则该修改应该得到允许。本申请要求保护一种高压自紧式法兰。原说明书和权利要求书虽然没有明确记载 β 与 α 的关系，但在 $\beta>\alpha$ 及 $\beta=\alpha$ 的情况下，均无法实现本申请说明书所记载的压力越高，自紧密封性

能越好的技术效果。可见，虽然 β<α 没有记载在原专利申请文件中，但本领域技术人员从原说明书和权利要求书中可以直接、明确地推导出，只有在 β<α 的情况下，才能实现本申请说明书所记载的技术效果，实现本申请的发明目的，β<α 已被原专利申请文件所隐含公开。此外，发明和实用新型专利申请文件的修改要求是，修改后的内容不得超出原说明书和权利要求书记载的范围。实施例是对发明或实用新型优选的具体实施方式的举例说明。只要符合上述要求，申请人在专利审查和复审过程中修改专利权利要求时，可以将其要求保护的技术方案限定为某一个具体的实施例，也可以基于该实施例重新合理概括权利要求。综上所述，植源公司对本申请的修改未超出原说明书和权利要求书记载的范围，符合专利法第三十三条的规定。

The SPC, in the second-instance trial, held that Article 33 of the Patent Law allows applicants to amend their patent application documents, but such amendments must not exceed the disclosure of the original specification and claims for invention and utility model patent applications. The scope of the original specification and claims should be determined from the perspective of those skilled in the art, based on the technical content disclosed in the original specification and claims. The scope should include the following: (i) the content explicitly expressed in words, graphics, or other means in the original specification, including its drawings, and in the claims; and (ii) the content that those skilled in the art can directly and unambiguously deduce from the original specification and claims. Even though the added content in the Claims is not explicitly described in the original patent application document, if it is implicitly disclosed in the original document and can be directly and unambiguously deduced by those skilled in the art, based on the original specification and claims and the purpose of the invention, then such amendment should be allowed. In this case, the application sought protection for a high-pressure self-locking flange. Although the original specification and claims did not explicitly describe the relationship between β and α, it was clear from the original specification and claims that the technical effect of better self-tightening sealing performance cannot be achieved when $\beta>\alpha$ or $\beta=\alpha$. Therefore, even though $\beta<\alpha$ was not described in the original patent application documents, those skilled in the art could directly and unambiguously deduce from the original specification and claims that this relationship is necessary to achieve the technical effect described in the application. Thus, $\beta<\alpha$ was implicitly disclosed in the original patent application documents. Furthermore, the requirement for amending invention and utility model patent applications is that the amendment must not exceed the disclosure of the original specification and claims. The examples of embodiments provided in the specification are merely illustrations of specific preferred embodiments for implementing the invention or utility model. As long as the amendment meets the above requirement, applicants can limit their protected technical solutions to a specific embodiment or reasonably generalize their claims based on that embodiment when amending their patent claims during the examination and reexamination process. Therefore, the amendment made by Zhiyuan to this Application did not exceed the disclosure of the original specification and claims, and was in compliance with Article 33 of the Patent Law.

3. 缺少必要技术特征的判断
Determination on lack of necessary technical features

【裁判要旨】

[Judgment Digest]

判断独立权利要求是否缺少必要技术特征，需要结合说明书中记载的发明目的等内容，基于对权利要求的合理解释得出结论。只有当本领域技术人员通过阅读权利要求书、说明书和附图对独立权利要求进行合理解释后，仍认为其不能解决发明所要解决的技术问题时，才能认定独立权利要求缺少必要技术特征。

To ascertain whether independent claims lack necessary technical features, the conclusion should be reached on the basis of a reasonable interpretation of the claims in combination with the invention purpose as contained in the description. The lack of necessary technical features in an independent claim may be ascertained only when a person skilled in the art still considers that the independent claim cannot solve the technical problem to be allegedly solved by the invention after reasonably interpreting the independent claim by reading the claims, description and drawings.

【关键词】

[Keywords]

专利　无效宣告　必要技术特征　权利要求合理解释

Patent; invalidation; necessary technical features; reasonable interpretation of claims

【案号】

[Case Number]

（2021）最高法知行终 987 号

(2021) SPC IP Admin. Final 987

【基本案情】

[Case Facts]

在上诉人国家知识产权局与上诉人原田工业株式会社（以下简称原田株式会社)、被上诉人东莞友华通信配件有限公司（以下简称友华公司）发明专利权无效行政纠纷案中，涉及专利权人为原田株式会社、专利号为201510121116.5、名称为“天线装置”的发明专利（以下简称本专利)。友华公司请求国家知识产权局宣告本专利权利要求全部无效。国家知识产权局对此作出第37938号无效宣告请求审查决定（以下简称被诉决定)，宣告本专利权利要求部分无效，在原田株式会社于2018年9月3日提交的权利要求1-8的基础上继续维持该专利权有效。友华公司不服，认为本专利权利要求1缺少“伞形振子的一部分位于绝缘底座上方”等必要技术特征，全部权利要求不具备创造性，向北京知识产权法院（以下简称一审法院）提起诉讼。一审法院经审理认为，权利要求1记载的技术方案囊括了伞形振子全部配置于导电底座上方而不位于绝缘底座上方的情形，而该情形下是无法实现本专利说明书中所述“使绝缘底座上的伞形振子的接地面为车体且使实质的高度变高，进而能够提高接收信号的灵敏度”的发明目的。故本专利权利要求1缺少“伞形振子的一部分位于绝缘底座上方”这一必要技术特征。据此，一审法院判决撤销被诉决定，责令国家知识产权局重作。国家知识产权局、原田株式会社均不服，向最高人民法院提起上诉。最高人民法院于2022年8月10日判决撤销原判，驳回友华公司的诉讼请求。

In the administrative dispute over invalidation of invention patent between the appellants, CNIPA and Harada Industry Co., Ltd. (hereinafter referred to as “Harada”), and the appellee, Dongguan Youhua Communication Accessories Co., Ltd. (hereinafter referred to as “Youhua”), Harada was the patent holder of the patent “Antenna Assembly” (hereinafter referred to as the

"Patent") with patent No. 201510121116. 5. Youhua requested that CNIPA declare all claims of the Patent invalid. CNIPA issued Decision on Request for Invalidation No. 37938 (hereinafter referred to as the "disputed decision"), declaring part of the claims of the Patent to be invalid and maintaining the validity of the Patent based on Claims 1 – 8 submitted by Harada on September 3, 2018. Youhua was dissatisfied and filed a lawsuit with the Beijing Intellectual Property Court (hereinafter referred to as the "Court of First Instance"), arguing that Claim 1 of the Patent lacked necessary technical features such as "Part of the umbrella-shaped oscillator is located above the insulating base," and that none of the Claims contained inventive steps. After the trial, the Court of First Instance found that the technical solution described in Claim 1 covered the situation where the entire umbrella-shaped oscillator was located on the conductive base rather than above the insulating base, and it was impossible to achieve the purpose of the invention stated in the specification, "making the grounding surface of the umbrella-shaped oscillator on the insulating base the same as the vehicle body and increasing the received signal sensitivity by increasing the actual height". Therefore, Claim 1 of the Patent lacked the necessary technical feature of "Part of the umbrella-shaped oscillator is located above the insulating base." Based on this, the Court of First Instance revoked the disputed decision and ordered CNIPA to re-decide. CNIPA and Harada were dissatisfied and appealed to the SPC. On August 10, 2022, the SPC ruled to revoke the original judgment and dismiss Youhua's claims.

【裁判意见】

[Judge's Opinion]

最高人民法院二审认为，在判断独立权利要求是否缺少必要技术特征时，应考虑说明书中记载的发明目的等内容，基于对权利要求的合理解释得出结论。理由如下：第一，无论适用哪一法律条款判断专利权利要求是否应当授权或者维持有效，权利要求的解释应当保持一致。换言之，在专利授权确权程序中应当基于对权利要求的同一解释，判断专利权利要求是否符合专利法和《中华人民共和国专利法实施细则》（以下简称专利法实施细则）有关条款的规定。第二，结合说明书对权利要求作出合理解释，其关键在于“合理”。这意味着在解释时既要以权利要求的内容为准，又不能脱离说明书和附图，包括发明目的等内容在内的说明书及附图均可以用于解释权利要求。在此标准下，不会因权利要求的解释问题架空专利法实施细则第二十条第二款的规定。第三，要求独立权利要求具备必要技术特征，本意在于规范权利要求的撰写。如果社会公众不能实现权利要求所确定的技术方案以解决技术问题，或者权利要求的保护范围与技术贡献不相符，可以通过专利法的其他条款解决。如果本领域技术人员根据对权利要求的合理解释可以得出其具备解决技术问题的全部必要技术特征的结论，社会公众的利益不会受到损害。相反，在本领域技术人员根据对权利要求的合理解释可以得出其具备解决技术问题的全部必要技术特征的情况下，仅因申请人在独立权利要求中没有进一步详细记载技术特征而不予授权，会导致对申请人撰写专利文件的要求与其创新程度不相适应，背离专利法鼓励发明创造的立法目的。因此，只有当本领域技术人员通过阅读权利要求书、说明书和附图对独立权利要求进行合理解释后仍不能认为其可以解决发明所要解决的技术问题时，才能认定独立权利要求缺少必要技术特征。

The SPC, in the second-instance trial, believed that when determining whether independent claims lack necessary technical features, it is necessary to consider the purpose of the invention stated in the specification, among other factors, and the conclusion should be reached based on a reasonable interpretation of the claims. The reasons are as follows: First, regardless of which legal provisions are applicable to determine whether patent claims should be

granted or maintained, the interpretation of claims should be consistent. In other words, during the patent granting and confirmation process, a consistent interpretation of the claims should be applied to determine whether the claims comply with the relevant provisions of the Patent Law and the *Implementing Regulations of the Patent Law of the People's Republic of China* (hereinafter referred to as the "Implementing Regulations of the Patent Law"). Second, when making a reasonable interpretation of the claims based on the specification, the key lies in "reasonableness". This means that the interpretation should be based on the content of the claims and should not deviate from the specification and drawings. The specification and drawings, including the stated purpose of the invention, can be used to interpret the claims. Under this standard, the interpretation of the claims does not override the provisions of Paragraph 2, Article 20 of the Implementing Regulations of the Patent Law. Third, the requirement for independent claims to possess necessary technical features is intended to regulate the drafting of claims. If the public cannot implement the technical solution defined by the claims to solve the technical problem, or if the protection scope of the claims does not match the technical contribution, other provisions of the Patent Law can be used to address the issue. If it can be concluded based on a reasonable interpretation of the claims by a person skilled in the art that the claims possess all the necessary technical features to solve the technical problem, the interests of the public will not be harmed. Conversely, in cases where a person skilled in the art can conclude, based on a reasonable interpretation of the claims, that the claims possess all the necessary technical features to solve the technical problem, denying patent granting solely because the applicant did not further specify the technical features in the independent claims would result in requirements for patent drafting being disproportionate to the degree of innovation, which goes against the legislative purpose of encouraging invention and creation under the Patent Law. Therefore, only when a person skilled in the art, after reading the claims, specification, and drawings and making a reasonable interpretation, still cannot consider the independent claims as possessing all the necessary technical features to solve the technical problem addressed by the invention, can it be determined that the independent claims lack necessary technical features.

本案中，权利要求1既限定了天线底座由绝缘底座和导电底座构成且导电底座比绝缘底座小，又限定了伞形振子配置在天线底座的上方。按照本领域技术人员的通常理解，上述限定已经表达了伞形振子的一部分位于绝缘底座上方的含义，而且本领域技术人员通过阅读说明书和权利要求书亦能够合理地予以确定，实施例记载的相关内容亦与发明目的相符，友华公司所举之示例为脱离本领域技术人员对技术方案合理理解的极端示例。故根据本领域技术人员对权利要求1限定内容的合理解释，本专利独立权利要求不缺少“伞形振子的一部分位于绝缘底座上方”的必要技术特征。因权利要求1已具备能解决至少一个本专利所要解决技术问题的技术特征，故其不缺少必要技术特征。

In this case, Claim 1 specified that the antenna base is composed of an insulating base and a conductive base, with the conductive base being smaller than the insulating base, and that the umbrella-shaped oscillator is positioned above the antenna base. According to the usual understanding of a person skilled in the art, the above limitations have already expressed the meaning that a part of the umbrella-shaped oscillator is located above the insulating base, and through reading the specification and claims, a person skilled in the art can reasonably determine this. The relevant content recorded in the embodiments also matches the purpose of the invention. The example given by Youhua is an extreme example that departs from the reasonable interpretation

of the technical solution by a person skilled in the art. Therefore, based on the reasonable interpretation of the limited content of Claim 1 by a person skilled in the art, the independent claim of the Patent did not lack the necessary technical features of "Part of the umbrella-shaped oscillator is located above the insulating base." As Claim 1 already had the technical features to solve at least one technical problem addressed by the Patent, it was not lacking necessary technical features.

4. 最接近现有技术的选取
Selection of the closest prior art

【裁判要旨】

[Judgment Digest]

选取最接近现有技术的核心考虑因素是，该现有技术与发明创造是否针对相同或者近似的技术问题、拥有相同或者近似的技术目标；优选考虑因素是，该现有技术与发明创造的技术方案是否足够接近。关于技术方案是否接近的判断，一般可以考虑发明构思、技术手段等因素。其中技术手段的近似度可以主要考虑现有技术公开技术特征的数量。本领域技术人员基于特定现有技术方案是否具有获得发明创造的合理成功预期，通常并非确定本专利最接近现有技术的要件因素或者优选因素。

The core consideration for selecting the closest prior art is whether the prior art and the invention address the same or similar technical problems and have the same or similar technical objectives; the preferred factor is whether the prior art is sufficiently close to the technical solution of the invention. When determining whether the technical solution is close enough, considerations are generally given to such factors as inventive concept and technical means. As for the degree of approximation of technical means, consideration is mainly given to the number of disclosed technical features of the prior art. Whether a person skilled in the art has a reasonable expectation of success in obtaining the invention based on a particular prior art solution is not usually an elementary or preferred factor in determining the closest prior art for the involved patent.

【关键词】

[Keywords]

专利　无效宣告　最接近现有技术　要件因素　优选因素

Patent; invalidation; the closest prior art; essential factors; preferred factors

【案号】

[Case Number]

（2019）最高法知行终 235 号

（2019）SPC IP Admin. Final 235

【基本案情】

[Case Facts]

在上诉人诺华股份有限公司（以下简称诺华公司）与被上诉人国家知识产权局、原审第三人戴某良发明专利权无效行政纠纷案中，诺华公司系专利号为 201110029600. 7、名称为“含有缬沙坦和 NEP 抑制剂的药物组合物”的发明专利（以下简称本专利）的专利权人。戴某良申请宣告本专利权无效。国家知识产权局认为，一是本专利权利要求1、2 相对于附件 13 与附件 12、14、15 的结合不具备创造性；二是有关补充实验数据不应接受也不能证明缬沙坦（AII 拮抗剂）和沙库巴曲（NEP 抑制剂）的组合具有抗高血压的协同作用。故宣告本专利权全部无效。诺华公司不服，向北京知识产权法院（以下简称一审法院）提起诉讼。一审法院判决驳回诺华公司的诉讼请求。诺华公司不服，向最高人民法院提起上诉，主张一审判决和被诉决定应当考虑而没有考虑“合理的成功预期”，其认为作为创造性判断起点的最接近现有技术应

当至少是“有前景”的技术方案，即本领域技术人员有一定合理成功预期基于最接近现有技术能够得到专利技术方案。如果本领域技术人员无法理性预期问题能够得到解决，则其不会产生改进动机。本领域技术人员在本专利优先权日面对附件 13 没有得到本专利要求保护的药物组合的合理预期。最高人民法院于 2021 年 6 月 30 日判决驳回上诉，维持原判。

In the administrative dispute between the appellant, Novartis (Taiwan) Co., Ltd. (hereinafter referred to as "Novartis"), and the appellees, CNIPA and Dai (the third party in the first instance) regarding invalidation of the invention patent titled "Drug combination comprising Valsartan and NEP Inhibitor" with patent No. 201110029600. 7 (hereinafter referred to as the "Patent"), of which Novartis was the patent holder, Dai filed an application to declare the Patent invalid. CNIPA held that, firstly, Claims 1 and 2 of the Patent lacked inventive steps compared to the combination of Annex 13 with Annexes 12, 14, and 15; secondly, the supplementary experimental data should not be accepted and could not prove the synergistic effect of combining Valsartan (AII antagonist) and Sacubitril (NEP inhibitor) in treating hypertension. Therefore, CNIPA declared the patent invalid in its entirety. Novartis disagreed and filed a lawsuit with the Beijing Intellectual Property Court (hereinafter referred to as the "Court of First Instance"), which ruled to dismiss Novartis' Claims. Dissatisfied with the judgement, Novartis appealed to the SPC, arguing that the first-instance judgment and the contested ruling should have considered the concept of "Reasonable expectation of success". Novartis contended that the closest prior art, as the starting point for inventive step assessment, should be at least a "promising" technical solution, meaning that those skilled in the art would have a reasonable expectation of obtaining a patentable technical solution based on the closest prior art. If the skilled person could not reasonably expect the problem to be solved, they would lack the motivation to make improvements. Novartis argued that on the priority date of the Patent (i. e., the filing or priority date), a person skilled in the art could not have reasonably expected to arrive at the claimed drug combination protected by the Patent when confronted with Annex 13 (i. e., the closest prior art). On June 30, 2021, the SPC dismissed the appeal and affirmed the original judgment.

【裁判意见】

[Judge's Opinion]

最高人民法院二审认为，原则上，选取最接近现有技术的核心考虑因素是，该现有技术与发明创造是否针对相同或者近似的技术问题、拥有相同或者近似的技术目标。在此基础上，进一步的优选考虑因素是，该现有技术与发明创造的技术方案是否足够接近。本领域技术人员基于最接近现有技术是否具有获得发明创造的合理成功预期，通常取决于申请日或者优先权日是否存在阻碍其获得发明创造的认知局限。但此系确定最接近现有技术后，认定发明创造是否是显而易见的考虑因素，通常并非确定本专利最接近现有技术的要件因素或者优选因素。对于申请保护的发明创造而言，即便选择了与其具有相同技术问题、技术目标且技术方案足够接近的现有技术作为最接近现有技术，本领域技术人员仍然可能基于申请日或者优先权日的技术认知或者研发条件局限等，不具有获得发明创造的合理成功预期，进而难以产生将其他现有技术或者公知常识与该最接近现有技术结合获得发明创造技术方案的动机，但这并不影响该最接近现有技术作为拟制的发明起点的资格。当然，如果所谓最接近的现有技术明显不具有可行性，本领域技术人员通常不会基于该不具有可行性的现有技术研发完成发明创造，故该不具有可行性的现有技术原则上不适宜作为评价专利创造性的最接近现有技术。

The SPC, in the second-instance trial, held that the core consideration

for selecting the closest prior art, in principle is whether the prior art and the invention address the same or similar technical problems and have the same or similar technical objectives; the preferred factor is whether the prior art is sufficiently close to the technical solution of the invention. Whether a person skilled in the art would have a reasonable expectation of success in achieving the invention based on the closest prior art often depends on the cognitive limitations existing at the application or priority date that may hinder their ability to achieve the invention. However, this is a consideration for determining whether the invention is obvious or not after identifying the closest prior art. It is not a determining factor or a preferred factor for establishing the closest prior art to this Patent. Even if the closest prior art is selected based on having the same technical problem, technical objective, and a sufficiently close technical solution to the invention for the protection of the claimed invention, a person skilled in the art may still lack a reasonable expectation of success in achieving the invention due to their technical knowledge or research and development constraints at the application or priority date. Therefore, they may find it difficult to have the motivation to combine other prior art or common knowledge with the closest prior art to arrive at the inventive technical solution. However, this does not affect the qualification of the closest prior art as the starting point for the invention. Of course, if the so-called closest prior art is obviously not feasible, a person skilled in the art would generally not develop the invention based on such unfeasible prior art. Therefore, such unfeasible prior art is not suitable for evaluating the inventive step of the patent as the closest prior art.

本案中，诺华公司以药物作用机理复杂、存在无法实现技术效果的具体实施例等为由，主张本领域技术人员不具有基于附件 13 获得本专利技术方案的合理成功预期，进而主张附件 13 不构成适格的最接近现有技术。上述理由本质上是以本领域技术人员存在认知局限为由，主张缺乏合理的成功预期。如前所述，本领域技术人员基于最接近现有技术是否具有获得发明创造的合理成功预期，原则上并非判断某一现有技术是否具备作为创造性评价中最接近现有技术的考虑因素，该因素更适宜在“三步法”的第三步中予以考虑。诺华公司基于上述理由否定附件13最接近现有技术资格的主张缺乏依据。

In this case, Novartis argued that the person skilled in the art would not have a reasonable expectation of success in obtaining the claimed technical solution based on Annex 13, citing reasons such as the complex mechanism of action of the drug and the absence of specific embodiments demonstrating the achievable technical effect. Therefore, Novartis maintained that Annex 13 did not constitute eligible closest prior art. Essentially, these arguments were based on the cognitive limitations of the person skilled in the art and claimed a lack of reasonable expectation of success. As mentioned earlier, whether the person skilled in the art has a reasonable expectation of success in achieving the invention based on the closest prior art is not the determining factor for judging whether a particular prior art qualifies as the closest prior art for the purpose of inventive step assessment. This factor was more suitable to be considered in the third step of the “Three-step approach”. Novartis' argument that Annex 13 did not qualify as the closest prior art lacks basis.

诺华公司还主张，因附件13承认AII拮抗剂和NEP抑制剂药物作用机理的不可预测性，且未提供任何结论，故其属于明显不具有可行性的现有技术，不能作为最接近现有技术。对此，分析如下：首先，附件13记载，“由AII受体拮抗剂或肾素抑制剂与NEP抑制剂的组合得到的提高的效果因为多种原因而不可预期”。根据该记载，不可预期的内容是药物组合“提高的效果”即协同效果，而非本专利实际要解决的技术问题即药物组合治疗高血压的效果。其次，附件13公开了AII拮抗

剂和 NEP 抑制剂的组合能够治疗高血压的技术方案，且载明了有关实验方法、实验结论、给药方式、治疗剂量等技术信息，对于有关药物组合的药用功能给出了明确结论。因此，本领域技术人员并不会仅仅因为“由 AII 受体拮抗剂或肾素抑制剂与 NEP 抑制剂的组合得到的提高的效果因为多种原因而不可预期”这一记载即认为附件 13 明显不具有可行性。故此，诺华公司关于因附件 13 属于明显不具有可行性的现有技术而不能作为最接近现有技术的主张，亦缺乏依据。

Novartis further argued that Annex 13 acknowledges the unpredictability of the mechanism of action of AII antagonist and NEP inhibitor and does not provide any conclusions, making it an obviously unworkable prior art that cannot be considered the closest prior art. In response to this argument, the analysis was as follows: Firstly, Annex 13 stated that "The enhanced effects obtained from the combination of AII receptor antagonist or renin inhibitor with NEP inhibitor are unpredictable for various reasons." According to this statement, the unpredictability referred to the "Enhanced effects" or synergistic effects of the drug combination, rather than the specific technical issue addressed by the present patent, i.e., the therapeutic effect of the drug combination in treating hypertension. Secondly, Annex 13 disclosed a technical solution of combining AII antagonist and NEP inhibitor for the treatment of hypertension. It also provided technical information including experimental methods, experimental results, administration methods, therapeutic dosages, and clearly concluded the pharmaceutical function of the drug combination. Therefore, persons skilled in the art would not consider Annex 13 as obviously unworkable solely based on the statement that "The enhanced effects obtained from the combination of AII receptor antagonist or renin inhibitor with NEP inhibitor are unpredictable." Therefore, Novartis' argument that Annex 13 was obviously unworkable and could not be considered the closest prior art also lacks basis.

5. “合理的成功预期”在专利创造性判断中的考量 Consideration of “reasonable expectation of success” in determining non-obviousness of a patent

【裁判要旨】

[Judgment Digest]

“合理的成功预期”可以作为判断发明创造是否显而易见时的考虑因素。综合考虑专利申请日的现有技术状况、技术演进特点、创新模式及条件、平均创新成本、整体创新成功率等，本领域技术人员有动机尝试从最接近现有技术出发并合理预期能够获得专利技术方案的，可以认定该专利技术方案不具备创造性。“合理的成功预期”仅要求达到对于本领域技术人员而言有“尝试的必要”的程度，不需要具有“成功的确定性”或者“成功的高度盖然性”。

A “reasonable expectation of success” can be a factor to consider in terms of non-obviousness assessment. Where a person skilled in the art has the motive to attempt from the closest prior art and reasonably expect of obtaining the patented technical solution after comprehensively considering the status of prior art as at the date of filing, features of technical evolution, innovation model and conditions, average innovation cost and overall innovation success rate, it can be determined that the patented technical solution is obvious. The “reasonable expectation of success” only needs to reach the degree of having “necessity to try” for a person skilled in the art, rather than such degree as “certainty of success” or “high probability of success”.

【关键词】

[Keywords]

专利　无效宣告　创造性　显而易见　合理的成功预期

Patent; invalidation; inventive step; obviousness; reasonable expectation of success

【案号】

[Case Number]

(2019) 最高法知行终 235 号

(2019) SPC IP Admin. Final 235

【裁判意见】

[Judge's Opinion]

在上诉人诺华股份有限公司与被上诉人国家知识产权局、原审第三人戴某良发明专利权无效行政纠纷案中，最高人民法院指出，在最接近的现有技术已经公开了两类已知化合物组合的药用功能的前提下，本专利实际上是研发一种具体的具有药用效果的组合物。此时，对于具体化合物组合的药用效果"合理的成功预期"是判断"结合启示"的重要考虑因素。如果本领域技术人员对于具体化合物组合的药用效果没有"合理的成功预期"，专利申请人仍然作出了尝试，并获得了相应的具有药用功能的具体组合物技术方案，那么该具体药用组合物技术方案通常会被认定为具有创造性。如果本领域技术人员对于该具体化合物组合的药用效果具有"合理的成功预期"，此时只有在验证具体的具有药用效果的组合物需要付出创造性劳动，或者取得了预料不到的技术效果的情况下，该具体的药用组合物技术方案才会被认为具备创造性。

In the administrative dispute over invalidation of invention patent between the appellant, Novartis, and the appellees, CNIPA and Dai (the third party in the first instance), the SPC pointed out that in the scenario where the closest prior art has already disclosed the pharmaceutical functions of two known compound combinations, the present patent essentially involves the development of a specific combination with pharmaceutical effects. In this case, the "reasonable expectation of success" regarding the pharmaceutical effects of the specific compound combination is an important factor in determining the "motivation to combine". If there is no "reasonable expectation of success" among the person skilled in the art regarding the pharmaceutical effects of the specific compound combination, and yet the patent applicant still made attempts and obtained a specific combination with corresponding pharmaceutical functions, then this specific pharmaceutical combination would generally be considered as creative. However, if persons skilled in the art have a "reasonable expectation of success" regarding the pharmaceutical effects of the specific compound combination, then this specific pharmaceutical combination would only be deemed creative if it requires creative effort to verify the specific pharmaceutical effects or if it achieves unforeseeable technical effects.

应予说明的是，对于“合理的成功预期”的判断，至少应当注意以下两个问题：一是“合理的成功预期”系本领域技术人员在本专利申请日或者优先权日，基于其技术认知和本领域普遍实验条件，对从现有技术出发得到专利技术方案的成功可能性的客观评估和理性预测，其不取决于专利申请人的主观意愿。二是“合理的成功预期”仅要求达到本领域技术人员认为有“尝试的必要”的程度，而无须具有“成功的确定性”或者“成功的高度盖然性”。具有“合理的成功预期”通常不以实施预期的尝试必然或者高度可能实现技术目标或者解决技术问题为前提，仅要求本领域技术人员综合考虑具体领域的现有技术状况、技术演进特点、创新模式及条件、平均创新成本、整体创新成功率等因素后，仍然不会放弃该种尝试即可。

It should be noted that in the evaluation of "reasonable expectation of success," at least two issues should be considered: first, the "reasonable ex-

pectation of success" is an objective assessment and rational prediction by the person skilled in the art, based on their technical knowledge and common experimental conditions in the art, on the likelihood of obtaining the patented technical solution from the prior art as of the filing date or priority date of the patent. It is not subject to the subjective intention of the patent applicant. Second, the "reasonable expectation of success" only needs to reach the degree of having "necessity to attempt" for a person skilled in the art, rather than such degree as "certainty of success" or "high probability of success". It usually does not require the premise that the attempt will inevitably or is highly likely to achieve the technical goal or solve the technical problem, but only requires persons skilled in the art not to give up the attempt after comprehensively considering the status of prior art in the specific field, features of technical evolution, innovation models and conditions, average innovation cost, an overall innovation success rate, etc.

诺华公司主张，本领域技术人员对本专利技术方案即使用缬沙坦（AII 拮抗剂）和沙库巴曲（NEP 抑制剂）的组合治疗高血压，不具有合理的成功预期，主要基于以下理由：AII 拮抗剂和 NEP 抑制剂显示出相反且复杂的生理作用；最接近现有技术承认 AII 拮抗剂和 NEP 抑制剂作用机理的不可预测性，并且没有提供任何结论；AII 拮抗剂和 NEP 抑制剂的组合中存在无法实现降血压效果的“坏点”。对此，最高人民法院分析如下：附件 13 作为最接近的现有技术，公开了 AII 拮抗剂和 NEP 抑制剂的组合能够治疗高血压的技术方案，且载明了有关实验方法、实验结论、给药方式、治疗剂量等技术信息，其为本领域技术人员选择具体的 AII 拮抗剂和具体的 NEP 抑制剂以治疗高血压提供了明确的技术启示。在附件 13 对于类型化药物组合的药用功能已有明确指引，具体的药物组合又存在其他选择的情况下，即便具备有关药用功能的具体药物组合研发不具有“成功的确定性”，其亦不足以证明本领域技术人员会放弃基于附件 13 研发具有降血压功能的具体 AII 拮抗剂和具体 NEP 抑制剂的组合，不足以否定本领域技术人员的“合理的成功预期”。

Novartis argued that the person skilled in the art did not have a reasonable expectation of success in treating hypertension using the combination of valsartan (an AII antagonist) and sacubitril (an NEP inhibitor), mainly based on the following reasons: AII antagonist and NEP inhibitor exhibited opposite and complex physiological effects; the closest prior art acknowledged the unpredictability of the mechanisms of action of AII antagonist and NEP inhibitor, and did not provide any conclusion; there was a “drawback” in the AII antagonist/NEP inhibitor combination, i. e., it could not achieve the effect of lowering blood pressure. In this regard, the SPC analyzed as follows: Annex 13, as the closest prior art, disclosed a technical solution that the combination of AII antagonist and NEP inhibitor can be used to treat hypertension, and it set forth the technical information such as experimental methods, experimental conclusions, administration methods, therapeutic doses, etc., which provided a clear technical inspiration for persons skilled in the art to choose specific AII antagonist and NEP inhibitor to treat hypertension. Given that there were clear guidelines on the therapeutic functions of typified drug combinations in Annex 13 and other options existed for the specific drug combination, even if there was no “certainty of success” in developing a specific drug combination with the desired therapeutic functions, it is not enough to prove that persons skilled in the art will give up developing specific AII antagonist and NEP inhibitor combinations based on Annex 13, nor enough to negate their “reasonable expectation of success”.

6. 发明构思差异对改进动机及技术启示的影响 Influence of difference in inventive concept on improvement motive and technical teaching

【裁判要旨】

[Judgment Digest]

在采用“三步法”判断发明创造是否具备创造性的过程中，判断本领域技术人员是否会对最接近的现有技术产生改进动机以及是否有将作为现有技术的对比文件相结合的技术启示时，如果发明与最接近的现有技术之间在发明构思上存在明显差异，则通常可以认定本领域技术人员不会有改进最接近的现有技术以得到本发明的动机；如果作为现有技术的对比文件之间在发明构思上存在明显差异，则通常可以认定现有技术不存在将上述对比文件结合以得到本发明的技术启示。

In the course of adopting the “three-step method” to determine whether an invention is non-obvious, when determining whether a person skilled in the art will have a motive to improve the closest prior art and whether there is a technical teaching that will combine the references in prior art, if there is an obvious difference between the invention and the closest prior art in the inventive concept, it could generally be deemed that a person skilled in the art will not have the motivation to improve the closest prior art to obtain the invention; and if there is an obvious difference in the inventive concept among prior art references, it could generally be deemed that the prior art does not have the technical teaching of combining the aforementioned prior art references to obtain the invention in question.

【关键词】

[Keywords]

专利申请　驳回复审　改进动机　技术启示　发明构思

Patent application; reexamination of rejection; motive for improvement; technical teaching; inventive concept

【案号】

[Case Number]

(2022) 最高法知行终 316 号

(2022) SPC IP Admin. Final 316

【基本案情】

[Case Facts]

在上诉人郑州泽正技术服务有限公司（以下简称泽正公司）与被上诉人国家知识产权局发明专利申请驳回复审行政纠纷案中，涉及申请号为 201510248436.7、名称为“一种克氏针折弯装置”的发明专利申请（以下简称本申请）。国家知识产权局作出第 215237 号复审请求审查决定（以下简称被诉决定），维持其于 2019 年 2 月 1 日对本申请作出的驳回决定。泽正公司不服被诉决定，向北京知识产权法院（以下简称一审法院）提起诉讼，一审法院经审查判决驳回泽正公司的诉讼请求。泽正公司不服，向最高人民法院提起上诉。最高人民法院于 2022 年 12 月 2 日判决撤销原判和被诉决定，国家知识产权局重新作出决定。

In the administrative dispute between the appellant, Zhengzhou Zezheng Technical Services Co., Ltd. (hereinafter referred to as “Zezheng”), and the appellee, CNIPA, over the reexamination of rejection its patent application for the invention “A K-wire Bending Device” (hereinafter referred to as “the Application”) with application No. 201510248436.7, CNIPA issued Reexamination Decision No. 215237 (hereinafter referred to as the “Disputed Decision”) to uphold its rejection decision made on February 1, 2019. Disagreeing with the Disputed Decision, Zezheng filed a lawsuit with the Beijing Intellectual Property Court (hereinafter referred to as the “Court of First Instance”), which dismissed Zezheng's Claims after the trial, followed by Zezheng's appeal

to the SPC. On December 2, 2022, the SPC ruled to revoke the original judgment and the Disputed Decision, while CNIPA was ordered to make a new decision.

【裁判意见】

[Judge's Opinion]

最高人民法院二审认为，发明构思，是指在发明创造的完成过程中，发明人为了解决所面临的技术问题在谋求解决方案的过程中所提出的技术改进思路，决定了发明进行技术改进的途径和最终形成的技术方案的构成。采用“三步法”判断发明是否具有创造性过程中，在判断本领域技术人员是否会对最接近的现有技术产生改进动机以及是否有将作为现有技术的对比文件进行结合的技术启示时，如果发明与最接近的现有技术之间在发明构思上存在较大差异，则本领域技术人员通常不会有改进最接近的现有技术以得到本发明的动机；如果作为现有技术的对比文件之间在发明构思上存在较大差异，则本领域技术人员通常也难以产生将两个发明构思不同的对比文件进行结合以得到本发明的技术启示。本申请与对比文件 1 均是以 CN87212315U 专利为基础说明现有技术中存在的问题，二者面对需要解决的技术问题相同。本申请的具体结构组成，触头的旋转平面垂直于尖嘴钳的头部，但平行于钳子转轴轴线方向。由此，触头能够围绕尖嘴钳的头部旋四周旋转。而对比文件 1 的具体结构组成，拨块的旋转平面平行于固定轴的轴线方向，但垂直于钳子转轴轴线方向，拨块只能在固定轴的一面旋转。由上分析可见，本申请与对比文件 1 二者使克氏针弯曲的部件，在具体结构组成、相互位置关系设置、技术效果方面存在明显差异。基于对比文件 1 给出的技术教导，本领域技术人员不会想到将固定轴（底座 5）替换成尖嘴钳，进而也不会想到将“对比文件 1 中折弯底座 5 替换成尖嘴钳，利用尖嘴钳进行克氏针夹持”，也即本领域技术人员不会产生将对比文件 1 改进为本申请的动机。同时，对比文件 2 中的尖嘴钳的头部作为旋转轴就是尖嘴钳长度方向的中心轴，尖嘴钳长度方向的中心轴垂直于钳子转轴，而触头绕钳子转轴转动，触头的旋转平面也轴垂直于钳子转轴，尖嘴钳长度方向的中心轴和触头的旋转平面平行，触头不可能绕尖嘴钳长度方向的中心轴旋转，所以对比文件 2 的触头没有绕尖嘴钳长度方向的中心轴旋转的可能，故对比文件 2 没有给出将“对比文件 1 中折弯底座 5 替换成尖嘴钳，利用尖嘴钳进行克氏针夹持”的技术启示。

The SPC, in its second-instance trial, held that the inventive concept refers to the technological improvement ideas proposed by inventors during the process of invention and creation, which aims to solve the technical problems they face. It determines the approach to technical improvement and the final composition of the technical solution. When using the “Three-step method” to determine whether an invention involves an inventive step, if there is significant difference in inventive concept between the invention and the closest prior art, it is unlikely that those skilled in the art will have the motivation to improve the closest prior art to obtain the invention. Similarly, if there is significant difference in inventive concept between two comparative documents serving as the prior art, it is also difficult for those skilled in the art to combine the two comparative documents with different inventive concepts to obtain the technical inspiration for the invention. In this application, both the present Application and the Comparison Document 1 are based on the CN87212315U patent to illustrate the existing problems in the prior art, and both address the same technical problem that needs to be solved. The specific structural composition of the present Application is that the rotation plane of the contact head is perpendicular to the head of the pliers but parallel to the axial direction of the pliers. Consequently, the contact head can rotate around the head of the pliers. On the other hand, the specific structural composition of Comparison Document 1 is that the rotation plane of the pawl is parallel to the axis direc-

tion of the fixed shaft but perpendicular to the axial direction of the pliers, and the pawl can only rotate on one side of the fixed shaft. From the above analysis, it can be seen that there are obvious differences between the present Application and the Comparison Document 1 in terms of specific structural composition, mutual positional relationship setting, and technical effects regarding the components that bend the Kirschner wire. Based on the technical teaching provided by the Comparison Document 1, those skilled in the art would not think of replacing the fixed shaft (Base 5) with a pair of pliers, and therefore would not come up with the motivation to improve the Comparison Document 1 to arrive at the present Application, i. e., "replacing the bending base 5 in the Comparison Document 1 with a pair of pliers and using the pair of pliers to clamp K-wire". Furthermore, in Comparison Document 2, the head of the pliers serves as the rotation axis, which is the central axis in the length direction of the pliers. The central axis in the length direction of the pliers is perpendicular to the axial direction of the pliers, and the contact head rotates around the pliers' axial direction. The rotation plane of the contact head is also perpendicular to the axial direction of the pliers, and the central axis in the length direction of the pliers is parallel to the rotation plane of the contact head. Thus, the contact head cannot rotate around the central axis in the length direction of the pliers. Therefore, the Comparison Document 2 did not provide any technical inspirations for "replacing the bent base 5 in the Comparison Document 1 with a pair of pliers and using the pair of pliers to perform K-wire clamping".

7. 新颖性宽限期的适用
Application of novelty grace period

【裁判要旨】

[Judgment Digest]

专利法关于新颖性宽限期中的“他人未经申请人同意而泄露其内容”的规定，核心在于他人违背申请人意愿公开发明创造的内容。具体判断时，可以综合考虑申请人的主观意思和客观行为，即申请人主观上是否愿意公开或者是否放任公开行为的发生，客观上是否采取了一定保密措施使其发明创造不易被公众所知晓。他人违反明示保密义务或者违反根据社会观念、商业习惯所应承担的默示保密义务，擅自公开发明创造内容的，构成违背申请人意愿，属于“他人未经申请人同意而泄露其内容”。

The core of the provision in the Patent Law on grace period for novelty based on “disclosure by others without the consent of the applicant” lies in disclosure against the will of the applicant. In specific judgment, consideration can be given to the applicant’s subjective intention and objective act. In other words, whether or not the applicant is subjectively willing to disclose or indulges such disclosure, and whether or not the applicant has objectively taken certain confidentiality measures to make it difficult for the public to access the invention. Where others disclose the invention without authorization and thus in violation of the express confidentiality obligation, or such implied confidentiality obligation as required by social norms and business practices, then it can be deemed that such act goes against the will of the applicant and conforms with the concept of “disclosure by others without the consent of the applicant”.

【关键词】

[Keywords]

专利　无效宣告　新颖性宽限期　未经申请人同意的公开

Patent; invalidation; novelty grace period; unauthorized disclosure

【案号】

[Case Number]

(2020) 最高法知行终 588 号

(2020) SPC IP Admin. Final 588

【基本案情】

[Case Facts]

在上诉人北京奇虎科技有限公司（以下简称奇虎公司）、北京奇智商务咨询有限公司（以下简称奇智公司）与被上诉人国家知识产权局、原审第三人北京江民新科技术有限公司（以下简称江民公司）外观设计专利权无效行政纠纷案中，奇虎公司、奇智公司是专利号为201430324283.6、名称为“带图形用户界面的电脑”的外观设计专利（以下简称本专利）的专利权人。江民公司于2016年8月8日向原国家知识产权局专利复审委员会（以下简称专利复审委员会）提出了无效宣告请求，请求宣告本专利权无效。江民公司提交的证据1为北京市长安公证处（2016）京长安内经证字第18612号公证书复印件，该公证书显示访问卡饭论坛，在该论坛中找到标题为“360安全卫士10下载地址”的帖子，该帖子显示发帖时间为2014年8月19日，点击所列链接地址，下载文件“setup_ 10_ priv. exe”，通过百度搜索7-Zip软件下载并安装，将“setup_ 10_ priv. exe”文件通过安装好的7-Zip软件提取到文件夹，点击所提取文件中的“360safe. exe”文件运行该软件，其页面左上角显示“360安全卫士10.0Beta”。专利复审委员会及北京知识产权法院均认为任何非特定人通过7-Zip软件均可解压缩涉案软件，获得相关的界面设计内容，该软件的界面设计实际上已处于为公众所知的状态，故而证据1属于现有设计；奇虎公司、奇智公司提交的证据不足以证明本专利申请日前体验用户负有明示或默示的保密义务，所述下载软件不属于专利法第二十四条第三项所规定的不丧失新颖性宽限期的情形。奇虎公司、奇智公司不服，向最高人民法院提起上诉。最高人民法院于2021年5月31日判决撤销原判和被诉决定，国家知识产权局重新作出决定。

In the administrative dispute over invalidation of design patent between the appellants, Beijing Qihoo Technology Co., Ltd. (hereinafter referred to as "Qihoo") and Beijing Qizhi Business Consulting Co., Ltd. (hereinafter referred to as "Qizhi"), and the appellees, CNIPA and Beijing Jiangmin New Sci. & Tec. Co., Ltd. (hereinafter referred to as "Jiangmin", the third party in the first instance), Qihoo and Qizhi were the patent holders of the design patent "Computer with Graphical User Interface" (hereinafter referred to as the "Patent") with patent No. 201430324283.6. Jiangmin filed an invalidation request with the Patent Reexamination Board of the former State Intellectual Property Office (hereinafter referred to as the "Patent Reexamination Board") on August 8, 2016, requesting the invalidation of the Patent in question. The Exhibit 1 submitted by Jiangmin was a copy of notarization [Jing Chang an Nei Jing Zheng Zi No. 18612 (2016)] from Beijing Chang'an Notary Public Office, which showed access to the Kafan Forum where a post titled "360 Security Guard 10 Download Link" was found. The post indicated that it was posted on August 19, 2014. By clicking on the provided link, the file "setup_ 10_ priv. exe" was downloaded. Then, downloading 7-Zip software through Baidu and installing it, extracting the "setup_ 10_ priv. exe" file into the folder using the installed 7-Zip software and clicking the extracted "360safe. exe" file, "360 Security Guard 10. 0 Beta" was displayed in the top-left corner of the interface. Both the Patent Reexamination Board and Beijing

Intellectual Property Court considered that the interface design of the software was publicly known since it could be extracted by any non-specific person using the 7-Zip software. Therefore, Exhibit 1 was deemed as prior art. The evidence submitted by Qihoo and Qizhi was insufficient to prove that there was an explicit or implicit obligation of confidentiality imposed on the experience users, prior to the filing date of the Patent. The downloaded software mentioned did not fall under the circumstances specified in Paragraph 3, Article 24 of the Patent Law, which would exempt it from losing novelty during the grace period. Dissatisfied with the decision, Qihoo and Qizhi filed an appeal to the SPC, which, on May 31, 2021, ruled to revoke the original judgment and the Disputed Decision, and ordered the CNIPA to make a new decision.

【裁判意见】

[Judge's Opinion]

最高人民法院二审认为，根据专利法第二十四条第三项的规定，申请专利的发明创造在申请日以前六个月内，他人未经申请人同意而泄露其内容的，不丧失新颖性。他人未经申请人同意而泄露其内容所造成的公开，其核心在于他人违背申请人意愿而将发明创造的内容公开，其具体表现形式包括但不限于：他人未遵守明示的保密义务或者根据社会观念、商业习惯所应承担的默示的保密义务而将发明创造的内容公开；他人用威胁、欺诈或者间谍活动等非法手段从发明人或者申请人那里得知发明创造的内容而后造成的公开，等等。判断是否违背申请人意愿的公开时，可以从申请人主观的意思表示和客观的行为综合考虑，即申请人主观上是否愿意将其发明创造的内容公开，或者放任公开行为的发生；客观上是否采取一定保密措施确保其发明创造不被公众所容易知晓。

The SPC, in the second-instance trial, held that according to Paragraph 3, Article 24 of the Patent Law, any invention/creation for which a patent is applied shall not lose its novelty if, within six months before the filing date of the application, it was disclosed by any person without the consent of the applicant. The core of this provision lies in disclosure against the will of the applicant. Specific manifestations of such disclosure include, but are not limited to: disclosure of the content of the invention/creation by others violating explicit confidentiality obligations or implied confidentiality obligations based on social norms or commercial practices; disclosure by others after obtaining knowledge of the content of the invention/creation through illegal means such as threats, fraud, or espionage, etc. When determining whether the disclosure is made against the applicant's will, subjective expression of intention and objective behaviors of the applicant can be considered comprehensively, that is, whether the applicant is subjectively willing to disclose the content of the invention/creation, or allows the occurrence of the disclosure; and objectively, whether certain confidentiality measures have been taken to ensure that the invention/creation is not easily known to the public.

本案中，现有的证据 1 可以证明在专利申请日之前发帖人将带有本专利图形用户界面设计的软件公开在卡饭论坛上，但其安装界面提示的是“仅供试用”并要求输入体验码，仅有部分能够获得体验资格的用户可以试用该软件。其后，跟帖人发布 7-Zip 软件下载提示，使得公众可以通过 7-Zip 软件下载使用该软件。需要指出的是，奇虎公司和奇智公司认可 2014 年 8 月 19 日卡饭论坛上的软件链接属于内部测试，但主张发帖人未经同意泄露软件内容。此外，根据证据 2 的内容，获得优先体验资格的用户进一步披露了所述软件内容。对此，具体分析如下：

In this case, the existing Exhibit 1 could prove that the poster disclosed software with the patented graphical user interface design on the Kafan Forum before the patent filing date. However, the installation interface indicated “For trial use only” and required an experience code, allowing only a limited number of users who qualified for the trial to use the software. Subsequently,

another user posted a download prompt for the 7-Zip software, making it accessible to the public to download and use the software. It should be noted that Qihoo and Qizhi acknowledged that the software link on the Kafan Forum on August 19, 2014 was for internal testing, but they argued that the poster disclosed the software content without consent. Additionally, according to the content of Exhibit 2, users who obtained priority experience qualification further disclosed the software content. In this regard, the specific analysis was as follows:

第一，就发帖人而言，首先，其明确表示该软件“仅供获得优先体验资格的用户试用”，并要求输入体验码。从发帖人的意思表示以及其采用体验码限制措施可知，其主观上并不愿意将所述软件的内容公开，也没有证据证明其存在放任所述软件公开行为发生的意愿；客观上其采取了要求输入体验码的保密措施确保该软件内容不被公众所容易知晓。因此，发帖人已经按照专利申请人的要求履行不公开的义务，未公开所述软件，其不属于专利法第二十四条第三项规定的“他人”。其次，通过发帖人上述行为，根据社会观念和软件内测的商业惯例，作出7-Zip软件下载提示的跟帖人应当明知或者应知发帖人或者软件权利人有保密的意思和行为，并因此负有默示保密义务。但是，跟帖人违背了基于社会观念及商业惯例所承担的默示保密义务，披露了所述软件的非正常打开方式并向社会公众呈现出软件中的图形用户界面，违背专利申请人的意愿，应当属于专利法第二十四条第三项规定的“他人未经申请人同意而泄露其内容”的情形。

Firstly, as for the person who posted the thread, he/she explicitly stated that the software is only for trial use by users who have obtained a priority experience qualification and require an experience code to access it. From the expression of the poster's intention and the use of the experience code as a restriction measure, it can be inferred that the poster subjectively did not want to disclose the content of the software and there is no evidence to prove his/her intention to make the content of the software public. Objectively, he/she had taken measures to require an experience code to ensure that the content of the software was not easily known to the public. Therefore, the poster was not considered as one of the "Others" under Paragraph 3, Article 24 of the Patent Law. Secondly, based on social norms and commercial practices related to software testing, the follow-up person who provided 7-Zip software prompt should have known or should know that the poster or the software right holder intended to keep the information confidential, and therefore, he/she has an implicit obligation of confidentiality. However, the follow-up person violated the implicit obligation of confidentiality that is typically expected based on social norms and commercial practices, disclosed the unconventional method of accessing the software and presented the graphic user interface of the software to the public, which goes against the will of the patent applicant and falls under the situation specified in Paragraph 3, Article 24 of the Patent Law, which prohibits others from disclosing the content without the consent of the applicant.

第二，就可以获得优先体验资格的用户而言，由于体验中心页面对领取体验码的用户存在保密承诺的要求，体验用户应当遵守其保密约定。专利申请人的真实意图在于所述下载软件仅限于供具有资格的用户试用、体验，而体验码一般是对试用者资格的限制。因此，虽然体验码并非密码，但其所起到的作用与密码基本相同，均是限定接触到该软件的人员的范围。故对于可以获得优先体验资格的用户，其当然具有明示的保密义务，其违反约定的保密义务泄露申请人的发明创造属于专利法第二十四条第三项规定的情形。

As for users who can obtain the priority experience qualification, due to the confidentiality commitment required by the experience center page for re-

ceiving the experience code, experience users should comply with their confidentiality agreements. The true intention of the patent applicant is that the downloaded software in question is limited to trial use only by qualified users, and the experience code is generally used to limit the scope of people who have access to the software. Therefore, although the experience code is not a password, its role is basically the same as a password, both of which limit the scope of personnel who have access to the software. Therefore, for those who can obtain the priority experience qualification, they certainly have an explicit obligation of confidentiality, and any violation of their confidentiality obligations to disclose the invention or creation of the applicant belongs to the situation specified in Paragraph 3, Article 24 of the Patent Law.

综上，证据 1 因跟帖人提示行为导致所述下载软件呈现的图形用户界面设计处于能够为公众得知的状态，且其时间早于本专利的申请时间，故属于本专利申请日之前公开的现有设计，但由于证据 1 所述软件公开行为属于专利法第二十四条第三项所规定的不丧失新颖性宽限期的情形，故证据 1 不能作为在先设计的对比文件。

In summary, Exhibit 1 showed that the graphic user interface design presented by the downloaded software was in a state that can be known to the public due to the prompting behavior of the follow-up person, and its time was earlier than the filing date of the Patent. However, the public disclosure behavior of the software mentioned in Exhibit 1 belonged to the situation specified in Paragraph 3, Article 24 of the Patent Law, which did not affect the novelty grace period. Therefore, Exhibit 1 could not be used as a prior art for comparison.

8. 具有一定缺陷的技术方案是否具备实用性

Whether technical solution with certain defects has practicality

【裁判要旨】

[Judgment Digest]

实用性要求发明或者实用新型专利申请能够产生积极效果，但不要求其毫无缺陷；只要存在的缺陷没有严重到使有关技术方案无法实施或者无法实现其发明目的的程度，就不能仅以此为由否认该技术方案具备实用性。

Speaking of practicality, it simply requires that an invention or utility model patent application can produce positive effects, but it does not require that such invention or utility model does not have any defects; as long as the defects are not severe enough to make it impossible to implement relevant technical solution or realize its invention purpose, it shall not be deemed that such technical solution is of no practicality merely because of such minor defects.

【关键词】

[Keywords]

专利申请　驳回复审　实用性　积极效果　缺陷

Patent application; reexamination of rejection; practicality; positive effects; defect

【案号】

[Case Number]

(2022)最高法知行终 68 号

(2022) SPC IP Admin. Final 68

【基本案情】

[Case Facts]

在上诉人厦门吉达丽鞋业有限公司（以下简称吉达丽公司）与被上诉人国家知识产权局实用新型专利申请驳回复审行政纠纷案中，吉达丽公司为申请号为 201820174833.3、名称为“一种鞋子”的实用新型专利申请（以下简称本申请）的申请人。国家知识产权局认为本申请的技术方案明显无益，脱离了社会需要，不具备实用性。故宣告维持其作出的驳回本申请的决定。吉达丽公司不服，向北京知识产权法院（以下简称一审法院）提起诉讼。一审法院认为本申请存在固有缺陷、明显无益、脱离社会需要，不具备实用性，判决驳回吉达丽公司的诉讼请求。吉达丽公司不服，向最高人民法院提起上诉。最高人民法院于 2022 年 6 月 28 日作出判决，撤销原判和被诉决定，并由国家知识产权局重新作出审查决定。

In the administrative dispute between the appellant, Xiamen Fullah Sugah Footwear Co., Ltd. (hereinafter referred to as "Fullah Sugah") and the appellee, CNIPA, over the reexamination of rejection patent application for the utility model "A Kind of Shoes" (hereinafter referred to as the "Application") with application No. 201820174833.3, of which Fullah Sugah was the applicant. Considering that the patented technical solution was obviously useless, had no social demand, and lacked applicability, CNIPA maintained its decision of rejecting the application. Then, Fullah Sugah filed a lawsuit to the Beijing Intellectual Property Court (hereinafter referred to as the "Court of First Instance"), which ruled to dismiss Fullah Sugah's Claims based on the ground that the Application had inherent defects, was obviously useless, had no social demand, and lacked utility. Subsequently, Fullah Sugah filed an appeal to the SPC. The SPC made a judgment on June 28, 2022, revoking the original verdict and the Disputed Decision, and ordered CNIPA to make a new decision.

【裁判意见】

[Judge's Opinion]

最高人民法院二审认为，专利授权的实用性要求申请专利的发明或者实用新型能够产生积极效果，并不要求发明或者实用新型毫无缺点。事实上，任何技术方案都不能是完美无缺的。只要存在的缺点或者不足之处没有严重到使有关技术方案根本无法实施或者根本无法实现其发明目的的程度，就不能因为存在这样或者那样的缺点或者不足之处，否认该技术方案具备实用性。申请中存在的缺陷可能恰恰是申请人进行下一步研发的方向，如此才能不断促使研发人员进行发明创造并推动科技进步。

The SPC, in the second-instance trial, held that the requirement of applicability for patent authorization requires that the invention or utility model applied for patent should have positive effects, and does not require that the invention or utility model should be completely without defects. In fact, no technical solution can be perfect. As long as the shortcomings or deficiencies are not severe enough to render the technical solution completely impractical or incapable of achieving its intended purpose, the applicability of the technical solution should not be denied based on such shortcomings or deficiencies. The existing defects in the application may precisely indicate the direction for the applicant's further research and development, which can continuously stimulate inventors to create and promote technological progress.

本案中，虽然如被诉决定和一审判决所述，向本申请所涉空心容腔中填充指甲油、药膏、香水等物品以及取用、更换上述内容物可能会存在一定不便，但上述物品因被填充进鞋子的空心容腔内，使用人出行时无须单独携带便可随时取用，能够在一定程度上满足社会需要，从而产生积极有益的社会效果，并非明显无益。被诉决定以及一审判决仅因本

申请的技术方案可能存在一定缺陷就直接认定该方案无积极效果，不符合专利法关于实用性的认定标准。

In this case, although, as mentioned in the disputed decision and the first-instance judgment, there may be some inconvenience in filling the hollow cavity of the shoe with nail polish, ointment, perfume, and the like, as well as in accessing and replacing the contents, these items are readily accessible without the need to carry them separately when they are filled into the hollow cavity of the shoe, which can meet certain social needs to some extent and produce positive and beneficial social effects. Therefore, it could not be considered obviously useless. The disputed decision and the first-instance judgment directly concluded that the technical solution lacked a positive effect solely based on the possibility of certain defects, which did not comply with the determination criteria for applicability under the Patent Law.

9. 零部件外观设计一般消费者的判断 Determination of ordinary consumers in the case of design of parts and components

【裁判要旨】

[Judgment Digest]

外观设计产品的一般消费者，通常包括在产品交易、使用过程中能够观察到或者会关注产品外观的人。如果产品的功能和用途决定了其只能被作为组装产品的部件使用，该组装产品的最终用户在正常使用组装产品的过程中无法观察到部件的外观设计，则一般消费者主要包括该部件的直接购买者、安装者。

The ordinary consumers in the case of design patent usually refer to those who can observe or pay attention to the appearance of the product in question in the course of transaction and usage. If a product can only be used as a part or component of the assembled product due to its function and usage, and the end user of the assembled product cannot observe the design of such part or component in the normal use of such assembled product, then the ordinary consumers shall mainly refer to the direct procurement staff or installers of such part or component.

【关键词】

[Keywords]

外观设计专利　无效宣告　组装产品部件　一般消费者

Design patent; invalidation; part or component of assembled product; ordinary consumers

【案号】

[Case Number]

（2021）最高法知行终 464 号

（2021）SPC IP Admin. Final 464

【基本案情】

[Case Facts]

在上诉人国家知识产权局与被上诉人东莞市昶通通讯科技有限公司（以下简称昶通公司）、原审第三人中航光电精密电子（深圳）有限公司（以下简称中航公司）外观设计专利权无效行政纠纷案中，涉及专利权人为昶通公司、专利号为 201630657867.4、名称为“线缆连接器”的外观设计专利（以下简称本专利）。中航公司就本专利向国家知识产权局提出无效宣告请求。国家知识产权局认为，本专利这类连接器主要用于连接柔性电路板，起到连接和导电的作用，其功能主要是通过产品的形状来实现，因此，该类产品的一般消费者更为关注产品的形状，特别是与电路板连接处的具体设计以及导电端子、导电片凹槽的分布。本专利与对比设计的区别点 1、3、4 属于局部细微差异；区别点 2 中部属

于本领域较为常见的设计，底部齿状凹凸与对比设计相符，上下部的浅浮雕凹槽一般消费者关注较低。上述区别点尚不足以对产品整体视觉效果产生显著影响，本专利不符合专利法第二十三条第二款的规定。国家知识产权局作出被诉决定，宣告本专利权全部无效。昶通公司认为，本专利与对比设计具有明显区别，故向北京知识产权法院（以下简称一审法院）提起诉讼。一审法院认为，本专利产品的“一般消费者”不应当是使用该外观设计产品制造出的成品的最终用户。本专利与对比设计的区别点 1、2、3 均不属于局部细微差异，能够引起一般消费者的注意。本专利与对比设计具有明显区别，符合专利法第二十三条第二款的规定，遂判决撤销被诉决定，国家知识产权局重新作出决定。国家知识产权局不服，向最高人民法院提起上诉。最高人民法院于 2022 年 8 月 9 日判决撤销原判，驳回昶通公司的诉讼请求。

In the administrative dispute between the appellant, CNIPA, and the appellees, Dongguan Changtong Communication Technology Co., Ltd. (hereinafter referred to as "Changtong") and AVIC Optoelectronic Precision Electronics (Shenzhen) Co., Ltd. (hereinafter referred to as "AVIC", the third party in the first instance), concerning invalidation of the design patent "Cable Connector" (hereinafter referred to as the "Patent") with patent No. 201630657867.4, Changtong was the patentee, who filed a request for invalidation of the Patent with the CNIPA. CNIPA considered that this type of connector is primarily used for connecting flexible circuit boards and serves the purpose of connection and conductivity. Its function is mainly achieved through the shape of the product. Therefore, ordinary consumers of this type of product pay more attention to the shape of the product, especially the specific design of the connection with the circuit board and the distribution of conductive terminals and grooves. According to CNIPA, the differences between the Patent and the prior designs were minor and localized in Points 1,

3, and 4. The design of the middle part of Point 2 was common in the art, and the tooth-shaped projection at the bottom matched the prior design. The shallow relief grooves on the upper and lower parts were of less concern to ordinary consumers. These differences were not sufficient to significantly affect the overall visual effect of the product and the Patent did not comply with the provisions of Paragraph 2, Article 23 of the Patent Law. Therefore, CNIPA made the disputed decision, declaring the Patent invalid in its entirety. Changtong believed that there were significant differences between the Patent and the prior designs, and filed a lawsuit with Beijing Intellectual Property Court (hereinafter referred to as the "Court of First Instance"). The Court of First Instance held that the "ordinary consumers" of the product covered by the design patent should not be end users of the finished product manufactured using this design. The differences between the Patent and the prior designs in Points 1, 2, and 3 were not minor and localized, but rather noticeable by ordinary consumers. The Patent had significant differences from the prior designs and complied with the provisions of Paragraph 2, Article 23 of the Patent Law. Thus, the Court of First Instance ruled to revoke the disputed decision and ordered CNIPA to make a new decision. Dissatisfied with the judgement, CNIPA appealed to the SPC. On August 9, 2022, the SPC ruled to revoke the original judgment and dismissed Changtong's claim.

【裁判意见】

[Judge's Opinion]

最高人民法院二审在确认被诉决定所归纳的相同点的基础上，综合各方意见，重新归纳了本专利与对比设计的相同点与区别点，认为：外观设计产品的一般消费者，通常包括在产品交易、使用过程中能够看到产品外观的所有消费者。如果产品的功能和用途决定了其只能被作为组装产品的部件使用，组装产品的最终用户在正常使用组装产品的过程中

仍然能够看到该部件的外观设计，则一般消费者既包括该部件的直接购买者、安装者，也包括组装产品的最终用户。如果组装产品的最终用户在正常使用组装产品的过程中无法看到部件的外观设计，则一般消费者应主要包括该部件的直接购买者、安装者。本案中，本专利为线缆连接器，主要用于连接柔性电路板，其作为电子产品部件被安装在 PCB 板上使用。电子产品制造完成后，最终用户无法看到本专利的外观设计，故本专利产品的一般消费者主要为直接购买、安装线缆连接器的群体。

Based on the confirmation of similarities summarized in the disputed decision, the SPC, in the second-instance trial, comprehensively summarized the similarities and differences between the Patent and the prior designs, taking into account the opinions of all parties involved. It held that the "ordinary consumers" of the design patent primarily include all consumers who can see the appearance of the product during the product transaction and use process. If the function and purpose of the product determine that it can only be used as a component of an assembled product, and the final users of the assembled product can still see the design of that component in the normal use process, the ordinary consumers should include not only the direct purchasers and installers of that component but also the final users of the assembled product. If the final users of the assembled product cannot see the appearance design of the component in the normal use process, the ordinary consumers should primarily include the direct purchasers and installers of that component. In this case, the Patent is a cable connector mainly used for connecting flexible circuit boards. It is installed on PCB boards as a component of electronic products. After the electronic products are manufactured, the final users cannot see the design of the Patent. Therefore, the ordinary consumers of the patented product primarily refer to the group of individuals who directly purchase and install the cable connector.

10. 兼具功能性和美观性的设计对整体视觉效果的影响 Impact of functional and aesthetic designs on the overall visual effect

【裁判要旨】

[Judgment Digest]

当产品某个部位的设计非为功能唯一限定时，该部位设计对于整体视觉效果的影响取决于一般消费者对其关注主要出于功能考虑还是美感考虑。如果一般消费者在产品正常使用时对该部位的关注主要出于相关功能而非视觉美感的考虑，则可以认定该部位的设计对整体视觉效果难以产生显著影响。

When the design of a part of a product is not the only available design subjected to its functions, the impact of such design on the overall visual effect depends on whether general consumer's focus is primarily on its functions or aesthetic aspect. If the general consumer mainly focuses on functions rather than on aesthetic aspect in the course of the normal usage of the product, it can be deemed that it is difficult for such design to remarkably influence the overall visual effect.

【关键词】

[Keywords]

外观设计专利　无效宣告　功能性　美观性　整体视觉效果　显著影响

Design patent; invalidation; functionality; aesthetics; overall visual effect; significant impact

【案号】

[Case Number]

(2021) 最高法知行终 464 号

(2021) SPC IP Admin. Final 464

【裁判意见】

[Judge's Opinion]

在上诉人国家知识产权局与被上诉人东莞市昶通通讯科技有限公司、原审第三人中航光电精密电子（深圳）有限公司外观设计专利权无效行政纠纷案中，最高人民法院指出，本专利设计1与对比设计的相同点占据了产品正面绝大部分空间比例，对一般消费者而言已经形成了基本一致的整体视觉印象。区别点1、3-5属于局部细微差异或一般消费者在产品正常使用过程中不容易看到的。区别点2即产品背面的设计，根据本专利图片中所显示的产品结构，结合产品的功能、用途，本专利只能将背面贴合PCB板进行安装。安装后，产品背面的设计因与PCB板贴合，视觉上无法看到。一般消费者在产品正常使用时，虽然如昶通公司所主张的能够看到产品背面的设计，但上述使用方式决定了其对产品背面的关注不会基于视觉美感的考虑，而是主要基于相关功能的考虑，本专利背面设计虽非功能唯一限定，但其兼具的有一定美感的视觉效果因产品安装后难以呈现，不会使一般消费者在产品正常使用中予以关注。一般消费者不会对本专利产生明显不同于现有设计的整体视觉印象。故本专利设计1与对比设计相比不具有明显区别。

In the administrative dispute over invalidation of the design patent between the appellant, CNIPA, and the appellees, Dongguan Changtong Communication Technology Co., Ltd., and AVIC Optoelectronic Precision Electronics (Shenzhen) Co., Ltd. (the third party in the first instance), the SPC pointed out that, firstly, the similarities between Design 1 of this Patent and the prior designs occupy the overwhelming majority of the front space of the product and have formed a basic uniform overall visual impression for ordinary consumers. Secondly, Differences 1 and 3-5 are local and subtle differences or are not easy to be seen by ordinary consumers in the normal use of the product. Difference 2 refers to the design on the back of the product. According to the product structure shown in the pictures of this Patent and combined with the functions and uses of the product, this Patent can only install the back of the product close to the PCB board. After installation, the design on the back of the product cannot be seen visually because it is closely connected to the PCB board. Although ordinary consumers can see the design on the back of the product during normal use, as claimed by Changtong, their attention to the back of the product is mainly based on relevant functions rather than aesthetic considerations. While the back design of this patent is not solely limited to functionality and does possess certain aesthetic visual effects, these effects are difficult to showcase once the product is installed. As a result, ordinary consumers do not pay particular attention to it during the normal use of the product and they will not have an overall visual impression of the Patent that is significantly different from the existing designs. Therefore, Design 1 of the Patent does not have significant differences compared to the prior art.

11. 专利权期限届满通知的可诉性
Justiciability of notice on patent expiration

【裁判要旨】

[Judgment Digest]

国家知识产权局基于专利权已因权利期限届满而终止的既定法律事实作出的专利权终止通知，并未对专利权人的权利义务产生实际影响，也未实际产生行政法意义上的法律效果，一般属于不可提起行政诉讼的行政行为。

If China National Intellectual Property Administration (CNIPA) issues a notice of patent termination based on the established legal fact that the patent

has come to an end due to the expiration of validity period, then such notice neither has actually affected the rights and obligations of the patentee, nor has it actually produced any substantive legal effect in the sense of administrative law, and thus generally speaking no administrative lawsuit can be filed against such notice as issued by CNIPA.

【关键词】

[Keywords]

行政行为　专利权终止通知　行政诉讼　受案范围

Administrative act; notice of termination of patent right; administrative litigation; scope of case acceptance

【案号】

[Case Number]

（2022）最高法知行终 54 号

（2022）SPC IP Admin. Final 54

【基本案情】

[Case Facts]

在上诉人吴某德与被上诉人国家知识产权局专利其他行政行为案中，涉及专利权人为吴某德、专利号为 200410064310.6、名称为“快速密封装置及其制造方法和新的用途以及快速密封方法”的发明专利（以下简称涉案专利）。吴某德于 2004 年 8 月 19 日提出涉案专利申请时，明确该申请系申请号为 98110707.9、申请日为 1998 年 3 月 11 日的原申请的分案申请。2018 年 3 月 15 日，国家知识产权局向吴某德发出专利权终止通知（以下简称被诉通知），告知吴某德根据 2008 年修正的专利法第四十二条（对应 1992 年修正的专利法第四十五条）的规定，涉案专利权因保护期届满于 2018 年 3 月 11 日终止。吴某德不服被诉通知，认为国家知识产权局审查程序违法，应在专利权终止后延长专利权保护期，故向北京知识产权法院（以下简称一审法院）提起诉讼，请求判令撤销被诉通知。一审法院经审理后判决驳回吴某德的诉讼请求。吴某德不服，向最高人民法院提起上诉，主张本案应适用新修订的专利法延长涉案专利权的保护期限，请求撤销一审判决。最高人民法院于 2022 年 5 月 5 日裁定撤销原判，驳回吴某德的起诉。

In the appeal case between the appellant, Wu, and the appellee, CNIPA, regarding other administrative acts related to the invention patent "Quick Sealing Device and Its Manufacturing Method, New Use, and Quick Sealing Method" (hereinafter referred to as the "Patent") with patent No. 200410064310.6, Wu was the patentee. When Wu filed the Patent application on August 19, 2004, it was explicitly stated that the application was a divisional application of the original application with application No. 98110707.9 and a filing date of March 11, 1998. On March 15, 2018, CNIPA issued a Notice of Termination of Patent Right (hereinafter referred to as the "Contested Notice") to Wu, informing him that according to Article 42 of the amended Patent Law (2008) [corresponding to Article 45 of the amended Patent Law (1992)], the patent right was terminated on March 11, 2018 upon the expiration of the protection period. Wu disagreed with the Contested Notice, claiming that the CNIPA's examination procedure was illegal and that the patent protection period should be extended after the termination of the patent right. Therefore, he filed a lawsuit with Beijing Intellectual Property Court (hereinafter referred to as the "Court of First Instance"), requesting the revocation of the Contested Notice. After the trial, the Court of First Instance ruled to dismiss Wu's claim. Dissatisfied with the judgement, Wu appealed to the SPC, arguing that the newly amended Patent Law should be applied in this case to extend the protection period of the Patent and requested the revocation of the first-instance judgment. On May 5, 2022, the SPC ruled to revoke the original judgment and rejected Wu's lawsuit.

【裁判意见】

[Judge's Opinion]

最高人民法院二审认为，基于专利权已经届满，吴某德作为专利权人的权利终止已属既定的法律事实，被诉通知的作出与否对专利权人的权利义务关系未产生实际影响。被诉通知既无发生法律效果的意思表示，也未在实际上产生行政法意义上的法律效果，属于不可提起行政诉讼的行政告知行为。吴某德的起诉不属于行政诉讼的受案范围，应予驳回。

The SPC, in its second-instance trial, held that since the patent right had already expired, the termination of Wu's rights as the patentee was an established legal fact. The issuance or non-issuance of the Contested Notice did not have any practical impact on the rights and obligations of the patentee. The Contested Notice neither constituted a declaration of legal effect nor produced administrative legal effects in the sense of administrative law. It was an administrative notification that could not give rise to administrative litigation. Therefore, Wu's lawsuit did not fall within the scope of administrative litigation and should be dismissed.

12. 许诺销售行为的认定 Identification of offering for sale

【裁判要旨】

[Judgment Digest]

被诉侵权人销售产品的意思表示内容明确、具体时，即可以认定其存在专利法所规定的许诺销售行为；该意思表示缺少有关价格、供货量以及产品批号等可能影响合同成立的内容，并不影响对许诺销售行为的认定。

When the accused infringer's expression of intention to sell products is clear and specific, it can be identified that such accused infringer conducts an act of offering for sale as stipulated in the Patent Law; and even if the expression of intention lacks such contents as price, supply quantity and product batch number that may affect the establishment of the contract, the identification of offering for sale will not be affected thereby.

【关键词】

[Keywords]

专利　许诺销售　合同成立　行政裁决

Patent; offering for sale; establishment of contract; administrative decision

【案号】

[Case Number]

(2021) 最高法知行终 451 号

(2021) SPC IP Admin. Final 451

【基本案情】

[Case Facts]

在上诉人南京恒生制药有限公司（以下简称恒生公司）与被上诉人江苏省南京市知识产权局（以下简称南京市知识产权局）、原审第三人拜耳知识产权有限责任公司（以下简称拜耳公司）专利行政裁决案中，涉及专利号为00818966.8、名称为“取代的噁唑烷酮和其在血液凝固领域中的应用”的发明专利（以下简称本专利）。恒生公司在一审庭审中认可涉案网站及展板上展示的产品“利伐沙班”落入本专利修改后的权利要求保护范围。恒生公司认为，其没有对涉案产品标注价格和供货量，涉案产品并未处于可以销售的状态，其宣传涉案产品的目的不是销售，没有销售涉案产品的意思表示，其展示涉案产品的行为属于针对计划开发利伐沙班仿制药的企业的定向投送，因此不构成许诺销售。

其不服宁知（2019）纠字5号专利侵权纠纷案件行政裁决，向江苏省南京市中级人民法院（以下简称一审法院）提起诉讼，请求撤销南京市知识产权局作出的上述行政裁决。一审法院认为，恒生公司已经明确作出销售涉案产品的意思表示。至于恒生公司是否具备生产、销售本专利产品的相应资质和生产能力以及是否具有实际可供销售的产品，都不是认定许诺销售的必要条件，不能改变恒生公司的行为性质。恒生公司的行为构成专利侵权。恒生公司不服，向最高人民法院提起上诉，主张其行为不构成许诺销售，即使构成许诺销售行为，也属于专利法规定的药品和医疗器械行政审批例外，因此不构成侵权。最高人民法院于2022年6月22日判决认定恒生公司的行为属于许诺销售，不属于专利法规定的药品和医疗器械行政审批例外，构成侵权。

In the appeal case between the appellant, Nanjing Hencer Pharmaceutical Co., Ltd., (hereinafter referred to as "Hencer"), and the appellees, Nanjing Intellectual Property Office of Jiangsu Province (hereinafter referred to as "Nanjing Intellectual Property Office") and Bayer Intellectual Property GmbH (hereinafter referred to as "Bayer", the third party in the first instance), it involved an invention patent titled "Substituted Oxazolidinone and Its Application in the Field of Blood Coagulation" (hereinafter referred to as the "Patent") with application No. 00818966.8. In the first-instance trial, Hencer acknowledged that the product "Rivaroxaban" displayed on the relevant website and exhibition board fell within the protection scope of the amended claims of the Patent. Hencer argued that it did not indicate the price and supply quantity of the product, and the product was not in a state of being ready for sale. The purpose of promoting the product was not for sales, and there was no intention to sell the product. Its display of the product involved was targeted at companies planning to develop generic drugs of Rivaroxaban, therefore not constituting offering for sale. Dissatisfied with the administrative decision [Ning Zhi (2019)Jiu Zi No. 5] in patent infringement dispute case, Hencer filed a lawsuit with Nanjing Intermediate People's Court (hereinafter referred to as the "Court of First Instance"), requesting the revocation of the above-mentioned administrative decision made by Nanjing Intellectual Property Office. The Court of First Instance held that Hencer had clearly expressed its intention to sell the product in question. Whether Hencer had the corresponding qualifications and production capacity to produce and sell the patented product, and whether it had actual products available for sale, were not necessary conditions for determining an offering for sale, and could not change the nature of Hencer's act, which constituted patent infringement. Dissatisfied with the judgment, Hencer appealed to the SPC, arguing that its act did not constitute an offering for sale. Even if it constituted an offering for sale, it fell within the administrative approval exception as stipulated in the Patent Law for drugs and medical devices, and therefore did not constitute infringement. On June 22, 2022, the SPC ruled that Hencer's act constituted an offering for sale, and did not fall within the administrative approval exception stipulated in the Patent Law for drugs and medical devices, and constituted infringement.

【裁判意见】

[Judge's Opinion]

最高人民法院二审认为，首先，恒生公司对于许诺销售侵权行为的法律理解存在错误。第一，许诺销售行为既可以针对特定对象，又可以针对不特定对象。根据《最高人民法院关于审理专利纠纷案件适用法律问题的若干规定》第十八条的规定，专利法第十一条、第六十九条所称的许诺销售，是指以做广告、在商店橱窗中陈列或者在展销会上展出等方式作出销售商品的意思表示。将产品通过陈列或演示、列入销售征订单、列入推销广告或者以任何口头、书面或其他方式向特定或不特定对象明确表示销售意愿的行为即构成许诺销售。许诺销售既可以面向

特定对象，也可以面向不特定对象，针对特定对象作出销售商品意思表示的定向投送亦属于许诺销售。第二，许诺销售行为既可以是发出要约，也可以是发出要约邀请。根据《最高人民法院关于审理侵犯专利权纠纷案件应用法律若干问题的解释（二）》第十九条的规定，产品买卖合同依法成立的，人民法院应当认定属于专利法第十一条规定的销售。许诺销售行为的目的指向销售行为，是一种法定的、独立的侵权行为方式，其民事责任承担不以销售是否实际发生为前提。许诺销售在性质上系销售者的单方意思表示，并非以产品处于能够销售的状态为基础，只要存在明确表示销售意愿的行为即可认定为许诺销售。当双方达成合意时，即不再属于许诺销售的范畴，而是属于销售。因此，当销售产品的意思表示内容明确、具体时，即可认定存在许诺销售行为。缺少有关价格、供货量以及产品批号等关于合同成立的条款，并不影响对许诺销售行为的认定。

The SPC, in its second-instance trial, held that: (1) Hencer had an erroneous understanding of the legal concept of infringement by offering for sale. Firstly, offering for sale can be directed towards both specific and non-specific targets. According to Article 18 of *Several Provisions of the Supreme People's Court on Issues concerning the Application of Law in the Trial of Cases on Patent Disputes*, the offering for sale as mentioned in Articles 11 and 69 of the Patent Law refers to making a sales offer or expression by means of advertising, displaying in shop windows, or exhibiting at trade fairs, among other methods. The act of displaying or demonstrating products, including them in sales orders, featuring them in promotional advertisements, or expressing a clear intention to sell through any oral, written, or other means to specific or non-specific individuals constitutes an offering for sale. Offering for sale can be directed towards specific or non-specific individuals. Targeted delivery of sales offers to specific individuals also falls within the scope of offering for sale. Secondly, offering for sale can be either an offer or an invitation for offer. According to Article 19 of *the Interpretation of the Supreme People's Court on Several Issues Concerning the Application of Law in the Trial of Patent Infringement Dispute Cases (II)*, when a purchase and sale contract is legally formed, the people's court should determine it as a sale under Article 11 of the Patent Law. Offering for sale, with the intent to engage in sales activities, is a legally recognized and independent form of infringement. The assumption of civil liability does not depend on whether the sale actually takes place. Offering for sale constitutes unilateral expression of the seller's intent, and it is not based on the product being in a sellable state. As long as there is a clear expression of intent to sell, it can be recognized as an offering for sale. Once the parties reach an agreement, it is no longer considered an offering for sale but rather a sale. Therefore, when the expression of intent to sell the product is clear and specific, it can be recognized as an offering for sale. The absence of specific contract terms regarding price, supply quantity, or product batch number does not affect the determination of an offering for sale.

其次，恒生公司销售涉案产品的意思表示明确、具体，其关于并无销售涉案产品意思表示的上诉主张与事实不符。第一，根据审理查明的事实，恒生公司在其官网“外销产品（制剂产品）”“外销产品（原料药产品）”栏目分别展示“利伐沙班片 Rivaroxaban Tablets”“利伐沙班 Rivaroxaban API”，在其官网“产品中心”栏目展示“利伐沙班片 Rivaroxaban Tablets”，产品包装上印制标注恒生公司注册商标。恒生公司和生命能公司参加“第十八届世界制药原料药中国展”，展板上有恒生公司和生命能公司的注册商标，展示有“Rivaroxaban API”（利伐沙班原料药）并配有包装瓶图片，展示有“Rivaroxaban Tablets”（利伐沙班片）并配有包装盒及包装瓶图片，标注产品规格为 10mg。根据商标法的规定，商标作为区别商品和服务来源的重要标志，商标使用人对其

使用商标的商品质量负责。恒生公司将其公司的注册商标使用在涉案产品的包装盒上，其使用商标的行为本身明确指示了商品的来源为恒生公司。从恒生公司对商标的使用目的可知，其通过使用商标，使他人了解涉案产品来源于恒生公司。对于浏览恒生公司官网以及参加展会的不特定对象而言，恒生公司通过在官网、展会上展示印有其注册商标的涉案产品图片等行为，传递了销售涉案产品的信息，其销售涉案产品的意思表示是明确、具体的。第二，本案没有证据证明恒生公司的宣传行为针对的是特定对象，且如上所述，针对特定对象作出销售意思表示的定向投送亦属于许诺销售。恒生公司在网站和展会上宣传展示的涉案产品面向不特定对象，虽然不具备合同的必备条款，仍属于许诺销售行为。恒生公司是否有实际的销售行为，销售行为是否违反了药品管理的法律规定，均不影响其构成许诺销售侵权行为的事实。至于恒生公司在其官网展示的“利伐沙班片”下方标注了原研药公司及原研商品，在展会展板下方标注“根据《美国联邦法规》（CFR）第35篇第271（e）（1）小节的规定，受专利法保护的产品可用于研究和开发用途”的行为，属于针对涉案产品所进行的说明，其实质是服务于通过恒生公司许诺销售了解到涉案产品的他人购买该产品，同样不影响其构成许诺销售侵权行为的事实。

(2) Hencer's expression of intent to sell the product in question was clear and specific, and its claim that it had no intention to sell the product involved was inconsistent with the facts. Firstly, according to the facts ascertained in the trial, Hencer displayed “Rivaroxaban Tablets” and “Rivaroxaban API” in the “Exported Products (Preparation Products)” and “Exported Products (Drug Substances)” sections on its official website respectively, displayed “Rivaroxaban Tablets” in the “Product Center” section, and printed the company's registered trademark on the product packaging. Hencer and Life Energy Company participated in the “18th CPHI China”. The booth displayed

the registered trademarks of Hencer and Life Energy Company. It also showed "Rivaroxaban API" (Rivaroxaban Active Pharmaceutical Ingredients) with pictures of packaging bottles, and "Rivaroxaban Tablets" with pictures of packaging boxes and bottles, indicating a product strength of 10 mg. According to the Trademark Law, the trademark is an important symbol for distinguishing the source of goods and services, and the trademark user shall be responsible for the quality of the goods using the trademark. Hencer used its registered trademark on the packaging box of the product involved, which clearly indicated that the source of the goods was Hencer. From the purpose of Hencer's use of the trademark, it conveyed the information that the product involved came from Hencer through the use of the trademark. For the non-specific entities who browsed the official website of Hencer and participated in the exhibition, Hencer's intent to sell the product involved was clearly and specifically indicated by displaying pictures of the product with its registered trademark on the official website and exhibition. Secondly, there was no evidence providing that Hencer's promotion activities were targeted at specific entities, and as mentioned above, targeted delivery of sales offers to specific entities was also an offering for sale. The promotion and display of the product involved by Hencer on its website and exhibition were aimed at non-specific entities. Although there were no necessary terms of a contract, it still constituted an offering for sale. Whether Hencer had actual sales behavior and whether the sales behavior violated the drug administration regulations would not affect the fact that it constituted an infringement by offering for sale. As for the statement that "Rivaroxaban Tablets" displayed on Hencer's website was followed by the original drug company and original drug product, and the statement under the exhibition board that "Products protected by patent law can be used for research and development purposes according to 35 CFR § 271 (e)

(1)," which belonged to the explanation of the product involved, in essence, it is to serve those who obtained the information of the product involved from Hencer's offering for sale to purchase the product, and it also did not affect the fact that it constituted an infringement by offering for sale.

综上所述，恒生公司未经专利权人拜耳公司的许可，通过网站、展会向不特定对象作出销售涉案产品的意思表示，且涉案产品落入本专利权保护范围，被诉裁决和一审判决关于恒生公司实施了许诺销售侵权行为的事实认定以及法律适用正确，予以维持。

Therefore, Hencer, without the permission of the patentee, Bayer, expressed its intention to sell the product involved to unspecified entities through websites and exhibitions, and the product involved fell within the protection scope of the Patent. The Disputed Decision and the first-instance judgment were upheld as the fact ascertained that Hencer had committed an infringement by offering for sale was correct and the law was applied correctly.

13. 针对不确定第三人的许诺销售行为不属于药品和医疗器械行政审批例外 Offering for sale to an uncertain third party is not an exceptional case in terms of administrative approval for drugs and medical devices

【裁判要旨】

[Judgment Digest]

专利法关于药品和医疗器械行政审批的侵权例外仅适用于为了获得仿制药品和医疗器械行政审批所需要的信息而实施专利的行为人以及为前述行为人获得行政审批而实施专利的行为人。后一主体以药品和医疗器械行政审批例外为由提出抗辩时，应当以前一主体的实际存在为前提和条件。后一主体针对不确定的第三人而非实际存在且已与其建立特定交易联系的前一主体许诺销售专利产品的，不具备适用药品和医疗器械行政审批侵权例外的前提和条件。

The infringement-related exception in the Patent Law with respect to administrative approval of drugs and medical devices only applies to those who exploit patent for the purpose of obtaining the information required for administrative approval of drugs and medical devices, and those who exploit patent for the aforementioned patent exploiters to obtain the administrative approval. If any latter patent exploiter defends on the ground of administrative approval exception for drugs and medical devices, the actual existence of the former patent exploiter should be the prerequisite and condition. If the latter patent exploiter offers to sell the patented product to uncertain third party rather than the former patent exploiter itself with whom it has established a specific transaction relationship, then it should be deemed that there is no prerequisite or condition for application of the aforementioned exception.

【关键词】

[Keywords]

专利　许诺销售　药品行政审批例外　行政裁决

Patent; offering for sale; exception for administrative approval of drugs; administrative decision

【案号】

[Case Number]

（2021）最高法知行终 451 号

（2021）SPC IP Admin. Final 451

【裁判意见】

[Judge's Opinion]

在上诉人南京恒生制药有限公司与被上诉人江苏省南京市知识产权局、原审第三人拜耳知识产权有限责任公司专利行政裁决案中，最高人民法院指出，我国法律对药品和医疗器械规定了严格的行政审批制度，生产厂商为了获得行政审批需要的数据和其他信息，需要进行长时间的大量研究、分析和临床实验等活动。为了在专利权保护期届满后及时推出仿制药品和医疗器械，保障社会公众及时获得价格低廉的药品和医疗器械，同时避免客观上延长专利权的保护期限，2008 年修正的专利法在第六十九条第五项增加了关于仿制药品和医疗器械不视为侵犯专利权的规定。根据该项规定，为提供行政审批所需要的信息，在专利保护期内制造、使用、进口专利药品或者专利医疗器械的行为以及在专利保护期内专门为其制造、进口专利药品或者专利医疗器械的行为，不视为侵犯专利权。专利法的立法目的是保护专利权人的合法权益，鼓励发明创造，推动发明创造的应用，提高创新能力，促进科学技术进步和经济社会发展。合法的专利权利保护是原则，法定不侵权的规定是例外。因此，在适用专利法第六十九条第五项时应当进行严格解释而非宽泛解释，依法从抗辩主体及其具体行为等方面进行分析认定。

In the appeal case between the appellant, Nanjing Hencer Pharmaceutical Co., Ltd., and the appellees, Nanjing Intellectual Property Office of Jiangsu Province and Bayer Intellectual Property GmbH (the third party in the first instance), the SPC pointed out that China's laws strictly regulate the administrative approval procedure for drugs and medical devices. In order to obtain the data and other information required for administrative approval, manufacturers need to conduct extensive research, analysis, and clinical trials for a long time. To ensure the timely launch of generic drugs and medical devices after the patent protection period expires, and to provide the public with affordable medications and medical devices, while avoiding objectively extending the patent protection period, the Patent Law was amended in 2008 to add a provision in Paragraph 5, Article 69, stating that the production and sale of generic drugs and medical devices shall not be deemed as infringement of patent rights. According to this provision, the act of manufacturing, using, or importing patented drugs or medical devices during the patent protection period solely to provide administrative approval-related information, as well as the act manufacturing or importing patented drugs or medical devices specifically for the aforementioned act during the patent protection period, are not considered as patent infringements. The legislative purpose of the Patent Law is to protect the legitimate rights and interests of patentees, encourage invention-creation, promote the application of invention-creation, improve innovative capabilities, and promote scientific and technological progress and economic and social development. The legitimate patent protection is universally applicable, while the statutory non-infringement provision is an exception. Therefore, when applying Paragraph 5, Article 69 of the Patent Law, a strict interpretation instead of a broad interpretation should be adopted, and analysis and determination should be made based on the defense subject and its specific behavior according to law.

首先，关于药品和医疗器械行政审批例外条款的抗辩主体及其条件。药品和医疗器械行政审批例外条款包含两种类型的主体：一是为了获得仿制药品和医疗器械行政审批所需要的信息而实施专利的行为人；二是为该行为人专门实施专利的行为人。前一主体系为自己申请行政审批，后一主体系为帮助前一主体申请行政审批，后一主体以药品和医疗器械行政审批例外为由提出抗辩时，应以前一主体的实际存在为前提和条件。恒生公司称其在官网和展会宣传涉案产品，受众对象是准备申请注册利伐沙班产品的企业，据此主张其属于合法的抗辩主体。经审查，

恒生公司没有提交存在某个生产利伐沙班药品的行政审批申请人的证据。恒生公司客观上通过官网和展会宣传作出了向不特定对象销售涉案产品的意思表示，没有事实表明其仅向准备申请注册利伐沙班产品的特定企业进行了宣传。恒生公司自己也非申请利伐沙班药品需要进行行政审批的主体。因此，恒生公司不符合药品和医疗器械行政审批例外抗辩的主体条件。

First, regarding subjects and conditions for the defense based on the exception clause for administrative approval of drugs and medical devices. The exception clause for administrative approval of drugs and medical devices includes two types of subjects: those who exploit the patent in order to obtain the information required for administrative approval of generic drugs and medical devices, and those who specifically exploit the patent for the aforementioned patent exploiters. The former subject applies for administrative approval on their own, while the latter subject assists the former in applying for administrative approval. When the latter subject raises a defense based on the exception clause for administrative approval of drugs and medical devices, it should be premised on the actual existence of the former subject. Hencer claimed that it was a legitimate defense subject since the product involved promoted on its official website and at exhibitions was targeted at companies preparing to apply for registration of Rivaroxaban products. However, upon examination, Hencer did not provided evidence of the existence of an administrative approval applicant for the production of Rivaroxaban. Objectively, it had made implicit statements through its official website and exhibitions indicating its intention to sell the product in question to unspecified entities, and there was no evidence suggesting that it had only promoted the product to specific enterprises preparing to apply for registration of Rivaroxaban products. Hencer itself was not a subject that requires administrative approval to manufacture Rivaroxaban drugs. Therefore, Hencer did not meet the subject conditions for the defense based on the exception clause for administrative approval of drugs and medical devices.

其次，关于药品和医疗器械行政审批例外的行为范围。药品和医疗器械行政审批例外条款所调整的行为是，为提供行政审批所需要的信息，为自己申请行政审批而实施“制造、使用、进口”行为，以及专门为前一主体申请行政审批而实施“制造、进口”行为，均不包括许诺销售行为。本案中，恒生公司实施的行为是向不特定对象许诺销售涉案产品，系以销售为目的而非以获取行政审批所需的信息为目的，超出了药品和医疗器械行政审批例外所规定的后一主体可以实施的“制造、进口”行为范围。恒生公司关于如果不通过涉案宣传行为就无法了解到有开发利伐沙班仿制药计划的企业的辩解，既与法律明文规定不符，又实际上不合法地压缩了专利权人在专利保护期内的合法利益空间。在药品专利权存续期间，未经许可实施不属于药品和医疗器械行政审批例外情形的许诺销售行为，可能导致不特定对象推迟向专利权人购买专利产品等后果，实质上削弱了对专利权人合法权益的保护。被诉裁决和一审判决认定恒生公司的许诺销售行为不属于药品和医疗器械行政审批例外规定的侵权行为例外，予以维持。

Second, regarding the scope of actions regulated by the exception clause for administrative approval of drugs and medical devices. The actions regulated by the exception clause for administrative approval of drugs and medical devices include the “Manufacturing, use, and import” actions carried out in order to provide the information required for administrative approval applied on their own, as well as the “manufacturing and import” actions specifically carried out to apply for administrative approval for the former subject, and both do not include the act of offering for sale. In this case, the action taken by Hencer was offering to sell the product in question to unspecified entities.

This behavior is aimed at sales rather than obtaining the information required for administrative approval, which exceeds the scope of "Manufacturing and import" that the latter subject is allowed to perform under the exception clause for administrative approval of drugs and medical devices. Hencer's defense that it would not have known about the companies planning to develop generic Rivaroxaban drugs without the said promotional activities is not in line with the clear provisions of the law. Furthermore, it illegitimately restricts the legitimate interests of the patentee during the patent protection period. During the term of a drug patent, unauthorized act of offering for sale that does not fall within the administrative approval exception for drugs and medical devices may result in unspecified entities delaying the purchase of patented products from the patentee, thereby substantially undermining the protection of the patentee's legitimate rights and interests. Both the Disputed Decision and the first-instance judgment concluded that Hencer's act of offering for sale did not fall within the infringement-related exception defined by the exception clause for administrative approval of drugs and medical devices, and therefore, they were upheld.

二、专利民事案件
Ⅱ. Civil Patent Cases

14. 说明书中技术用语特别界定和具体实施方式的区分 Distinction between the special definition of technical terms and specific embodiment in the description

【裁判要旨】

[Judgment Digest]

解释专利权利要求时，需要准确识别说明书记载的相关内容属于对权利要求用语的特别界定还是该权利要求的具体实施方式。说明书对此有明确表述的，以其表述为准；没有明确表述的，应当综合考量发明目的、发明构思、相关用语所属权利要求意图保护的技术方案等因素，从整体上予以考量。

In the construction of claims, it is necessary to accurately identify whether the relevant contents as contained in the description are special definition or specific embodiment of the claims. If there is clear expression in the description, such expression should prevail; if not, consideration should be given to such factors as the invention purpose, invention concept, and the technical solution under the protection of the claims that contain the relevant terms.

【关键词】

[Keywords]

专利　侵权　权利要求解释

Patent; infringement; construction of claims

【案号】

[Case Number]

(2020) 最高法知民终 580 号

(2020) SPC IP Civil Final 580

【基本案情】

[Case Facts]

在上诉人广州华欣电子科技有限公司（以下简称华欣公司）与被上诉人广州诚科商贸有限公司（以下简称诚科公司）、广州君海商贸有限公司（以下简称君海公司）、广州兆科电子科技有限公司（以下简称兆科公司）、峻凌电子（东莞）有限公司（以下简称峻凌公司）、佛山市厦欣科技有限公司（以下简称厦欣公司）侵害发明专利权纠纷案中，涉及专利号为 201010235151.7、名称为“一种触摸屏及其多路采样的方法”的发明专利（以下简称涉案专利）。华欣公司作为涉案专利的被许可人，认为诚科公司、君海公司、兆科公司、峻凌公司、厦欣公司未经许可大量制造、销售、许诺销售侵害涉案专利权的产品，且主观侵权恶意非常明显，故向广州知识产权法院（以下简称一审法院）提起诉讼，请求判令被诉侵权人停止侵害并连带赔偿经济损失 1000 万元和维权合理开支 20 万元。一审法院认为，被诉侵权产品仅是 12 块电路板及可由该 12 块电路板拼接成的一个电路框，缺少屏结构或触摸屏体，相应的触摸检测区没有载体，即无涉案专利权利要求 1 的触摸检测区，被诉侵权技术方案没有落入涉案专利权的保护范围，故华欣公司诉讼请求不能成立。华欣公司不服，向最高人民法院提起上诉，主张一审法院错误认定权利要求中“一种触摸屏”及“触摸检测区”必须要为实体屏结构，进而对于被诉侵权产品是否落入涉案专利权保护范围的认定存在错误。最高人民法院于 2021 年 10 月 16 日判决撤销原判，五被诉侵权人停止侵害，诚科公司、君海公司、兆科公司共同赔偿华欣公司经济损失 292.6 万元及维权合理开支 20 万元，峻凌公司、厦欣公司分别对前述赔偿金额中部分金额承担连带责任。

In the appeal case between the appellant, Guangzhou Huaxin Electronic Technology Co., Ltd. (hereinafter referred to as "Huaxin"), and the appellees, Guangzhou Chengke Trading Co., Ltd. (hereinafter referred to as "Chengke"), Guangzhou Junhai Trading Co., Ltd. (hereinafter referred to as "Junhai"), Guangzhou Zhaoke Electronic Technology Co., Ltd. (hereinafter referred to as "Zhaoke"), Junling Electronics (Dongguan) Co., Ltd. (hereinafter referred to as "Junling"), and Foshan Xiaxin Technology Co., Ltd. (hereinafter referred to as "Xiaxin"), regarding a dispute over infringement of an invention patent, the invention patent titled "A Touch Screen and Its Multi-Channel Sampling Method" (hereinafter referred to as the "Patent") with patent No. 201010235151.7 was involved. Huaxin, as a licensee of the Patent, claimed that Chengke, Junhai, Zhaoke, Junling, and Xiaxin had manufactured, sold, and offered to sell a significant number of infringing products without permission, showing obvious subjective infringement intent. Therefore, it filed a lawsuit with Guangzhou Intellectual Property Court (hereinafter referred to as the "Court of First Instance"), seeking an injunction to stop the infringement and joint compensation for economic losses of CNY 10 million and reasonable expenses of CNY 200 thousand. The Court of First Instance held that the accused infringing products were only 12 circuit boards and a circuit frame composed of these 12 circuit boards, lacking a screen structure or touch screen body. The corresponding touch detection area did not have a carrier, so in other words, it did not include the touch detection area as claimed

in Claim 1 of the Patent, and the accused infringing technical solution did not fall within the protection scope of the Patent. Therefore, Huaxin's Claims were dismissed. Dissatisfied with the judgment, Huaxin appealed to the SPC, arguing that the Court of First Instance wrongly interpreted "A touch screen" and "Touch detection area" in the Claims as requiring a physical screen structure, which resulted in a wrong determination on whether the accused infringing products fell within the protection scope of the Patent. On October 16, 2021, the SPC ruled to quash the original judgment and ordered the five accused infringers to cease the infringement. Chengke, Junhai, and Zhaoke should jointly compensate Huaxin for its economic losses totaling CNY 2, 926, 000 and reasonable expenses totaling CNY 200, 000. Junling and Xiaxin should be severally liable for partial amounts of the aforementioned compensation.

【裁判意见】

[Judge's Opinion]

最高人民法院二审认为，对专利权利要求进行解释时，需注意要准确识别说明书记载的相关内容属于对权利要求用语的特别界定还是具体实施方式。在说明书中没有明显的提示性语句，无法仅从形式上判断说明书记载的相关内容属于对权利要求相关用语的特别界定还是具体实施方式的情况下，应当结合发明目的、发明构思以及发明要求保护的技术方案，从整体上予以考量。如果说明书记载的相关内容属于对权利要求中出现的、本领域中没有确切含义的自造词作出的专门定义；或者属于对权利要求相关用语做出的有别于本领域通常含义的特别说明，则应当认定说明书记载的相关内容属于对权利要求用语的特别界定；除此之外，一般应认定为属于权利要求的具体实施方式。需注意的是，判断特别界定与具体实施方式时，通常先要确定权利要求中的相关用语在本技术领域是否具有通常含义，这往往需要引入本领域的技术词典、技术手册、工具书、教科书、国家或者行业技术标准等属于本领域技术人员已经取得一致认识的公知常识性证据，作为确定通常含义的依据。当然，主张相关事实的当事人，应就此举证或者进行充分说明。

The SPC, in its Second Instance trial, held that when constructing patent Claims, it is necessary to accurately identify whether the relevant contents contained in the description are special definitions of terms used in the Claims or specific embodiment of the Claims. If there is no obvious indicative statement in the description, and it is not possible to determine whether the relevant contents contained in the description are special definition or specific embodiment of the Claims based solely on its form, consideration should be given to such factors as the invention purpose, invention concept, and the technical solution protected by the patent Claims. If the relevant contents in the description are special definitions of self-coined terms that appear in the Claims and do not have a precise meaning in the art, or if they provide special explanations that differ from the ordinary meanings in the art of the terms used in the Claims, then it should be determined that the relevant contents contained in the description constitute special definitions of the terms used in the Claims. Otherwise, it is generally deemed as a specific embodiment of the Claims. It should be noted that when determining whether it is a special definition or a specific embodiment, it is usually necessary to first determine whether the relevant term in the Claim has an ordinary meaning in the relevant technical field. This often requires the introduction of technical dictionaries, handbooks, reference books, textbooks, national or industry technical standards, and other publicly known common knowledge of professionals in the field as evidence to ascertain the ordinary meaning. Of course, the party who asserts relevant facts should present evidence or provide sufficient explanation regarding this matter.

具体到本案中，涉案专利说明书记载的相关内容为触摸屏的具体实施方式而非特别界定。根据说明书所记载的涉案专利的技术领域、背景技术、发明内容等可知，涉案专利的发明点并不在于改进触摸屏的材质和结构，而在于一种能够提高触摸屏响应速度的多路采样方法及所对应的电路。说明书中所记载的具体实施方式的内容，也是围绕着涉案专利所提出的一种新的多路采样方法和电路而展开，在涉案专利触摸屏是否包含实体屏结构这一技术点上，说明书并没有对此作出有别于通常意义的特别说明。基于上述关于触摸屏的解释并结合涉案专利说明书关于触摸检测区并未作出特别界定的情况，本领域技术人员可以清楚地理解，涉案专利权利要求 1 中的触摸检测区应为红外发射管与红外接收管之间的空间区域，其并非必须依赖于有形的实体材料而存在。综上所述，涉案专利权利要求 1 的主题名称中的触摸屏应理解为既包括带有实体屏结构的接触式触摸屏，也包括不带有实体屏结构的非接触式触摸屏；触摸检测区应为红外发射管与红外接收管之间的空间区域，并非必须依赖于有形的实体材料而存在。

In this case, the relevant content contained in the Patent description is a specific embodiment of the touch screen rather than a special definition. Based on the technical field, background technology, and invention content described in the description of the Patent, it is evident that the inventive point of the Patent does not lie in improving the material and structure of the touch screen, but rather in a multi-channel sampling method and corresponding circuitry that can enhance the response speed of the touch screen. The specific embodiment recorded in the description also revolves around the new multi-channel sampling method and circuitry proposed by the Patent. Regarding the technical aspect of whether the patented touch screen includes a physical screen structure, the description does not provide any special explanation contrary to the ordinary meaning. Based on the above interpretation of the touch screen and considering that the description of the Patent does not offer any special definition for the touch detection area, persons skilled in the art can clearly understand that the touch detection area mentioned in Claim 1 of the Patent refers to the spatial region between the infrared emitters and infrared receivers, which does not necessarily exist relying on tangible physical materials. Therefore, it can be concluded that the term "Touch screen" in the subject-matter of Claim 1 of the Patent should be understood to encompass both the touch screen with physical screen structure (contact-type) and touch screen without physical screen structure (non-contact type). Additionally, the touch detection area refers to the spatial region between the infrared emitters and infrared receivers, which does not necessarily exist relying on tangible physical materials.

15. 权利要求解释中外部证据使用规则
Rules for external evidence in the construction of claims

【裁判要旨】

[Judgment Digest]

说明书对于权利要求中的技术术语没有作出特别界定的，应当首先按照本领域技术人员对于该技术术语的通常理解，而非直接按照日常生活中的通常含义进行解释。本领域技术人员对于技术术语的通常理解，可以结合有关技术词典、技术手册、工具书、教科书、国家或者行业技术标准等公知常识性证据，并可优选与涉案专利技术所属领域相近程度更高的证据予以确定。

Where the technical terms in the claims are not specifically defined in the description, they should be first construed in accordance with the general un-

derstanding of a person skilled in the art, rather than directly in accordance with the common meaning in daily life. The general understanding of the technical terms of a person skilled in the art can be determined in combination with such commonsense evidence as relevant technical dictionaries, technical manuals, tools, textbooks, national or industry technical standards as well as preferably selected evidence as similar as possible to the field to which the involved patent belongs.

【关键词】

[Keywords]

专利　侵权　权利要求解释　外部证据　公知常识

Patent; infringement; construction of claims; external evidence; common general knowledge

【案号】

[Case Number]

（2020）最高法知民终580号

（2020）SPC IP Civil Final 580

【裁判意见】

[Judge's Opinion]

在上诉人广州华欣电子科技有限公司（以下简称华欣公司）与被上诉人广州诚科商贸有限公司、广州君海商贸有限公司、广州兆科电子科技有限公司（以下简称兆科公司）、峻凌电子（东莞）有限公司（以下简称峻凌公司）、佛山市厦欣科技有限公司侵害发明专利权纠纷案中，最高人民法院指出，对专利权利要求进行解释时，需注意权利要求解释应当基于本领域技术人员的认知能力，并在本领域的技术背景和知识体系下进行合理解释。在说明书对于权利要求中的技术术语没有作出特别界定的情况下，应当按照本领域技术人员对于该技术术语的通常理解进行解释，而不是诉诸该技术术语在日常生活中的通常含义进行解释。相关技术词典、技术手册、工具书、教科书、国家或者行业技术标准等公知常识性证据，一般根据其与涉案专利技术所属领域的相近程度，作为认定本领域的技术背景和知识体系的相应证据。具体到本案中，触摸屏属于在本领域中已有确切含义的技术术语。根据各方当事人提交的《多媒体计算机实用检修技术（教程）》《多媒体技术应用基础》《计算机操作装配与维修》等本领域公知常识性证据的记载，对于本领域技术人员而言，权利要求 1 主题名称中的“触摸屏”，可以理解为既包括带有实体屏结构的接触式触摸屏，也包括不带有实体屏结构的非接触式触摸屏。并且，可以进一步认定，不带有实体屏结构的非接触式触摸屏属于本领域的公知常识。一审法院优先运用与涉案专利技术领域距离较远的《现代汉语词典》、百度百科等非本领域工具作为依据解释涉案专利中触摸屏，脱离本领域的技术背景和知识体系，结论有所不当，应予纠正。基于相同理由，华欣公司、兆科公司、峻凌公司等二审中提交的用于解释涉案专利权利要求 1 的公知常识证据之外的其他现有技术证据，缺乏相应证明力，不予采信。

In the appeal case between the appellant, Guangzhou Huaxin Electronic Technology Co., Ltd. (hereinafter referred to as “Huaxin”), and the appellees, Guangzhou Chengke Trading Co., Ltd., Guangzhou Junhai Trading Co., Ltd., Guangzhou Zhaoke Electronic Technology Co., Ltd. (hereinafter referred to as “Zhaoke”), Junling Electronics (Dongguan) Co., Ltd. (hereinafter referred to as “Junling”), and Foshan Xiaxin Technology Co., Ltd., regarding a dispute over infringement of an invention patent, the SPC pointed out that when constructing patent Claims, it is necessary to consider the cognitive ability of persons skilled in the art and to explain the terms reasonably based on the technical background and knowledge system in the art. Where the technical terms in the Claims are not specifically defined in the description, they should be first interpreted in accordance with the general under-

standing of a person skilled in the art, rather than directly in accordance with the common meaning in daily life. Relevant technical dictionaries, manuals, reference books, textbooks, national or industry technical standards, and other common general knowledge are usually used as corresponding evidence to determine the technical background and knowledge system in the art, depending on their proximity to the technical field to which the patent belongs. Specific to this case, "touch screen" is a technical term with a definite meaning in the art. According to the *Practical Maintenance Technology for Multimedia Computers, Fundamentals of Multimedia Technology Applications, Computer Assembly and Repair,* and other common knowledge evidences submitted by the parties, persons skilled in the art can understand that the term "touch screen" in the subject-matter of Claim 1 of the Patent encompasses both touch screens with physical screen structures and touch screens without physical screen structures. It can further be determined that touch screens without physical screen structures are common general knowledge in the art. The Court of First Instance had improperly relied on non-domain reference books such as *Modern Chinese Dictionary* and Baidu Baike, which are further from the technical field of the Patent, and deviated from the technical background and knowledge system in the art when interpreting the touch screen in the Patent. Its conclusion was inappropriate and should be corrected. Based on the same reasoning, other existing technical evidences submitted by Huaxin, Zhaoke, Junling, etc., during the Second Instance trial to construct Claim 1 of the Patent, beyond common general knowledge evidence, lack corresponding probative force and should not be adopted.

16. 主题名称对于权利要求保护范围的限定作用

Restrictive effect of the subject-matter on protection scope of patent claims

【裁判要旨】

[Judgment Digest]

专利主题名称本身构成或隐含了具体技术特征，或者系权利要求所限定的技术方案与现有技术的区别所在的，其对于权利要求的保护范围具有实质限定作用。

Where the subject-matter of the patent itself constitutes or implies specific technical features, or demonstrates the distinction between the technical solution defined by the claims and prior art, then the aforementioned subject-matter has a substantial restrictive effect on the protection scope of the claims.

【关键词】

[Keywords]

专利　侵权　主题名称　保护范围　限定作用

Patent; infringement; subject-matter; protection scope; restrictive effect

【案号】

[Case Number]

（2020）最高法知民终 1469 号

（2020）SPC IP Civil Final 1469

【基本案情】

[Case Facts]

在上诉人北京极智嘉科技有限公司（以下简称极智嘉公司）与被上诉人深圳市海柔创新科技有限公司（以下简称海柔公司）、百世物流科技（中国）有限公司佛山分公司（以下简称百世物流佛山分公司）侵害发明专利权及发明专利临时保护期使用费纠纷案中，涉及专利权人

为极智嘉公司、专利号为 201810557067.3、名称为“货架命中方法、装置、服务器和介质”的发明专利（以下简称涉案专利）。极智嘉公司认为，海柔公司未经许可，制造、销售、许诺销售落入涉案专利权保护范围的产品，百世物流佛山分公司未经许可，使用落入涉案专利权保护范围的产品，均侵害了涉案专利权，故向广州知识产权法院（以下简称一审法院）提起诉讼，请求判令海柔公司、百世物流佛山分公司停止侵害并连带赔偿经济损失、维权合理开支及涉案专利公布日至授权公告日期间的合理使用费共计 330 万元。一审法院认为，被诉侵权产品未落入涉案专利权保护范围，判决驳回极智嘉公司的诉讼请求。极智嘉公司不服，向最高人民法院提起上诉。最高人民法院于 2021 年 4 月 8 日判决驳回上诉，维持原判。

In the appeal case between the appellant, Beijing Geek+ Technology Co., Ltd. (hereinafter referred to as “Geek+”), and the appellees, Hai Robotics Co., Ltd. (hereinafter referred to as “Hai Robotics”), and Foshan Branch of Best Logistics Technology (China) Co., Ltd. (hereinafter referred to as “Best Foshan”), regarding a dispute over infringement of invention patent and invention patent royalties during the temporary protection period, an invention patent titled “Shelf Hitting Method, Device, Server and Medium” (hereinafter referred to as the “Patent”) with the patentee, Geek+, and patent No. 201810557067.3 was involved. Geek+ contended that Hai Robotics had manufactured, sold, and offered to sell products falling within the protection scope of the Patent without permission, while Best Foshan had used products falling within the protection scope of the Patent without permission, both of which infringed upon the Patent. Therefore, Geek+ filed a lawsuit with Guangzhou Intellectual Property Court (hereinafter referred to as the “Court of First Instance”), requesting the court to order Hai Robotics and Best Foshan to cease infringement and jointly compensate for its economic losses, rights protection expenses, and reasonable royalty fees totaling CNY 3.3 million from the publication date of the Patent until the date of authorization announcement. The Court of First Instance held that the accused infringing products did not fall within the protection scope of the Patent and thus rejected Geek+'s claims. Dissatisfied with the judgement, Geek+ appealed to the SPC. On April 8, 2021, the SPC ruled to dismiss the appeal and affirm the original judgment.

【裁判意见】

[Judge's Opinion]

最高人民法院二审认为，确定专利权的保护范围，应当考虑主题名称。主题名称对于权利要求保护范围的实际限定作用，取决于该主题名称对于权利要求所保护的主题本身产生何种影响。因此，有必要区分情形进行类型化分析。第一种情形，也是最典型的情形，即主题名称构成或隐含具体技术特征，属于此种情形的主题名称对于专利权的保护范围无疑具有限定作用。第二种情形，主题名称被用于区分现有技术。无论主题名称的抽象概括程度如何，如果其被用于区分现有技术，则意味着该主题名称具有类似权利要求特征部分的地位或功能，于此情形下，应认为主题名称对权利要求的保护范围具有限定作用。第三种情形，主题名称和特征部分的术语之间具有重述或引用的关系。如果同一技术术语在主题名称和技术特征中重复出现，使得它们之间互相参证解释的可能性显著提高，导致主题名称和特征部分从语义解释角度而言难以区分，于此情形下，亦应认为主题名称对权利要求的保护范围具有限定作用。

The SPC, in its Second Instance trial, held that when determining the protection scope for a patent, the subject-matter of the patent should be considered. The actual restrictive effect of the subject-matter on the protection scope of a patent claim depends on the impact of the subject-matter on the subject that the patent claim intends to protect. Therefore, it is necessary to

differentiate and conduct typological analysis based on the situation: The first and most typical situation is that the subject-matter of the patent constitutes or implies specific technical features. In this case, the subject-matter has an undeniable restrictive effect on the protection scope of the patent claim. The second situation is when the subject-matter is used to distinguish existing prior art. Regardless of the degree of abstractness of the subject-matter, if it is used to distinguish existing prior art, it means that the subject-matter has a similar status or function as the feature part of the patent claim, in which case the subject-matter should be considered to have a restrictive effect on the protection scope of the patent claim. The third situation is when there is repetition or reference between technical terms in the subject-matter and feature part. If the same technical term is repeatedly used in both the subject-matter and feature part, which increases the possibility of mutual reference and interpretation between them, making it difficult to distinguish the subject-matter from the feature part from a semantic interpretation perspective, then the subject-matter should also be considered to have a restrict effect on the protection scope of the patent claim.

本案中，权利要求 1 的主题名称为“一种货架命中方法”，其对于该项权利要求的保护范围具有限定作用，该限定作用主要体现在对涉案专利权利要求 1 所保护的技术方案具体应用领域的限定。第一，前已述及，如果主题名称被用于区分现有技术，则意味着该主题名称具有类似权利要求特征部分的地位或功能。根据涉案专利说明书“背景技术”记载的内容，涉案专利权利要求 1 提出的拣货方案，是对“‘货到人’机器人系统搬运货架”这一拣货方案的改进和优化。这种改进、优化方案显然有别于涉案专利说明书背景技术所描述的原先更为原始的“利用穿梭小车等传统自动化分拣设备搬运通常仅存放一种商品的货位”的拣货方案。鉴此，应认为涉案专利权利要求 1 主题名称中“货架”的含义不同于“货位”的含义，“‘货到人’机器人系统搬运货架”的技术方案亦明显有别于“穿梭小车等传统自动化分拣设备搬运货位”的技术方案。因涉案专利权利要求 1 的主题名称呈现出区分现有技术的特点，故该主题名称对于涉案专利权利要求 1 的保护范围具有限定作用。第二，前已述及，如果同一技术术语在主题名称和技术特征中重复出现，使得彼此从语义解释角度而言难以区分，则应认为主题名称对权利要求的保护范围具有限定作用。涉案专利权利要求 1 除了在主题名称中出现“货架”一词外，在特征部分的多处地方亦出现“货架池”“货架”等技术术语。鉴于“货架”这一技术术语在涉案专利权利要求 1 的主题名称和特征部分重复出现，使得彼此从语义解释角度而言难以区分，故应认为涉案专利权利要求 1 的主题名称对于该项权利要求的保护范围具有限定作用。第三，涉案专利说明书“发明内容”“具体实施方式”记载的相关内容，进一步印证了“货架”与“货位”各自具有特定的含义。根据涉案专利说明书的记载内容，涉案专利说明书系将“货架”作为“货位”的集合，“货位”系存放于“货架”之上，并强调涉案专利实施的是命中“货架”的方法。因此，“货架”与“货位”二者的含义并不相同。

In this case, the subject-matter of Claim 1 is “a shelf hitting method”, which has a restrictive effect on the protection scope of this claim. This restriction mainly lies in the specific application field of the technical solution protected by Claim 1. Firstly, as mentioned before, if the subject-matter is used to distinguish existing prior art, it means that the subject-matter has a similar status or function as the feature part of the claim. According to the “background technology” stated in the patent description, the picking scheme proposed in Claim 1 is an improvement and optimization of the “goods-to-person robot system for handling shelves” scheme, which clearly differs from the original and more primitive picking scheme described in the “background

technology" of the patent description, that is, using traditional automated sorting equipment such as shuttle cars to handle storage locations typically storing only one type of product. Therefore, it should be recognized that the meaning of "shelf" in the subject-matter of Claim 1 is different from that of "storage location", and the technical solution of "goods-to-person robot system for handling shelves" is obviously different from the technical solution of "using traditional automated sorting equipment such as shuttle cars to handle storage locations". As the subject-matter of Claim 1 exhibits the characteristic of distinguishing existing prior art, it can be concluded that the subject-matter has a restrictive effect on the protection scope of Claim 1 of the Patent. Secondly, as mentioned before, if the same technical term appears repeatedly in both the subject-matter and the technical feature, making it difficult to distinguish each other from a semantic interpretation perspective, then the subject-matter should be considered to have a restrictive effect on the protection scope of the Claim. In addition to the term "shelf" appearing in the subject-matter, technical terms such as "shelf pool" and "shelf" also appear in multiple places in the feature part of Claim 1. Since the term "Shelf" appears repeatedly in both the subject-matter and the feature part of Claim 1, making it difficult to distinguish each other from a semantic interpretation perspective, it should be acknowledged that the subject-matter of Claim 1 has a restrictive effect on the protection scope of this Claim. Thirdly, the relevant content in the "content of the invention" and "embodiments" in the patent description further confirms the specific meanings of "shelf" and "storage location". According to the contents of the patent description, "shelf" is a collection of "storage locations", with the "storage locations" placed on the "shelf", emphasizing that the claimed invention is a method of hitting the "shelf". Therefore, the meanings of "shelf" and "storage location" are not the same.

本案中，海柔公司的拣选方法是精准命中仅盛放一种商品的料箱，故“命中料箱”相当于“命中货位”。因此，在涉案专利权利要求 1 的主题名称已经将该项权利要求所保护的技术方案的应用领域限定于“命中货架”的情况下，海柔公司被诉侵权的“命中料箱”的方法应认为未落入涉案专利权利要求 1 的保护范围。

In this case, Hai Robotics' picking method precisely hits bins that only contain one product. Therefore, “hitting bins” is equivalent to “hitting storage locations”. Considering that the subject-matter of Claim 1 has already limited the application field of the protected technical solution to “hitting shelves”, Hai Robotics' accused infringing method of “hitting bins” should be deemed outside the protection scope of Claim 1.

17. 背景技术、发明目的在等同侵权判断中的考量 Taking background technology and invention purpose into account in determination of equivalent infringement

【裁判要旨】

[Judgment Digest]

如果本领域技术人员完整阅读权利要求书、说明书和附图后认为，涉案专利的发明目的之一是克服某项背景技术的技术缺陷，且其系以摒弃该背景技术方案的方式来克服该技术缺陷，则不应再通过认定等同侵权将含有该技术缺陷的技术方案纳入专利权保护范围。

Where after reading the claims, description and drawings, a person skilled in the art is of the opinion that one of the invention purposes of the involved patent is to overcome the technical defect of a certain background technology by discarding the technical solution of the background technology, the

technical solution with such technical defect should not be put under the protection of the patent by applying the doctrine of equivalents.

【关键词】

[Keywords]

专利　侵权　等同　背景技术　发明目的　技术缺陷

Patent; infringement; equivalent; background technology; objective of the invention; technical defect

【案号】

[Case Number]

(2021) 最高法知民终 860 号

(2021) SPC IP Civil Final 860

【基本案情】

[Case Facts]

在上诉人佛山市宝索机械制造有限公司（以下简称宝索公司）与被上诉人佛山市南海区德昌誉机械制造有限公司（以下简称德昌誉公司）、河北金博士集团有限公司（以下简称金博士公司）侵害实用新型专利权纠纷案中，涉及专利权人为宝索公司、专利号为201621299560.2、名称为“以机械压合纸卷的封口装置”的实用新型专利（以下简称涉案专利）。涉案专利限定的挤压机构是用以将纸卷按压在第一夹压件的边缘处，并使得纸卷圆周面在第一夹压件的边缘处形成由凹陷部和未凹陷部组成的台阶状形变。被诉侵权产品的挤压机构是将纸卷按压在第一夹压件和第二夹压件的边缘处，并使得纸卷圆周面在第一夹压件和第二夹压件的边缘处形成类似台阶状的形变。宝索公司向河北省石家庄市中级人民法院（以下简称一审法院）提起诉讼，认为上述技术特征构成等同特征，主张德昌誉公司、金博士公司侵害其专利权。一审法院判决驳回宝索公司的诉讼请求。宝索公司不服，向最高人民法院提起上诉。最高人民法院于 2021 年 8 月 9 日判决驳回上诉，维持原判。

In the appeal case between the appellant, Baosuo Paper Machinery Manufacture Co., Ltd. (hereinafter referred to as "Baosuo"), and the appellees, Foshan Nanhai Dechangyu Paper Machinery Manufacturing Co., Ltd. (hereinafter referred to as "Dechangyu"), and Hebei Jinboshi Group Co., Ltd. (hereinafter referred to as "Jinboshi"), regarding a dispute over infringement of utility model patent, an utility model patent titled "A Sealing Device that Mechanically Compresses Paper Rolls" (hereinafter referred to as the "Patent") with the patentee, Baosuo, and patent No. 201621299560.2 was involved. The extrusion mechanism defined by the Patent is used to press the paper roll at the edge of the first pressing member, causing the circumferential surface of the paper roll to form a step-like deformation consisting of a recessed part and an unrecessed part at the edge of the first pressing member. The accused infringing extrusion mechanism presses the paper roll at the edges of both the first pressing member and the second pressing member, causing the circumferential surface of the paper roll to form a similar step-like deformation at the edges of both pressing members. Baosuo filed a lawsuit with Shijiazhuang Intermediate People's Court of Hebei Province (hereinafter referred to as the "Court of First Instance"), claiming that the above-mentioned technical feature constituted an equivalent feature, and Dechangyu and Jinboshi had infringed upon its patent. The Court of First Instance ruled to dismiss Baosuo's claims. Then, Baosuo appealed to the SPC, which, on August 9, 2021, ruled to dismiss the appeal and affirm the original judgment.

【裁判意见】

[Judge's Opinion]

最高人民法院二审认为，根据涉案专利说明书第［0002］和第［0003］段记载可知，涉案专利技术方案所要解决的技术问题正是在于

对纸卷机械压合封口方式的改进，以期解决现有技术中封口质量不高的缺陷。特别地，涉案专利说明书明确指出，公开号为 CN105293196A 的中国专利申请采用夹钳夹压封口的技术方案存在封口质量极不稳定的缺陷，该方法的封口质量依赖于夹具能否在纸卷圆周面上挤压出凸出于纸卷圆周面的压合部。尽管该背景技术中未明确是否存在挤压机构，但是根据本领域普通技术人员的常识，为了能在纸卷圆周面上挤压出凸出于纸卷圆周面的压合部，夹具与纸卷圆周面之间需存在一定挤压力以期形成形变以便压合，该形变显然是形成在夹具的两个夹钳的边缘处。而涉案专利目的是提供一种以机械压合纸卷的封口装置，以克服上述背景技术的缺陷，即涉案专利的技术方案正是针对该背景技术存在的技术缺陷而提出。涉案专利说明书具体实施方式第［0025］段对台阶状形变的具体形成方式和位置作了进一步的说明，其中明确记载挤压机构施加适当压力使得纸卷的圆周面在第一夹压件的边缘处形成由凹陷部和未凹陷部组成的台阶状形变。可见，涉案专利技术方案改进背景技术中在两个夹钳边缘处形成形变的技术手段，采用通过挤压机构施压在第一夹压件边缘处形成台阶状形变，即涉案专利技术方案的形成正是在该背景技术的基础上作出的改进。被诉侵权产品的挤压机构是将纸卷按压在第一夹压件和第二夹压件的边缘处以形成形变，与背景技术在夹具的两个夹钳的边缘处形成形变的技术手段相比并无实质性差异，与涉案专利技术特征 1 相比，两者技术手段差异明显。因此，被诉侵权产品的该技术特征与涉案专利相应技术特征不构成等同技术特征。

The SPC, in its Second Instance trial, held that according to [0002] and [0003] paragraphs in the patent description, the technical problem to be solved by the patented technical solution is precisely the improvement of the sealing method by mechanically compressing paper rolls, with the aim to address the low sealing quality issue in the prior art. Specifically, the patent description explicitly points out the defect of extremely unstable sealing quality in the technical solution using clamp compression sealing as described in Chinese patent application CN105293196A. The sealing quality of this method relies on whether the fixture can squeeze out a protruding compression section on the circular surface of the paper roll. Although it is not explicitly stated in the background technology whether there is an extrusion mechanism, it is common general knowledge for those skilled in the art that in order to extrude a protruding compression section on the circular surface of the paper roll, there needs to be a certain extrusion force between the fixture and the circular surface to induce deformation for compression sealing. This deformation clearly occurs at the edges of the two clamps of the fixture. On the other hand, the purpose of the Patent is to provide a sealing device that mechanically compresses paper rolls to overcome the defect of the aforementioned background technology. In other words, the technical solution of the Patent is precisely aimed at addressing the technical defect existing in the background technology. The specific formation method and position of the step-shaped deformation are further explained in [0025] paragraph of the patent description, which clearly states that the extrusion mechanism applies appropriate pressure to form a step-shaped deformation consisting of a recessed part and an unrecessed part at the edge of the first pressing member on the circular surface of the paper roll. It can be seen that the patented technical solution improves the technical means in the background technology for forming deformation at the edges of two clamps, which is achieved by applying pressure through an extrusion mechanism to create a stepped deformation at the edge of the first pressing member. In other words, the technical solution of the Patent is exactly an improvement made based on the aforementioned background technology. The extrusion mechanism of the accused infringing product compresses the paper roll at the edges of the first and second pressing members to induce deformation,

which is not substantially different from the technical means of forming deformation at the edges of the clamps in the background technology. Compared with Technical Feature 1 of the Patent, the technical means of the accused infringing product clearly exhibit differences. Therefore, the corresponding technical features of the accused infringing product and the Patent did not constitute equivalent technical features.

18. 同日申请的发明专利与实用新型专利的衔接保护 Coordinated protection of the invention patent and utility model patent with the same technical solution and the same date of filing

【裁判要旨】

[Judgment Digest]

申请人就同样的发明创造于同日申请实用新型专利和发明专利，在获得实用新型专利授权后，为取得发明专利授权而放弃实用新型专利权。其就他人在实用新型专利授权日至发明专利授权日期间未经许可实施专利技术方案的行为，可以循以下途径请求救济：一是对于实用新型专利授权日至发明专利申请公布日期间未经许可实施专利技术方案的行为，可以侵害实用新型专利权为由请求救济；二是对于发明专利申请公布日至授权日期间未经许可实施专利技术方案的行为，可选择以支付发明专利临时保护期使用费或者侵害实用新型专利权为由请求救济。

Where an applicant applies for both a utility model patent and an invention patent for the same technical solution on the same day, after obtaining the grant of utility model patent, the applicant may choose to give up such utility model patent for obtaining the grant of invention patent. Under such circumstances, if any other party embodies the patented technical solution without authorization between the date of grant of the utility model patent and the date of grant of the invention patent, the applicant can seek for relief in the following ways: (1) as for embodying the patented technical solution without authorization between the date of grant of the utility model patent and the date of publishing the application of the invention patent, the applicant can seek for relief on the ground of infringement upon the utility model patent; (2) as for embodying the patented technical solution without authorization between the date of publishing the application of the invention patent and the date of grant of the invention patent, the applicant can seek for relief on the ground of either payment of royalties for the temporary protection period of the invention patent or infringement upon the utility model patent.

【关键词】

[Keywords]

发明　实用新型　同日申请　侵权　临时保护期使用费　衔接保护

Invention; utility model; application on the same day; infringement; royalties during the temporary protection period; coordinated protection

【案号】

[Case Number]

（2020）最高法知民终 1738 号

（2020）SPC IP Civil Final 1738

【基本案情】

[Case Facts]

在上诉人湖南五新隧道智能装备股份有限公司（以下简称五新公司）与被上诉人北京新能正源智能装备有限公司（以下简称新能正源公司）等侵害专利权纠纷案中，涉及新能正源公司同日申请并获得授权的专利号为 201720132080.5、名称为“用于拱架的吊装夹具、抓手机构和拱架台车”的实用新型专利和专利号为 201710078689.3、名称

为“用于拱架的吊装夹具、抓手机构和拱架台车”的发明专利。新能正源公司在发明专利临时保护期内取得侵权证据，并在发明专利授权公告后向陕西省西安市中级人民法院（以下简称一审法院）提起诉讼，主张五新公司制造、销售的拱架安装车侵害其涉案专利权，请求判令停止侵害并赔偿经济损失及维权合理开支共计 108 余万元。一审法院经审理，判决五新公司停止侵害并赔偿经济损失及维权合理开支 100 万元。五新公司不服，向最高人民法院提起上诉。最高人民法院于 2022 年 11 月 2 日判决改判五新公司赔偿经济损失 20 万元、维权合理开支 8 万余元。

In the appeal case between the appellant, Hunan Wuxin Tunnel Intelligent Equipment Co., Ltd. (hereinafter referred to as "Wuxin"), and the appellee, Beijing Xinneng Zhengyuan Equipment Co., Ltd. (hereinafter referred to as "Xinneng Zhengyuan"), regarding a dispute over patent infringement, the utility model patent with patent No. 201720132080.5 and the invention patent with patent No. 201710078689.3, both titled "Lifting Clamp, Gripping Mechanism and Arch Frame Trolley for Arch Frame", which were applied for and granted on the same day by Xinneng Zhengyuan, were involved. Xinneng Zhengyuan obtained evidence of infringement during the temporary protection period of the invention patent and filed a lawsuit with Xi'an Intermediate People's Court of Shaanxi Province (hereinafter referred to as the "Court of First Instance") after the invention patent was granted, claiming that the arch frame installation vehicle manufactured and sold by Wuxin infringed upon its patent. It requested that the court order Wuxin to stop the infringement and compensate for its economic losses and reasonable expenses for rights protection totaling more than CNY 1.08 million. After the trial, the Court of First Instance ruled that Wuxin should stop the infringement and compensate Xinneng Zhengyuan CNY 1 million for its economic losses and reasonable expenses for rights protection. Dissatisfied with the judgment, Wuxin appealed to the SPC. On November 2, 2022, the SPC ruled to change the original judgment. Wuxin was ordered to compensate Xinneng Zhengyuan CNY 200 thousand for its economic losses and more than CNY 80 thousand for reasonable expenses for rights protection.

【裁判意见】

[Judge's Opinion]

最高人民法院二审认为，专利法允许申请人同日对同样的发明创造既申请实用新型专利又申请发明专利，是为了全面保障发明创造申请人的权益，故不能因为发明专利申请获得授权而否定申请人此前依据实用新型专利申请所获得的利益。申请人就同样的发明创造于同日申请实用新型专利和发明专利，在获得实用新型专利授权后为取得发明专利授权而声明放弃实用新型专利权，此种情形下，就他人在实用新型专利授权日至发明专利授权日期间未经许可实施专利技术方案的行为，专利权人可循以下途径请求公力救济：一是对于实用新型专利授权日至发明专利申请公布日期间未经许可实施专利技术方案的行为，可以侵害实用新型专利权为由请求救济；二是对于发明专利申请公布日至授权日期间未经许可实施专利技术方案的行为，可以支付发明专利临时保护期使用费为由请求救济，亦可以侵害实用新型专利权为由请求救济。

The SPC, in the Second Instance trial, held that according to the Patent Law, an applicant may simultaneously apply for a utility model patent and an invention patent for the same invention-creation on the same day. This is done to fully safeguard the rights and interests of the inventors. Therefore, the grant of an invention patent should not deny the benefits obtained by the applicant based on the earlier application for a utility model patent. Where an applicant applies for both utility model patent and invention patent for the same invention-creation on the same day, after obtaining the grant of utility model patent, the applicant may choose to give up such utility model patent for obtai-

ning the grant of invention patent. Under such circumstances, if any other party embodies the patented technical solution without authorization between the date of grant of the utility model patent and the date of grant of the invention patent, the applicant can seek for relief in the following ways: (1) as for embodying the patented technical solution without authorization between the date of grant of the utility model patent and the date of publishing the application of the invention patent, the applicant can seek for relief on the ground of infringement upon the utility model patent; (2) as for embodying the patented technical solution without authorization between the date of publishing the application of the invention patent and the date of grant of the invention patent, the applicant can seek for relief on the ground of either payment of royalties for the temporary protection period of the invention patent or infringement upon the utility model patent.

本案中，涉案发明专利申请经过修改，其在授权公告前要求保护的范围与涉案实用新型专利授权公告的保护范围不同，不构成同样的发明创造，可以分别获得授权。但两专利的权利要求均经过无效程序中的修改，并在修改后的权利要求的基础上维持有效。由于修改前的权利要求自始无效，故两专利权的保护范围应自始以修改后的权利要求为准。涉案实用新型专利和涉案发明专利修改后存在保护范围相同的权利要求，构成同样的发明创造。因此，本案实质上仍然涉及两专利权衔接保护的问题，可以参照适用上述规则。对于新能正源公司的诉讼主张，首先，专利法中关于同日申请的实用新型和发明专利的规定是为了全面保障发明创造申请人的权益而作出的特殊制度安排，既能使申请人较早地获得专利权保护，同时又维护专利的先申请制度、保护期限制度以及禁止重复授权制度。本案中虽然权利人未放弃实用新型专利权，但同样涉及同日申请的、存在相同保护范围的发明和实用新型专利应如何保护的问题。参照上述分析，权利人对于他人未经许可在实用新型专利授权日至发明专利授权日这段期间的实施行为，有权以实用新型专利权作为权利基础主张侵权损害赔偿责任。其次，在被诉侵权行为从实用新型专利授权之日持续至发明专利授权之后的情况下，不能苛求当事人在主张权利时对请求权基础作出准确区分，人民法院可以就此进行释明。如果权利人基于发明专利权主张权利，且主张的侵权损害赔偿范围及于实用新型专利权有效期间，人民法院可以一并处理，属于诉的客体合并，不违反法律规定，亦符合同日申请发明和实用新型专利的制度目的。此种情形下，权利人无须再另行主张发明专利临时保护期使用费，有利于纠纷的实质解决和减轻当事人的讼累。需要指出的是，本案的特殊之处在于，涉案实用新型专利系因未缴纳年费而终止，故从涉案发明专利授权日至涉案实用新型专利因未缴纳年费而终止这段期间，有两项保护范围相同的专利权利要求同时处于有效状态。基于专利权的有效推定原则，在本案侵权诉讼中不能否定任一项专利权的有效性，但理应择一保护，不能重复保护。将涉案发明创造相关侵权纠纷合并审理，能更合理地处理这一特殊情况所带来的问题。最后，本案中一审法院未对上述问题予以明确，新能正源公司在二审中主张其侵权损害赔偿诉请涵盖五新公司等在涉案实用新型专利授权日至涉案发明专利授权日期间的专利实施行为，新能正源公司的该项主张系对其一审主张的损害赔偿范围的进一步澄清，不属于在二审程序中新增的诉讼请求，可以对此进行审理，无须征得其他当事人的同意。

In this case, the invention patent application has undergone modifications, and the protection scope requested before the grant announcement is different from the protection scope of the utility model patent granted. Therefore, they do not constitute the same invention-creation and can be granted separately. However, both patent claims have been modified during the invalidation proceedings and the modified claims are maintained as valid. Since the pre-modification claims are deemed invalid from the beginning, the protection

scope for both patents should be based on the modified claims from the beginning. As the modified utility model patent and invention patent have overlapping claims in terms of protection scope, they constitute the same invention-creation. Therefore, the case still involves the issue of coordinated protection of the two patents, and the above rules can be applied. Regarding the claims made by Xinneng Zhengyuan, first, the provisions in the Patent Law regarding patents of utility model and invention filed on the same day are special arrangements made to fully protect the rights of inventors. It allows the applicant to obtain patent protection at an earlier stage while maintaining the principles of the first-to-file system, limitations on the protection period, and prohibitions on repetitive grants. Although the right holder did not abandon the utility model patent in this case, the issue of how to protect the invention and utility model patents filed on the same day with the same protection scope still arises. Referring to the above analysis, the right holder has the right to claim compensation on the ground of infringement upon the utility model patent for embodying the patented technical solution without authorization between the date of grant of the utility model patent and the date of grant of the invention patent. Second, if the accused infringing acts continue from the date of grant of the utility model patent and the date of grant of the invention patent, it is not necessary to strictly distinguish the basis of claims when asserting rights. The people's court can provide clarification on this matter. If the right holder claims compensation for infringement upon the invention patent and the scope of claims extends to the validity period of the utility model patent, the people's court can treat it together as a merged subject matter of the lawsuit, which does not violate legal provisions and is consistent with the purpose of the system for filing invention and utility model patents on the same day. Under such circumstances, the right holder does not need to separately claim royalties during the temporary protection period of the invention patent, which is advantageous for the substantive resolution of the dispute and reduces the litigation burden on the parties. It should be noted that the special aspect of this case is that the utility model patent involved was terminated due to non-payment of annuities. Therefore, from the date of grant of the invention patent to the date of termination of the utility model patent, there are two patent claims with the same protection scope in a valid state. Based on the presumption of patent validity, neither patent right can be denied in the infringement litigation of this case, but a choice must be made for protection, and double protection cannot be granted. Consolidating the related infringement disputes over the invention-creation in this case allows for a more reasonable treatment of the issues arising from this special situation. Furthermore, the Court of First Instance did not provide a clear answer to the above issue. In the Second Instance, Xinneng Zhengyuan claimed that its claim for damages covers the patent embodiments of Wuxin and others from the date of grant of the utility model patent to the date of grant of the invention patent. This claim by Xinneng Zhengyuan further clarifies its claim for damages in the First Instance and does not constitute a new claim in the Second Instance. Therefore, it can be treated in the trial without obtaining the consent of other parties.

综上所述，本案的案由应确定为侵害专利权纠纷，如涉及损害赔偿问题的审理，则本案的审理范围不仅包括涉案发明专利授权日之后的损害赔偿，还包括涉案实用新型专利授权日至涉案发明专利授权日期间的损害赔偿。

Based on the above, the cause of action in this case should be determined as a patent infringement dispute. If the trial involves the issue of damages, the scope of the trial should not only include damages after the date of grant of the invention patent, but also damages from the date of grant of the utility model

patent to the date of grant of the invention patent.

19. 被诉侵权产品制造者的认定 Identification of manufacturer of the accused infringing product

【裁判要旨】

[Judgment Digest]

侵害专利权纠纷中，被诉侵权产品上标识有真实且指向明确的经营主体信息（企业名称、企业地址、销售热线、注册商标等），被诉侵权人不能提交足以推翻的相反证据的，可以认定该标识指向的经营主体构成被诉侵权产品的制造者。

In the case of patent infringement, where the accused infringing products carry a label showing true and specific information of the business entity (such as name, domicile, sales hotline, registered trademark, *etc.*) and the accused infringer fails to present sufficient contrary evidence, the business entity as shown on the label can be deemed as the manufacturer of the accused infringing products.

【关键词】

[Keywords]

专利　侵权　被诉侵权产品制造者　举证责任

Patent; infringement; manufacturer of the accused infringing product; burden of proof

【案号】

[Case Number]

（2021）最高法知民终 1784、1840 号

（2021）SPC IP Civil Final 1784&1840

【基本案情】

[Case Facts]

在上诉人比肯灯饰国际有限公司（以下简称比肯公司）与被上诉人中山市名派照明电器有限公司（以下简称中山名派公司）、江西名派光电科技有限公司（以下简称名派光电公司）、江西名派投资管理集团有限公司（以下简称名派投资公司）侵害发明专利权纠纷两案中，涉及专利权人为比肯公司、专利号为200680032396.1、名称为“组合的灯具和天花板风扇”以及专利号为200880131045.5、名称为“组合的天花板风扇和灯具”的发明专利（以下简称涉案专利）。比肯公司认为，中山名派公司、名派光电公司、名派投资公司制造销售的被诉侵权产品落入涉案专利权的保护范围，构成侵权，故向广州知识产权法院（以下简称一审法院）提起诉讼，请求判令停止侵权，每案赔偿损失15万元。一审法院认为，现有证据难以证明中山名派公司、名派光电公司或者名派投资公司实施了被诉侵权行为，也没有其他证据证明存在虚假陈述，中山名派公司、名派光电公司、名派投资公司共同认为被诉侵权产品属于假冒其商标和企业名称的假冒商品，这属于消极事实无须举证。一审法院判决驳回比肯公司的诉讼请求。比肯公司不服，向最高人民法院提起上诉，主张中山名派公司、名派光电公司、名派投资公司实施了被诉侵权行为。最高人民法院于2022年6月28日判决中山名派公司、名派光电公司停止侵权，每案赔偿损失15万元。

In the two appeal cases between the appellant, Beacon Lighting International Limited (hereinafter referred to as “Beacon”), and the appellees, Zhongshan Mingpai Lighting Appliances Co., Ltd. (hereinafter referred to as “Zhongshan Mingpai”), Jiangxi Mingpai Optoelectronics Technology Co., Ltd. (hereinafter referred to as “Mingpai Optoelectronics”), and Jiangxi Mingpai Investment Management Group Co., Ltd. (hereinafter referred to as “Mingpai Investment”), regarding a dispute over infringement of invention pa-

tents, an invention patent titled "Combined Lamp and Ceiling Fan" with patent No. 200680032396.1 and another invention patent titled "Combined Ceiling Fan and Lamp" with patent No. 200880131045.5 (hereinafter referred to as the "Patents"), were involved, both belonging to the patentee, Beacon. Beacon claimed that the accused infringing products manufactured and sold by Zhongshan Mingpai, Mingpai Optoelectronics, and Mingpai Investment fell within the protection scope of the Patents, constituting infringement. Therefore, it filed a lawsuit with Guangzhou Intellectual Property Court (hereinafter referred to as the "Court of First Instance"), requesting an order to stop the infringement and seeking a compensation of CNY 150,000 for each case. The Court of First Instance held that the existing evidence was insufficient to prove that Zhongshan Mingpai, Mingpai Optoelectronics, or Mingpai Investment have engaged in the accused infringing acts, nor was there any other evidence to prove false statements. Zhongshan Mingpai, Mingpai Optoelectronics, and Mingpai Investment jointly argued that the accused infringing products were counterfeit goods infringing their trademarks and company names, which were negative facts that did not require evidence. The Court of First Instance dismissed Beacon's claims. Dissatisfied with the decision, Beacon appealed to the SPC, claiming that Zhongshan Mingpai, Mingpai Optoelectronics, and Mingpai Investment committed the accused infringing acts. On June 28, 2022, the SPC ruled that Zhongshan Mingpai and Mingpai Optoelectronics should stop the infringement and pay CNY 150,000 as compensation for each case.

【裁判意见】

[Judge's Opinion]

最高人民法院二审认为，基于下述事实，可以认定名派光电公司、中山名派公司实施了共同制造、销售被诉侵权产品的行为。首先，比肯公司提交的公证书客观、真实，可以证明被诉侵权产品购买事实。第一，经审查，公证书记载的取证时间真实。销售单手写“订货时间2019年1月10日、2019年1月11日提货”与公证书记载的取证时间2019年1月11日相符，POS签购单机打时间“2018/01/11”与POS机的日期设置有关，不足以影响公证书的记载内容。第二，公证书记载的产品销售价格真实。销售单手写单价“730”，并划去“收定金200元”，可以印证比肯公司关于2019年1月10日预付定金200元、1月11日公证取证时支付余款530元的解释合理，不影响公证书的记载内容。第三，公证书记载的公证取证地点真实。公证取证地点位于十里河灯饰城。根据公证书所附照片，销售门店展示的营业执照和出具的销售单上的经营场所均为“沈阳市铁西区沈新东路27号十里河灯具城一楼B区×××”的事实，公证书关于取证地点的记载真实。比肯公司关于公证书所附照片有一张自带“辽宁省沈阳市于洪区黄海路”文字标记系公证处位于沈阳市于洪区以及公证处相机设置原因所致的解释合理，故予以采信。此外，关于公证处出具的《认证说明》加盖有公证处公章，其来源和真实性可以确认，具有证明效力。其次，基于现有证据可以初步认定被诉侵权产品系由名派光电公司、中山名派公司共同制造、销售。被诉侵权产品标记的企业名称、注册商标“MIPAI”和公司地址均为名派光电公司的真实企业信息，标记的全国服务热线“4008306×××”和销售热线“0760-8768×××6”均为中山名派公司的企业联系方式；被诉侵权产品制造于2017年6月，此时中山名派公司是名派光电公司注册商标“MIPAI”的被许可使用人；被诉侵权产品销售门店展示的“MIPAI”中国驰名商标铭牌、“PHILIPS”精英合作伙伴铭牌分别由名派光电公司和中山名派公司持有，名派光电公司、中山名派公司对上述事实的真实性予以确认，且被诉侵权产品销售门店为“MIPAI”名派照明专营店经营模式，以及POS签购单商户名称为“沈阳市名派照明经销处”的事实，足以使相关消费者确认该销售门店与中山名派公司、

名派光电公司存在关联关系，为其确认的授权经销商。根据上述事实，结合日常生活经验，现有证据已经能够初步证明被诉侵权产品系由名派光电公司、中山名派公司共同制造、销售。最后，在现有证据已经可以初步证明相关事实成立的可能性较大的情况下，主张该事实不成立的一方当事人应提供相应证据或者其他充分理由以实质性削弱现有证据的证明力；不能提供证据或者提供的证据或者理由不足以实质性削弱现有证据的证明力并使其达不到证明标准的，可以认定现有证据证明的事实成立。本案中，中山名派公司、名派光电公司、名派投资公司虽辩称被诉侵权产品系假冒其商标和企业名称，但在一审中并未提交任何证据加以证明。另外，本案被诉侵权行为发生于 2019 年 1 月 11 日，直至 2021 年 11 月 23 日本案二审询问时，中山名派公司、名派光电公司、名派投资公司并未对沈阳市铁西区众明照明灯饰经销处经营处采取任何维权举措，其放任他人侵权行为不符合常理。中山名派公司、名派光电公司、名派投资公司虽于 2021 年 12 月 20 日对沈阳市铁西区众明照明灯饰经销处的经营者章某微提起侵害商标权诉讼，但因其诉讼行为发生在本案二审询问后，亦难以认定为市场经营者的正常维权行为。结合中山名派公司、名派光电公司、名派投资公司以与章某微和解为由对该案撤回起诉，却不能应本院要求提供章某微的真实联系信息及其对被诉侵权产品来源情况说明的事实，中山名派公司、名派光电公司、名派投资公司前述维权诉讼的真实目的存疑。综上所述，在中山名派公司、名派光电公司、名派投资公司不能提交有效反证的情形下，故对三公司关于被诉侵权产品为假冒产品的抗辩主张不予支持。

The SPC, in its Second Instance trial, held that based on the following facts, it can be determined that Mingpai Optoelectronics and Zhongshan Mingpai have jointly engaged in the manufacturing and sale of the accused infringing products. Firstly, the notarized documents submitted by Beacon are objective and true, which can prove the purchase of the accused infringing products. Upon examination, the time of obtaining evidence as recorded in the notarized documents is authentic. The handwritten sales order stating "order placed on January 10, 2019, and picked up on January 11, 2019" corresponds to the recorded time of obtaining evidence, January 11, 2019, in the notarized documents. The machine-printed purchase receipt date "2018/01/11" is related to the date setting of the POS machine and is not sufficient to affect the contents of the notarized documents. Secondly, the sales prices recorded in the notarized documents are authentic. The handwritten unit price on the sales order is "730", and the crossed-out "prepaid CNY 200" confirms Beacon's explanation that a deposit of CNY 200 was paid on January 10, 2019, and the remaining balance of CNY 530 was paid during the notarization process on January 11, which does not affect the contents of the notarized documents. Thirdly, the location of obtaining evidence as recorded in the notarized documents is authentic. The place of obtaining evidence is located in Shilihe Lighting City. According to the attached photos in the notarized documents, the displayed business license and the address of operation on the issued sales order all indicate "No. ×××, Block B, 1F, Shilihe Lighting City, 27 Shenxin East Road, Tiexi District, Shenyang City", which confirms the authenticity of the location of obtaining evidence recorded in the notarized documents. Beacon's explanation that one of the photos attached to the notarized documents bears the text "Huanghai Road, Yuhong District, Shenyang City, Liaoning Province" due to the location of the notary office being in Yuhong District and the setting of the notary office's camera is reasonable, so it is accepted as credible information. In addition, the Certification Statement issued by the notary office with the official seal of the notary office can confirm its source and authenticity, so it has evidential effect. Secondly, based on the existing evidence, it can be preliminarily determined that the accused infrin-

ging products are jointly manufactured and sold by Mingpai Optoelectronics and Zhongshan Mingpai. The business name, registered trademark "MIPAI", as well as the company address marked on the accused infringing products, is the authentic corporate information of Mingpai Optoelectronics. The national hotline "4008306×××" and the sales hotline "0760-8768×××6" marked on the accused infringing products are the contact information of Zhongshan Mingpai. The accused infringing products were manufactured in June 2017, at which time Zhongshan Mingpai was the licensee authorized to use the registered trademark "MIPAI" of Mingpai Optoelectronics. The "MIPAI - China Well-known Trademark" plaque and "PHILIPS Elite Partner" plaque displayed in the sales stores of the accused infringing products are held by Mingpai Optoelectronics and Zhongshan Mingpai. Mingpai Optoelectronics and Zhongshan Mingpai have confirmed the authenticity of the above facts. Moreover, the sales stores of the accused infringing products operate under the model of "MIPAI" Mingpai Lighting Exclusive Store, and the merchant name on the POS purchase receipt is "Shenyang Mingpai Lighting Distribution Office". These facts are sufficient for relevant consumers to confirm the association between the sales stores and Zhongshan Mingpai and Mingpai Optoelectronics, thereby recognizing them as authorized distributors. Based on the above facts and combined with daily life experience, the existing evidence is sufficient to preliminarily prove that the accused infringing products are jointly manufactured and sold by Mingpai Optoelectronics and Zhongshan Mingpai. Furthermore, in a situation where the existing evidence can already preliminarily prove the likelihood of the established facts, a party claiming that such facts are not true should provide corresponding evidence or other sufficient reasons to substantively weaken the probative force of the existing evidence. If it fails to provide evidence or the evidence or reasons provided are insufficient to substantially weaken the probative force of the existing evidence and do not meet the standard of proof, the established facts based on the existing evidence can be deemed as true. In this case, Zhongshan Mingpai, Mingpai Optoelectronics, and Mingpai Investment argued that the accused infringing products counterfeited their trademarks and company names, but they did not submit any evidence to prove this in the First Instance. Moreover, the alleged infringing acts occurred on January 11, 2019, and until the Second Instance interrogation on November 23, 2021, Zhongshan Mingpai, Mingpai Optoelectronics, and Mingpai Investment did not take any measures to protect their rights against Shenyang Tiexi District Zhongming Lighting Distribution Office, which is unreasonable. Although Zhongshan Mingpai, Mingpai Optoelectronics, and Mingpai Investment filed a trademark infringement lawsuit against Zhang, the operator of Shenyang Tiexi District Zhongming Lighting Distribution Office, on December 20, 2021, the lawsuit was initiated after the Second Instance interrogation of this case, so it cannot be considered a normal act of rights protection by market operators. Considering that Zhongshan Mingpai, Mingpai Optoelectronics, and Mingpai Investment withdrew their lawsuit in this case claiming settlement with Zhang, but failed to provide the true contact information of Zhang and an explanation of the source of the accused infringing products as required by the court, the true purpose of their aforementioned rights protection lawsuit is questionable. Therefore, in the absence of valid counter-evidence from Zhongshan Mingpai, Mingpai Optoelectronics, and Mingpai Investment, their defense claim that the accused infringing products were counterfeits is not supported.

20. 涉及多物理实体的多主体实施方法专利的侵权判定 Determination on infringement on a method patent involving multiple physical objects and multiple entities for implementation

【裁判要旨】

[Judgment Digest]

专利侵权判定中所谓的“全面覆盖原则”，是指同一被诉侵权技术方案应当覆盖权利要求中的全部技术特征，而不必然要求同一主体的行为覆盖权利要求中的全部技术特征。对于需借助多个物理实体才能完成的通信领域的多主体实施的方法专利而言，不应因为任何一方制造者未完整实施专利技术方案而使其都得以免除侵权责任。关于制造者是否实施了侵权行为的认定，仍然应当判断该制造者是否以生产经营为目的将专利方法的实质内容固化在被诉侵权产品中，且该行为或者行为结果对权利要求的技术特征被全面覆盖起到不可替代的实质性作用。

The all elements rule adopted in determining patent infringement means that the accused infringing technical solution should cover all technical features as contained in the claim in question, but it does not necessarily require that the acts carried out by one particular accused infringer individually must cover all technical features as contained in that claim. As to the method patent in the field of telecommunication embodied by multiple accused infringers which needs to be facilitated by multiple physical objects, any manufacturer involved therein should not be exempted from its liabilities simply because it does not fully embody the patented technical solution. For determining whether the manufacturer commits the act of infringement, the decision should still rely on whether the manufacturer incorporates the substantial content of the patented method into the accused infringing product for the purpose of business operation and whether the aforementioned act or the result of such act has an irreplaceable substantive effect on the full coverage of all technical elements as contained in the claim in question.

【关键词】

[Keywords]

发明专利　标准必要专利　侵权　多物理实体　多主体实施　方法专利　全面覆盖原则

Invention patent; standard essential patent; infringement; multiple physical objects; implementation by multiple entities; method patent; all elements rule

【案号】

[Case Number]

(2022) 最高法知民终 817 号

(2022) SPC IP Civil Final 817

【基本案情】

[Case Facts]

在上诉人苹果电脑贸易（上海）有限公司（以下简称苹果电脑上海公司）与被上诉人西安西电捷通无线网络通信股份有限公司（以下简称西电捷通公司）、原审被告西安市国美电器有限公司侵害发明专利权纠纷案中，涉及专利权人为西电捷通公司、专利号为 02139508. X、名称为“一种无线局域网移动设备安全接入及数据保密通信的方法”的发明专利（以下简称涉案专利），涉案专利系无线局域网鉴别和保密基础结构（WAPI）标准的一项标准必要专利。西电捷通公司与苹果公司（Apple Inc.）签订有专利许可合同，合同到期日为 2028 年 12 月 28 日，合同中约定了 2010 年至 2014 年的许可费用，2014 年之后的许可费用应于 2014 年底前重新谈判确定。由于双方对 2014 年之后的许可费用一直未达成一致，西电捷通公司主张苹果公司的全资子公司苹果电脑上

海公司销售相关型号终端产品（iPhone、iPad）侵害其涉案专利权，向陕西省高级人民法院（以下简称一审法院）提起诉讼，请求判令停止侵害并赔偿经济损失及合理开支共计 1.5 亿元。一审法院经审理，判决苹果电脑上海公司停止侵害并赔偿经济损失及维权合理开支 1.43 亿余元。苹果电脑上海公司不服一审判决，向最高人民法院提起上诉。最高人民法院于 2022 年 12 月 30 日判决撤销原审判决停止侵害的判项，维持赔偿经济损失及维权合理开支 1.43 亿余元的判项。

In the appeal case between the Appellant, Apple Computer Trading (Shanghai) Co., Ltd. (hereinafter referred to as "Apple Shanghai"), and the Appellees, China Iwncomm Co., Ltd. (hereinafter referred to as "Iwncomm"), and Xi'an Gome Electrical Appliances Co., Ltd. (the defendant in the First Instance), regarding a dispute over infringement of invention patent, an invention patent titled "A Method for Secure Access and Confidential Communication of WLAN Mobile Devices" (hereinafter referred to as the "Patent") with the patentee, Iwncomm, and patent No. 02139508. X, was involved. This Patent was an SEP (Standard essential patent) for the implementation of the WLAN Authentication and Privacy Infrastructure (WAPI) Standard. Iwncomm and Apple Inc. had signed a patent license agreement with an expiration date on December 28, 2028. The agreement stipulated the licensing fees for the period from 2010 to 2014, and the licensing fees after 2014 should be renegotiated by the end of 2014. As the two parties failed to reach an agreement on the licensing fees after 2014, Iwncomm claimed that Apple Inc.'s wholly-owned subsidiary, Apple Shanghai, has infringed its patent by selling certain models of terminal products (iPhone, iPad), and therefore, filed a lawsuit with Shaanxi High People's Court (hereinafter referred to as the "Court of First Instance"), requesting an order to cease the infringement and compensation for its economic losses and reasonable expenses totaling CNY 150 million. After the trial, the Court of First Instance ruled that Apple Shanghai should cease the infringement and compensate for Iwncomm's economic losses and reasonable expenses for rights protection totaling more than CNY 143 million. Dissatisfied with the judgment, Apple Shanghai appealed to the SPC. On December 30, 2022, the SPC rendered a judgment revoking the First Instance judgment regarding the cessation of infringement, but upholding the judgment regarding the compensation for economic losses and reasonable expenses for rights protection totaling more than CNY 143 million.

【裁判意见】

[Judge's Opinion]

最高人民法院二审认为，首先，涉案专利为合法有效的专利，多侧撰写式的权利要求亦为专利审查实践中允许的权利要求撰写方式，该类专利权在被授权后应当得到有效的保护。涉案专利的特点在于，其要求保护的方法并非仅涉及服务器和终端的交互，而是涉及移动终端、无线接入点、认证服务器三个物理实体，最终由终端用户完整执行实施专利方法的过程。另外，涉案专利要求保护的内容就是通过认证服务器实现移动终端和无线接入点双向认证的无线网络安全机制，必须有三方参与才能实现发明目的，涉案专利方法的全部实质内容客观上无法集成在同一个物理实体中。因此，仅借助其中任何一方的单一产品，不借助其他装置或者依赖其他网络条件，均不可能完整地实施涉案专利方法。涉案专利属于必须借助多个物理实体才能完成的多主体实施的方法专利，其与仅涉及服务器和终端交互的多主体实施的方法专利存在一定差异。在适用多主体实施的方法专利侵权判断标准时，应当结合涉案专利三方实体交互的实际情况，妥善考虑如何在不损害社会公众利益的情况下有效保护该类专利的权利人的合法权利。

The SPC, in its Second Instance trial, held that the Patent is a legally valid patent, and the multi-party drafting style of the claims is an acceptable

drafting method in patent examination practice. Such patents should be effectively protected once granted. The characteristic of the Patent is that the method it seeks to protect not only involves the interaction between servers and terminals but also involves three physical objects: mobile terminals, wireless access points, and authentication servers. The complete embodiment of the patented method is ultimately carried out by the end users. Furthermore, the Patent seeks to protect a wireless network security mechanism that achieves mutual authentication between mobile terminals and wireless access points through an authentication server. In order to achieve the intended purpose of the invention, the participation of all three entities is necessary. The entirety of the essential content of the patented method cannot be objectively integrated into a single physical object. Therefore, it is not possible to fully implement the patented method by simply relying on any single product without the use of other devices or dependence on other network conditions. The Patent belongs to a method patent that requires the involvement of multiple physical objects and multi-entity implementation, and it differs from a method patent involving only the interaction between servers and terminals and multi-entity implementation. When applying the infringement judgment criteria for method patents involving multi-entity implementation, the actual situation of the three-object interaction in the Patent should be taken into account, and due consideration should be given to how to effectively protect the legitimate rights of the patentee without harming the public interest.

其次，专利侵权判定中所谓的“全面覆盖原则”是指同一被诉侵权技术方案应覆盖权利要求中的全部技术特征，而不必然要求同一主体的行为覆盖权利要求中的全部技术特征。不同主体共同实施的行为，既包括共同故意实施的行为，也包括共同过失实施的行为，还包括故意与过失行为结合实施的行为，即数个行为人虽主观过错程度不一，但各自行为相结合而实施的行为，造成他人损害的，也可以构成共同侵权行为。对于必须借助多个物理实体才能完成的通信领域的多主体实施的方法专利而言，其技术方案的实质内容被固化在不同装置中，即不同装置的制造者实施的行为相结合，使得终端用户只需要正常操作其所持有的终端设备，即能够机械地重演专利的技术方案。对于该类专利而言，只有多个物理实体制造者的共同行为才能使权利要求中的全部技术特征被终端用户机械重演的技术方案全面覆盖。因此，不应因为任何一方制造者未完整实施专利技术方案而使其都得以免除侵权责任。判断其中任何一方制造者是否实施了侵权行为，仍然应当判断该制造者是否以生产经营为目的将专利方法的实质内容固化在被诉侵权产品中，且该行为或行为结果对权利要求的技术特征被全面覆盖起到不可替代的实质性作用。特别应当注意的是，该固化的实质内容及不可替代的实质性作用不仅包括与用户交互的内容及其作用，还包括与其他执行端交互的内容及其作用。

Secondly, the “all elements rule” adopted in determining patent infringement means that the same accused infringing technical solution should cover all technical features as contained in the claim in question, but it does not necessarily require that the acts carried out by one particular accused infringer individually must cover all technical features as contained in that claim. The acts performed by different entities jointly include intentional acts, negligent acts, and both intentional and negligent acts. That is to say, if several actors jointly commit an act, whether intentionally or negligently, and cause harm to others, it may constitute joint infringement, regardless of the subjective fault level of each actor. For method patents in the field of communication that require the involvement of multiple physical objects and multi-entity implementation, the substantial content of their technical solution is incorporated in different devices. In other words, the acts carried out by different device manu-

facturers combine to allow end users to mechanically replicate the patented technical solution simply by operating the terminal device they possess. For such patents, only the collective acts of multiple physical object manufacturers can fully cover all the technical features as contained in the claim and enable the patented technical solution to be mechanically replicated by end users. Therefore, any manufacturer involved therein should not be exempted from its liabilities simply because it does not fully embody the patented technical solution. For determining whether the manufacturer commits the act of infringement, the decision should still rely on whether the manufacturer incorporates the substantial content of the patented method into the accused infringing product for the purpose of business operation and whether the aforementioned act or the result of such act has an irreplaceable substantive effect on the full coverage of all technical elements as contained in the Claim in question. It should be noted that the incorporated substantial content and irreplaceable substantive effect include not only the content and function of interaction with users but also the content and function of interaction with other execution ends.

最后，按照上述判断方式认定侵权，对于必须借助多个物理实体才能完成的多主体实施的方法专利并不会必然给予过度保护。第一，前已述及，对于该类专利应当给予保护而非拒绝保护。如果基于各个物理实体的制造者固化的内容，终端用户只需正常操作所持终端设备即可机械重演专利技术方案，则在此情况下，各制造者均从专利技术方案中获益，而使得专利权人的利益受损。按照上述判断方式认定侵权，能够合理平衡专利权人和有关行为实施者的利益。而如果坚持其中任何一方固化技术内容的行为都无法构成侵权行为，要求构成侵权必须具备“明知”“侵权专用品”等条件，或者要求专利权人证明被诉侵权人为生产经营目的自己直接实施了测试等行为，则对专利权人过于严苛，无法为该类型的专利提供有效保护。第二，上述判断标准仍然坚持固化的内容应为实质内容，固化行为或结果对技术特征被全面覆盖应起到不可替代的实质性作用。相应的审查能够避免专利权人任意将不同主体实施的方法步骤写入权利要求并以此扩大可主张权利的范围。第三，由于侵权技术方案系由不同主体完成，在确定赔偿范围时应当考虑当事人在案件中的具体主张和被诉侵权行为对于损害后果所起的作用。相应的审查认定能够避免权利人通过向不同实施主体重复主张许可费或侵权赔偿而获得过度保护。

Moreover, according to the aforementioned judgment criteria for determining infringement, it does not necessarily result in excessive protection for method patents that require the involvement of multiple physical objects and multi-entity implementation. Firstly, as previously mentioned, protection should be granted to this type of patent instead of denied. If end users can mechanically reproduce the patented technical solution simply by operating the terminal device they possess based on the incorporated content by each physical object manufacturer, then in this case, all manufacturers benefit from the patented technical solution, while the interests of the patentee are harmed. By using the aforementioned judgment criteria for determining infringement, a reasonable balance can be achieved between the interests of the patentee and the doers of relevant acts. However, if the act of incorporating the technical content by either party cannot constitute an act of infringement, and requirements such as "knowingly" or the presence of "infringing-specific products" are needed to establish infringement, or if the patentee is required to prove that the accused infringer directly carried out testing or other acts for production purposes, it would be excessively stringent on the patentee and unable to provide effective protection for this type of patent. Secondly, the aforementioned judgment criteria still adhere to the principle that the incorporated con-

tent should be substantive and the incorporation act or the result of such act should have an irreplaceable substantive effect on the full coverage of all technical features as contained in the claim. This examination ensures that the patentee does not arbitrarily include method steps embodied by different entities in the claims to expand the scope of claimable rights. Thirdly, since the infringing technical solution is embodied by different entities, when determining the scope of compensation, the specific allegations of the parties involved and the role of the accused infringing act in the resulting damages should be considered. This examination and determination prevent the patentee from obtaining excessive protection by repeatedly claiming license fees or infringement compensation from different implementing entities.

具体而言，涉案专利是一种多主体实施的方法专利，涉及移动终端、无线接入点、认证服务器三个物理实体相互配合实现全部技术方案。由于涉案专利的发明目的为提供一种以双向认证机制保障移动终端接入安全性的方法，移动终端、无线接入点、认证服务器均为参与认证的主体，故在移动终端、无线接入点、认证服务器中固化的相关技术内容均为使得双向认证机制得以实现的实质内容，对于完成整个技术方案而言作用都是不可替代的。正是因为移动终端、无线接入点、认证服务器各自的制造商都固化了涉案专利的相关实质技术内容，使得终端用户可以根据自己的需求，通过在移动终端的正常操作，启用 WAPI 功能，触发涉案专利技术方案的自动执行。并且，涉案专利的最终目的是为移动终端提供一种安全的、高保密性的接入无线局域网的方法，移动终端是触发技术方案实施的必不可少的部分，移动终端的固化方应当是实施涉案专利技术的最大受益者。至于终端用户下载证书的行为，只是正常使用终端设备的行为。因此，在本案被诉侵权产品中固化涉案专利中移动终端相关技术内容的行为构成侵权行为。

Specifically, the Patent is a method patent that involves multiple entities collaborating to embody the entire technical solution. The collaboration occurs among three physical objects: a mobile terminal, a wireless access point, and an authentication server. Since the patented invention aims to provide a method to ensure the security of mobile terminal access through a two-way authentication mechanism, all three physical objects involved, namely the mobile terminal, wireless access point, and authentication server, are essential to the authentication process, and the relevant technical content incorporated by each physical object manufacturer is substantive and plays an irreplaceable role in fully covering the technical features necessary to embody the patented technical solution. It is precisely because the relevant technical content has been incorporated by the manufacturers of the mobile terminal, wireless access point, and authentication server, that end-users can activate the WAPI function and trigger the automatic execution of the patented technical solution through normal operation of the mobile terminal. Moreover, the ultimate goal of the Patent is to provide a secure and highly confidential method for mobile terminals to access the WLAN, with the mobile terminal being an indispensable part of triggering the embodiment of the technical solution. As such, the manufacturer of the mobile terminal is the primary beneficiary of embodying the patented technology. As for the behavior of end-users downloading certificates, it is merely a normal use of the terminal device. Therefore, the act of incorporating the relevant technical content related to the mobile terminal from the Patent into the accused infringing products constitutes an infringement.

21. 专利默示许可的认定

Identification of implied patent license

【裁判要旨】

[Judgment Digest]

专利权人主动向被诉侵权人提供并意图使其实施专利技术方案，但未披露其专利权，直至被诉侵权人实施完毕方才请求侵权救济，被诉侵权人主张其已获得专利权人默示许可的，人民法院可予支持。

The accused infringer's claim that it has obtained a patent license by acquiescence can be supported by court, if the patentee voluntarily provides the patented technical solution to the accused infringer and intends to cause the accused infringer to embody such technical solution without any disclosure of its patent rights, but requests for relief after the accused infringer completes the embodiment.

【关键词】

[Keywords]

专利　侵权　诚实信用　主动提供　隐瞒权利　怠于主张权利　默示许可

Patent; infringement; good faith; voluntary provision; concealment of patent right; negligent in asserting rights; implied license

【案号】

[Case Number]

(2022) 最高法知民终 139 号

(2022) SPC IP Civil Final 139

【基本案情】

[Case Facts]

在上诉人江苏固耐特围栏系统股份有限公司（以下简称固耐特公

司）与被上诉人厦门高诚信工程技术有限公司（以下简称高诚信公司）、厦门中联永亨建设集团有限公司（以下简称中联永亨公司）、原审被告河北振兴金源丝网集团有限公司、原审第三人华庭工程设计有限公司（以下简称华庭公司）侵害发明专利权纠纷案中，涉及专利权人为固耐特公司、专利号为201110403257.8、名称为“围栏柱及具有该围栏柱的围栏系统”的发明专利（以下简称涉案专利）。固耐特公司认为，安装在福建省翔安监狱监区工程项目（以下简称涉案工程）的防攀爬围栏采用的技术方案落入涉案专利权的保护范围，高诚信公司、中联永亨公司分别是该工程的代建单位、施工单位，该两公司的行为侵害了固耐特公司享有的涉案专利权，应当承担相应的侵权责任。固耐特公司向福建省厦门市中级人民法院（以下简称一审法院）提起诉讼，请求判令高诚信公司、中联永亨公司停止侵害并赔偿其经济损失（含维权合理开支）300万元。一审法院认为，固耐特公司的行为应视为其许可在涉案工程中使用涉案专利，故判决驳回固耐特公司的诉讼请求。固耐特公司不服，向最高人民法院提起上诉，主张其向涉案工程设计单位华庭公司提供设计图是推荐涉案专利的商业推广行为，而非专利许可。最高人民法院于2022年12月15日判决驳回上诉，维持原判。

In the appeal case between the Appellant, Jiangsu GoldNet Fencing System Co., Ltd. (hereinafter referred to as “GoldNet”), and the Appellees, Xiamen Gaochengxin Engineering Technology Co., Ltd. (hereinafter referred to as “Gaochengxin”), Xiamen Central United Invariable Group Co., Ltd. (hereinafter referred to as “CUIG”), Hebei Zhenxing Jinyuan Screen Group Co., Ltd. (the defendant in the First Instance), and Huating Engineering Design Co., Ltd. (hereinafter referred to as “Huating”, the third party in the First Instance), regarding a dispute over infringement of invention patent, an invention patent titled “Fence Post and Fence System with the Fence Post” (hereinafter referred to as the “Patent”) with the patentee, GoldNet, and pa-

tent No. 201110403257.8, was involved. GoldNet claimed that the technical solution used in the anti-climbing fence installed in the Xiang'an Prison Area Project in Fujian Province (hereinafter referred to as the "Project") fell within the protection scope of the Patent. Gaochengxin and CUIG were the general contractor and construction contractor for the Project, respectively. GoldNet argued that their acts infringed upon its patent right and should bear corresponding liability for infringement. Therefore, it filed a lawsuit with Xiamen Intermediate People's Court of Fujian Province (hereinafter referred to as the "Court of First Instance"), requesting the court to order Gaochengxin and CUIG to cease the infringement and compensate for its economic losses (including reasonable expenses for safeguarding rights) totaling CNY 3 million. The Court of First Instance held that GoldNet's act should be considered as allowing the use of the Patent in the Project, thus rejecting its claims. Dissatisfied with the judgment, GoldNet appealed to the SPC, arguing that providing design drawings to Huating, the design agency for the Project, was a commercial promotion activity recommending the Patent and not a patent license. On December 15, 2022, the SPC ruled to dismiss the appeal and affirm the original judgment.

【裁判意见】

[Judge's Opinion]

最高人民法院二审认为，专利法第十一条规定，发明和实用新型专利权被授予后，除本法另有规定的以外，任何单位或者个人未经专利权人许可，都不得实施其专利，即不得为生产经营目的制造、使用、许诺销售、销售、进口其专利产品，或者使用其专利方法以及使用、许诺销售、销售、进口依照该专利方法直接获得的产品。专利侵权判定的关键在于实施专利是否获得专利权人的许可。如果获得了专利权人的明示许可，行为人实施专利的行为自然不属于专利法第十一条所规定的侵害专利权的行为；如果行为人实施专利虽未获得专利权人明示许可，但结合具体案情，根据专利权人的行为可以推断其具有默示许可的意思表示，则可以认定行为人实施专利的行为不构成侵害专利权。

The SPC, in the Second Instance trial, held that according to Article 11 of the Patent Law, after the grant of the patent right for an invention or utility model, except where otherwise provided for in this Law, no entity or individual may, without the permission of the patentee, exploit the patent, that is, make, use, offer to sell, sell, or import the patented product, or use the patented process, and use, offer to sell, sell, or import the product directly obtained by the patented process, for production or business purposes. The key to determining patent infringement lies in whether the exploitation of the patent has obtained the permission of the patentee. If the act is expressively permitted by the patentee, the act of exploiting the patent does not fall under the acts that infringe the patent right as defined in Article 11 of the Patent Law. If the accused infringer exploits the patent without obtaining explicit permission from the patentee, but based on the specific circumstances of the case, it can be inferred from the acts of the patentee that it has an implied license, then it can be determined that the accused infringer's exploitation of the patent does not constitute a patent infringement.

本案中，首先，固耐特公司提供设计图的时间晚于华庭公司与涉案工程的发包单位福建省翔安监狱（以下简称翔安监狱）签订设计合同的时间，且相关图纸内容明确指向了涉案工程，可见固耐特公司对于其向华庭公司提供的设计方案将用于涉案工程系属明知。其次，2015 年 2 月至 10 月，固耐特公司与华庭公司就涉案工程设计事宜持续沟通，其间根据华庭公司要求对设计方案进行了修改，最终确定的设计图明确标注有防攀爬围栏的长宽尺寸、材质规格、样式参数等技术要求，可以确定作为权利人的固耐特公司深度参与了涉案工程的设计工作。再次，经

查明，涉案工程的施工图中关于防攀爬围栏的设计方案与固耐特公司发送给华庭公司电子邮件的相关内容相符，系涉案专利技术方案。而代建合同、施工合同均明确约定了该设计方案不得随意变更，高诚信公司、中联永亨公司严格履行相关合同必然会导致实施涉案专利的结果。最后，固耐特公司早已知晓涉案工程的发包人和实际使用单位为翔安监狱，但固耐特公司并未将相关专利情况告知翔安监狱，也未告知高诚信公司和中联永亨公司。固耐特公司故意隐瞒上述关键事实的行为，使翔安监狱丧失了在实际施工前要求华庭公司更改设计方案，或与华庭公司就设计费重新进行协商议价的机会，从而导致被纳入设计图的专利技术方案成为涉案工程的不可替代之方案。迟至工程竣工前半年左右，固耐特公司才发出告知提醒函，意图收取专利许可费，此种做法不符合诚实信用原则，极易导致发生纠纷。

In this case, firstly, it can be seen that GoldNet knew clearly that the design scheme they provided to Huating would be used for the Project, because the time when GoldNet provided the design drawings was later than the time when Huating signed the design contract with the contracting unit of the Project, Fujian Xiang'an Prison (hereinafter referred to as "Xiang'an Prison"), and the content of relevant drawings clearly pointed to the Project. Secondly, from February to October 2015, GoldNet and Huating continued to communicate on the design matters of the Project, during which the design scheme was modified based on Huating's requirements. The final design drawing clearly marked the technical requirements such as the size, material, specifications, style, and parameters of the anti-climbing fence. It can be determined that GoldNet, as the patentee, was deeply involved in the design work of the Project. Thirdly, it was found that the design scheme for the anti-climbing fence in the construction drawings of the Project matched the relevant content in the email sent by GoldNet to Huating, which was the patented technical solution in this case. Both the construction agency contract and construction contract explicitly stipulated that the design scheme should not be changed without permission. Gaochengxin's and CUIG' s strict performance of relevant contracts would inevitably lead to exploitation of the Patent. Finally, GoldNet had already known that the contracting party and the actual user of the Project were Xiang'an Prison, but it did not inform Xiang'an Prison of the Patent, nor did it inform Gaochengxin and CUIG. GoldNet's intentional concealment of the above key facts caused Xiang'an Prison to lose the opportunity to require Huating to modify the design scheme before actual construction or to renegotiate and bargain for the design fee with Huating, which resulted in the patented technical scheme included in the design drawing becoming the irreplaceable scheme of the Project. Only about half a year before the completion of the Project, GoldNet sent out a notice of reminder intending to collect patent license fees, which does not comply with the principle of good faith and is likely to lead to disputes.

综上所述，在权利人固耐特公司明知其提供的设计方案用于涉案工程，且深度参与了设计工作，涉案工程亦严格按照图纸施工的情况下，应认定固耐特公司默示许可相关主体在涉案工程中实施涉案专利。固耐特公司主张代建单位高诚信公司及施工单位中联永亨公司侵害涉案专利，缺乏事实和法律依据。

Based on the above, it should be recognized that in this case, GoldNet knew clearly that the design scheme they provided would be used for the Project and was deeply involved in the design work. Furthermore, the Project was strictly constructed according to the drawings. Therefore, it should be deemed that GoldNet impliedly licensed the relevant parties to exploit the Patent in the Project. GoldNet's argument that the general contractor, Gaochengxin, and the construction contractor, CUIG, had infringed upon the Patent lacks factu-

al and legal basis.

22. 现有技术抗辩基础事实的合法性
Legality of basic facts for prior art defense

【裁判要旨】

[Judgment Digest]

任何人不得从违法行为中获益。被诉侵权人或者其授意的第三人违反明示或者默示的保密义务公开专利技术方案，被诉侵权人依据该非法公开的事实状态主张现有技术抗辩的，人民法院不予支持。

No one shall obtain any benefits from his own illegal act. If the accused infringer disclosed or instigated any third party to disclose the patented technical solution in violation of its express or implied confidentiality obligations and then afterwards defends on the ground of prior art based on the aforementioned illegal disclosure, such defense should not be supported by people's courts.

【关键词】

[Keywords]

专利　侵权　现有技术抗辩　保密义务　违约公开　违法公开

Patent; infringement; prior art defense; confidentiality obligation; breach of confidentiality; illegal disclosure

【案号】

[Case Number]

(2020) 最高法知民终 1568 号

(2020) SPC IP Civil Final 1568

【基本案情】

[Case Facts]

在上诉人上海环莘电子科技有限公司（以下简称环莘公司）与被

上诉人广东法瑞纳科技有限公司（以下简称法瑞纳公司）、江苏水乡周庄旅游股份有限公司（以下简称周庄旅游公司）、北京镇边网络科技股份有限公司（以下简称镇边公司）侵害实用新型专利权纠纷案中，涉及专利权人为环莘公司、专利号为201820194071.3、名称为“一种应用于自动租售终端系统的连接手柄”的实用新型专利（以下简称涉案专利）。环莘公司向江苏省苏州市中级人民法院（以下简称一审法院）提起诉讼，主张在周庄旅游公司管理的旅游景区内使用的共享儿童手推车的连接手柄落入涉案专利保护范围。上述被诉侵权产品系法瑞纳公司制造并销售给镇边公司，并由镇边公司使用在周庄旅游公司管理的景区内租赁给游客使用，三公司的行为构成侵害环莘公司的涉案专利权。环莘公司在涉案专利申请日前曾向法瑞纳公司采购儿童推车租赁设备并签订采购合同，法瑞纳公司依约完成产品制造并在涉案专利申请日前将产品交付承运人运输。法瑞纳公司据此提出先用权抗辩以及现有技术抗辩。一审法院认为，被诉侵权技术方案于相关产品交付承运人运输后即因投入市场而被公开，法瑞纳公司的现有技术抗辩成立。故驳回环莘公司的诉讼请求。环莘公司不服，向最高人民法院提起上诉。二审经审理查明，环莘公司与法瑞纳公司的采购合同约定儿童推车租赁设备及相关设计的专利权属于环莘公司，法瑞纳公司对环莘公司的儿童推车租赁设备的知识产权、产品资料、业务模式、软件功能负有保密义务。法瑞纳公司在须知网公开文章及图片的行为属于违反合同保密义务的披露行为。最高人民法院于2021年7月9日判决撤销原判，法瑞纳公司停止侵害并赔偿经济损失50万元及维权合理开支2万余元，镇边公司、周庄旅游公司对其中维权合理开支承担连带责任。

In the appeal case between the Appellant, Shanghai Huanxin Electronic Technology Co., Ltd. (hereinafter referred to as “Huanxin”), and the Appellees, Guangdong Farina Technology Co., Ltd. (hereinafter referred to as “Farina”), Jiangsu Shuixiang Zhouzhuang Tourism Co., Ltd. (hereinafter re-

ferred to as "Zhouzhuang Tourism"), and Beijing Zhenbian Network Technology Co., Ltd. (hereinafter referred to as "Zhenbian"), regarding a dispute over infringement of utility model patent, a utility model patent titled "A Connecting Handle for Automatic Renting and Selling Terminal System" (hereinafter referred to as the "Patent") with the patentee, Huanxin, and patent No. 201820194071. 3, was involved. Huanxin filed a lawsuit with Suzhou Intermediate People's Court of Jiangsu Province (hereinafter referred to as the "Court of First Instance"), claiming that the connecting handle used in shared children's strollers within the tourist attractions managed by Zhouzhuang Tourism fell within the protection scope of the Patent. The alleged infringing products were manufactured by Farina and sold to Zhenbian, which then used them for rental purposes within the tourist attractions managed by Zhouzhuang Tourism. The acts of the three companies constituted infringement upon Huanxin's patent right. Prior to the filing date of the Patent, Huanxin had purchased children's stroller rental equipment from Farina and signed a purchase contract. Farina completed the production of the products as agreed and delivered them to the carrier for transportation before the filing date of the Patent. Based on this, Farina raised a defense of prior use as well as a defense of prior art. The Court of First Instance held that the alleged infringing technical solution had been publicly disclosed after the related products were delivered to the carrier for transportation and entered the market, and that Farina's defense of prior art was established. Therefore, Huanxin's Claims were rejected. Huanxin refused to accept the judgement and appealed to the SPC. Through the trial in the Second Instance, it was founded that the patent rights to the children's stroller rental equipment and related designs stipulated in the purchase contract between Huanxin and Farina belong to Huanxin. Farina has the obligation to keep confidential regarding the intellectual property, product information, business model, and software functions of children's stroller rental equipment of Huanxin. Farina's act of publishing articles and pictures on Xuzhi. net constitutes a disclosure that violates the contractual confidentiality obligation. On July 9, 2021, the SPC ruled to revoke the original judgment. Farina should cease the infringement and compensate Huanxin for its economic losses totaling CNY 500, 000 as well as reasonable expenses for safeguarding rights totaling over CNY 20, 000. Zhenbian and Zhouzhuang Tourism should bear joint and several liability for the said reasonable expenses.

【裁判意见】

[Judge's Opinion]

最高人民法院二审认为，综合案件相关事实，法瑞纳公司将相关产品交付承运并未导致被诉侵权技术方案为公众所知，一审法院关于相关产品交付承运人运输后即投入市场而导致被诉侵权技术方案被公开的认定有所不当，予以纠正。关于法瑞纳公司依据其在须知网公开的文章及图片主张现有技术抗辩的问题，一方面，现有技术抗辩制度可以防止社会公众遭受不当授权的专利权人提出的侵权诉讼的侵扰，在无效宣告行政程序之外提供更为便捷的救济措施；另一方面，其也为善意使用现有技术的社会公众提供一种稳定的合理预期，可以对自身行为进行合理预测和评价。但是，民事主体从事民事活动，应当遵循诚信原则，同时不得违反法律和公序良俗，这是民法的基本原则。作为一项民事诉讼中的侵权抗辩事由，现有技术抗辩的行使也应遵循上述民法基本原则，被诉侵权人在有关抗辩事由中应当是善意或者无过错的一方，任何人不能因自身违法或不当行为而获得利益。如果被诉侵权人主张现有技术抗辩的现有技术，系由其本人或者由其授意的第三人违反明示或者默示保密义务而公开的技术方案，则该被诉侵权人不得依据该项现有技术主张现有技术抗辩，否则将使得被诉侵权人因自身违法公开行为而获得利益，明显违反民法基本原则和专利法立法精神。根据环莘公司与法瑞纳公司的

协议，法瑞纳公司负有保密义务，该公司未经专利权人环莘公司同意而公开涉案专利技术方案，违反合同义务，其行为具有违法性和可责难性，基于前述有关民法基本原则，其不能依据该项现有技术主张现有技术抗辩。

The SPC, in the Second Instance trial, considered the relevant facts of the case and found that the delivery of the products by Farina to the carrier did not result in the alleged infringing technical solution being known to the public. The Court of First Instance's determination that the alleged infringing technical solution was publicly disclosed after the products were delivered to the carrier for transportation and entered the market was deemed inappropriate and should be corrected. Regarding Farina's defense of prior art based on the articles and pictures it published on Xuzhi. net, the current prior art defense system serves two purposes. On the one hand, it prevents the social public from being disturbed by infringement lawsuits brought by patentees who have been improperly granted patents, providing a more convenient remedy outside the administrative procedure for invalidation. On the other hand, it provides a stable and reasonable expectation for the social public to use the prior art in good faith, enabling them to make reasonable predictions and evaluations of their own acts. When conducting civil activities, civil subjects should adhere to the principle of good faith and must not violate laws and public order and morals, which are basic principles of the Civil Law. As a defense ground in civil litigation, the exercise of defense of prior art should also follow the above-mentioned basic principles. The alleged infringer should be the innocent or non-negligent party in relation to the defense ground. No one shall obtain benefits from his own illegal or improper acts. If the alleged infringer raises a defense of prior art based on the technical solution that has been disclosed in violation of express or implied confidentiality obligations by itself or by a third party instructed by it, it cannot rely on that technical solution to assert the defense of prior art. Otherwise, it would allow the alleged infringer to benefit from its own illegal disclosure, which clearly violates the basic principles of the Civil Law and the legislative spirit of the Patent Law. According to the agreement between Huanxin and Farina, Farina had a confidentiality obligation and its disclosure of the patented technical solution without the consent of the patentee, Huanxin, constituted a violation of the contractual obligation. Such act is illegal and blameworthy. Based on the aforementioned basic principles of the Civil Law, Farina cannot claim the defense of prior art based on the patented technical solution.

23. 合法来源抗辩的适用对象 Applicable litigants of legitimate source defense

【裁判要旨】

[Judgment Digest]

合法来源抗辩的适用对象限于专利侵权产品的使用者、许诺销售者、销售者，具体包括使用、许诺销售、销售专利侵权产品或者使用、许诺销售、销售依照专利方法直接获得的专利侵权产品的情形，原则上不包括使用专利方法的情形。

Legitimate source defense only applies to the litigants who use, offer for sale or sell the infringing products, specifically including the following circumstances including use, offer for sale or sale of infringing products, or use, offer for sale or sale of such infringing products as directly obtained through using the patented method, but in principle, excluding the circumstance where the defendant itself uses the patented method.

【关键词】

[Keywords]

专利　侵权　临时保护期　方法专利　使用方法专利　合法来源抗辩

Patent; infringement; period of temporary protection; method patent; use of method patent; legitimate source defense

【案号】

[Case Number]

（2021）最高法知民终 434 号

（2021）SPC IP Civil Final 434

【基本案情】

[Case Facts]

在上诉人中集安瑞环科技股份有限公司（以下简称南通中集公司）、中集安瑞科投资控股（深圳）有限公司（以下简称安瑞科公司）、中国国际海运集装箱（集团）股份有限公司（以下简称国际海运公司）与被上诉人靖江市亚泰物流装备有限公司（以下简称靖江亚泰公司）、原审被告成都焊研威达科技股份有限公司（以下简称成都焊研公司）、南通汇达智能设备有限公司（以下简称南通汇达公司）侵害发明专利权及发明专利临时保护期使用费纠纷案中，涉及专利号为 201510465803.9、名称为“罐式容器装配台及装配方法”的发明专利（以下简称涉案专利）。南通中集公司、安瑞科公司、国际海运公司认为，成都焊研公司制造、销售，南通汇达公司销售了被诉侵权的罐式容器装配台，靖江亚泰公司购买并利用被诉侵权装配台制造罐式容器产品的行为侵害了涉案专利权，故向江苏省南京市中级人民法院（以下简称一审法院）提起诉讼，请求判令成都焊研公司、南通汇达公司、靖江亚泰公司停止侵害并赔偿损失。一审法院认为，靖江亚泰公司于临时保护期内购买被诉侵权产品，在该范围内的使用行为不构成侵权。南通中集公司等不服,向最高人民法院提起上诉,主张靖江亚泰公司在涉案专利授权后使用被诉侵权产品及实施专利方法的行为已侵害涉案专利权。最高人民法院于2022年11月18日改判靖江亚泰公司停止侵害并赔偿经济损失及维权合理开支5389137.83元。

In the appeal case between the Appellants, CIMC Safeway Technologies Co., Ltd. (hereinafter referred to as "Nantong CIMC"), CIMC Enric Investment Holdings (Shenzhen) Ltd. (hereinafter referred to as "Enric"), and China International Marine Containers (Group) Co., Ltd. (hereinafter referred to as "CIMC"), and the Appellees, Jingjiang Asian-Pacific Logistics Equipment Co., Ltd. (hereinafter referred to as "Jingjiang Asian-Pacific", the defendant in the First Instance), Chengdu Hanyan Weida Technology Co., Ltd. (hereinafter referred to as "Chengdu HYWD"), and Nantong Huida Intelligent Equipment Co., Ltd. (hereinafter referred to as "Nantong Huida"), regarding a dispute over infringement of invention patent and invention patent royalties during the temporary protection period, an invention patent titled "Tank Container Assembly Platform and Assembly Method" (hereinafter referred to as the "Patent"), with patent No. 201510465803.9, was involved. Nantong CIMC, Enric, and CIMC argued that Chengdu HYWD manufactured and sold, while Nantong Huida sold, the accused infringing tank container assembly platform, and Jingjiang Asian-Pacific purchased and utilized the accused infringing assembly platform to manufacture tank container products, all of which infringed upon the Patent. Therefore, they filed a lawsuit with Nanjing Intermediate People's Court of Jiangsu Province (hereinafter referred to as the "Court of First Instance"), requesting an order for Chengdu HYWD, Nantong Huida, and Jingjiang Asian-Pacific to cease the infringement and compensate for the losses. The Court of First Instance held that Jingjiang Asian-Pacific's purchase and use of the accused infringing product

during the temporary protection period did not constitute an infringement. Dissatisfied with the judgment, Nantong CIMC and the others appealed to the SPC, claiming that Jingjiang Asian-Pacific's use of the accused infringing product and embodiment of the patented method after the grant of the Patent constituted an infringement upon the Patent. On November 18, 2022, the SPC changed the original judgment and ordered Jingjiang Asian-Pacific to cease the infringement and compensate for the economic losses and reasonable expenses totaling CNY 5,389,137.83.

【裁判意见】

[Judge's Opinion]

最高人民法院二审认为，靖江亚泰公司以合法来源抗辩主张不侵权的主张不能成立。首先，合法来源抗辩是免除赔偿责任的抗辩，是保护善意第三人制度在专利法中的具体体现，其适用对象限于专利侵权产品的使用者、销售者、许诺销售者，具体包括使用、许诺销售、销售专利侵权产品或者使用、许诺销售、销售依照专利方法直接获得的产品的情形，而不包括使用专利方法的情形。合法来源抗辩并不适用于使用专利方法的行为，不应突破现行法律和司法解释的规定对使用专利方法的侵权行为适用合法来源抗辩。

The SPC, in the Second Instance trial, held that Jingjiang Asian-Pacific's defense of legitimate source, claiming non-infringement, could not be established. Firstly, the legitimate source defense is a defense to exempt liability for compensation, specifically reflecting the protection of the innocent third-party system in patent law. Its application is limited to the litigants who use, offer for sale, or sell the infringing products, specifically including the following circumstances: use, offer for sale, or sale of infringing products, or use, offer for sale, or sale of such infringing products as directly obtained through using the patented method, but in principle, excluding the circumstance where the defendant itself uses the patented method. The legitimate source defense does not apply to acts of using a patented method and should not exceed the provisions of current laws and judicial interpretations regarding the application of legitimate source defense to infringing acts of using a patented method.

其次，就专利侵权产品而言，合法来源抗辩实质上受到产品物理条件的限制，被诉侵权人并不能永久实施专利技术方案，支持专利侵权产品合法来源抗辩不会过分损害专利权人的利益；而就侵权使用专利方法而言，其原则上不具有上述基于产品物理条件的限制，一旦对侵权使用专利方法的行为适用合法来源抗辩，被诉侵权人将得以永久实施专利技术方案，从而过分损害专利权人的利益。

Secondly, with regard to the patent - infringing products, legitimate source defense is essentially limited by the physical conditions of the product, and the accused infringer cannot permanently embody the patented technical solution. Supporting the legitimate source defense for patent-infringing products will not excessively harm the interests of the patentee. However, with regard to the infringing use of a patented method, there is no such limitation. If the legitimate source defense is applied to acts of infringing use of a patented method, the accused infringer will be able to permanently embody the patented technical solution, which will excessively harm the interests of the patentee.

最后，专利侵权产品合法来源抗辩不能及于以使用专利侵权产品的方式侵权使用专利方法的行为。产品专利和方法专利的保护范围延伸性不同。方法专利的保护范围可以延及依照专利方法直接获得的产品，但产品专利的保护范围仅及于产品本身而不延及以使用专利产品的方式使用的方法。专利侵权产品合法来源抗辩本质上是对专利产品保护范围的限制，在该保护范围本身就不延及以使用专利产品的方式使用的方法的

情况下，合法来源抗辩亦不能延及相关侵权使用专利方法的行为。

Lastly, the legitimate source defense for patent-infringing products does not extend to the infringing use of a patented method via using patent-infringing products. The protection scope for product patents differs from method patents. The protection of a method patent can extend to products directly obtained through the patented method, but the protection of a product patent only covers the product itself and does not extend to the method of using the patented product. The legitimate source defense for patent-infringing products essentially limits the protection scope for the patented product. In cases where the protection scope itself does not cover the method of using the patented product, the legitimate source defense cannot be extended to acts of infringing use of the relevant patented method.

24. “三无产品”合法来源抗辩的认定 Determination on legitimate source defense regarding “three-no products”

【裁判要旨】

[Judgment Digest]

被诉侵权产品无生产厂厂名、厂址、产品质量检验合格证明等标识，可以作为认定销售商未尽合理注意义务的重要考量因素。

If the accused infringing products have no manufacturer's name, no production site, and no certificate of quality inspection, then such “three-no” status may be taken into account as an important factor in determining whether the seller fails to perform its duty of reasonable care.

【关键词】

[Keywords]

专利　侵权　合法来源　“三无产品”

Patent; infringement; legitimate source defense; three-no products

【案号】

[Case Number]

（2021）最高法知民终1138号

（2021）SPC IP Civil Final 1138

【基本案情】

[Case Facts]

在上诉人源德盛塑胶电子（深圳）有限公司（以下简称源德盛公司）与被上诉人南宫市新中昊通讯门市（以下简称新中昊门市）侵害实用新型专利权纠纷案中，涉及专利号为201420522729.0、名称为“一种一体式自拍装置”的实用新型专利（以下简称涉案专利）。源德盛公司为专利权人，认为新中昊门市销售的被诉侵权产品侵害了涉案专利权，故向河北省石家庄市中级人民法院（以下简称一审法院）提起诉讼，请求判令：新中昊门市立即停止侵害并赔偿经济损失2万元（包括维权合理开支）。一审法院认为新中昊门市销售的被诉侵权产品落入涉案专利权保护范围，但合法来源抗辩成立，不应承担赔偿责任，仅判决新中昊门市停止侵权，驳回源德盛公司的其他诉讼请求。源德盛公司不服，向最高人民法院提起上诉，主张被诉侵权产品无生产厂家、厂址、产品质量合格证明等标识，属于“三无产品”，新中昊门市主观上存在过错，且新中昊门市所提供的证据不能证明被诉侵权产品是从“深圳恒泰数码”购买。最高人民法院于2022年1月27日改判新中昊门市赔偿源德盛公司经济损失及维权合理开支共计2000元。

In the appeal case between the Appellant, Winners' Sun Plastic Electronics (Shenzhen) Co., Ltd. (hereinafter referred to as “Winners' Sun”),

and the Appellee, Nangong Xinzhonghao Communication Store (hereinafter referred to as "Xinzhonghao Store"), regarding a dispute over infringement of utility model patent, a utility model patent titled "An Integrated Selfie Device" (hereinafter referred to as the "Patent") with the patentee, "Winners' Sun", and patent No. 201420522729.0, was involved. Winners' Sun claimed that the accused infringing products sold by Xinzhonghao Store infringed upon the Patent and therefore filed a lawsuit with Shijiazhuang Intermediate People's Court of Hebei Province (hereinafter referred to as the "Court of First Instance"), requesting the court to order Xinzhonghao Store to immediately cease the infringement and compensate for its economic losses (including reasonable expenses for safeguarding rights) totaling CNY 20,000. The Court of First Instance held that the accused infringing products sold by Xinzhonghao Store fell within the protection scope of the Patent, but the legitimate source defense was established, and Xinzhonghao Store should not be held liable for compensation. The court only ordered Xinzhonghao Store to cease the infringement and dismissed the other claims made by Winners' Sun. Dissatisfied with the judgement, Winners' Sun appealed to the SPC, claiming that the accused infringing products had no manufacturer, factory address, and product certificate, indicating that they were "three-no" products. Xinzhonghao Store had subjective fault and the evidence provided by Xinzhonghao Store could not prove that the accused infringing products were purchased from "Shenzhen Hengtai Digital". On January 27, 2022, the SPC revised the judgment and ordered Xinzonghao Store to compensate Winners' Sun CNY 2,000 for economic losses and reasonable expenses for safeguarding rights.

【裁判意见】

[Judge's Opinion]

最高人民法院二审认为，销售者合法来源抗辩的成立，需要同时满足被诉侵权产品具有合法来源的客观要件和销售者无主观过错的主观要件。被诉侵权产品具有合法来源，是指销售者通过合法的进货渠道、通常的买卖合同等正常商业方式取得所售产品。对于客观要件，销售者应当提供符合交易习惯的相关证据；对于主观要件，销售者应当证明其实际不知道且不应当知道其所售产品系制造者未经专利权人许可而制造并售出。上述两个要件相互关联。首先，新中昊门市在本案一审程序中主张合法来源抗辩提交的仅为淘宝网订单页打印件，两笔订单的淘宝用户会员名不一致，淘宝网交易时间距离源德盛公司取证时间间隔长达一年以上，且在“深圳恒泰数码”淘宝网店已查找不到相应自拍杆产品，仅凭新中昊门市提供的淘宝网订单页所显示的产品照片，无法确认与被诉侵权产品是否完全相同。其次，被诉侵权产品上没有生产厂家、厂址、质量合格证明等标识，可作为认定销售商是否尽到合理注意义务的重要考虑因素。新中昊门市自述以4.5元的较低价格于2016年2月、4月先后两次从同一家网店购进多个自拍杆，虽然其声称不知道所购为“三无产品”，但从其在时隔两个月后再次购买相同产品，其经营的线下店铺实际出售“三无产品”来判断，可以认定其对自拍杆无标识的情况是知晓的，没有尽到销售商的合理注意义务。且本案经过一审、二审，新中昊门市亦未补充提交其他证据。故新中昊门市关于被诉侵权产品具有合法来源的抗辩理由不能成立，仍应当承担停止侵害、赔偿损失的民事责任。关于侵权赔偿数额的确定，综合考虑本案侵权行为发生地在河北省南宫市，当地经济发展水平不高，新中昊门市只是从事零售业务的个体经营户，侵权主观过错不大，经营规模小，被诉侵权产品利润微薄，销售量非常有限，侵权情节较轻，且源德盛公司已在全国各地就涉案专利提起批量诉讼，进行溯源维权等因素，酌定新中昊门市赔偿源德盛公司经济损失1000元、维权合理开支1000元。

The SPC, in the Second Instance trial, held that the legitimate source defense by the seller requires the objective requirement that the alleged infrin-

ging product has a legitimate source and the subjective requirement that the seller has no subjective fault. The legitimate source means that the seller obtains the product through legitimate channels, customary sales contracts, and other normal commercial methods. For the objective requirement, the seller should provide relevant evidence that conforms to transaction practices. For the subjective requirement, the seller should prove that it actually did not know and could not have known that the product it sold was manufactured and sold by the manufacturer without permission from the patentee. These two requirements are interrelated. Firstly, in the First Instance trial, Xinzhonghao Store claimed a legitimate source defense but only submitted printed Taobao order pages as evidence. The two orders had different Taobao user names, and the time between Taobao transactions and the time when Winners' Sun obtained the evidence was more than one year. Furthermore, the corresponding selfie sticks could not be found in the "Shenzhen Hengtai Digital" store on Taobao. Based only on the product photos displayed on the Taobao order page provided by Xinzhonghao Store, it was impossible to confirm whether they were exactly the same as the infringing products. Secondly, whether there are manufacturer, factory address, and quality certification markings on the infringing products can be an important consideration in determining whether the seller fulfilled its duty of care. Xinzhonghao Store stated that it purchased multiple selfie sticks twice from the same online store at a low price of CNY 4.5 each in February and April 2016. Although it claimed not to know they were "three-no" products, it could be inferred from its later purchase of the same product and the fact that its offline shop actually sold "three-no" products that Xinzhonghao Store was aware of the absence of markings on the selfie sticks and it did not fulfill the duty of care as a seller. Moreover, Xinzhonghao Store did not submit any other evidence throughout the First and Second Instance trials. Therefore, its defense of having a legitimate source for the infringing products cannot stand. It should still bear the civil liabilities of ceasing the infringement and compensating for losses. Regarding the amount of compensation for the infringement, considering that the infringement occurred in Nangong City, Hebei Province, which has a relatively low level of economic development, Xinzhonghao Store is only a small-scale individual retail business, its subjective fault for the infringement was not significant, and the profit from the infringing product was meager with very limited sales volume, the infringement can be deemed minor. Taking into account Winners' Sun's nationwide mass litigation to protect their patent rights, the court decided that Xinzhonghao Store should compensate Winners' Sun for economic losses of CNY 1,000 and reasonable expenses of CNY 1,000 for protecting their rights.

25. 使用租赁产品的合法来源抗辩
Legitimate source defense regarding the use of leased products

【裁判要旨】

[Judgment Digest]

被诉侵权使用者能够证明其使用的侵权产品系付费租赁而来，租赁价格合理且符合商业惯例，专利权利人未进一步提供足以推翻的相反证据的，可以认定被诉侵权使用者的合法来源抗辩成立。

Where the accused infringing user can prove that it rents the infringing product at a reasonable price in line with business practices, and the patentee fails to present sufficient evidence to the contrary effect, such legitimate source defense can be supported by court.

【关键词】

[Keywords]

专利　侵权　租赁使用　合法来源抗辩

Patent; infringement; use of leased products; legitimate source defense

【案号】

[Case Number]

（2021）最高法知民终 1118 号

（2021）SPC IP Civil Final 1118

【基本案情】

[Case Facts]

在上诉人中铁电气化局集团有限公司（以下简称中铁公司）与被上诉人北京波森特岩土工程有限公司（以下简称波森特公司）侵害发明专利权纠纷案中，涉及专利号为 98101332.5、名称为“底端带有夯扩头的混凝土桩的施工设备”的发明专利（以下简称涉案专利）。波森特公司认为，中铁公司在土建工程施工中使用多台被诉侵权产品进行施工，侵害了涉案专利权，故向北京知识产权法院（以下简称一审法院）提起诉讼，请求判令中铁公司立即停止制造、使用被诉侵权产品进行施工的行为，中铁公司向波森特公司赔偿 200 万元。一审法院认为，被诉侵权产品落入涉案专利权利要求 1 的保护范围。中铁公司存在制造、使用行为，故判决中铁公司赔偿波森特公司经济损失 60 万元。中铁公司不服，向最高人民法院提起上诉。最高人民法院于 2022 年 10 月 10 日判决撤销原判，驳回波森特公司的全部诉讼请求。

In the appeal case between the Appellant, China Railway Electrification Bureau Group Co., Ltd. (hereinafter referred to as “CREB”), and the Appellee, Beijing Puissant Geotechnical Engineering Co., Ltd. (hereinafter referred to as “Puissant”), regarding a dispute over infringement of invention patent, an invention patent titled “Construction Equipment for Concrete Pile with Tamping and Expansion Head at the Bottom" (hereinafter referred to as the "Patent"), with patent No. 98101332.5, was involved. Puissant alleged that CREB used multiple infringing products during construction of civil engineering projects, which infringed upon the Patent. Therefore, it filed a lawsuit with Beijing Intellectual Property Court (hereinafter referred to as the "Court of First Instance"), requesting an order for CREB to immediately cease manufacturing and using the infringing products for construction, and compensate Puissant CNY 2 million. The Court of First Instance held that the accused infringing products fell within the protection scope of Claim 1 of the Patent. As CREB engaged in the manufacturing and use of such products, it was ordered to compensate Puissant for its economic losses totaling CNY 600 thousand. Then, CREB appealed to the SPC. On October 10, 2022, the SPC ruled to revoke the original judgment and reject all claims of Puissant.

【裁判意见】

[Judge's Opinion]

最高人民法院二审认为，为生产经营目的使用、许诺销售或者销售不知道是未经专利权人许可而制造并售出的专利侵权产品，能证明该产品合法来源的，不承担赔偿责任。本案中，在案证据可以证明中铁公司将涉案工程分包给菏建公司、中兵公司和世纪滕迈公司。上述分包单位通过合法、正常的商业租赁方式向案外人租赁被诉侵权产品并用于涉案工程施工。该租赁方式符合建筑施工行业的一般惯例和特点，租赁价格也比较合理，故可以推定中铁公司对于该使用行为主观无过错。在波森特公司未进一步提供足以推翻上述推定的相反证据的情况下，应当认定中铁公司使用的被诉侵权产品具有合法来源，其主张的合法来源抗辩成立。

The SPC, in the Second Instance trial, held that if it can be proven by evidence that the patent-infringing products used, offered for sale, or sold for

production and business purposes are obtained from a legitimate source without knowing the lack of permission from the patentee, then the infringer shall not be held liable for compensation. In this case, the evidence showed that CREB subcontracted the project to Hejian Company, Zhongbing Company, and Century Tenmai Company. These subcontractors legally and normally leased the accused infringing products from unrelated third parties for the construction of the project. Such lease was in line with the general practices and characteristics of the construction industry, and the leasing prices were reasonable. Therefore, it can be presumed that CREB had no subjective fault regarding the use of these products. In the absence of further evidence provided by Puissant to overturn this presumption, it should be determined that the accused infringing products used by CREB have a legitimate source, and thus, the legitimate source defense raised by CREB is established.

26. 合法来源抗辩的主观要件 Subjective elements of legitimate source defense

【裁判要旨】

[Judgment Digest]

是否守法规范经营和谨慎理性交易可以作为合法来源抗辩主观要件审查的重要考量因素。主张合法来源抗辩的使用者曾向权利人购买使用涉案技术制造的产品并且依约负有相关技术保密义务，后又于专利授权后以明显低于权利人专利产品售价的价格向他人购买相同产品的，其对产品的权利瑕疵负有更高的注意义务。使用者不能证明其已履行上述注意义务的，对其合法来源抗辩可不予支持。

Operating business in compliance with laws and transacting with prudence and rationality can be taken as important factors for consideration in reviewing subjective elements of legitimate source defense. Where the user who raises the legitimate source defense purchased from the patentee the products manufactured with the technical scheme in question before the filing date of the patent and is therefore obligated to keep in secrecy the relevant technology, but such user then purchases the same products from others at a price significantly lower than the selling price of the patented products upon grant of patent, such user should bear stricter duty of reasonable care with respect to the defects in rights of the products. Where the user cannot prove that it has fulfilled the aforementioned obligation, its legitimate source defense can not be supported.

【关键词】

[Keywords]

专利　侵权　使用者　合法来源抗辩　主观要件

Patent; infringement; user; legitimate source defense; subjective element

【案号】

[Case Number]

(2022) 最高法知民终 593 号

(2022) SPC IP Civil Final 593

【基本案情】

[Case Facts]

在上诉人深圳市华创众成智能装备有限公司（以下简称华创众成公司）与上诉人深圳市宏贲科创有限公司（以下简称宏贲公司）、深圳市宏贲科创有限公司东莞分公司（以下简称宏贲东莞分公司）、广东嘉拓新能源科技有限公司东莞分公司（以下简称嘉拓东莞分公司）等侵害发明专利权纠纷案中，涉及专利号为 201610239004.4、名称为“一种带托盘的电池上下料系统及方法”的发明专利（以下简称涉案专

利）。华创众成公司认为，宏贲公司、宏贲东莞分公司未经许可，制造、销售落入涉案专利权保护范围的产品，嘉拓东莞分公司明知上述产品为侵权产品，仍购买并使用，均构成对涉案专利权的侵害，故向广州市知识产权法院（以下简称一审法院）提起诉讼，请求判令宏贲公司等停止侵害并赔偿经济损失和维权合理开支。一审法院认为，被诉侵权产品落入涉案专利权保护范围。嘉拓公司在购买被诉侵权产品之前，曾向华创众成公司购买涉案专利产品，两次购买行为中的销售方代表均为何某凌，而何某凌正是涉案专利的发明人之一，可见嘉拓东莞分公司知道或应当知道涉案专利的存在且被诉侵权产品系侵害涉案专利权的产品，嘉拓东莞分公司的合法来源抗辩不符合主观要件，依法不能成立，判决宏贲公司、宏贲东莞分公司停止侵害，宏贲公司、宏贲东莞分公司赔偿华创众成公司经济损失 489600 元，嘉拓东莞分公司赔偿华创众成公司经济损失 10 万元，宏贲公司、宏贲东莞分公司、嘉拓东莞分公司共同赔偿华创众成公司维权合理开支 5 万元。嘉拓东莞分公司不服，向最高人民法院提出上诉，主张其为购买被诉侵权产品支出的合理对价，不知道涉案专利的存在及所购买设备系侵权产品的事实，不应承担停止侵害及赔偿损失责任。最高人民法院于 2022 年 12 月 12 日判决驳回上诉，在纠正原审判决关于维权合理开支判项未确定履行期限的基础上，维持原判。

In the appeal case between the Appellant, Shenzhen Huachuang Zhongcheng Intelligent Equipment Co., Ltd. (hereinafter referred to as "Huachuang Zhongcheng"), and the Appellees, Shenzhen Hongben Technology Innovation Co., Ltd. (hereinafter referred to as "Hongben"), Dongguan Branch of Shenzhen Hongben Technology Innovation Co., Ltd. (hereinafter referred to as "Hongben Dongguan Branch"), and Dongguan Branch of Guangdong Cvatop New Energy Technology Co., Ltd. (hereinafter referred to as "Cvatop Dongguan Branch"), regarding a dispute over infringement of invention patent, an invention patent titled "A Battery Loading and Unloading System and Method with Tray" (hereinafter referred to as the "Patent"), with patent No. 201610239004.4, was involved. Huachuang Zhongcheng argued that Hongben and Hongben Dongguan Branch had manufactured and sold products that fell within the protection scope of the Patent without permission, while Cvatop Dongguan Branch knowingly purchased and used the infringing products, all of which infringed upon the Patent. Therefore, it filed a lawsuit with Guangzhou Intellectual Property Court (hereinafter referred to as the "Court of First Instance"), requesting an order for Hongben and the other defendants to cease the infringement and compensation for its economic losses and reasonable expenses for safeguarding rights. The Court of First Instance found that the accused infringing products indeed fell within the protection scope of the Patent. Before purchasing the accused infringing products, Cvatop had previously purchased the patented products from Huachuang Zhongcheng. The sales representative on both occasions was He, one of the inventors of the Patent. It can be seen that Cvatop Dongguan Branch knew or should have known about the existence of the Patent and that the accused infringing products infringed upon the Patent. The legitimate source defense raised by Cvatop Dongguan Branch did not meet the subjective requirement and could not be established under the law. The Court of First Instance ruled that Hongben and Hongben Dongguan Branch should cease the infringement and compensate Huachuang Zhongcheng for its economic losses totaling CNY 489,600; Cvatop Dongguan Branch should compensate Huachuang Zhongcheng for its economic losses totaling CNY 100,000; Hongben, Hongben Dongguan Branch, and Cvatop Dongguan Branch should jointly compensate Huachuang Zhongcheng for the reasonable expenses incurred for safeguarding rights, amounting to CNY 50,000. Cvatop Dongguan Branch appealed to the SPC, ar-

guing that it should not be held liable for ceasing the infringement and compensating for the losses because it paid a reasonable price for the accused infringing products and was unaware of the existence of the Patent and the fact that the purchased equipment was an infringing product. On December 12, 2022, the SPC ruled to dismiss the appeal and affirm the original judgment while correcting the original judgment by specifying the deadline for the performance of the reasonable expenses for safeguarding rights.

【裁判意见】

[Judge's Opinion]

最高人民法院二审认为，合法来源抗辩性质上属于专利侵权损害赔偿责任豁免的例外情形，其成立需要同时满足被诉侵权产品具有合法来源这一客观要件和销售者、使用者无主观过错这一主观要件。被诉侵权人提出合法来源抗辩的，应当首先审查该主体是否守法规范经营、谨慎理性交易。本案中，嘉拓东莞分公司曾向专利权人华创众成公司购买使用涉案技术制造的产品并且负有相关的保密义务，在华创众成公司任职的涉案专利发明人之一何某凌离职加入宏贲公司后，嘉拓东莞分公司通过何某凌以明显低于专利产品的价格向宏贲公司购买相同产品，其应当对产品权利瑕疵产生合理怀疑，进而具有更高的注意义务。但嘉拓东莞分公司未举证证明已审慎审查所售产品的权利瑕疵问题，故不应认定其无主观过错。关于嘉拓东莞分公司主张其系基于对何某凌的信任进行交易的抗辩理由，本院认为，涉案产品系工业产品，交易双方重点关注的因素通常是产品的功能、质量、价格等，而非纯粹依赖个人之间的信任关系。并且，嘉拓公司与宏贲公司于 2018 年 1 月 8 日签订的设备订购协议书中载明的宏贲公司联系人为肖某良，表明嘉拓公司在没有何某凌参与的情况下也与宏贲公司进行了交易，其主张的基于信任关系而向宏贲公司购买被诉侵权产品的理由显然难以成立。综上，嘉拓东莞分公司作为理性的市场交易主体，在先期购买专利产品并负有保密义务的情况下，对于购买同类产品应当负有合理注意义务，但嘉拓东莞分公司并未善尽合理注意义务，不属于善意使用者，不符合合法来源抗辩的主观要件，其提出的合法来源抗辩不能成立。

The SPC, in the Second Instance trial, held that legitimate source defense is an exceptional circumstance where liability for patent infringement damages is exempted. Its establishment requires the simultaneous satisfaction of two criteria: the objective requirement that the accused infringing product has a legitimate source and the subjective requirement that the seller or user is free from subjective fault. When the accused infringer raises a legitimate source defense, the court should first examine whether the party in question conducted lawful and normative business operations and exercised reasonable and prudent judgment in the transaction. In this case, Cvatop Dongguan Branch had previously purchased products made using the patented technology from the patentee, Huachuang Zhongcheng, and was bound by confidentiality obligations. When one of the inventors of the Patent, He, left Huachuang Zhongcheng and joined Hongben, Cvatop Dongguan Branch purchased the same products from Hongben at a price significantly lower than that of the patented product. As a result, Cvatop Dongguan Branch should have been suspicious of potential legal defects in the products and exercised a higher level of due diligence. However, Cvatop Dongguan Branch failed to demonstrate that it had carefully considered the possible legal issues with the products sold. Therefore, Cvatop Dongguan Branch was not considered free from subjective fault. Regarding Cvatop Dongguan Branch's argument that it relied on trust in He when conducting the transaction, the court held that for industrial products like the accused infringing products, the focus of the transaction is typically on factors such as functionality, quality, and price, rather than purely on trust between individuals. Furthermore, the equipment purchase agreement be-

tween Cvatop Dongguan Branch and Hongben, which was signed on January 8, 2018, identified Xiao as the contact person for Hongben, indicating that Cvatop Dongguan Branch had transacted with Hongben without He's involvement. As a result, Cvatop Dongguan Branch's argument that it purchased the accused infringing products based purely on trust was not persuasive. In summary, Cvatop Dongguan Branch, as a rational market participant who had previously purchased the patented product and was bound by confidentiality obligations, had a reasonable duty of care when purchasing similar products. However, it failed to exercise due care and did not qualify as a bona fide user nor meet the subjective requirement for the legitimate source defense. Therefore, Cvatop Dongguan Branch's legitimate source defense cannot be established.

27. 标准必要专利侵权案件中的禁令救济 Injunctive reliefs in standards-essential patent infringement cases

【裁判要旨】

[Judgment Digest]

在标准必要专利侵权纠纷案件中适用《最高人民法院关于审理侵犯专利权纠纷案件应用法律若干问题的解释（二）》第二十六条之规定判断是否判令停止侵害时，除考虑国家利益、公共利益外，还可以考虑涉案专利的性质、当事人的过错、涉案专利权的权利状态和判令附条件停止侵害的必要性，以及专利权人的利益保障方式等因素。当涉案专利在性质上属于实施强制性标准所无法避开的必要专利时，判令被诉侵权人承担停止侵害的民事责任应当更为审慎，更应重点综合考虑当事人的主观过错程度、当事人之间是否存在利益失衡、损害赔偿是否能够充分弥补专利权人损失、停止侵害是否影响社会公共利益等因素。

In deciding whether to order to cease the infringement in a standard essential patent(SEP) infringement case pursuant to Article 26 of *the Interpretation of the Supreme People's Court on Several Issues concerning the Application of Law in the Trial of Patent Infringement Dispute Cases (II)*, in addition to national and public interests, considerations may also be given to such factors as the nature of the involved patent, the fault of the involved parties, the status of right of the involved patent, the necessity to order conditional cease of infringement and the way to protect the patentee's interests. When the involved patent by its nature is an essential patent that cannot be avoided in implementing compulsory standards, then people's courts should be more prudent when ordering the accused infringer to cease the infringement and should further take into account such factors as the degree of subjective fault of the involved parties, whether there is interest imbalance between the involved parties, whether the damages can fully cover the patentee's losses, and whether ceasing the infringement will affect public interests.

在标准必要专利侵权纠纷案件中，可以根据案件具体情况，对停止侵害判决附加条件。例如，在判令标准必要专利实施者停止侵害的同时，可以给予其修改技术方案的合理宽限期，或者可以明确其停止侵害的义务至其实际支付充分的损害赔偿或符合 FRAND 原则的许可费时止。

In SEP infringement cases, the decision to cease infringement can be made with conditions based on specific circumstances of the case. For instance, when the SEP implementer is ordered to cease the infringement, a reasonable grace period can be offered for the implementer to amend the technical solution or it can be made clear that the obligation of the implementer to cease the infringement exists until the full damages or license fees that comply

with FRAND are actually paid up.

【关键词】

[Keywords]

标准必要专利　侵权　停止侵害　附条件判决

Standard essential patent; infringement; cessation of infringement; conditional judgment

【案号】

[Case Number]

(2022) 最高法知民终 817 号

(2022) SPC IP Civil Final 817

【裁判意见】

[Judge's Opinion]

在上诉人苹果电脑贸易（上海）有限公司与被上诉人西安西电捷通无线网络通信股份有限公司、原审被告西安市国美电器有限公司侵害发明专利权纠纷案中，最高人民法院二审认为，对于侵害专利权的行为，根据侵权责任法的一般原理和有关侵权责任承担方式的规定，原则上应当承担停止侵害的民事责任。但是，在具体案件中，基于国家利益、社会公共利益、具体权利状态以及当事人的主观过错等因素，在特殊情况下可以不判令被诉侵权人承担停止侵害的民事责任，但可通过充分的损害赔偿等责任的承担弥补专利权人相应的损失。本案中，苹果电脑上海公司实施了侵害涉案专利权的行为，对于是否应判令苹果电脑上海公司停止侵害，至少可考虑以下因素：

In the appeal case between the Appellant, Apple Computer Trading (Shanghai) Co., Ltd., and the Appellees, China Iwncomm Co., Ltd., and Xi'an Gome Electrical Appliances Co., Ltd. (the defendant in the First Instance), regarding a dispute over infringement of invention patent, the SPC held in the Second Instance trial that, according to the general principles of tort liability law and relevant provisions on the modes of tort liability, the infringing party should, in principle, generally bear the civil liability of ceasing the infringement. However, in specific cases, based on factors such as national interests, public interests, specific rights status, and the subjective fault of the parties involved, the accused infringer may not be ordered to cease the infringement under special circumstances. Instead, the patentee's corresponding losses can be compensated through sufficient damages. In this case, Apple Shanghai had conducted acts that infringed upon the Patent. Factors to be considered in determining whether Apple Shanghai should be ordered to cease infringement include, but are not limited to:

其一，涉案专利的性质。涉案专利不仅是标准必要专利，而且是实施强制性标准所无法避开的必要专利，这一事实使得涉案专利具有更多社会公共利益的因素，是否应当判令停止侵害更应注意综合考虑当事人的主观过错程度、当事人之间是否存在利益失衡、损害赔偿是否能够充分弥补专利权人损失、停止侵害是否影响社会公共利益等因素。首先，GB15629. 11-2003 标准和第 1 号修改单均为“GB”标号的强制性标准。虽然 2004 年第 44 号公告推迟了 GB 15629. 11—2003 标准强制实施的时间，但 2006 年发布的第 1 号修改单明确载明本修改单的 7. 3. 2. 8 和第 8 章为强制性的，其余为推荐性的，而涉案专利涉及的即为第 8 章的内容。苹果电脑上海公司与西电捷通公司在二审中亦对 WAPI 标准事实上已经强制实施不持异议。因此，WAPI 标准在本案中可以被认定为强制性标准。一审法院基于 WAPI 标准为推荐性标准考虑是否判令停止侵害，不尽准确、妥当。其次，因实施强制性标准导致的侵权行为，专利实施者无法通过改变技术方案避免侵权，特别是在专利技术只是终端产品整体使用的技术方案的一部分时，如果判令停止侵害，则意味着专利权人对权利的行使可能导致专利实施者完全退出相关商品的市场竞争。考虑到涉案专利只是被诉侵权 iPhone 或 iPad 产品所使用的整体技术方

案中的一部分，其作用占比相对较低，如果判决结果导致专利实施者退出市场，可能会使专利权人和专利实施者之间的利益显著失衡。因此，在审理侵害涉及强制性标准的必要专利纠纷时，判令承担停止侵害的民事责任应当更为慎重，不宜仅因构成侵权即简单判令停止侵害，还应综合前述各种因素作出判断。

(1) The nature of the Patent. In this case, the Patent is not only a Standard Essential Patent (SEP) but also a necessary patent that cannot be avoided when implementing mandatory Standards. This fact brings in more social public interest factors, and the decision to order a cessation of infringement should carefully consider factors such as the subjective fault of the parties involved, whether there is an imbalance of interests between the parties, whether the compensation for damages can adequately compensate the patentee's losses, and whether the cease of infringement would affect social public interests. Firstly, both Standard GB 15629. 11-2003 and its Amendment No. 1 are mandatory Standards with the "GB" mark in China. Although the implementation of Standard GB 15629. 11-2003 was postponed by Announcement No. 44 in 2004, Amendment No. 1, issued in 2006, explicitly states that Section 7. 3. 2. 8 and Chapter 8 thereof are mandatory while the rest are recommended, and the Patent relates to the content of Chapter 8. Apple Shanghai and Iwncomm did not object to the fact that WAPI Standard had already been mandatorily implemented during the Second Instance trial. Therefore, the WAPI Standard can be recognized as a mandatory Standard in this case. It was inaccurate and inappropriate for the Court of First Instance to consider whether to order a cessation of infringement based on the WAPI Standard being considered as a recommended Standard. Secondly, when infringement occurs due to the implementation of a mandatory Standard, when implementing mandatory Standard, the patent exploiter cannot avoid infringe-

ment by changing the technical solution, especially when the patented technology is only a part of the overall technical solution used in the end product. If a cessation of infringement is ordered, the patentee's exercise of the patent right may cause the patent exploiter to completely withdraw from the market competition of related goods. Considering that the Patent is only a part of the overall technical solution used in the accused infringing products like iPhone or iPad, its contribution is relatively low. If the judgment results in the patent exploiter exiting the market, it may significantly unbalance the interests between the patentee and the patent exploiter. Therefore, when adjudicating SEP infringement disputes involving mandatory standards, the decision to order a civil liability of ceasing the infringement should be made more cautiously. It should not simply order a cessation of infringement based solely on the existence of infringement but should take into account the various factors mentioned above.

其二，当事人的过错。对于标准必要专利许可的 FRAND 谈判，当事人应当本于善意行为人、循诚信原则进行协商，如果标准必要专利的专利权人行为符合 FRAND 原则，而实施者存在明显过错，即便对于强制性标准，也可以在综合考虑各种因素后支持专利权人停止侵害的诉讼请求。本案中，苹果公司无正当理由严重拖延 2014 年以后继续获得许可的谈判，并质疑获得专利许可的必要性，其在本案苹果电脑上海公司被诉侵权期间的行为具有明显过错，苹果电脑上海公司也构成共同过错方，苹果公司和苹果电脑上海公司并非有意愿继续获得许可的善意、诚信的实施者。涉案仲裁裁决认定西电捷通公司在 2014 年后的谈判中没有违反其 FRAND 义务，苹果电脑上海公司表示认可该仲裁裁决，根据在案证据体现的事实，本案中可以认定西电捷通公司在关于继续许可的谈判过程中并无过错。虽然西电捷通公司在 WAPI 标准的形成过程中仅声称该标准可能涉及其专利，并未载明具体的专利信息，但考虑到西电

捷通公司在本案中主张的是 2014 年之后苹果电脑上海公司构成侵权的行为，此时基于苹果公司与西电捷通公司 2014 年之前的专利许可合同的签订与履行情况，苹果公司和苹果电脑上海公司对西电捷通公司主张涉案专利为标准必要专利早已明知，故该事实不影响对本案中双方当事人过错的整体认定。基于上述考虑，一审判决判令苹果电脑上海公司承担停止侵害的法律责任并无明显不当。但是，在本案中西电捷通公司主张权利的期间之后，苹果公司已于 2018 年 3 月提起仲裁程序，以解决双方之间有关继续许可的纠纷。现仲裁裁决已确定符合 FRAND 原则的许可费率，且西电捷通公司和苹果电脑上海公司在本案中均表示认可该仲裁裁决。因此，对于本案被诉侵权期间之后实施相关专利的行为，可以按照专利许可合同约定的内容及仲裁裁决确定的许可费率继续履行合同。故在本案西电捷通公司主张权利的期间之后，特别是涉案仲裁裁决和一审判决作出之后，苹果公司和苹果上海公司的主观状态发生了变化，本案有关专利许可合同履行问题的事实基础亦发生了变化，这些变化减缓了判令被诉侵权人承担停止侵害民事责任的必要性和紧迫性。

(2) The fault of the parties involved. In FRAND negotiations for SEP, the parties should conduct negotiations in good faith and adhere to the principle of honesty and credibility. Even for mandatory Standards, if the SEP patentee's behavior complies with FRAND and the exploiter has obvious faults, the court can support the patentee's request to cease infringement after comprehensive consideration of various factors. In this case, Apple Inc. had no justifiable reason to significantly delay negotiations for licenses after 2014 and questioned the necessity of obtaining patent licenses. Its behavior during the period when Apple Shanghai was accused of infringement was clearly at fault, making both Apple Inc. and Apple Shanghai liable for their joint fault. Neither Apple Inc. nor Apple Shanghai demonstrated good faith or honesty in their intention to obtain licenses. The arbitration ruling determined that Iwn-

comm did not violate its FRAND obligations during negotiations after 2014, and Apple Shanghai agreed with that ruling. Based on the evidence in the case, it can be determined that Iwncomm had no fault in the negotiations for continued license. Although Iwncomm only claimed that its patent might be involved in the formation of the WAPI Standard without specifying the exact patent information, considering Iwncomm's assertion that Apple Shanghai's alleged infringement occurred after 2014, and Apple Inc.' s and Iwncomm's previous patent licensing contract had been signed and implemented before 2014, Apple Inc. and Apple Shanghai should have known Iwncomm's assertion that the Patent was an SEP. Therefore, this fact does not affect the overall determination of the fault of both parties in the case. Based on the above, the First Instance judgement, which ordered Apple Shanghai to cease the infringement, was not obviously inappropriate. However, following Iwncomm's assertion of rights, Apple Inc. initiated arbitration proceedings in March 2018 to resolve their dispute over continued licensing. The arbitration ruling has determined a FRAND licensing fee, and both Iwncomm and Apple Shanghai have acknowledged and accepted the arbitration ruling in the case. Therefore, for the exploitation of the relevant patent after the accused infringement period, the contract can continue to be performed in accordance with the content of the patent license contract and the licensing fee determined by the arbitration ruling. As a result, following Iwncomm's assertion of rights in the case, particularly after the arbitration ruling and the First Instance judgment were made, there was a change in the subjective mindset of Apple Inc. and Apple Shanghai. Additionally, the factual basis for the performance of the patent license contract also changed. These changes mitigated the necessity and urgency of ordering the accused infringer to bear the civil liability of ceasing the infringement.

其三，涉案专利权的权利状态和判令附条件停止侵害的必要性。考虑到标准必要专利的特殊性，在因该类专利引发的侵权纠纷中，可以根据当事人过错、停止侵害是否可能导致当事人之间出现严重利益失衡等案件具体情况，附条件地作出停止侵害的判决。一方面，可以在前述特殊情况下，考虑在判令标准必要专利实施者停止侵害的同时，对于执行停止侵害判项给予其修改技术方案的合理宽限期；另一方面，如果标准必要专利实施者通过支付充分的损害赔偿或者以符合 FRAND 原则的许可费的方式支付许可使用费，则停止侵害的判项可以不再执行。本案中，可以结合涉案专利权的权利状态，对是否以及如何适用附条件停止侵害判决予以考虑。但因涉案专利权的期限为 2002 年 11 月 6 日至 2022 年 11 月 5 日，涉案专利权于 2022 年 11 月 6 日终止，即涉案专利的权利状态在二审期间发生了重大变化。基于该事实，继续维持判令苹果电脑上海公司承担停止侵害的民事责任已经失去法律基础。

(3) The status of the patent right and the need for a conditional order to cease the infringement. Considering the special nature of an SEP, in infringement disputes arising from such patents, it is possible to make a conditional judgment to cease infringement based on factors such as the parties' faults and whether ceasing the infringement could lead to a serious imbalance of interests between the parties. On the one hand, under the aforementioned special circumstances, the exploiter of an SEP may be granted a reasonable grace period to modify its technical solution while being ordered to cease the infringement. On the other hand, if the exploiter of an SEP pays sufficient damages or offers a license fee consistent with FRAND, the order to cease infringement may no longer be enforced. In this case, whether and how to apply a conditional judgment to cease infringement can be considered based on the status of the Patent. However, since the term of the Patent was from November 6, 2002 to November 5, 2022, and the Patent expired on November 6, 2022, there has

been a significant change in the status of the Patent during the appeal period. Based on this fact, there is no longer a legal basis to maintain the judgment that Apple Shanghai should bear the civil liability of ceasing the infringement.

其四，专利权人的利益保障方式。在因标准必要专利引发的侵权纠纷中，如果判令停止侵害可能使双方当事人的利益显著失衡，但专利权人的利益可以通过足额赔偿等责任的承担予以保障，则可以在综合考量前述各种有关因素的基础上通过判决专利实施者承担足额赔偿等法律责任，替代停止侵害的法律责任。本案中，基于上述分析，如果判令停止侵害，则判决结果可能会导致专利实施者退出相关商品市场，使专利权人和专利实施者的利益显著失衡。相反，判令专利实施者足额赔偿可以使专利权人的利益得到保障。

(4) The way to protect the interests of the patentee. In infringement disputes arising from SEPs, ordering the infringer to cease the infringement may significantly unbalance the interests of both parties, but the interests of the patentee can be protected by taking responsibility, such as paying sufficient compensation, then instead of ceasing the infringement, a judgment can be made to order the exploiter to bear legal liability, such as paying sufficient compensation. In this case, based on the above analysis, by ordering the exploiter to cease the infringement, the judgment may lead to the exploiter's withdrawal from the relevant product market, resulting in a significant imbalance of interests between the patentee and the exploiter. On the contrary, ordering the exploiter to pay sufficient compensation can protect the interests of the patentee.

综上所述，一审法院判决苹果电脑上海公司停止侵害，在裁判作出时具有一定的事实和法律基础，并无明显不当。并且，停止制造固化了涉案方法专利实质内容的产品必然意味着制造者自身不得销售固化该方法专利的产品，否则难以实现制造者停止侵害的法律效果，基于苹果公

司和苹果电脑上海公司之间的共同行为，一审判决判令苹果电脑上海公司停止销售行为，亦无明显不当。但是，在本案西电捷通公司主张权利的期间之后，特别是一审判决作出后，涉及专利许可合同履行问题的基本事实、专利实施者的主观状态及涉案专利的权利状态发生了重大变化；同时，本案可以认定涉案专利为实施强制性标准的必要专利。基于对本案事实和法律问题的综合评判，二审中继续维持一审判决判令苹果电脑上海公司承担停止侵害的民事责任既无必要、亦无可能。因此，对于一审判决关于停止侵害的判项，对此予以调整。

In conclusion, the Court of First Instance's judgment to order Apple Shanghai to cease the infringement had a certain factual and legal basis at the time of the ruling and was proper. Moreover, ceasing the manufacturing of products that embody the essential content of the patented method necessarily means that the manufacturers cannot sell products that embody such patented method themselves. Otherwise, it would be difficult to achieve the legal effect of the manufacturer's ceasing of the infringement. Considering the joint acts between Apple Inc. and Apple Shanghai, the First Instance judgment to order Apple Shanghai to cease the sales activities was also proper. However, following Iwncomm's assertion of rights in the case, particularly after the First Instance judgment was rendered, significant changes occurred regarding the basic facts related to the performance of the patent license contract, the subjective condition of the patent exploiter, and the rights status of the Patent. Meanwhile, the Patent can be identified as an essential patent for implementing a mandatory Standard. Based on a comprehensive assessment of the facts and legal issues in this case, it is neither necessary nor feasible to maintain the civil liability of ceasing the infringement imposed on Apple Shanghai in the Second Instance trial. Therefore, adjustments should be made to the First Instance judgment regarding the injunction to cease the infringement.

28. 侵害零部件产品专利损害赔偿计算基础的选择
Choice of the basis for calculating damages for patent-infringing parts and components

【裁判要旨】

[Judgment Digest]

侵害零部件产品专利权的损害赔偿计算基础，可以根据产品零部件与使用该零部件的产品整体的销售模式，零部件对于产品整体利润的贡献程度，零部件与产品整体是否存在协同效应，产品整体是否存在多项专利技术方案以及相关的价格、销量、利润等数据的可获得性等因素，选择确定以零部件或者该零部件所属的产品整体作为损害赔偿计算基础。若有关侵权零部件产品为耗材且通常向终端用户单独销售，在产品整体中的功能和作用相对独立，与产品其他部件的协同作用不显著，销售价格、销售数量、利润率等证据较为充分的，宜选择零部件产品作为损害赔偿计算基础。

When calculating damages incurred by patent-infringing parts and components, people's court may consider the following factors including sales models for such parts and components as well as for the products containing them, the degree of contribution of such parts and components to the overall profit of the products containing them, whether there is any synergistic effect between the two, whether the product in question has multiple patented technical solutions, and availability of the relevant price, sales volume, profit margin, etc, so as to choose the parts and components or the product containing them as the calculation basis. If the patent-infringing parts and components are consumables usually sold separately to end users, with functions and roles relatively independent from the product containing them, having no significant synergy with other parts or components of the product, and there is

sufficient evidence on sales price, sales volume and profit margin, then it is appropriate to take such parts and components as the basis for calculating the damages.

【关键词】

[Keywords]

专利　侵权　零部件专利　实际损失

Patent; infringement; part and component patent; actual losses

【案号】

[Case Number]

（2020）最高法知民终 589 号

（2020）SPC IP Civil Final 589

【基本案情】

[Case Facts]

在上诉人广州市彩标立体眼镜有限公司（以下简称彩标公司）与上诉人广州市柏拉图新材料有限公司（以下简称柏拉图公司）侵害发明专利权纠纷案中，涉及专利权人为彩标公司、专利号为201410132116.0、名称为“一种旋转式眼镜清洗设备及其清洗篮”的发明专利（以下简称涉案专利）。彩标公司认为，柏拉图公司制造、销售、许诺销售的 3D 眼镜清洗机及其配套清洗篮落入涉案专利权保护范围，故向广州知识产权法院（以下简称一审法院）提起诉讼，请求判令柏拉图公司停止侵害并赔偿损失。一审法院认为，被诉侵权产品的清洗篮落入涉案专利权保护范围，清洗机未落入涉案专利权保护范围；以包括清洗篮在内的清洗机整机的价格作为计算基础，综合考虑利润率、贡献率，判决柏拉图公司停止侵害并赔偿损失 1327980 元及维权合理开支。彩标公司、柏拉图公司均不服，向最高人民法院提起上诉。最高人民法院于 2021 年 3 月 24 日判决维持原审关于判赔数额的判项。

In the appeal case between the Appellant, Guangzhou Caibiao 3D Glasses Co., Ltd. (hereinafter referred to as "Caibiao"), and the Appellee, Guangzhou Plato New Material Co., Ltd. (hereinafter referred to as "Plato"), regarding a dispute over infringement of invention patent, an invention patent titled "A Rotating Eyeglass Cleaning Device and Its Cleaning Basket" (hereinafter referred to as the "Patent"), with the patentee, Caibiao, and patent No. 201410132116. 0, was involved. Caibiao contended that the 3D eyeglass cleaning machine and its accompanying cleaning basket manufactured, sold, and offered for sale by Plato fell within the protection scope of the Patent. Therefore, it filed a lawsuit against Plato with Guangzhou Intellectual Property Court (hereinafter referred to as the "Court of First Instance"), requesting that Plato cease the infringement and compensate for its losses. The Court of First Instance held that the cleaning basket of the Accused Infringing Product fell within the protection scope of the Patent, while the cleaning machine did not. The damages should be calculated based on the price of the entire cleaning machine, including the cleaning basket, taking into account profit margin and contribution rate. Therefore, it ordered Plato to cease the infringement and compensate for Caibiao's economical losses totaling CNY 1, 327, 980 and reasonable expenses for safeguarding its rights. Both Caibiao and Plato appealed to the SPC. On March 24, 2021, the SPC upheld the original judgment regarding the amount of compensation.

【裁判意见】

[Judge's Opinion]

最高人民法院二审认为，侵害发明、实用新型专利权的产品系另一产品的零部件的，人民法院应当根据该零部件本身的价值及其在实现成品利润中的作用等因素合理确定赔偿数额。无论选取产品整体还是专利所覆盖的最小可销售单元作为计算基础，在正确考虑利润率及专利技术方案对产品整体贡献率的情况下，最终计算得出的损害赔偿数额均属合

理。如何选择，取决于市场因素、技术因素等以及数据的可获得性等。就市场因素而言，需要考虑整个产品的市场需求驱动力是来源于零部件还是产品整体。就技术因素而言，需要考虑产品零部件与整体是否存在协同效应，同一产品中是否存在多项专利技术方案等。一般而言，由于零部件的价格和利润信息相对更难获取，在具体案件中还需要考虑获得零部件的价格和利润信息的可行性。本案中，被诉侵权产品的清洗篮落入涉案专利权保护范围，清洗机未落入涉案专利权的保护范围。从产品设计看，清洗篮与清洗机可以拆分；从商业实践看，清洗篮被作为类似耗材的产品可单独销售。故可以认定，清洗篮的单独销售价格已经能够体现其所包含的技术方案价值以及其作为零部件与产品整体的协同价值等。根据彩标公司提交的证据，万达两个年度项目中清洗篮的销售数量、销售价格均可单独计算，故在可以单独计算零部件的销售金额的情况下，可以选择将清洗篮作为计算基础，以彩标公司适当的专利产品利润率、专利贡献率计算损害赔偿。首先，2017—2019 年度的万达 3D 眼镜清洗机及耗材集中采购项目中，柏拉图公司中标后的销售数量即为彩标公司因被侵权造成的销售量减少，取整数确定为 1300 个，清洗篮单价为 1600 元，据此可以计算彩标公司因侵权造成的销售金额的减少。其次，根据《商品单位成本评估报告》披露的数据，扣除销售、管理和财务等费用，彩标公司的利润率在 66%以下。最后，在计算实际损失金额时，已排除了其他部件在清洗机整体中所占比例等影响因素，即专利贡献率确定为 100%。根据上述因素，一审法院判决的赔偿经济损失数额 1327980 元，系在利润率 66% 以下确定，并无明显不当，予以维持。

The SPC held in the Second Instance trial that if a product that infringes upon an invention patent or a utility model patent is a component of another product, the amount of compensation should be reasonably determined based on factors such as the value of the component itself and its contribution to the overall profit of the finished product. Whether to select the entire product or the smallest saleable unit covered by the patent as the basis for calculation, the calculated amount of damages is reasonable when correctly considering the profit margin and the contribution rate of the patented technical solution to the overall product. The choice depends on market factors, technological factors, and the availability of data, among others. With regard to market factors, it is necessary to consider whether the demand for the entire product is driven by the component or the product as a whole. With regard to technical factors, it is necessary to consider whether there is a synergistic effect between the component and the whole product, and whether there are multiple patented technical solutions in the same product. In general, it is more difficult to obtain price and profit information on components, so the feasibility of obtaining such information needs to be considered in specific cases. In this case, the cleaning basket of the Accused Infringing Product falls within the protection scope of the Patent, while the cleaning machine does not. From a product design perspective, the cleaning basket and cleaning machine can be separated, and from a business practice perspective, the cleaning basket can be sold as a consumable product separately. Therefore, it can be determined that the separate sales price of the cleaning basket already reflects its value in terms of technical solution and synergy with the overall product as a component. According to the evidence submitted by Caibiao, the sales quantity and price of the cleaning basket could be calculated separately in two annual projects of Wanda, so the cleaning basket could be selected as the basis for calculation, and compensation for damages caused by patent infringement could be calculated based on Caibiao's appropriate profit margin and patent contribution rate for relevant products. Firstly, in the centralized procurement projects concerning Wanda 3D glasses cleaning machine and consumables in 2017-2019, the number of

units sold after Plato was awarded the bid was determined to be 1300, which was the decrease in Caibiao's sales caused by the infringement, and the unit price of the cleaning basket was CNY 1, 600. Based on this, the reduction in sales amount caused by the infringement can be calculated. Secondly, according to the data disclosed in the Evaluation Report on Unit Cost of Commodity, Caibiao's profit margin was below 66% after deducting the sales expenses, management expenses, and financial expenses. Finally, when calculating the amount of actual losses, other factors such as the proportion of other components in the overall cleaning machine were excluded, and the patent contribution rate was determined to be 100%. Based on these factors, the compensation for economic losses totaling CNY 1, 327, 980 as ruled by the Court of First Instance was determined to be below the profit rate of 66%, and was not obviously inappropriate, so it shall be upheld.

29. 侵权人对外宣称的经营业绩可以作为计算损害赔偿的依据

Business performance announced by the infringer may be taken as the basis for calculating damages

【裁判要旨】

[Judgment Digest]

专利权利人主张以侵权人对外宣传的经营规模作为损害赔偿计算依据，侵权人抗辩该经营规模属于夸大宣传，并非经营实绩，但未提交证据证明其实际侵权经营规模的，人民法院可以依据该对外宣传的经营规模作为损害赔偿计算依据。

If the patentee claims that damages should be calculated based on the business scale announced by the infringer itself, while the infringer defends that such business scale is exaggerated and hence does not represent the actual business performance but fails to submit evidence to prove its actual business scale in connection with the infringement, then people's courts can take the infringer's self-announced business scale as the basis for calculating damages.

【关键词】

[Keywords]

专利　侵权　侵权责任　赔偿计算　自我宣传业绩

Patent; infringement; liability for infringement; compensation calculation; self-promotion performance

【案号】

[Case Number]

（2021）最高法知民终 1066 号

（2021）SPC IP Civil Final 1066

【基本案情】

[Case Facts]

在上诉人福州百益百利自动化科技有限公司（以下简称百益百利公司）与被上诉人上海点挂建筑技术有限公司（以下简称点挂公司）、张某彬侵害实用新型专利权纠纷案中，涉及专利号为 201320534267.X、名称为“结固式锚栓”的实用新型专利（以下简称涉案专利）。百益百利公司认为，点挂公司、张某彬于 2017 年开始积极推广第三代点挂安装技术，其中“点挂专用抗拉拔保护锚栓”落入涉案专利权的保护范围，构成侵权，故向上海知识产权法院（以下简称一审法院）提起诉讼，请求判令停止侵害、赔偿损失 250 万元。一审法院认为，点挂公司、张某彬主张的抵触申请抗辩成立，故判决驳回百益百利公司的诉讼请求。百益百利公司不服，向最高人民法院提起上诉，主张被诉侵权产品技术方案与抵触申请公开的内容不同。最高人民法院于 2022 年 5 月 23 日判决撤销原判，点挂公司、张某彬停止侵害，赔偿损失 250

万元。

In the appeal case between the Appellant, Fuzhou Baiyi Baili Automation Technology Co., Ltd. (hereinafter referred to as "Baiyi Baili"), and the Appellees, Shanghai Diangua Construction Technology Co., Ltd. (hereinafter referred to as "Diangua") and Zhang, regarding a dispute over infringement of utility model patent, a utility model patent titled "A Mechanical Expansion Anchor Bolt" (hereinafter referred to as the "Patent"), with patent No. 201320534267. X, was involved. Baiyi Baili argued that Diangua and Zhang had actively promoted the third-generation point-hanging installation technology since 2017, and the "Special anti-pullout protection anchor bolt for point-hanging" fell within the protection scope of the Patent, constituting infringement. Therefore, it filed a lawsuit with Shanghai Intellectual Property Court (hereinafter referred to as the "Court of First Instance"), requesting an injunction to cease the infringement and compensate for its losses totaling CNY 2. 5 miliion. The Court of First Instance held that the conflicting application defense raised by Diangua and Zhang was established, and therefore dismissed Baiyi Baili's Claims. Then, Baiyi Baili appealed to the SPC, claiming that the technical solution of the Accused Infringing Product was different from the content disclosed in the conflicting application. On May 23, 2022, the SPC ruled to revoke the original judgment and ordered Diangua and Zhang to cease the infringement and compensate for the losses totaling CNY 2. 5 million.

【裁判意见】

[Judge's Opinion]

最高人民法院二审认为，点挂公司、张某彬主张的抵触申请抗辩不成立。被诉侵权产品是点挂公司和张某彬积极推广的第三代点挂安装技术产品配件，点挂公司和张某彬在2017年宣称其累计施工面积已达200万平方米以上，且其通过宣传册和官方网站对相关工程案例进行了宣传展示，点挂公司副总经理在2019年2月24日仍通过微信朋友圈对第三代点挂施工工程进行宣传展示。点挂公司和张某彬对上述事实虽持有异议，认为200万平方米为夸大宣传，相关工程案例为借鉴合作方的案例，且相关工程并未使用被诉侵权产品。但是，点挂公司和张某彬并未提交有效反证证明其实际施工量，其主张夸大宣传依据不足；点挂公司和张某彬亦不提交其实际使用的锚栓配件，其主张未使用被诉侵权产品与事实不符，不能成立。在以上事实基础上，参考百益百利公司主张的每平方米所需被诉侵权产品平均用量约为5根、专利产品销售单价为3.57元、3.27元不等以及合理利润率认定赔偿数额，点挂公司和张某彬侵权获利应不低于250万元。综合考虑点挂公司和张某彬经营规模，因其侵权时间长、侵权范围广、侵权恶意明显，以及百益百利公司为本案支出的律师费、公证费等合理维权费用等因素，依法对百益百利公司主张的250万元赔偿数额予以全额支持。

The SPC, in the Second Instance trial, held that the conflicting application defense raised by Diangua and Zhang was not established. The Accused Infringing Products were accessories of the third-generation point-hanging installation technology actively promoted by Diangua and Zhang. In 2017, Diangua and Zhang claimed that their cumulative construction area had exceeded 2,000,000 m^2 and showcased relevant engineering cases through brochures and official websites. The Deputy General Manager of Diangua continued to promote and showcase third-generation point-hanging construction projects through WeChat Moments on February 24, 2019. Although Diangua and Zhang disputed the above facts, claiming that 2,000,000 m^2 was exaggerated and the engineering cases were borrowed from cooperative partners, and that the Accused Infringing Products were not used in the relevant projects, they failed to provide valid evidence to prove their actual construction volume. Their claim of exaggerating the construction area lacked sufficient basis. Dian-

gua and Zhang also did not submit the anchor bolt accessories they actually used, and their claim of not using the Accused Infringing Products was inconsistent with the facts and therefore not established. Based on the above facts and referring to Baiyi Baili's claim that the average usage of the Accused Infringing Products per square meter was approximately 5 pieces, with a sales price ranging from CNY 3. 57 to CNY 3. 27 per piece, as well as the reasonable profit margin, Diangua and Zhang's profits from infringement should be no less than CNY 2. 5 million. Considering the business scale of Diangua and Zhang, their long duration of infringement, wide scope of infringement, obvious malicious intent, as well as the reasonable legal fees and notarization expenses incurred by Baiyi Baili for safeguarding its rights, the Court fully supported the CNY 2. 5 million compensation claimed by Baiyi Baili.

30. 侵权和解后再次销售相同侵权产品的惩罚性赔偿责任

Punitive damages in case of re-selling identical infringing product after reaching settlement with patentee

【裁判要旨】

[Judgment Digest]

侵权人与专利权利人就有关销售侵权产品行为的纠纷达成和解后，再次销售相同侵权产品的，可以认定其构成故意侵权且情节严重；专利权利人请求适用惩罚性赔偿，并主张参照在先和解协议约定的赔偿数额作为计算基础的，人民法院可以依法予以支持。

If the infringer sells products identical to previously-infringing products once again after reaching a settlement agreement with the patentee on sale of such previously-infringing products, then the infringer can be deemed to have committed intentional infringement with serious circumstances, in which scenario if the patentee claims for punitive damages and also taking the amount of damages as agreed upon in the aforementioned agreement as calculation basis, such claim can be supported by people's courts.

【关键词】

[Keywords]

专利　侵权和解　重复侵权　惩罚性赔偿　赔偿数额计算

Patent; infringement settlement; repeated infringement; punitive damages; calculation of damages

【案号】

[Case Number]

（2022）最高法知民终 871 号

（2022）SPC IP Civil Final 871

【基本案情】

[Case Facts]

在上诉人金某海与被上诉人郑东新区白沙镇百佳五金机电劳保建材经营部（以下简称百佳经营部）、原审被告郑州佰发商贸有限公司（以下简称佰发公司）侵害发明专利权纠纷案中，涉及专利号为01125315.0、名称为“反向地面刨毛机”的发明专利（以下简称涉案专利）。金某海认为，百佳经营部在双方和解后再次销售同种被诉侵权产品，构成重复侵权，故向河南省郑州市中级人民法院提起诉讼，请求适用惩罚性赔偿判令百佳经营部等赔偿金某海经济损失及合理费用共计25 万元。一审法院认为，虽然百佳经营部存在侵权的故意，但未达到情节严重程度，不符合适用惩罚性赔偿的条件，故适用法定赔偿确定百佳经营部赔偿金某海经济损失及维权合理开支共计 1 万元。金某海不

服，向最高人民法院提起上诉，请求改判百佳经营部赔偿经济损失及维权合理开支共计10万元或发回重审。最高人民法院于2022年10月10日判决撤销原判，改判百佳经营部承担惩罚性赔偿责任，赔偿金某海经济损失及维权合理开支共计6万元。

In the appeal case between the Appellant, Jin, and the Appellees, Baisha Town Baijia Hardware, Electromechanical Equipment, PPE & Building Materials Store in Zhengdong New District (hereinafter referred to as "Baijia Store") and Zhengzhou Baifa Trading Co., Ltd. (hereinafter referred to as "Baifa", the defendant in the First Instance), regarding a dispute over infringement of invention patent, an invention patent titled "A Reverse Ground Shaver" (hereinafter referred to as the "Patent"), with patent No. 01125315.0, was involved. Jin argued that after reaching a settlement agreement, Baijia Store's act of continuing to sell the same infringing products constituted a repeated infringement. Therefore, he filed a lawsuit with Zhengzhou Intermediate People's Court of Henan Province, requesting the application of punitive damages and demanding Baijia Store compensate for his economic losses and reasonable expenses totaling CNY 250,000. The Court of First Instance held that although Baijia Store had the intent to infringe, the severity of the circumstance did not meet the conditions for punitive damages. Therefore, the Court determined a statutory compensation for Baijia Store's economic losses and reasonable expenses totaling CNY 10,000. Dissatisfied with the judgment, Jin appealed to the SPC, requesting a revised judgment to award compensation of CNY 100,000 for his economic losses and reasonable expenses or a retrial. On October 10, 2022, the SPC ruled to revoke the original judgment and impose punitive damages on Baijia Store, ordering it to compensate for Jin's economic losses and reasonable expenses totaling CNY 60,000.

【裁判意见】

［Judge's Opinion］

最高人民法院二审认为，在本案之前，金某海曾因百佳经营部销售被诉侵权产品向一审法院提起专利侵权诉讼，后双方达成《和解协议》，百佳经营部承诺停止侵权并赔偿经济损失及合理费用共计3万元。百佳经营部在经历前案诉讼后，已明知金某海系涉案专利权人，也明知其销售被诉侵权产品侵害涉案专利权，但在前案中作出停止侵权承诺并支付赔偿款后，仍然再次销售被诉侵权产品，具有侵权的故意，构成重复侵权，属于《最高人民法院关于审理侵害知识产权民事案件适用惩罚性赔偿的解释》第四条规定的“其他可以认定为情节严重的情形”。百佳经营部主观上存在侵权故意且侵权情节严重，应承担惩罚性赔偿责任。关于赔偿数额，本案中，虽然各方当事人均未举证证明权利人因被侵权的实际损失、侵权人侵权获利或可供参考的专利许可使用费等，但是考虑到本案百佳经营部在前案达成和解协议后不到两个月内即发生再次侵权行为，侵权持续时间较短，侵权获利有限，以及涉案专利于2021年8月10日到期，本案为批量维权性质等因素，酌情以前案《和解协议》约定赔偿数额为计算基数，确定由百佳经营部承担惩罚性赔偿责任，赔偿金某海经济损失及为制止侵权行为所支付的合理开支共计6万元。

The SPC held in the Second Instance trial that before this case, Jin had filed a patent infringement lawsuit against Baijia Store for selling the Accused Infringing Products, and the two parties reached a Settlement Agreement where Baijia Store promised to cease the infringement and compensate for Jin's economic losses and reasonable expenses totaling CNY 30, 000. After the previous lawsuit, Baijia Store was aware that Jin was the patentee of the Patent and that selling the Accused Infringing Products would infringe on the Patent. Despite making a promise to cease infringement and paying compensation in

the previous case, Baijia Store still sold the Accused Infringing Products, demonstrating intentional infringement and constituting repeated infringement, which falls under the "Other circumstances that can be deemed as serious" in Article 4 of *Interpretation of the Supreme People's Court on the Application of Punitive Damages in Civil Cases of Intellectual Property Infringement*. As Baijia Store had the subjective intent to infringe and the circumstance was serious, it should bear the liability for punitive damages. Regarding the amount of damages, although none of the parties provided evidence to prove the actual losses suffered by the patentee, the profits gained by the infringer from the infringement, or a reasonable royalty for reference, the Court considered that Baijia Store had committed the infringement again within two months of reaching a settlement agreement in the previous case, the duration of infringement was short, the profits gained from infringement were limited, and the Patent expired on August 10, 2021. Additionally, this case related to mass litigation. Therefore, the Court used the compensation amount agreed upon in the previous Settlement Agreement as the basis for calculating punitive damages. Baijia Store was ordered to pay a total of CNY 60,000 in compensation for Jin's economic losses and reasonable expenses incurred to cease the infringement.

31. 专利权人在专利无效程序中的支出一般不属于专利侵权案件中的维权合理开支

The patentee's expenses incurred by patent invalidation proceedings shall generally not be deemed as reasonable expenses for remedies in patent infringement cases

【裁判要旨】

[Judgment Digest]

侵害专利权纠纷案件中，专利权人请求将涉案专利权无效宣告程序中产生的费用列为维权合理开支的，一般不予支持。

If in a patent-infringement civil case, the patentee claims for the expenses incurred in the proceedings on invalidation of the involved patent in the name of reasonable expenses for remedies, then such claim shall generally not be supported by people's court.

【关键词】

[Keywords]

专利　侵权　无效宣告费用　维权合理开支

Patent; infringement; expenses for invalidation procedures; reasonable expenses for remedies

【案号】

[Case Number]

(2022) 最高法知民终 1165 号

(2022) SPC IP Civil Final 1165

【基本案情】

[Case Facts]

在上诉人辽宁金立电力电器有限公司（以下简称金立公司）与被上诉人丹阳市金诺电器有限公司（以下简称金诺公司）、原审被告南通市神舟兴华电气有限公司（以下简称神舟公司）侵害发明专利权纠纷案中，涉及专利权人为金诺公司、专利号为201611245881.9、名称为“一种用于三角立体卷铁心变压器的条形分接开关”的发明专利（以下简称涉案专利）。金诺公司主张由金立公司制造并销售、神舟公司销售的涉案产品侵害其专利权，故向江苏省苏州市中级人民法院提起诉讼，请求判令金立公司停止侵害，并赔偿金诺公司经济损失75万元、维权合理开支共计11万元；请求判令神舟公司停止侵害并就上述赔偿承担连带责任。一审法院认为，被诉侵权产品落入了涉案专利权保护范围，构成侵权，判令金立公司停止生产、销售被诉侵权产品并赔偿金诺公司经济损失40万元，维权合理开支11万元（包括金诺公司专利无效程序中为维护专利有效而支出的10万元与本案中的1万元维权合理开支）；判令神州公司停止使用被诉侵权产品。金立公司不服，向最高人民法院提起上诉，主张被诉侵权产品并未落入涉案专利权保护范围，一审认定赔偿数额过高。最高人民法院于2022年12月5日判决维持一审关于金立公司停止侵害、赔偿40万元经济损失的判项，改判金立公司向金诺公司支付维权合理开支2万元。

In the appeal case between the Appellant, Liaoning Jinli Electric Power Electrical Appliance Co., Ltd. (hereinafter referred to as "Jinli"), and the Appellees, Danyang Jinnuo Electric Appliance Co., Ltd. (hereinafter referred to as "Jinnuo") and Nantong Shenzhou Xinghua Electric Co., Ltd. (hereinafter referred to as "Shenzhou", the defendant in the First Instance), regarding a dispute over infringement of invention patent, an invention patent titled "A Strip Tap Changer for Triangular 3D Winding Core Transformer" (hereinafter referred to as the "Patent"), with the patentee, Jinnuo, and patent No. 201611245881.9, was involved. Jinnuo claimed that the accused infringing products manufactured and sold by Jinli, as well as the products sold by Shenzhou, infringe upon its patent right. Therefore, it filed a lawsuit with Suzhou Intermediate People's Court of Jiangsu Province, requesting an order for Jinli to cease the infringement and compensate for its economic losses totaling CNY 750,000 and reasonable expenses for remedies totaling CNY 110,000; and requesting an order for Shenzhou to cease the infringement and to bear joint liability for the aforementioned compensation. The Court of First Instance held that the accused infringing products fell within the protection scope of the Patent, constituting infringement. Therefore, it ordered Jinli to cease the production and sales of the accused infringing products, and compensate for Jinnuo's economic losses totaling CNY 400,000 and reasonable expenses for remedies totaling CNY 110,000 (including CNY 100,000 spent by Jinnuo to maintain the validity of the Patent in the invalidation procedure and CNY 10,000 for the present case); and ordered Shenzhou to cease the use of the accused infringing products. Dissatisfied with the ruling, Jinli appealed to the SPC, arguing that the accused infringing products did not fall within the protection scope of the Patent and that the compensation amount awarded in the First Instance was too high. On December 5, 2022, the SPC upheld the First Instance judgment that Jinli should cease the infringement and compensate for Jinnuo's economic losses totaling CNY 400,000, but revised the amount of reasonable expenses to be paid by Jinli to Jinnuo to CNY 20,000.

【裁判意见】

[Judge's Opinion]

最高人民法院二审认为，一审判决对于专利权人在诉讼程序的合理维权开支认定有误。首先，基于现行专利授权、确权审查制度的有限

性，一项专利权在授权时未必能被发现全部不符合专利法规定的情形，因此专利法第四十五条规定："自国务院专利行政部门公告授予专利权之日起，任何单位或者个人认为该专利权的授予不符合本法有关规定的，可以请求专利复审委员会宣告该专利权无效。"其次，专利权人依法享有自己实施、许可或禁止他人实施其专利的权利，并因该权利获得或者可以预期获得相应的经济利益。为维护该经济利益，专利法规定了其应当缴纳专利年费，这是维持其专利权存续的必要支出，对于专利权人因他人对其专利权提起无效而支出的包括代理费在内的必要费用，亦属于维持专利权存续的必要支出。再次，任何单位或者个人均有权宣告专利权无效，专利权人并不能据此要求提起无效宣告的单位或者个人支付专利权人为维护专利权有效而支出的必要费用，而在专利侵权程序中的被控侵权方亦是前述规定的任何单位或个人其中的一员，并无区别。最后，专利法第六十五条第一款规定："……赔偿数额还应当包括权利人为制止侵权行为所支付的合理开支。"据此可知，合理开支的产生系因制止违法侵权行为而产生的费用。专利无效宣告请求系请求人的正当权利行使，不属于导致专利权人产生维权费用的非法行为，提起无效宣告是被控侵权方对抗专利权人提起的侵害专利权诉讼的合法手段。因此，不能因为被诉侵权人提起专利无效而要求其在民事诉讼程序中支付专利权人在无效程序中支出的相关费用。同时，侵害专利权纠纷诉讼程序和专利权无效宣告程序为两个不同的程序，虽然具有一定相关性，但不宜将专利权无效宣告程序中当事人支出的费用在侵害专利权纠纷诉讼程序中作为合理开支一并予以支持。

The SPC held in the Second Instance trial that the First Instance judgment made an error in determining the patentee's reasonable expenses for remedies. Firstly, due to the limitations of the current patent grant and examination system, it is not always possible to discover all circumstances that do not comply with the provisions of the Patent Law during the grant process. Therefore, Article 45 of the Patent Law stipulates that "Where, starting from the date of the announcement of the grant of the patent right by the Patent Administration Department under the State Council, any entity or individual considers that the grant of the said patent right is not in conformity with the relevant provisions of this Law, it or he may request the Patent Administration Department under the State Council to declare the patent right invalid." Secondly, the patentees are entitled to exploit, license, or prohibit others from exploiting their patents, and they obtain or can expect to obtain corresponding economic benefits from these rights. To protect these economic interests, the Patent Law stipulates that the patentee must pay annual fees, which are necessary expenses for maintaining the validity of the patent right. The necessary expenses incurred by the patentee, including agency fees, for defending against invalidation requests by others are also considered necessary expenses for maintaining the validity of the patent right. Thirdly, any entity or individual has the right to declare a patent invalid. The patentee cannot demand that the party filing the invalidation request pay the necessary expenses incurred by the patentee to maintain the validity of the patent right. Similarly, in a patent infringement proceeding, the accused infringing party is also one of the entities or individuals mentioned above, without any distinction. Finally, Paragraph 1, Article 65 of the Patent Law states that: "... the amount of compensation shall also include the reasonable expenses paid by the right holder to cease the infringement." From this, it can be inferred that the reasonable expenses are the costs incurred to cease illegal infringement. The request for invalidation of a patent is the exercise of any individuals or entities' legitimate rights and does not constitute an illegal act that causes the patentee to incur litigation expenses. Filing an invalidation request is a legal means for the accused infringing party to counter the patentee's infringement lawsuit. Therefore, it is not appropriate to

require the accused infringing party to pay the related expenses incurred by the patentee in the invalidation process in a civil litigation procedure. At the same time, the procedures for resolving patent infringement disputes and patent invalidation are two separate procedures. Although they have certain relevance, it is not appropriate to consider the expenses incurred by the parties in the patent invalidation procedure as reasonable litigation expenses in the patent infringement dispute proceedings.

综上所述，专利权人在侵害专利权纠纷诉讼程序中支出的维权合理开支，一般应为该侵害专利权纠纷诉讼程序中专利权人为制止被诉侵权人的违法行为直接产生的相关费用。对于相关专利权无效宣告程序中产生的费用，无论无效宣告请求人是否为被诉侵权人，一般均不属于专利权人的维权合理开支的范围。

In summary, the reasonable expenses for remedies incurred by the patentee in a patent infringement dispute litigation should generally refer to the relevant costs directly generated by the patentee to cease the accused infringing party's illegal acts in that specific litigation. As for the expenses incurred in the related patent invalidation procedure, regardless of whether the requester of the invalidation is the accused infringing party or not, they generally do not fall within the scope of the patentee's reasonable expenses for remedies.

32. 合法来源抗辩成立仍可判令使用者负担维权合理开支

Even if a legitimate source defense is supported, people's courts can still order the accused user to bear the reasonable expenses for remedies

【裁判要旨】

[Judgment Digest]

专利权利人主张合法来源抗辩成立的侵权产品使用者负担维权合理开支的，人民法院可以视情予以支持。该合法来源抗辩成立的侵权使用者与其他侵权行为实施者同为被告时，维权合理开支的分担可以综合考虑其各自侵害行为所造成的损害、与专利权利人维权行为的因果关系或者关联程度、对专利权利人维权行为的顺利开展是否造成阻碍、是否导致维权费用增加等因素来确定。

If the patentee claims that the accused user of the infringing products, whose legitimate source defense is supported, should be liable for reasonable expenses for remedies, such claim can be supported by people's courts as it sees fit. When both the aforementioned infringing user and other infringers are co-defendants, which may result in allocating reasonable expenses for remedies among them, considerations should be given to such factors as damages caused by their respective acts of infringement, the causal relationship or the degree of association with the patentee's remedies, whether such acts impede the patentee's remedies, and whether such acts result in an increase in expenses for remedies.

【关键词】

[Keywords]

专利　侵权　使用者　合法来源抗辩　合理开支

Patent; infringement; user; legitimate source defense; reasonable expenses

【案号】

[Case Number]

（2021）最高法知民终1406号

（2021）SPC IP Civil Final 1406

【基本案情】

[Case Facts]

在上诉人莒县正大塑料机械修配厂（以下简称正大修配厂）、日照洁之源塑料制品有限公司（以下简称洁之源公司）与被上诉人瑞安市欧力机械有限公司（以下简称欧力公司）侵害发明专利权纠纷案中，涉及专利号为201410186797.9、名称为“节能高效型塑料造粒机”的发明专利（以下简称涉案专利）。欧力公司认为，正大修配厂所制造塑料造粒机（以下简称被诉侵权产品）的技术方案落入了涉案专利权利要求1的保护范围。正大修配厂提供该塑料造粒机给洁之源公司无偿使用，洁之源公司明知是侵权产品仍加以使用，二者均构成侵权且造成欧力公司的经济损失，故向山东省青岛市中级人民法院（以下简称一审法院）提起诉讼，请求判令正大修配厂停止制造、销售行为，洁之源公司停止使用行为，正大修配厂赔偿经济损失70万元，洁之源公司赔偿经济损失20万元，正大修配厂、洁之源公司共同承担欧力公司的维权合理开支5万元。一审法院认为，被诉侵权行为成立，且洁之源公司的合法来源抗辩不能成立，判决正大修配厂、洁之源公司停止侵害，正大修配厂赔偿经济损失及维权合理开支共计30万元，洁之源公司赔偿经济损失及维权合理开支共计3万元。正大修配厂、洁之源公司不服，向最高人民法院提起上诉，主张被诉侵权产品使用的是现有技术，且洁之源公司使用的被诉侵权产品系从正大修配厂购得，本案所维权合理开支亦应由制造者洁之源公司承担。最高人民法院于2022年6月6日改判正大修配厂赔偿欧力经济损失25万元，正大修配厂向欧力公司支付维权合理开支5万元，洁之源公司对其中的5000元承担连带清偿责任。

In the appeal case between the Appellants, Juxian Zhengda Plastic Machinery Repair Factory (hereinafter referred to as "Zhengda Repair Factory") and Rizhao Jiezhiyuan Plastic Products Co., Ltd. (hereinafter referred to as "Jiezhiyuan"), and the Appellee, Rui'an Ouli Machinery Co., Ltd. (hereinafter referred to as "Ouli"), regarding a dispute over infringement of invention patent, an invention patent titled "Energy-saving and Efficient Plastic Granulator" (hereinafter referred to as the "Patent"), with patent No. 201410186797.9, was involved. Ouli claimed that the technical solution used in the plastic granulator manufactured by Zhengda Repair Factory (hereinafter referred to as the "Accused Infringing Product") fell within the protection scope of Claim 1 of the Patent. Zhengda Repair Factory provided the Accused Infringing Product to Jiezhiyuan for free use, and despite knowing that it was an infringing product, Jiezhiyuan continued to use it, both of which constituted infringement and caused economic losses to Ouli. Therefore, Ouli filed a lawsuit with Qingdao Intermediate People's Court of Shandong Province (hereinafter referred to as the "Court of First Instance"), requesting that Zhengda Repair Factory cease the manufacturing and selling activities and compensate for its economic losses totaling CNY 700,000; that Jiezhiyuan cease using the product and compensate for its economic losses totaling CNY 200,000; and that Zhengda Repair Factory and Jiezhiyuan jointly bear Ouli's reasonable expenses for remedies totaling CNY 50,000. The Court of First Instance held that the alleged infringement was established while Jiezhiyuan's legitimate

source defense could not be established. It ruled that Zhengda Repair Factory and Jiezhiyuan shall cease the infringement, Zhengda Repair Factory shall compensate for Ouli's economic losses and reasonable expenses for remedies totaling CNY 300, 000, while Jiezhiyuan shall compensate for Ouli's economic losses and reasonable expenses for remedies totaling CNY 30, 000. Dissatisfied with the judgement, Zhengda Repair Factory and Jiezhiyuan appealed to the SPC, arguing that the Accused Infringing Product used prior art, Jiezhiyuan had obtained the product from Zhengda Repair Factory, and the reasonable expenses for remedies in this case should be borne by the manufacturer, Zhengda Repair Factory. On June 6, 2022, the SPC revised the original judgment and ordered that Zhengda Repair Factory should compensate for Ouli's economic losses totaling CNY 250, 000 and reasonable expenses for remedies totaling CNY 50, 000, while Jiezhiyuan should be jointly liable for CNY 5, 000 therein.

【裁判意见】

[Judge's Opinion]

最高人民法院二审认为，洁之源公司的合法来源抗辩成立。关于欧力公司所主张合理维权费用是否应由洁之源公司承担的问题。专利法第十一条第一款规定“使用”属于一种专利侵权行为；第六十五条第一款规定“侵犯专利权的赔偿数额……还应当包括权利人为制止侵权行为所支付的合理开支。”为了从源头上遏制侵权现象，积极引导专利权人从侵权产品的制造环节制止侵权行为，同时考虑到合法来源抗辩成立的侵权产品使用者主观上不具有侵权故意，现行立法及司法解释作出了免除其赔偿责任的制度设计，但合法来源抗辩作为一项免赔事由，并不能当然产生无须停止侵权、无须承担合理开支的法律效果。本案中，洁之源公司在其生产经营活动中使用了正大修配厂制造、销售的被诉侵权产品，该使用行为构成对涉案专利权的侵害。虽然洁之源公司的合法来源抗辩成立，但其使用行为的侵权属性并未得以改变，其仍需承担欧力公司为本案支出的合理维权费用。

The SPC, in the Second Instance trial, held that Jiezhiyuan's legitimate source defense was established. Regarding the issue of whether Jiezhiyuan should bear the reasonable expenses for remedies as claimed by Ouli, Paragraph 1, Article 11 of the Patent Law stipulates that "Use" constitutes a form of patent infringement, and Paragraph 1, Article 65 states that "the amount of compensation for patent infringement... shall also include the reasonable expenses incurred by the right holder to cease the infringement." In order to curb infringement at its source and actively guide patentees to prevent infringement from the manufacturing stage, the current legislation and judicial interpretations have provided a system that exempts the user of an infringing product, where his legitimate source defense is established and he has no subjective intent, from bearing compensation liability. However, the legitimate source defense, as a ground for exemption from compensation liability, does not automatically result in the legal effect of no need to cease the infringement or no need to bear reasonable expenses. In this case, Jiezhiyuan used the Accused Infringing Product manufactured and sold by Zhengda Repair Factory in its production and operation activities, which constituted infringement upon the Patent. Although Jiezhiyuan's legitimate source defense was established, the infringing nature of its behavior remained unchanged, and it still needed to bear the reasonable expenses incurred by Ouli for remedies in this case.

同时，专利侵权民事案件中的损失赔偿与专利权人的维权支出在法律性质上也有所差异。损失赔偿针对的是侵权行为给专利权人在研发成本、市场份额、交易机会等方面造成的损失，可根据专利权人的实际损失大小或侵权人的获利情况进行计算，需要考虑到被诉侵权产品的售价、数量、利润率、专利贡献度等因素。而合理开支包括律师费、公证

费、差旅费等在维权活动中据实支出的费用，属于专利权人为了获得侵权救济所支出的金钱成本，因此应由侵害行为的实施者承担。在同时存在制造者、使用者等多个侵害行为实施者的情况下，为获得侵权救济所支出的合理费用针对的是上述全部侵害行为，故各个侵害行为实施者均负有承担专利权人合理维权费用的义务。至于每个侵害行为实施者所应承担的具体数额，需根据其各自的侵害行为、与专利权人维权行为的因果关系或关联程度、对专利权人维权行为的顺利开展是否造成阻碍、是否导致维权费用增加等因素来确定。

Furthermore, in civil patent infringement cases, there are differences in the legal nature of compensation for damages and expenses incurred by the patentee for remedies. Compensation for damages aims at the losses suffered by the patentee in terms of research and development costs, market share, business opportunities, etc., as a result of the infringement. It can be calculated based on the actual losses suffered by the patentee or the profits obtained by the infringer. Factors such as the selling price, quantity, and profit margin of the Accused Infringing Product, as well as its contribution to the Patent, should be taken into account. On the other hand, reasonable expenses include the actual expenses incurred in rights protection activities, such as attorney fees, notary fees, travel expenses, etc. These expenses are the monetary costs incurred by the patentee in order to obtain infringement remedies. Therefore, they should be borne by the infringer. In cases where there are multiple infringers, such as manufacturers and users, the reasonable expenses incurred for obtaining infringement remedies are directed towards all the infringing acts mentioned above, and each infringer has an obligation to pay the reasonable expenses for remedies to the patentee. As for the specific amount that each infringer should bear, it should be determined based on factors such as their respective infringing acts, the causal relationship or degree of association with the patentee's rights protection activities, whether they hinder the smooth progress of the rights protection activities, and whether they result in increased rights protection expenses, etc.

结合该案具体情况，欧力公司在本案中要求由正大修配厂、洁之源公司承担的合理维权费用既是针对正大修配厂制造、销售被诉侵权产品行为，也是针对洁之源公司的使用侵权行为而支出，因此应由二者共同承担。

Considering the specific circumstances of this case, Ouli is requesting its reasonable expenses for safeguarding rights to be borne by both Zhengda Repair Factory (the manufacturer) and Jiezhiyuan (the user), because these expenses were incurred due to both the manufacturing and sales of the Accused Infringing Product by Zhengda Repair Factory and the use of the Accused Infringing Product by Jiezhiyuan. Therefore, it is appropriate for both parties to share the responsibility for these expenses.

33. 专利无效后对调解书已履行部分显失公平的认定 Identification of obvious unfairness of the fulfilled part of the mediation agreement after patent invalidation

【裁判要旨】

[Judgment Digest]

宣告专利权无效前已经支付的专利许可使用费与许可使用费总额之比，明显高于专利权被宣告无效前的许可期间与整个许可期限之比，当事人以不予返还明显违反公平原则为由请求返还的，人民法院可予支持。

Where the ratio of the license fee paid before the declaration of the patent

invalidation to the total amount of the license fee is obviously higher than the ratio of the license term before the declaration of the patent invalidation to the entire license term, if an involved party claims for return of the paid license fee on the ground that if not returned, it is obviously against the principle of fairness, then such claim can be supported by people's courts.

【关键词】

[Keywords]

专利权宣告无效　溯及力　专利权人的恶意　明显违反公平原则　返还许可使用费

Declaration of patent invalidation; retroactive effect; bad faith of the patentee; obviously contrary to the principle of fairness; refund of license fee

【案号】

[Case Number]

(2021) 最高法知民终 1986 号

(2021) SPC IP Civil Final 1986

【基本案情】

[Case Facts]

在上诉人尚某中与被上诉人柳州市柳南区浩千塑料制品厂（以下简称浩千厂）专利权宣告无效后返还费用纠纷案中，尚某中系名称为“纸碗或纸杯的筒纸片排版方法”、专利号为 200810233502. 3 的发明专利（以下简称涉案专利）专利权人。2018 年 10 月 31 日，尚某中以浩千厂侵害涉案专利权为由向广西壮族自治区柳州市中级人民法院提起诉讼。2018 年 11 月 16 日，根据双方自愿达成的协议，法院制作了民事调解书：(1) 浩千厂支付尚某中涉案专利许可使用费 22 万元（于 2018 年 11 月 16 日支付 12 万元，于 2019 年 8 月 10 日前支付 10 万元）；(2) 尚某中许可浩千厂在 2018 年 11 月 16 日至 2020 年 12 月 31 日期间，使用涉案专利生产同类型的产品。同日，浩千厂依据前述约定，向尚某中支付了许可使用费12万元。浩千厂未履行其余约定。2018年10月30日,案外人请求国家知识产权局宣告涉案专利权无效。国家知识产权局于2019年4月3日作出第39740号无效宣告审查决定(以下简称涉案无效决定),宣告涉案专利权全部无效。该决定经过司法程序已经发生法律效力。浩千厂遂诉至广西壮族自治区柳州市中级人民法院(以下简称一审法院),主张涉案专利权无效宣告的决定应对涉案调解书具有追溯力,尚某中应返还费用12万元及其利息。一审法院认为,涉案无效决定的决定日为2019年4月3日,涉案调解书记载的履行完毕日为2019年8月10日,且在该日前浩千厂亦未按约定支付余下费用,属于在宣告涉案专利权无效前人民法院作出的专利侵权调解书并未履行完毕的情形。基于此,涉案专利权无效宣告的决定应对涉案调解书具有追溯力,判令尚某中因涉案调解书的履行而获得的专利许可使用费12万元,应予如数返还给浩千厂。尚某中不服,向最高人民法院提起上诉。最高人民法院于2022年6月9日判决撤销原判,驳回浩千厂诉讼请求。

In the appeal case between the Appellant, Shang, and the Appellee, Liuzhou Liunan District Haoqian Plastic Products Factory (hereinafter referred to as "Haoqian Factory"), regarding a dispute over refund of license fee after a patent was declared invalid, an invention patent titled "Arrangement Method of Tubular Paper Pieces for Paper Bowls or Paper Cups" (hereinafter referred to as the "Patent"), with the patentee, Shang, and patent No. 200810233502.3, was involved. On October 31, 2018, Shang filed a lawsuit with Liuzhou Intermediate People's Court of Guangxi Zhuang Autonomous Region on the ground that Haoqian Factory had infringed upon the Patent. On November 16, 2018, a civil mediation agreement was reached voluntarily between the parties, and the Court produced a civil mediation document: (1) Haoqian Factory shall pay Shang a license fee of CNY 220,000 for the Patent (CNY 12,000 to be paid on November 16, 2018, and the remaining CNY 100,000 to be paid be-

fore August 10, 2019); (2) Shang shall grant Haoqian Factory a license to produce products of the same type using the Patent from November 16, 2018 to December 31, 2020. On the same day, Haoqian Factory paid Shang a license fee of CNY 120,000 in accordance with the aforementioned agreement. However, it failed to fulfill the remaining obligations. On October 30, 2018, a third party requested the China National Intellectual Property Administration (CNIPA) to declare the Patent invalid. On April 3, 2019, the CNIPA issued Decision No. 39740 on the invalidation examination (hereinafter referred to as the "Invalidation Decision"), declaring the Patent completely invalid. This decision became legally effective after going through the judicial process. Subsequently, Haoqian Factory filed a lawsuit with Liuzhou Intermediate People's Court of Guangxi Zhuang Autonomous Region (hereinafter referred to as the "Court of First Instance"), claiming that the decision on the invalidation of the Patent should have retroactive effect on the civil mediation document in question, and Shang should return the CNY 120,000 license fee and interest. The Court of First Instance held that the Invalidation Decision was made on April 3, 2019, while the deadline for the performance as stated in the civil mediation document was August 10, 2019. However, Haoqian Factory did not pay the remaining fees as agreed before that date. Therefore, it fell under the situation where the patent infringement mediation document issued by the people's court was not fully performed before the Patent was declared invalid. Based on this, the Invalidation Decision should have retroactive effect on the civil mediation document in question. It ruled that Shang should return to Haoqian Factory the CNY 120,000 license fee in full as obtained from the performance of the civil mediation document. Dissatisfied with the ruling, Shang appealed to the SPC. On June 9, 2022, the SPC decided to revoke the original judgment and dismiss the claims of Haoqian Factory.

【裁判意见】

[Judge's Opinion]

最高人民法院二审认为，专利法第四十七条第二款规定，宣告专利权无效的决定，对在宣告专利权无效前人民法院作出并已执行的专利侵权的判决、调解书，已经履行或者强制执行的专利侵权纠纷处理决定，以及已经履行的专利实施许可合同和专利权转让合同，不具有追溯力。基于专利的特殊性和维护社会经济秩序的需要，该款中“已执行”“已经履行或者强制执行”的法律文书或者合同的执行或者履行内容具有可分性或者阶段性时，不仅包括已经全部执行或者履行的法律文书或者合同，还包括已经部分执行或者履行的法律文书或者合同部分。因此，宣告专利权无效的决定对已经部分履行或执行的判决、调解书以及合同部分，同样不具有追溯力。涉案调解书是对尚某中与浩千厂在侵害发明专利权纠纷案中双方自愿达成的以专利许可使用为形式的和解协议的确认，该协议约定了分期履行义务，其中第一期款项于2018年10月31日已经履行完毕，该部分的履行时间在涉案无效决定的决定日前，该无效决定对已经履行的部分没有追溯力。

The SPC held in the Second Instance trial that according to Paragraph 2, Article 47 of the Patent Law, the decision declaring the patent right invalid shall have no retroactive effect on any judgment or mediation decision of patent infringement which has been pronounced and enforced by the people's court, on any decision concerning the settlement of a dispute over patent infringement which has been complied with or compulsorily executed, or on any contract of patent license or of assignment of patent right which has been performed prior to the declaration of the patent right as invalid. Given the special nature of patents and the need to maintain social and economic order, when the legal documents that have been “enforced” or “complied with or compulsorily executed”, or the performance of the contract in this provision is separable or in

phases, it should include not only legal documents or contracts that have been fully enforced or executed, but also those that have been partially enforced or executed. Therefore, the decision declaring the patent right invalid does not have retroactive effect on judgments, mediation decisions, nor contract parts that have been partially executed or enforced. The mediation agreement in question was a confirmation of the settlement agreement reached voluntarily between Shang and Haoqian Factory in the case of dispute over invention patent infringement, which took the form of a patent license. The agreement stipulates a performance obligation in phases, and the first installment was already fulfilled on October 31, 2018, earlier than the Invalidation Decision was made. Therefore, the Invalidation Decision did not have retroactive effect on the part of the agreement that had already been performed.

专利法第四十七条第二款规定，因专利权人的恶意给他人造成的损失，应当给予赔偿。专利权人明知其专利技术不具备专利性而取得专利权或者明知其专利权已经被宣告无效等情况，依然向他人主张权利，则属于该款中“专利权人的恶意”。本案中，首先，涉案专利系经过实质审查的发明专利，不存在明显不具备专利性的情形，也无证据证明尚某中存在故意规避法律或者以不正当手段获得专利权的行为；其次，虽然案外人是在涉案调解书生效日之前请求宣告涉案专利无效，但是，在双方达成和解协议之时无效宣告程序尚未进行实质审理，在浩千厂未就专利权有效性质疑或查询的情况下，尚某中对无效宣告请求的情况未进行主动说明，尚难认定构成恶意。因此，基于现有证据不能认定尚某中存在恶意。

Paragraph 2, Article 47 of the Patent Law stipulates that the damage caused to other persons in bad faith on the part of the patentee shall be compensated. If a patentee knows that his patented technology lacks novelty or has been declared invalid but still asserts his rights against others, it constitutes “bad faith” under this provision. In this case, first of all, the Patent is an invention patent that has undergone substantive examination, and there is no evidence to prove that Shang intentionally evaded the law or obtained the patent right by improper means. Secondly, although the third party requested the invalidation of the Patent before the effective date of the mediation agreement, the invalidation procedure had not undergone substantive examination when the parties reached the settlement agreement. In the absence of any challenge or inquiry by Haoqian Factory on the validity of the Patent, it is difficult to conclude that Shang acted in bad faith by not actively explaining the request for invalidation. Therefore, based on the existing evidence, it cannot be concluded that Shang acted in bad faith.

专利法第四十七条第三款规定，依照前款规定不返还专利侵权赔偿金、专利使用费、专利权转让费，明显违反公平原则的，应当全部或者部分返还。当专利被宣告无效之日前已支付的专利侵权赔偿金、专利使用费、专利转让费与许可使用费总金额之比，明显高于专利被宣告无效之日前实际使用专利技术的期间与整个许可使用期限之比的，则属于该款中“明显违反公平原则”。当然，对于是否存在返还的情形，应由被许可实施专利的人或被诉侵权人举证证明。根据在案材料可知，涉案调解书是对双方当事人在侵害发明专利权纠纷案中自愿协商达成的和解协议的确认，许可费用金额亦略低于涉案专利的其他侵权纠纷案判决的金额，且浩千厂也未能举证证明该金额明显超出正常范围。同时，涉案调解书是在专利侵权纠纷案中达成的以专利许可使用为形式的和解协议，浩千厂在涉案专利被宣告无效之日前已支付的 12 万元与许可使用费总金额 22 万元之比，相对于浩千厂在涉案专利被宣告无效之日前已实际使用涉案专利技术的期间与涉案调解书约定的许可使用期限之比，尚属合理，不存在显失公平之情形。因此，尚某中不返还浩千厂已经支付的 12 万元许可费不属于显失公平的情形。

According to Paragraph 3, Article 47 of the Patent Law, if, pursuant to the provisions of the preceding Paragraph, the patentee or the assignor of the patent right makes no repayment of damages for patent infringement, the fee for the exploitation of the patent, or of the price for the assignment of the patent right, which is obviously contrary to the principle of fairness, the whole of or part of the above-mentioned fees shall be repaid. If the ratio of the total amount of said damages or fees paid before the date on which the patent is declared invalid to the total amount of the patent license fee is significantly higher than the ratio of the period during which the patented technology was actually used before the invalidation date to the entire license period, it constitutes being "obviously contrary to the principle of fairness" under this provision. However, whether such damages or fees should be repaid should be proved by the licensee or the accused infringer. Based on the available evidence, the mediation agreement in question was a confirmation of the settlement agreement voluntarily reached by the parties in a case of dispute over invention patent infringement, the amount of the license fee was also slightly lower than the amount awarded in other patent infringement cases involving the Patent, and Haoqian Factory did not provided evidence to prove that the amount was significantly beyond the normal range. Moreover, the mediation agreement was a settlement agreement reached in the patent infringement dispute case, which took the form of a patent license. The ratio of CNY 120, 000 license fee paid by Haoqian Factory before the Patent was declared invalid to the total license fee of CNY 220, 000 was reasonable, relative to the ratio of the period during which the patented technology was actually used before the invalidation date to the license period specified in the mediation agreement. Therefore, Shang's refusal to repay the CNY 120, 000 license fee paid by Haoqian Factory was not obviously contrary to the principle of fairness.

34. 专利侵权诉讼中的非法证据认定

Identification of illegally obtained evidence in patent infringement lawsuits

【裁判要旨】

[Judgment Digest]

侵害专利权纠纷案件中，被诉侵权人主张专利权利人构成《最高人民法院关于适用〈中华人民共和国民事诉讼法〉的解释》第一百零六条规定的以违法方式取证的，可以结合专利权利人是否并无其他更为合适的取证途径、证据是否存在可能灭失的紧急情况、证据是否属于专利权救济的关键证据、他人权益因取证行为的受损是否明显小于专利权利人因取证行为的获益等因素综合判断。

If in a patent infringement case, the accused infringer claims that the patentee has obtained evidence in illegal ways under Article 106 of *the Interpretation of the Supreme People's Court on the Application of the Civil Procedure Law of the People's Republic of China*, a decision can be made by taking into account such factors as whether the patentee has no other appropriate method to collect the evidence, whether there are emergencies that could lead to loss of evidence, whether the evidence is critical for patent remedies, and whether the damages to other people's rights and interests due to the patentee's act of collecting evidence is obviously less than the benefits gained by the patentee due to such evidence collection.

【关键词】

[Keywords]

专利　侵权　非法证据　比例原则　必要性　实际损害

Patent; infringement; illegally obtained evidence; proportionality principle; necessity; actual damages

【案号】

[Case Number]

(2022) 最高法知民终 222 号

(2022) SPC IP Civil Final 222

【基本案情】

[Case Facts]

在上诉人莆田市坚强缝制设备有限公司(以下简称坚强公司)与被上诉人莆田市鑫派科自动化科技有限公司(以下简称鑫派科公司)侵害实用新型专利权纠纷案中,坚强公司认为鑫派科公司生产鞋眼松紧带所用的机器设备侵害其专利号为 201721078767.1、名称为"一种船袜下料机"的实用新型专利权,遂进入鑫派科公司的生产车间对该机器设备进行拍照。鑫派科公司发现后制止并报警,公安机关要求坚强公司删除所拍摄的全部照片,但坚强公司对其中的两张被诉侵权产品照片未予删除,后以该照片作为证据向福建省福州市中级人民法院(以下简称一审法院)提起本案侵权诉讼。一审法院认为,该照片系违法取得的证据,不应作为认定案件事实的依据,据此,一审判决驳回坚强公司的诉讼请求。坚强公司不服,向最高人民法院提起上诉,主张该照片应予采信,且能证明鑫派科公司实施了专利侵权行为。最高人民法院于 2022 年 11 月 23 日判决撤销原判,改判鑫派科公司停止侵害并赔偿坚强公司经济损失 10 万元以及为制止侵权所产生的合理支出 2000 元。

In the appeal case between the Appellant, Putian City Jianqiang Sewing Equipment Co., Ltd. (hereinafter referred to as "Jianqiang"), and the Appellee, Putian Xinpaike Automation Technology Co., Ltd. (hereinafter referred to as "Xinpaike"), regarding a dispute over infringement of utility model patent, Jianqiang claimed that Xinpaike's equipment used in the production of shoelace elastic bands infringed upon its utility model patent titled "A Sock Knitting Machine" with patent No. 201721078767.1. Jianqiang entered

Xinpaike's production workshop and took photos of the equipment. Upon discovering this, Xinpaike intervened and reported the incident to the police. The police requested Jianqiang to delete all the photos taken. However, Jianqiang did not delete two photos of the accused infringing product and later used these photos as evidence to file an infringement lawsuit against Xinpaike with Fuzhou Intermediate People's Court of Fujian Province (hereinafter referred to as the "Court of First Instance"). The Court of First Instance held that the photos were illegally obtained and should not be used as a basis for determining the facts of the case. Based on this, the Court dismissed Jianqiang's Claims. Dissatisfied with the ruling, Jianqiang appealed to the SPC, arguing that the photos should be admitted as evidence and could prove Xinpaike's patent infringement. On November 23, 2022, the SPC ruled to revoke the original judgment and ordered Xinpaike to cease the infringement and compensate for Jianqiang's economic losses totaling CNY 100,000 as well as reasonable expenses incurred to cease the infringement totaling CNY 2,000.

【裁判意见】

[Judge's Opinion]

最高人民法院二审认为，发现事实是民事诉讼的主要目标之一，对证据合法性的审查，应当兼顾程序正义与实体公正，根据具体的案情，从比例原则出发，综合考虑取证行为的必要性、取证行为造成的实际损害等因素，对民事诉讼中的证据是否属于非法证据并予以排除作出认定：（1）取证行为的必要性。如果法律已经为当事人设置了从对方当事人或第三人处获取证据的合法途径，当事人能够选择合法途径却弃而不用，则其非法取证行为所形成或者获取的证据不应被采纳。但是，如果客观上当事人并无其他更为合适的取证途径可以选择，或者存在证据可能灭失的紧急情况，当事人非通过轻微违法的方式取证其权益无法获得保护，则该取证行为可视为具有必要性。在知识产权侵权诉讼中，基

于权利客体的无形性，权利人“取证难”的问题客观存在。在侵权证据为被诉侵权人或者第三人所掌握的情况下，过分苛责取证方式，对取证行为的合法性作出比较狭窄的解释，将使得侵权事实难以查明，不利于知识产权的司法保护。（2）实际损害的考量。对民事诉讼中非法取证行为的认定，还需要考量该取证行为对他人合法权益造成了何种损害，该损害是否涉及刑事违法性或者触及他人重要民事权益等。通常，具有刑事违法性的取证行为，或者以侵害他人重要民事权益的方式形成或者获取的证据，应当作为非法证据在民事诉讼中予以排除。但是，对于以轻微行政或民事违法行为形成或者获取的查明案件基础事实的关键证据，其既未损害他人重要民事权益，亦未违反法律禁止性规定或者严重违背公序良俗，则不应不加区别直接予以排除。（3）比例原则的适用。对民事诉讼非法证据的认定，需要在轻微违法的取证行为给他人合法权益造成的损害与诉讼所要保护的利益（忽略取证行为的违法性所能够保护的利益）之间进行平衡，使二者保持适当、合理、均衡的比例关系。

The SPC held in the Second Instance trial that the discovery of facts is one of the main objectives of civil litigation. The examination of the legality of evidence should take into account both procedural justice and substantive fairness. Based on the specific circumstances of the case and the proportionality principle, the necessity of the evidence collection acts and the actual harm caused by these acts should be comprehensively considered when determining whether the evidence in civil litigation is illegal and should be excluded. First, regarding the necessity of the evidence collection acts. If the law has provided legal means for a party to obtain evidence from the opposing party or a third party, and the party chooses not to use these legal means, the evidence obtained through illegal means should not be admitted. However, if objectively there are no other suitable ways for the party to obtain evidence or if there is an urgent situation where the evidence may be lost and the party cannot protect its rights without resorting to a minor illegal means of obtaining evidence, then such illegal evidence collection acts can be considered necessary. In intellectual property infringement litigation, the issue of "difficulty in obtaining evidence" exists objectively due to the intangibility of the object of right. When the evidence of infringement is held by the alleged infringer or a third party, excessively strict interpretations of the legality of evidence collection methods would make it difficult to ascertain the facts of infringement, which is not conducive to the judicial protection of intellectual property rights. Second, regarding the actual harm. The determination of illegal evidence collection acts in civil litigation also requires consideration of the harm caused to the legitimate rights and interests of others and whether this harm involves criminal offenses or affects important civil rights of others. Generally, evidence obtained through acts that involve criminal offenses or that infringe upon others' important civil rights should be excluded as illegal evidence in civil litigation. However, for key evidence that establishes crucial facts obtained through minor administrative or civil violations, if it neither harms others' important civil rights nor violates prohibitive legal provisions or seriously violates public order and good customs, it should not be automatically excluded without distinction. Third, regarding the application of the proportionality principle. The determination of illegal evidence in civil litigation needs to balance the harm caused by minor illegal evidence collection acts to others' legitimate rights and the interests protected by the litigation (i. e., the interests that can be protected by ignoring the illegality of evidence collection acts), maintaining an appropriate, reasonable, and balanced proportionality relationship between the two.

本案中，坚强公司所提交的被诉侵权产品照片不属于非法证据，原因在于：其一，鑫派科公司未对外销售被诉侵权产品，除进入鑫派科公

司生产场所拍摄取证外，坚强公司难以通过其他方式从鑫派科公司或者第三人处获取初步证据，其取证行为具有必要性。而且，坚强公司在取证受阻后，及时请求市场监管部门立案调查，但由于市场监管部门作撤销案件处理，其维权目的无法借助执法部门的介入而实现。其二，坚强公司隐瞒身份进入鑫派科公司的生产场所进行拍摄取证，该行为未经过鑫派科公司许可，但并未对鑫派科公司的生产经营秩序或者其他重要民事权益造成严重妨碍或严重损害。公安机关要求坚强公司删除所拍摄的照片，属于履行社会治安管理职责的行为，不能仅基于此在民事诉讼中简单适用非法证据排除规则。其三，被诉侵权产品已经被鑫派科公司处理，亦无产品设计图纸，无法对被诉侵权产品实物进行比对，坚强公司所提交的两张照片成为查明本案事实的关键证据，如果不予采纳，将导致本案的技术事实无法查明，专利权人的权益无法维护。与之相应地，坚强公司的取证行为虽然对鑫派科公司的生产秩序造成了一定干扰，但并不能认定其侵害了鑫派科公司的重要权益。鑫派科公司主张该取证行为侵害了其商业秘密，但不能对商业秘密的内容、范围及载体作出明确陈述，故不能认定坚强公司实际侵害了鑫派科公司的商业秘密。鑫派科公司亦未举证证明其还因坚强公司的取证行为遭受了其他严重损害。据此，可以认为坚强公司取证行为的违法性对鑫派科公司权益的损害明显弱于忽略该违法性所能够保护的专利权人的利益。综上所述，坚强公司所提交的在鑫派科公司拍摄的两张被诉侵权产品照片可予采纳，作为查明本案技术事实的依据。

In this case, the photos of the accused infringing product submitted by Jianqiang should not be considered illegal evidence for the following reasons: Firstly, Xinpaike did not publicly sell the accused infringing product. Apart from entering Xinpaike's premises to gather evidence, it would be difficult for Jianqiang to obtain preliminary evidence from Xinpaike or a third party through other means. Therefore, its evidence collection acts were necessary.

Additionally, when Jianqiang faced obstacles in evidence collection, it promptly requested the market regulatory authority to investigate the case. However, due to the market regulatory authority's decision to withdraw the case, Jianqiang was unable to achieve the goal of protecting its rights through the intervention of law enforcement agencies. Secondly, Jianqiang concealed its identity and entered Xinpaike's production premises to collect evidence without permission. Although this act was unauthorized, it did not seriously disrupt Xinpaike's production and business operations or cause significant harm to Xinpaike's important civil rights. The request by the public security authorities for Jianqiang to delete the taken photos can be seen as their fulfillment of social security administration responsibilities. Therefore, this act alone cannot be the sole basis for excluding the illegal evidence in civil litigation. Thirdly, the accused infringing product has already been disposed of by Xinpaike, and there are no product design drawings available for comparison. Without the ability to compare the physical infringing product, the two photos submitted by Jianqiang become crucial evidence for determining the facts of the case. If not admitted, it would prevent the technical facts of the case from being ascertained and the rights of the patentee from being protected. Correspondingly, although Jianqiang's evidence collection acts caused some interference with Xinpaike's production order, it cannot be concluded that they infringed upon Xinpaike's important rights. Xinpaike claimed that these evidence collection acts infringed upon its trade secrets, but it failed to provide clear statements regarding the content, scope, and carrier of the trade secrets. Therefore, it cannot be determined that Jianqiang actually infringed upon Xinpaike's trade secrets. Xinpaike also failed to provide evidence proving that it suffered other significant damages as a result of Jianqiang's evidence collection acts. Based on these reasons, it can be argued that the illegality of

Jianqiang's evidence collection acts caused less harm to Xinpaike's rights compared to the interests of the patentee that would be protected by disregarding this illegality. Therefore, the two photos of the accused infringing product taken at Xinpaike's premises submitted by Jianqiang could be admitted as evidence to determine the technical facts of the case.

35. 专利权稳定性存疑时可引导当事人作出未来利益补偿承诺

Guiding the involved party to make commitment to future compensation if the patent validity remains doubtful

【裁判要旨】

[Judgment Digest]

专利侵权案件中涉案专利权稳定性存疑或者有争议时，人民法院可以视情采取继续审理并作出判决、裁定中止诉讼、裁定驳回起诉等不同处理方式，具体处理方式的选择主要取决于人民法院对涉案专利权稳定性程度的初步判断。为有效促进专利侵权纠纷解决，人民法院可以积极引导和鼓励专利侵权案件当事人基于公平与诚信之考虑，自愿作出双方双向或者单方单向的利益补偿承诺或者声明，即专利权利人可以承诺如专利权被宣告无效则放弃依据专利法第四十七条第二款所享有的不予执行回转利益；被诉侵权人可以承诺如专利权经确权程序被维持有效则赔偿有关侵权损害赔偿的利息。当事人自愿作出上述承诺的，人民法院应当将之作为专利侵权案件后续审理程序处理方式选择的重要考量因素。

Where, in a patent infringement case, the involved patent validity is in question or under dispute, people's court can, as it sees fit, continue the trial and render a judgment, or rule to suspend the case, or rule to dismiss the lawsuit, which depends on its preliminary judgment about the stability of the involved patent. In order to effectively promote the resolution of disputes over patent infringement, people's courts can actively guide and encourage the involved parties to voluntarily make bilateral or unilateral benefits compensation commitments or statements based on fairness and good faith. In other words, the patentee may waive his benefits under Paragraph 2 of Article 47 of the Patent Law(which prohibits restitution of rights and interests in the case of wrong-judgment enforcement) on the condition that the patent is invalidated; and the accused infringer may undertake to pay interests on the relevant infringement damages if the patent remains valid after the invalidation proceedings. Where the involved parties have voluntarily made the aforementioned undertakings, people's court should take it as an important factor in considering how to proceed with the patent infringement case.

【关键词】

[Keywords]

专利　侵权　专利权无效抗辩　专利权稳定性　未来利益补偿　承诺　处理方式选择

Patent; infringement; patent invalidity defense; stability of patent rights; compensation for future interests; commitment; choice of processing methods

【案号】

[Case Number]

(2022) 最高法知民终 124 号

(2022) SPC IP Civil Final 124

【基本案情】

[Case Facts]

在上诉人深圳市租电智能科技有限公司（以下简称租电公司）与

被上诉人深圳市森树强电子科技有限公司（以下简称森树强公司）、深圳市优电物联技术有限公司（以下简称优电公司）侵害实用新型专利权纠纷案中，租电公司以森树强公司、优电公司共同实施了侵害其享有的名称为“一种动态密码 USB 线材”的实用新型专利权（以下简称涉案专利权）的行为为由，向广东省深圳市中级人民法院（以下简称一审法院）起诉，请求判令森树强公司、优电公司停止侵害并连带赔偿 100 万元。森树强公司、优电公司提出专利权无效抗辩，理由系租电公司所享有的“一种动态密码墙壁充电器”实用新型专利权（以下简称关联专利权）已经被国家知识产权局作出无效宣告审查决定（以下简称第 41299 号审查决定）宣告无效，涉案专利也不符合授予专利权的条件。一审法院认定涉案实用新型专利和关联专利属于实质上的同一技术方案，关联专利权被宣告无效，涉案专利明显或者有极大可能属于不应获得授权的技术方案，其也不属于专利法保护的合法权益，森树强公司、优电公司的专利权无效抗辩成立。据此，一审法院判决驳回租电公司的诉讼请求。租电公司不服，向最高人民法院提起上诉，主张一审法院无权在民事案件中审查森树强公司、优电公司提出的无效抗辩的主张，关联专利并未公开涉案专利的全部技术特征，涉案专利具备创造性。本案二审审理过程中，森树强公司向国家知识产权局提出针对涉案专利权的无效宣告请求（以下简称本次专利确权程序），国家知识产权局已经受理。经二审合议庭对涉案专利权稳定性问题依法可能存在的处理方式进行释明，双方当事人分别自愿作出相应未来利益的补偿承诺。专利权人承诺的核心在于专利权被宣告无效时将返还全部有关侵权案件实际收益并给付相应利息；被诉侵权人承诺的核心在于专利权被确认有效时将支付全部侵权案件应付赔偿并给付相应利息。最高人民法院于 2022 年 6 月 22 日裁定撤销原判，驳回租电公司起诉。

In the appeal case between the Appellant, Shenzhen Uni-code Intelligent Technology Co., Ltd. (hereinafter referred to as "Uni-code"), and the Appellees, Shenzhen Senshuqiang Electronic Technology Co., Ltd. (hereinafter referred to as "Senshuqiang") and Shenzhen Youdian IoT Technology Co., Ltd. (hereinafter referred to as "Youdian"), regarding a dispute over infringement of utility model patent, Uni-code claimed that Senshuqiang and Youdian jointly infringed upon its utility model patent titled "A Dynamic Password USB Cable" (hereinafter referred to as the "Patent"), and therefore filed a lawsuit with Shenzhen Intermediate People's Court of Guangdong Province (hereinafter referred to as the "Court of First Instance"), requesting an order for Senshuqiang and Youdian to cease the infringement and jointly compensate it CNY 1 million. Senshuqiang and Youdian raised a patent invalidity defense, arguing that the utility model patent titled "A Dynamic Password Wall Charger" (hereinafter referred to as the "Associated Patent"), owned by Uni-code, had been declared invalid by the CNIPA in Decision No. 41299 (hereinafter referred to as the "Invalidation Decision"), and the Patent did not meet the conditions for patent granting. The Court of First Instance determined that the Patent and the Associated Patent were essentially the same technical solution, and since the Associated Patent had been declared invalid, it was evident or highly likely that the Patent should not have been granted nor enjoy legitimate protection under the Patent Law. The patent invalidity defense of Senshuqiang and Youdian was supported. Therefore, it ruled to dismiss the claims of Uni-code. Dissatisfied with the judgement, Uni-code appealed to the SPC, arguing that the Court of First Instance had no authority to examine Senshuqiang's and Youdian's patent invalidity defense in a civil case, and that the Associated Patent did not disclose all the technical features of the Patent, which possessed inventive step. During the Second Instance trial, Senshuqiang filed a request for invalidation of the Patent with the CNIPA (hereinafter referred to as the "Patent Confirmation Procedure"), which was

accepted. The Second Instance collegiate bench clarified the possible ways to handle the stability issue of the Patent according to the law, and the parties voluntarily made corresponding commitments regarding future compensation. The core of the patentee's commitment lies in returning all actual profits related to the infringement cases and paying corresponding interest if the patent is declared invalid, while the core of the accused infringer's commitment lies in paying full compensation for the infringement cases and corresponding interest if the patent is confirmed valid. On June 22, 2022, the SPC ruled to revoke the original judgment and dismissed Uni-code's lawsuit.

【裁判意见】

[Judge's Opinion]

最高人民法院二审认为，第一，在涉案专利权稳定性存疑或有争议的情况下，人民法院可以酌情对后续审理程序作出妥适处理。依据有关法律和司法解释的规定，专利侵权案件审理中对涉案专利权稳定性存疑或有争议时，人民法院至少可以有继续审理并作出判决、裁定中止诉讼、裁定驳回起诉三种处理方式，具体应采取哪种方式，主要取决于人民法院对涉案专利权稳定性程度的初步判断。一般而言，对于已经过专利授权确权程序中国务院专利行政部门实质审查判断的专利权，其稳定性相对较强，人民法院通常可以继续审理侵权案件并作出判决；对于未经国务院专利行政部门实质审查判断的专利权和其他有证据表明被宣告无效可能性较大的专利权，其稳定性相对不足，人民法院可以依据有关司法解释的规定视情对侵权案件裁定中止诉讼；对于已被国务院专利行政部门宣告无效但无效决定尚未确定发生法律效力的专利权，其稳定性明显不足，人民法院可以依据《最高人民法院关于审理侵犯专利权纠纷案件应用法律若干问题的解释（二）》第二条第一款的规定，对侵权案件裁定驳回起诉；对于有证据表明被宣告无效可能性极大的专利权，其稳定性明显不足的，虽然尚未被国务院专利行政部门宣告无效，但在专利确权程序已经启动的情况下，人民法院对侵权案件既可以裁定中止诉讼，也可以在必要时视情参照《最高人民法院关于审理侵犯专利权纠纷案件应用法律若干问题的解释（二）》第二条的规定裁定驳回起诉。

The SPC held in the Second Instance trial that firstly, when the stability of the Patent is in doubt or disputed, the people's court may handle subsequent proceedings appropriately. According to relevant laws and judicial interpretations, when the stability of the patent is in doubt or disputed in a patent infringement case, the court can at least adopt three methods of handling: continue the trial and render a judgment, rule to suspend the case, or rule to dismiss the lawsuit, which depends on its preliminary judgment about the stability of the involved patent. Generally speaking, for patents that have undergone substantive examination by the Patent Administration Department under the State Council in the patent confirmation process, their stability is relatively high, and the court can usually continue to try the infringement case and render a judgment; for patents that have not undergone substantive examination by the Patent Administration Department under the State Council and those with evidence indicating a high possibility of being declared invalid, their stability is relatively low, and the court may, depending on relevant judicial interpretations, rule to suspend the lawsuit in the infringement case; for patents that have been declared invalid by the Patent Administration Department under the State Council but the invalidation decision has not yet become legally effective, their stability is obviously insufficient, and the people's court can rule to dismiss the lawsuit according to Paragraph 1, Article 2 of the *Interpretation of the Supreme People's Court on Several Issues Concerning the Application of Law in the Trial of Patent Infringement Dispute Cases (II)*; for patents with evidence indicating a high possibility of being declared invalid and whose

stability is obviously insufficient, although they have not yet been declared invalid by the Patent Administration Department under the State Council, if the patent confirmation process has already started, the court may either suspend the lawsuit or dismiss the lawsuit, depending on the actual situation and referring to the provisions of Article 2 of the *Interpretation of the Supreme People's Court on Several Issues Concerning the Application of Law in the Trial of Patent Infringement Dispute Cases (II)*.

第二，基于本案现有事实和证据，可以得出涉案专利权稳定性明显不足的结论。本案已经查明，专利权人租电公司在申请涉案专利的同日申请了关联专利。该关联专利权已被发生法律效力的第 41299 号审查决定宣告全部无效。关联专利与涉案专利相比，区别技术特征仅在于，涉案专利为“一种动态密码 USB 线材，包括有 USB 插接头；其特征在于：所述的 USB 插接头的电源输出端经动态密码控制器连接充电接口”；关联专利为“一种动态密码墙壁充电器，包括有 AC 插头，连接 AC 插头的电源适配器模块。其特征在于：所述的电源适配器模块的输出端经动态密码控制器连接充电接口”。二者其余技术特征均相同。对于上述区别技术特征，根据涉案专利说明书及关联专利说明书可知，不论是 USB 线材还是采用 AC 插头的充电器均为现有技术，USB 插接头用于获取 5V 直流电，供数码产品充电；AC 插头用于插接在市电插座上获取 220V 或 110V 的交流电源，电源适配器模块将交流电源降压为低压直流输出，即 AC 插头与电源适配器连接后，用于提供低压直流输出电，供数码产品充电。森树强公司、优电公司主张，上述区别技术特征对于本领域技术人员而言，在涉案专利、关联专利中所起的作用、效果相同，属于惯用手段的直接替换。森树强公司在本案二审审理过程中也已就涉案专利权向国家知识产权局提出了无效宣告请求，其提交的证据与第 41299 号审查决定中的证据相同，无效理由也基本一致，国家知识产权局已经受理。基于上述涉案专利和关联专利均为未经实质审查即授权的实用新型专利，二者的区别技术特征仅系行业惯用和市场常见的 USB 插头与 AC 插头及与之配套使用的电源适配器的不同，且二者系同日申请，在关联专利权已被国家知识产权局宣告无效而森树强公司、优电公司也已就涉案专利向国家知识产权局提出宣告无效请求的情况下，涉案专利权被宣告无效的可能性极大，其专利权稳定性明显不足。

Secondly, based on the existing facts and evidence in this case, it can be concluded that the stability of the Patent is obviously insufficient. It has been found in the case that the patentee, Uni-code, applied for the Associated Patent on the same day as the application for the Patent. The Associated Patent has been declared invalid by the legally effective Examination Decision No. 41299. Comparing the Patent with the Associated Patent, the only difference in technical features is that the Patent is “a dynamic password USB cable, including a USB plug; characterized in that: the power output end of the USB plug is connected to the charging interface through a dynamic password controller”, while the Associated Patent is “a dynamic password wall charger, including an AC plug and a power adapter module connected to the AC plug; characterized in that: the output end of the power adapter module is connected to the charging interface through a dynamic password controller.” All other technical features of the two are the same. Regarding the above-mentioned difference in technical features, according to the descriptions of the Patent and the Associated Patent, both the USB cable and the charger with AC plug are prior arts. The USB plug is used to obtain 5V DC power supply for charging digital products, while the AC plug is used to plug into a household power socket to obtain 220V or 110V AC power supply, then the power adapter module reduces the AC power supply to low-voltage DC output. That is, after the AC plug is connected to the power adapter, it is used to provide low-voltage DC output power for charging digital products. Senshuqiang and Youdian

argued that the above-mentioned difference in technical features had the same role and effect in the Patent and the Associated Patent for those skilled in the art, belonging to direct substitution of common means in the industry. Senshuqiang has also filed an invalidation request for the Patent to the CNIPA during the Second Instance trial, with evidence submitted the same as that in Examination Decision No. 41299, and the reasons for invalidation being basically the same. The CNIPA has accepted the request. Based on the fact that both the Patent and the Associated Patent are utility model patents granted without substantive examination, the only difference in their technical features is the different use of USB plug and AC plug plus the power adapter that goes with it, which is common in the industry and the market, and the two were applied for on the same day, while the Associated Patent has been declared invalid by the CNIPA and Senshuqiang and Youdian have filed an invalidation request for the Patent to the CNIPA, the possibility of the Patent being declared invalid is extremely high, and its patent stability is obviously insufficient.

第三，本案中双方当事人自愿作出的有关涉案专利权稳定性问题的利益补偿承诺或声明，有利于彼此利益的实质平衡，人民法院也可将此作为对后续审理程序作出处理时的考量因素。本案中，在涉案专利权稳定性问题存疑且已经启动本次专利确权程序的情况下，经向当事人释明相关程序可能的走向和后果后，本案双方当事人分别针对本次专利确权程序可能的结果及因此可能对对方当事人利益造成的不利影响作出了相应的利益补偿承诺。二审法院认为，当事人所作有关利益补偿承诺系对各自民事权利和期待利益的自愿处分，内容并不违背法律规定，所作承诺系在充分考虑相关程序的可能走向和后果的基础上对彼此利益的合理预期和处分，能够较好地保障和合理地平衡专利侵权程序与专利确权程序交叉进行情况下当事人的程序利益和实体公正，符合公平原则和诚信原则，并具有实践可操作性。同时，在当事人自愿作出有关专利权稳定性问题的利益补偿承诺的情况下，无论人民法院后续是采取继续审理并作出判决、裁定中止诉讼、裁定驳回起诉三种处理方式中的哪一种方式，均可在实质上较好且有效地平衡保护双方当事人利益，也有利于人民法院结合具体案情就后续处理方式作出适当选择。

Thirdly, the voluntary compensation commitments or statements made by the parties in this case regarding the stability of the Patent are beneficial in achieving a substantive balance of interests. The court can also consider these commitments or statements when deciding on the subsequent proceedings. In this case, considering the uncertainty surrounding the Patent stability and the initiation of the Patent Confirmation Procedure, possible outcomes and consequences of which had been explained, both parties made respective commitments to compensate for the potential adverse impacts on each other's interests that may arise from the outcome of the Patent Confirmation Procedure. The Court of Second Instance believes that these commitments made by the parties are voluntary disposals of their respective civil rights and expected interests, which do not violate legal provisions. These commitments are based on a thorough consideration of the possible outcomes and consequences of relevant procedures, aiming to protect and reasonably balance the procedural interests and substantive justice of the parties in a situation where patent infringement proceedings intersect with patent confirmation procedures. This is in line with the principles of fairness and good faith, and is also practical. Moreover, in the case where the parties have voluntarily made commitments regarding the stability of the patent, regardless of which of the three methods of treatment the court chooses, namely to continue the trial and render a judgment, or to suspend the case, or to dismiss the lawsuit in the subsequent proceedings, it can effectively and fairly balance and protect the interests of both parties. It also allows the court to make an appropriate choice on follow-up methods of treat-

ment based on the specific circumstances of the case.

综合上述分析，涉案专利权稳定性明显不足，而被诉侵权人就涉案专利权稳定性问题所作相关利益补偿承诺也可以在本案裁定驳回起诉后未来专利权被确认有效时使得专利权人的相应利益得以保障，本案可以参照《最高人民法院关于审理侵犯专利权纠纷案件应用法律若干问题的解释（二）》第二条第一款、第二款的规定，按照裁定驳回起诉作出处理。专利权人可以在国家知识产权局就涉案专利权作出维持有效的审查决定确定发生法律效力后，另行提起诉讼，并可根据被诉侵权人在本案中所作利益补偿承诺主张权利。

Based on the above analysis, the stability of the Patent is obviously insufficient. However, the accused infringer’s commitments regarding the compensation for the stability of the Patent can safeguard the corresponding interests of the patentee if the Patent is confirmed as valid in the future after the lawsuit is dismissed in this case. The Court can rule to dismiss the lawsuit according to Paragraphs 1 and 2, Article 2 of the *Interpretation of the Supreme People’s Court on Several Issues Concerning the Application of Law in the Trial of Patent Infringement Dispute Cases (II)*. According to this interpretation, the patentee can initiate a separate lawsuit after a decision made by the CNIPA to maintain the validity of the Patent becomes legally effective. The patentee can also assert his rights based on the accused infringer’s commitments regarding the compensation made in this case.

36. 假冒专利行为的侵权定性及损害赔偿法律依据

Identification of patent counterfeiting as tort and legal basis for damages

【裁判要旨】

[Judgment Digest]

假冒他人专利行为与侵害专利权行为虽然均属于与专利相关的侵权行为，但其侵权行为样态、所侵害的法益、责任承担方式均有所不同。单纯假冒他人专利而未实施专利技术方案的行为，不构成专利法第十一条规定的侵害专利权行为，有关损害赔偿责任的认定应当适用民法典关于侵权损害赔偿的一般规定。

Although patent counterfeiting and patent infringement are both patent-related tort, they differ in their behavioral patterns, damaged legal interests and ways to take liabilities. Merely counterfeiting others' patents without embodying the patented technical solutions does not constitute patent infringement under Article 11 of the Patent Law, in which scenario the general provisions of *the Civil Code* for tort and damages shall apply.

【关键词】

[Keywords]

假冒专利　侵权　损害赔偿　法律依据

Patent counterfeiting; infringement; damages; legal basis

【案号】

[Case Number]

（2021）最高法知民终 2380 号

（2021）SPC IP Civil Final 2380

【基本案情】

[Case Facts]

在上诉人姚某君与被上诉人嘉兴捷顺旅游制品有限公司（以下简称捷顺公司）、原审被告上海寻梦信息技术有限公司（以下简称寻梦公司）假冒他人专利纠纷案中，涉及专利号为 201420624020.1、名称为“一种自挤水平板拖把”的实用新型专利（以下简称涉案专利）。捷顺公司认为，姚某君在其经营的拼多多店铺网页宣传其经营的是上述专利产品，构成假冒专利，请求判令姚某君赔偿捷顺公司经济损失 50 万元及维权合理开支合计 5 万元；判令寻梦公司承担连带责任。一审法院认为，姚某君未提供证据证明其经许可使用涉案专利号，其行为会使公众将被诉销售页面对应的产品使用的技术误认为是专利技术，构成假冒他人专利的行为，姚某君依法承担赔偿损失及支付合理维权费用的民事责任。捷顺公司未证明权利人损失和侵权人获利的事实，依照 2008 年修正专利法第六十五条规定，酌定姚某君赔偿捷顺公司经济损失及为制止侵权所支出的合理费用共计 10 万元。姚某君不服，向最高人民法院提起上诉，主张侵害专利标识的标记权与侵害专利权系不同概念，不能依照专利法第六十五条规定确定赔偿数额，应由捷顺公司另行举证其因专利号被他人标注造成的实际损失。最高人民法院认为，一审法院适用法律有误，但判决结果无明显错误，可予以维持，并于 2022 年 6 月 23 日判决驳回上诉，维持原判。

In the appeal case between the Appellant, Yao, and the Appellees, Jiaxing Jieshun Tourism Products Co., Ltd. (hereinafter referred to as "Jieshun"), and Shanghai Xunmeng Information Technology Co., Ltd. (hereinafter referred to as "Xunmeng"), regarding a dispute over patent counterfeiting, a utility model patent titled "A Self-squeezing Flat Mop" (hereinafter referred to as the "Patent"), with patent No. 201420624020.1, was involved. Jieshun argued that Yao promoted the sale of the aforementioned patented product on his Pinduoduo online store, which constituted patent counterfeiting. It requested a judgment ordering Yao to compensate for its economic losses totaling CNY 500, 000 and reasonable expenses for remedies totaling CNY 50, 000, as well as holding Xunmeng jointly liable. The Court of First Instance held that Yao failed to provide evidence proving his authorized use of the Patent. His act could lead the public to mistakenly believe that the technology used in the products sold on the accused sales page was patented technology, thus constituting patent counterfeiting. Yao should be liable for compensating the losses and paying reasonable expenses for remedies according to law. As Jieshun failed to prove the actual damages suffered by the right holder and the profits obtained by the infringer, according to Article 65 of the Patent Law amended in 2008, Yao was ordered to compensate Jieshun for its economic losses and reasonable expenses incurred to cease the infringement, totaling CNY 100, 000. Dissatisfied with the judgement, Yao appealed to the SPC, arguing that infringing the marking right of a patent and infringing the patent right itself were different concepts. Therefore, the amount of compensation should not be determined based on Article 65 of the Patent Law. Instead, Jieshun should provide separate evidence of the actual losses caused by the patent number being marked by others. The SPC held that the Court of First Instance had misapplied the law but found no obvious errors in the judgment, thus upholding the original judgment and dismissing the appeal on June 23, 2022.

【裁判意见】

[Judge's Opinion]

最高人民法院二审认为，专利法第十七条第二款规定，专利权人有权在其专利产品或者该产品的包装上标明专利标识。专利法实施细则第八十四条规定，在未被授予专利权的产品或者其包装上标注专利标识，或者未经许可在产品或产品包装上标注他人的专利号，属于专利法第六

十三条规定的假冒专利的行为。捷顺公司是涉案专利的专利权人，该专利合法有效。姚某君未经专利权人许可，在被诉销售页面展示有与涉案专利相同的产品名称、专利号，其行为会使相关公众将被诉销售页面对应的产品所实施的技术误认为是专利技术，侵害了专利权人的合法权益，且违反国家专利管理制度，属于假冒专利的行为。即使假冒专利的产品实际上并没有实施他人的专利技术方案，不具备专利产品应有的功能，但此类产品在市场上公开销售，可能影响专利产品的商誉，挤占专利权人制造、销售专利产品的市场空间。因此，假冒专利行为构成对专利标记权的侵害，属于侵权行为，专利权人可以要求行为人承担民事责任。

The SPC, in the Second Instance trial, held that according to Paragraph 2, Article 17 of the Patent Law, a patentee has the right to label the patent on its patented product or on the package of the said product. Article 84 of the Implementing Regulations of the Patent Law states that affixing a patent indication on a product which patent has not been granted or on the package of such product, or affixing the patent number of another person on a product or on the package of a product without authorization, constitutes an act of counterfeiting a patent as prescribed in Article 63 of the Patent Law. Jieshun is the patentee of the Patent, which is legally valid. Yao's act of displaying a product with the same name and patent number as the Patent on the accused sales page, without the patentee's authorization, could lead the relevant public to mistakenly believe that the technology embodied in the said product is the patented technology, which infringes upon the legitimate rights and interests of the patentee and violates the national patent management system. Therefore, it constitutes an act of counterfeiting a patent. Even if the product counterfeiting the patent does not actually embody the other's patented technical solution and lacks the functions that a patented product should have, such product being openly sold in the market may affect the reputation of the patented product and encroach upon the market space for the patentee's manufacturing and selling of the patented products. Therefore, counterfeiting a patent constitutes an infringement of the patent marking right and falls within the scope of infringement. The patentee can demand that the infringer bear civil liability.

假冒专利的行为与侵害专利权的行为并不相同。首先，二者的行为方式不同。专利法第六十条规定，未经权利人许可，实施其专利，即侵犯其专利权。根据专利法第十一条规定，任何单位或者个人未经专利权人许可，都不得实施其专利，即不得以生产经营为目的制造、使用、许诺销售、销售、进口其专利产品，或者使用其专利方法以及使用、许诺销售、销售、进口依照该专利方法直接获得的产品。即，专利法规定的侵害专利权，一般是指未经权利人许可实施其专利技术方案的行为，实施的具体方式在专利法第十一条中予以规定，而假冒专利并不实施专利技术方案。其次，假冒专利行为与侵害专利权行为所侵害的法益不同。侵害专利权行为所指向的是基于技术方案的专利权，而假冒专利行为侵害的是专利法第十七条所规定的标明专利标识的权利（即专利标记权)、国家专利管理秩序以及社会公众利益。最后，假冒专利行为与侵害专利权行为承担责任的方式也不同。即假冒专利可能承担民事责任、行政责任、刑事责任，其承担民事责任的法律依据应为规制侵权行为的一般民事法律。而侵害专利权行为所侵害的是专利权人的权益，依据专利法承担民事责任。

Counterfeiting a patent and infringing upon a patent are indeed different. Firstly, they are behaved differently. According to Article 60 of the Patent Law, exploiting a patent without the permission of the patentee constitutes an infringement upon the patent. Article 11 of the Patent Law stipulates that no entity or individual may, without the permission of the patentee, exploit the patent, that is, make, use, offer to sell, sell, or import the patented product,

or use the patented process, and use, offer to sell, sell, or import the product directly obtained by the patented process, for production or business purposes. In other words, infringing upon a patent as defined by the Patent Law generally refers to the act of exploiting the patented technical solution without the permission of the patentee, with specific embodiments specified in Article 11 of the Patent Law, while counterfeiting a patent does not involve the exploitation of a patented technical solution. Secondly, they affect different legal interests. Infringing upon a patent is directed at the patent based on the technical solution, while counterfeiting a patent infringes upon the right to mark the patent as defined in Article 17 of the Patent Law (i. e., the patent marking right), the national patent management order, and the interests of the public. Finally, they entail different forms of liability. Counterfeiting a patent may incur civil liability, administrative liability, and even criminal liability, with civil liability being based on general civil laws that regulate infringement acts. On the other hand, infringing upon a patent involves the infringement on the patentee's rights and entails civil liability based on the Patent Law.

本案中姚某君所实施的被诉行为系未经专利权人许可，在其销售网页上标注涉案专利的名称、专利号，但其相应的产品并未实施涉案专利技术方案，因此其行为仅构成假冒专利，侵害了捷顺公司的专利标记权，但并未侵害捷顺公司的涉案专利权。专利法第六十五条规定了侵害专利权的赔偿责任。假冒专利的行为并非侵害专利权的行为，故不能适用专利法第六十五条的规定计算侵权损害赔偿数额。

In the present case, the accused act committed by Yao constituted counterfeiting a patent as he labeled the name and patent number of the Patent on his sales webpage without the permission of the patentee. However, his corresponding product did not exploit the technical solution of the Patent. Therefore, his act only constituted counterfeiting a patent, which infringed upon

Jieshun's patent marking right but rather than its Patent. Article 65 of the Patent Law stipulates the compensation liability for infringing upon a patent. However, counterfeiting a patent is not equivalent to infringing upon a patent. Therefore, the damages cannot be calculated based on the provisions of Article 65 of the Patent Law.

本案中姚某君被诉假冒专利的行为，不仅仅在其销售网页标注涉案专利号，亦标明了专利名称“自挤水平板拖把”，并标明“专利产品防伪必究”，侵害了捷顺公司就涉案专利享有的专利标记权，可能使相关公众对涉案产品产生其相关技术是专利技术的误认，造成相关购买者的混淆，并进而侵占捷顺公司的市场空间，必然会给捷顺公司造成损失，其应当承担赔偿损失的民事责任。姚某君另案侵害捷顺公司“拖把（FC-44）”的外观设计专利权，又假冒捷顺公司的涉案专利，侵权主观故意明显。侵权责任法第六条规定，行为人因过错侵害他人民事权益，应当承担侵权责任。该法第十五条规定了承担侵权责任的主要方式。该法第十九条规定，侵害他人财产的，财产损失按照损失发生时的市场价格或者其他方式计算。本案中捷顺公司未证明其实际损失以及姚某君因侵权行为不当获利的情况，市场价格亦难以准确确定，但在案证据显示，涉案产品的销售单价为 29. 9 元至 39. 9 元，依据其销售网页显示销售量超过 10 万件，虽然该销售数据可能不尽准确，但亦可见其涉案产品销售额较大，给捷顺公司造成的损失也应较大。综合案件具体情况，酌情确定姚某君应赔偿捷顺公司 10 万元，鉴于一审判决确定的赔偿总额亦为 10 万元，因此不再作调整。

In the present case, Yao's act of counterfeiting a patent not only involved labeling the patent number on his sales webpage but also included the patent name “Self-Squeezing Flat Mop” and the phrase “anti-counterfeiting of patented product will be investigated”, which infringed upon Jieshun's patent marking right concerning the Patent. This may have caused confusion among

relevant consumers that the related technology of the product in question is patented technology, and thus results in a loss of market share for Jieshun. Therefore, Yao should bear civil liability for compensation for the damages caused. Additionally, in another case, Yao infringed upon Jieshun's design patent titled "Mop (FC-44)" and counterfeited Jieshun's Patent with clear subjective intent. According to Article 6 of the Tort Liability Law, one who is at fault for infringement upon a civil right or interest of another person shall be subject to tort liability, and Article 15 of the same law sets out the primary ways to bear tort liability. Article 19 of the Tort Liability Law stipulates that where a tort causes any harm to the property of another person, the amount of loss to the property shall be calculated in accordance with the market price at the time of occurrence of the loss or calculated otherwise. Although Jieshun did not prove its actual losses and Yao's profits from the infringement, and it is difficult to accurately determine the market price, the evidence presented in the case showed that the sales price of the disputed product was between CNY 29.9 to CNY 39.9, and the sales volume exceeded 100,000 pieces according to the sales webpage. Though this sales data may not be entirely accurate, it still showed that the sales revenue of the disputed product was significant, which should cause considerable damage to Jieshun. Taking into account the specific circumstances of the case, Yao was ordered to compensate Jieshun CNY 100,000. Since the First Instance judgment also determined a compensation amount of CNY 100,000, there is no need to adjust it.

37. 确认不侵害专利权纠纷的审理范围

Scope of adjudication in disputes over declaratory confirmation on patent non-infringement

【裁判要旨】

[Judgment Digest]

确认不侵害发明或者实用新型专利权纠纷案件中，人民法院应当要求专利权利人明确其侵权警告所主张的具体权利要求；专利权利人主张多个权利要求的，人民法院原则上应当对原告实施的技术方案是否落入每项权利要求保护范围予以审理。原告以实施现有技术为由请求确认不侵害涉案专利权的，人民法院还应当对争议技术方案是否属于现有技术予以审理。

In disputes over declaratory confirmation on non-infringement upon invention patents or utility model patents, people's courts should ask the patentee to clarify the specific claims as contained in its warning on patent infringement; where the patentee asserts more than one claim, people's courts shall, in principle, examine whether the technical solutions implemented by the plaintiff fall within the protection scope of each claim. Where the plaintiff requests for confirmation of non-infringement upon the involved patent on the basis of prior art, people's courts shall also examine whether the accused technical solution belongs to prior art.

【关键词】

[Keywords]

专利　确认不侵权　审理范围　多项权利要求　现有技术抗辩

Patent; declaratory confirmation on non-infringement; scope of trial; multiple claims; prior art defense

【案号】

[Case Number]

(2020) 最高法知民终 696 号

(2020) SPC IP Civil Final 696

【基本案情】

[Case Facts]

在上诉人刘某与被上诉人慈溪市博生塑料制品有限公司（以下简称博生公司）、黄某勇确认不侵害专利权纠纷案中，涉及专利号为201620853180.2、名称为"一种用于平板拖把挤水和清洗的拖把桶"的实用新型专利（以下简称涉案专利），专利权人为博生公司。2018 年 11 月 26 日，博生公司向业界同行发出公告，要求立即下架侵权产品，否则起诉后的侵权责任自负等等。刘某设计的"一款带桶挤水平板拖把"产品也属该类产品，其相关合作单位知悉博生公司的侵权公告后，要求刘某在确认其产品不构成对涉案专利的侵权后，方才同意开展进一步合作。后刘某多次与博生公司沟通未果，故向浙江省宁波市中级人民法院（以下简称一审法院）提起诉讼，请求确认其产品不侵害涉案专利权。博生公司在一审中明确涉案产品落入其涉案专利权利要求 1、2、3、4、7、18 的保护范围。一审法院仅对涉案产品是否落入涉案专利权利要求 1 的保护范围进行了认定，未对权利人主张的争议产品是否落入涉案专利权利要求 2、3、4、7、18 的保护范围进行认定。同时，一审法院认定刘某关于涉案产品使用的是现有技术的主张不能成立，故判决驳回刘某的诉讼请求。刘某不服，向最高人民法院提起上诉。二审诉讼程序中，涉案专利被案外人提起无效宣告请求，博生公司修改了权利要求，将授权文本中的权利要求 7、15 的附加技术特征以及权利要求 18 的部分附加技术特征加入到权利要求 1 中，删除原权利要求 4—6、8、9，并适应性调整了权利要求的编号。最高人民法院于 2021 年 9 月 28 日判决驳回上诉，维持原判。

In the appeal case between the Appellant, Liu, and the Appellees, Cixi Bosheng Plastic Products Co., Ltd. (hereinafter referred to as "Bosheng") and Huang, regarding a dispute over declaratory confirmation on non-infringement, a utility model patent titled "A Mop Bucket for Squeezing Water and Cleaning for Flat Mops" (hereinafter referred to as the "Patent") with the patentee, Bosheng, and patent No. 201620853180.2, was involved. On November 26, 2018, Bosheng issued a notice to industry peers, demanding the immediate removal of infringing products, warning of assuming infringement liability after prosecution, and so on. Liu had designed "A Flat Mop with Bucket for Squeezing Water" product that fell under the same category. Upon being informed of Bosheng's infringement notice, Liu's related cooperative partners requested him to confirm that his product does not infringe upon the Patent before agreeing to further cooperation. After multiple unsuccessful communications with Bosheng, Liu filed a lawsuit with Ningbo Intermediate People's Court of Zhejiang Province (hereinafter referred to as the "Court of First Instance"), seeking confirmation that his product does not infringe upon the Patent. In the First Instance trial, Bosheng explicitly claimed that the accused product fell within the protection scope of Claims 1, 2, 3, 4, 7, and 18 of the Patent. The Court of First Instance only determined whether the accused product fell within the protection scope of Claim 1 and did not make a determination regarding Claims 2, 3, 4, 7, and 18 as asserted by the patentee. Additionally, the Court of First Instance ruled that Liu's argument that the accused product uses prior art was not valid, thus dismissing Liu's lawsuit. Dissatisfied with the ruling, Liu appealed to the SPC. During the Second Instance litigation procedure, a third party filed an invalidation request against the Patent. Bosheng amended the Claims by incorporating the additional technical features of Claims 7 and 15 and a portion of the additional technical fea-

tures of Claim 18 into Claim 1, while deleting original Claims 4-6, 8, and 9, and making corresponding adjustments to the numbering of the Claims. On September 28, 2021, the SPC ruled to dismiss the appeal and affirm the original judgment.

【裁判意见】

[Judge's Opinion]

最高人民法院二审认为，在确认不侵害发明或实用新型专利权纠纷案件中，人民法院亦应要求权利人明确其主张的权利要求。权利人主张多个权利要求的，原则上可以首先审查争议产品技术方案是否落入权利人所主张的保护范围最大的权利要求的保护范围；如果审查结论是争议产品技术方案不落入该权利要求的保护范围，则当然亦不落入援引该权利要求的从属权利要求的保护范围；如果审查结论是争议产品技术方案落入保护范围最大的权利要求的保护范围，则通常还需要对争议产品技术方案是否落入权利人所主张的其他权利要求的保护范围进行审查。如果当事人主张争议产品使用的是现有技术的，还应对落入涉案专利权保护范围的技术特征与现有技术方案中的相应技术特征进行比对，并对争议产品是否使用的是现有技术进行认定。鉴于博生公司一审所主张的权利要求 1、2、3、4、7、18 在涉案专利无效宣告审查过程中，除权利要求 4 被删除外，其余或被保留或被加入到权利要求 1 中，经适应性调整后，成为修改后的权利要求 1、2、3、11，并被维持有效，故二审中争议产品是否构成对涉案专利权的侵害，应审查争议产品技术方案是否落入修改后的权利要求 1、2、3、11 的保护范围。二审比对了争议产品与涉案专利修改后的权利要求 1、2、3、11 中的相关技术特征，认定争议产品落入涉案专利上述权利要求的保护范围，构成对涉案专利权的侵害。一审判决虽遗漏认定争议产品技术方案是否落入博生公司一审主张的涉案专利权利要求的保护范围，但裁判结果正确，应予维持。

The SPC, in the Second Instance trial, held that in cases involving declaratory confirmation on non-infringement upon invention patent or utility model patent, the people's court should ask the patentee to clarify their asserted claims. If the patentee asserts multiple claims, the people's court shall, in principle, examine whether the technical solution of the disputed product falls within the protection scope of the claim with the broadest scope asserted by the patentee. If the examination concludes that the technical solution of the disputed product does not fall within the protection scope of that claim, it would also not fall within the protection scope of the dependent claims relying on that claim. However, if the examination concludes that the technical solution of the disputed product falls within the protection scope of the claim with the broadest scope, it is usually necessary to further examine whether the technical solution of the disputed product falls within the protection scope of other of the claims asserted by the patentee. If the party argues that the disputed product uses prior art, it is necessary to compare the technical features falling within the protection scope of relevant claims of the Patent with the corresponding technical features of the prior art to determine whether the disputed product uses such prior art. In this case, during the invalidation examination process of the Patent, except for Claim 4 being deleted, the other Claims asserted by Bosheng in the First Instance (Claims 1, 2, 3, 4, 7, and 18) were either retained or incorporated into Claim 1 after adaptive adjustment, resulting in amended Claims 1, 2, 3, and 11, which were maintained as valid. Therefore, in the Second Instance trial, the examination of whether the disputed product constituted an infringement upon the Patent should focus on whether the technical solution of the disputed product fell within the protection scope of the amended Claims 1, 2, 3, and 11. During the Second Instance trial, a comparison was made between the disputed product and the relevant technical features in the amended Claims 1, 2, 3, and 11 of the Patent. It

was determined that the disputed product fell within the protection scope of the aforementioned Claims, thus constituting infringement upon the Patent. Although the First Instance judgment failed to determine whether the technical solution of the disputed product fell within the protection scope of the Claims asserted by Bosheng in the First Instance, the outcome of the judgment was correct and should be upheld.

38. 确认不侵权之诉中“在合理期限内提起诉讼”的认定

Determination on “filing lawsuit within a reasonable period” in cases of declaratory confirmation on patent non-infringement

【裁判要旨】

[Judgment Digest]

提起确认不侵害知识产权之诉的原告应当举证证明被告“未在合理期限内提起诉讼”。所谓“合理期限”应当根据知识产权的权利类型及性质、案件具体情况，充分考量侵权行为证据发现的难易程度和诉讼准备所需合理时间等予以确定；所谓“诉讼”包括可以实质解决双方争议、消除被警告人不安状态的各种类型诉讼，如侵权诉讼、确权诉讼等。

The plaintiff who files a lawsuit for declaratory confirmation of non-infringement of intellectual property rights should present evidence to the effect that the defendant “fails to file a lawsuit within a reasonable period”. The so-called “reasonable period” should be determined in accordance with the type and nature of the intellectual property rights, the specific circumstances of the case, the difficulty to find out evidence of infringement and the reasonable time required for preparation of the lawsuit; the so-called "lawsuit" should include various types of lawsuits that can substantively resolve the dispute between both parties and eliminate the disturbing status of the party being warned, such as patent infringement lawsuit and patent ownership confirmation lawsuit.

【关键词】

[Keywords]

确认不侵权之诉　警告　催告　合理期限　诉讼类型

Lawsuit for confirmation of non-infringement; warnings; demands; reasonable period of time; type of action

【案号】

[Case Number]

（2021）最高法知民终 2460 号

（2021）SPC IP Civil Final 2460

【基本案情】

[Case Facts]

在上诉人威马中德汽车科技成都有限公司（以下简称威马成都公司）、威马汽车科技集团有限公司（以下简称威马集团公司）、威马智慧出行科技（上海）股份有限公司（以下简称威马上海公司）与被上诉人成都高原汽车工业有限公司（以下简称高原汽车公司）确认不侵害知识产权纠纷案中，威马成都公司、威马集团公司、威马上海公司（以下简称威马三公司）主张，2018 年 10 月，高原汽车公司向四川高院起诉称，威马成都公司申请的 8 项专利系其前员工利用在高原汽车公司工作期间所掌握的技术秘密所获得的专利，主张威马成都公司侵害其商业秘密，该案为（2018）川民初 121 号案（以下简称 121 号案）。其中 201610634961.7 号专利（以下简称 961.7 号专利）已于 2019 年 11

月 15 日被国家知识产权局驳回申请。立案后，高原汽车公司先后追加威马集团公司、威马上海公司为该案被告，并提交了补充证据，涉及威马三公司的 33 项专利。其中，201620823420.4 号专利（以下简称 420.4 号专利）因威马集团公司为避免重复授权放弃专利权。高原汽车公司在 121 号案开庭审理后撤诉，使得其是否行使诉权的意思表示回归到了一种不确定的状态，也导致威马三公司是否侵害其商业秘密处于不确定状态，严重影响正常生产经营。威马三公司于 2020 年 1 月 10 日向高原汽车公司邮寄催告函，书面催告高原汽车公司明确真实意图并行使诉权，但其签收满一个月后未作任何回应，故威马三公司向四川省成都市中级人民法院（以下简称一审法院）起诉请求判令高原汽车公司对其于 121 号案中主张的商业秘密不享有任何权利，威马三公司未实施侵害高原汽车公司商业秘密的不正当竞争行为、未侵害高原汽车公司任何权利，即威马三公司所申请的 41 项专利未侵害高原汽车公司在 121 号案中所主张的 10 个技术秘密。一审法院认定，高原汽车公司及其关联公司在本案起诉前，于 2019 年 5 月 16 日左右就前述 8 项专利及其他 34 项专利，向浙江省杭州市中级人民法院提起了 42 件专利权权属纠纷，以威马三公司及其员工不法获取技术资料、信息进而申请专利为由，要求确认前述专利申请权或专利权归高原汽车公司及其关联公司所有。该批案件后因管辖争议而移送至上海知识产权法院审理。因此，就诉争 8 项专利的技术获取、专利申请行为侵害高原汽车公司商业秘密的警告，高原汽车公司已在催告时间之前提起诉讼。据此，一审法院裁定驳回威马三公司的起诉。威马三公司不服，向最高人民法院提起上诉，请求撤销原裁定，责令一审法院继续审理。威马成都公司、威马集团公司主张，催告函涉及 8 项专利，上海知识产权法院仅立案受理高原汽车公司对其中 7 项专利的专利权或专利申请权权属提起的诉讼（以下简称上知系列案），高原汽车公司对 961.7 号专利并未提起诉讼，且上知系列案审理范围无法覆盖本案。上知系列案的案由为专利权或专利申请权权属纠纷，而本案系侵害商业秘密纠纷的确认不侵害知识产权纠纷，属侵权纠纷，两者性质及案由不同。威马上海公司除威马成都公司、威马集团公司前述提及的理由外，还认为上知系列案中威马上海公司并非案件当事人，因此，即使上知系列案与本案所涉及的专利存在部分重合，仍无法解决威马上海公司关于催告函中涉及的 8 项专利权利不稳定及威马上海公司不侵权的主张。最高人民法院于 2022 年 6 月 10 日裁定维持原裁定。

In the dispute over confirmation of non-infringement of intellectual property rights among the Appellants, WM Zhongde Automotive Technology Chengdu Co., Ltd. (hereinafter referred to as "WM Chengdu"), WM Motor Holdings Limited (hereinafter referred to as "WM Group"), WM Smart Mobility Technology (Shanghai) Co., Ltd. (hereinafter referred to as "WM Shanghai"), and the Appellee, Chengdu Gaoyuan Automobile Industry Co., Ltd. (hereinafter referred to as "Gaoyuan Automobile"), WM Chengdu, WM Group, and WM Shanghai (hereinafter referred to as the "Three WM Companies") claimed that in October 2018, Gaoyuan Automobile filed a lawsuit with the Sichuan High People's Court claiming that the eight patents applied for by WM Chengdu were patents obtained by its former employees using the technical secrets they had acquired during their employment with Gaoyuan Automobile, and claimed that WM Chengdu infringed on its trade secrets, which was the case of (2018) CMC No. 121 (hereinafter referred to as "Case 121"). Among them, patent No. 201610634961.7 (hereinafter referred to as Patent 961.7) was rejected for filing on November 15, 2019, by the China National Intellectual Property Administration. After the case was filed, Gaoyuan Automobile successively added WM Group and WM Shanghai as defendants in the case and submitted additional exhibits involving 33 patents of the Three WM Companies. Among which Patent No. 201620823420.4 (hereinafter referred

to as Patent 420. 4) was waived by WM Group in order to avoid duplicate licenses. Gaoyuan Automobile withdrew the case after the trial of Case 121, which made its intention of whether to exercise the right of action return to a state of uncertainty and also led to a state of uncertainty as to whether the Three WM Companies had infringed on its trade secrets, thus seriously affecting normal production and operation. The Three WM Companies mailed a reminder letter to Gaoyuan Automobile on January 10, 2020 to remind Gaoyuan Automobile in writing to clarify its true intention and to exercise its right to sue, but it did not make any response after one month of signing and receiving the reminder letter, and therefore, the Three WM Companies filed a lawsuit with the Chengdu Intermediate People's Court of Sichuan Province (hereinafter referred to as the "Court of First Instance") requesting an order to the effect that Gaoyuan Automobile did not have any rights to the trade secrets claimed by it in Case 121, and that the Three WM Companies had not committed acts of unfair competition infringing on Gaoyuan Automobile's trade secrets or infringed on any of the rights of Gaoyuan Automobile, i. e., the 41 patents filed by the Three WM Companies had not infringed on the 10 technical secrets claimed by Gaoyuan Automobile in Case 121. The Court of First Instance found that Gaoyuan Automobile and its affiliates filed 42 patent right ownership disputes with the Hangzhou Intermediate People's Court of Zhejiang Province on or about May 16, 2019 in respect of the aforesaid 8 patents and 34 other patents prior to the filing of this case, requesting confirmation of the aforesaid patent application rights or patent rights to be vested in Gaoyuan Automobile and its affiliates based on the fact that the Three WM Companies and its employees unlawfully obtained technical data and information and thus applied for patents. The cases were later transferred to the Shanghai Intellectual Property Court (hereinafter referred to as the SIPC) due to jurisdictional disputes. Therefore, in respect of the technology acquisition of the 8 patents in dispute and the warning of infringement of Gaoyuan Automobile's trade secrets by the patent application, Gaoyuan Automobile had filed a lawsuit before the time of the demand. Accordingly, the Court of First Instance ruled to dismiss the suits filed by the Three WM Companies. Unsatisfied, the Three WM Companies filed an appeal to the SPC, requesting that the original decision be revoked and the Court of First Instance be ordered to continue with the trial. WM Chengdu and WM Group claimed that the demand letter involved 8 patents, and the SIPC only accepted the lawsuits filed by Gaoyuan Automobile in respect of the ownership of the patent right or patent application right of 7 patents (hereinafter referred to as the SIPC' s Series Cases), and Gaoyuan Automobile did not file any lawsuit in respect of Patent 961. 7. Moreover, the trial scope of the SIPC' s Series Cases could not cover the present case. The causes of action in the SIPC' s Series Cases were disputes over the ownership of patents or patent application rights, whereas the present case was a dispute over the confirmation of non-infringement of intellectual property rights in a case of dispute over infringement of trade secrets, which is a dispute over infringement of intellectual property rights, and they are different in natures and causes of action. WM Shanghai, in addition to the reasons previously mentioned by WM Chengdu and WM Group, argued that WM Shanghai was not a party to the case in the SIPC' s Series Cases, and therefore, even if there was a partial overlap between the patents in the SIPC' s Series Cases and the patents involved in the present case, it still could not resolve WM Shanghai's claims that the rights in the eight patents involved in the demand were unstable and that WM Shanghai was not infringing the rights in the eight patents. The SPC ruled on June 10, 2022 to uphold the original ruling.

【裁判意见】

[Judge's Opinion]

最高人民法院二审认为，《最高人民法院关于知识产权民事诉讼证据的若干规定》第五条规定："提起确认不侵害知识产权之诉的原告应当举证证明下列事实：(一) 被告向原告发出侵权警告或者对原告进行侵权投诉；(二) 原告向被告发出诉权行使催告及催告时间、送达时间；(三) 被告未在合理期限内提起诉讼。" 为了平衡和保障知识产权权利人和被警告人的合法权益，允许被警告人在满足一定条件下，提起确认不侵权之诉，既是为了促使权利人尽快行使权利，避免双方知识产权纠纷长期处于不确定状态，也是为了尽量减少因知识产权权利人滥用权利给被警告的合法经营者增加负担。基于此，提起确认不侵害知识产权之诉，除了要满足民事诉讼法规定的起诉条件外，原告还必须提供初步证据证明《最高人民法院关于知识产权民事诉讼证据的若干规定》第五条限定的三项特别条件，缺少任何一项条件，提起确认不侵害知识产权之诉均不应当被受理。

The SPC held in the Second Instance that Article 5 of the *Several Provisions of the SPC on Evidence in Civil Procedures Involving Intellectual Property Rights* stipulates that "the plaintiff filing a lawsuit for confirmation of non-infringement of intellectual property rights shall adduce evidence to prove the following facts: (i) the defendant has warned the plaintiff of the infringement of the intellectual property rights or has made a complaint of infringement of the intellectual property rights against the plaintiff; (ii) the plaintiff has issued a demand to the defendant for exercising the right of action and the time of the demand and time of the service of the demand; (iii) the defendant has not instituted a lawsuit within a reasonable period of time." In order to balance and safeguard the legitimate rights and interests of intellectual property right holders and warned persons, the warned persons are allowed to file a lawsuit for confirmation of non-infringement if certain conditions are met, not only to prompt the right holders to exercise their rights as soon as possible, to avoid a long-term state of uncertainty of intellectual property disputes between the two parties, but also to minimize the burden added to the warned lawful operators due to the abuse of rights by the intellectual property right holders. Based on this, to file a lawsuit for confirmation of non-infringement of intellectual property rights, in addition to meeting the conditions for filing a lawsuit stipulated in the Civil Procedure Law, the plaintiff must also provide prima facie evidence to prove the three special conditions limited by the aforementioned Article 5 of the *Several Provisions of the SPC on Evidence in Civil Procedures Involving Intellectual Property Rights*, and in the absence of any one of these conditions, the filing of a lawsuit for confirmation of non-infringement of intellectual property rights shall not be admitted.

本案中，威马三公司已经举证证明其收到了高原汽车公司的侵权警告，且威马三公司已经向高原汽车公司发出诉权行使催告。

In this case, the Three WM Companies had already proved that it had received warnings of infringement from Gaoyuan Automobile, and the Three WM Companies had already sent a demand of exercising its right of action to Gaoyuan Automobile.

关于高原汽车公司是否在合理期限内提起诉讼，二审法院认为，首先，审查判断《最高人民法院关于知识产权民事诉讼证据的若干规定》第五条第三项规定的“被告未在合理期限内提起诉讼”要件，应当充分考量知识产权的无形财产权特性对于侵权行为证据发现和维权诉讼方式选择的深刻影响。其中，对于“合理期限”的判断，应当根据知识产权权利客体类型等案件具体情况，充分考量侵权行为证据发现的难易程度和诉讼准备所需时间等因素予以确定。对于“提起诉讼”的判断，应当包含可以实质解决双方争议、消除被警告人不安状态的所有诉讼形

式，如因侵害知识产权之诉和确认知识产权权利归属之诉，均以判断权利归属基础法律关系为前提，故，如果权利人提起的确权之诉涵盖了侵权警告中涉及的相关知识产权客体，则应当认定权利人已经“提起诉讼”。其次，根据在案事实，高原汽车公司无论2018年10月12日在四川高院提起121号侵害商业秘密诉讼，还是在2019年5月16日前后，向浙江省杭州市中级人民法院提起42件专利申请权或者专利权权属纠纷，均系基于高原汽车公司认为威马三公司及其相关员工等申请相关专利的行为侵害了高原汽车公司的技术秘密。显然，121号案件的审理范围和后续42件专利申请权或者专利权权属纠纷案件审理范围均以审查判断相关技术成果归属基础法律关系为前提。因此，高原汽车公司虽然撤回了121号案件的起诉，但保留了相关专利申请权或者专利权权属纠纷案件的起诉，且高原汽车公司提起相关专利申请权或者专利权权属纠纷的时间早于威马三公司发出催告函的时间，故应当认定高原汽车公司已经在发出警告后在合理期限内提起诉讼。再次，关于121号案件中高原汽车公司提起诉讼时明确主张权利的961.7号专利所涉相关技术方案，因高原汽车公司目前提起的专利申请权或者专利权权属纠纷未予涉及，威马三公司是否有权提起确认本案不侵害知识产权之诉的问题，因高原汽车公司针对121号案件第一次主张权利的8项专利中的7项提起专利权权属纠纷诉讼时，国家知识产权局驳回961.7号专利申请决定已经生效，高原汽车公司未就961.7号专利技术方案提起相关专利申请权权属纠纷诉讼，可以视为高原汽车公司已经撤回针对961.7号专利所涉技术方案的侵权警告。因此，威马三公司针对961.7号专利所涉技术方案不具备提起确认不侵权诉讼的条件。最后，关于121号案件起诉后高原汽车公司扩大主张权利范围涉及的其余33项专利，威马三公司是否有权提起确认不侵权之诉的问题，对于其中所涉及的420.4号专利，因威马集团公司为避免重复授权放弃专利权，专利权已经失效，高原汽车公司未就该项专利提起相关专利权权属纠纷诉讼，可以视为高原汽车公司已经撤回针对该专利所涉技术方案的侵权警告。对于其余32项专利，根据在案证据，高原汽车公司均已在威马三公司提起本案诉讼前向上海知识产权法院、上海市高级人民法院提起相关专利权权属纠纷诉讼，故威马三公司针对121号案件涉及的其余33项专利所涉技术方案亦不具备提起确认不侵权诉讼的条件。综上所述，威马三公司提起本案确认不侵害知识产权之诉，不符合《最高人民法院关于知识产权民事诉讼证据的若干规定》第五条规定的起诉条件，一审法院裁定驳回威马三公司的起诉，并无不当。

Regarding whether Gaoyuan Automobile filed a lawsuit within a reasonable period, the Court of Second Instance held that, firstly when examining and judging the element of "the defendant's failure to file a lawsuit within a reasonable period of time" stipulated in Item 3 of Article 5 of the *Several Provisions of the SPC on Evidence in Civil Procedures Involving Intellectual Property Rights*, full consideration should be given to the profound impact of the characteristics of intangible property rights of intellectual property rights on the discovery of evidence of infringement and the choice of litigation methods for the protection of rights. Among them, for the judgment of a "reasonable period", it should be determined according to the specific circumstances of the case, such as the type of intellectual property right object, taking into full consideration the difficulty of discovering the evidence of infringement and the time required for the preparation of the litigation, and other factors. The judgment of "filing a lawsuit" should include all forms of litigation that can substantially resolve the dispute between the two parties and eliminate the uneasy state of the person being warned, such as the lawsuit on infringement of intellectual property rights and the lawsuit on confirmation of ownership of intellectual property rights, both of which are based on the premise of judging the underlying legal relationship of ownership of the rights, so, if the right holder

has filed a lawsuit for confirmation of rights covering the relevant intellectual property objects involved in the infringement warnings, the right holder should be recognized as having "filed a lawsuit". Secondly, according to the facts of the case, whether Gaoyuan Automobile filed Case 121 on infringement of trade secrets in the Sichuan High People's Court on October 12, 2018, or filed the case in the Hangzhou Intermediate People's Court of Zhejiang Province on or about May 16, 2019, involving disputes over the ownership of 42 patent applications rights or patents, all of them were based on Gaoyuan Automobile's belief that the Three WM Companies' and its relevant employees' applications for the relevant patents infringed on Gaoyuan Automobile's technical secrets. Obviously, the trial scope of Case 121 and the trial scope of the subsequent dispute over the ownership of 42 patent applications or patent rights are premised on the examination and judgment of the basic legal relationship of the ownership of the relevant technical achievements. Therefore, although Gaoyuan Automobile withdrew the prosecution of Case 121, it retained the prosecution on the disputes over the ownership of the relevant patent applications or patents, and the time when Gaoyuan Automobile filed the disputes over the ownership of the relevant patent applications or patents was earlier than the time when the Three WM Companies sent out the demand letter, and therefore it should be recognized that Gaoyuan Automobile had filed the lawsuit within a reasonable period after sending out the warnings. Thirdly, as the dispute over the ownership of the patent application right or patent right filed by Gaoyuan Automobile did not involve the relevant technical solutions of Patent 961. 7, which was explicitly claimed by Gaoyuan Automobile when it filed the lawsuit in Case 121, as to whether the Three WM Companies have the right to file a lawsuit on confirmation of non-infringement of intellectual property rights in the present case, it can be considered that Gaoyuan Automobile has withdrawn the infringement warning against the technical solution covered by Patent 961. 7 as the decision of the China National Intellectual Property Administration to reject the application of Patent 961. 7 had already come into effect when it filed a lawsuit on the ownership dispute over 7 out of the 8 patents claimed by Gaoyuan Automobile for the first time in Case 121 and Gaoyuan Automobile did not file a lawsuit on the ownership dispute over the patent application in respect of the technical solutions of Patent 961. 7. Therefore, the Three WM Companies do not have the conditions for filing a lawsuit for confirmation of non-infringement with respect to the technical solutions covered by Patent 961. 7. Finally, regarding whether the Three WM Companies have the right to file a lawsuit for confirmation of non-infringement on the remaining 33 patents involved in the expansion of the scope of rights claimed by Gaoyuan Automobile after the filing of Case 121, with regard to Patent 420. 4 involved therein, it can be considered that Gaoyuan Automobile has withdrawn the warning of infringement against the technical solution involved in the patent, as the patent right has lapsed due to the abandonment of the patent right by WM Group in order to avoid duplicate licenses, and Gaoyuan Automobile has not filed a lawsuit concerning patent ownership disputes in connection with the patent. For the remaining 32 patents, according to the evidence in the case, Gaoyuan Automobile had filed lawsuits with Shanghai Intellectual Property Court and Shanghai High People's Court for patent ownership disputes before the Three WM Companies filed the present lawsuit, and therefore, the Three WM Companies did not have the conditions to file lawsuits for confirmation of non-infringement upon technical solutions covered by the remaining 33 patents involved in Case 121. To sum up, the Three WM Companies' filing of this lawsuit for confirmation of non-infringement of intellectual property rights did not meet the conditions for filing a lawsuit as stipulated in Article 5 of the *Several*

Provisions of the SPC on Evidence in Civil Procedures Involving Intellectual Property Rights, and there was nothing improper that the Court of First Instance ruled to dismiss the lawsuit filed by the Three WM Companies.

39. 权属争议期间登记的 PCT 申请人的善良管理义务 Bona-fide management obligations of PCT applicant registered during the dispute over patent application ownership

【裁判要旨】

[Judgment Digest]

PCT 申请权权属争议期间，登记的 PCT 申请人无正当理由未尽善良管理义务，致使 PCT 申请效力终止的，应当对实际权利人承担赔偿损失的民事责任；实际权利人亦有过错的，可以酌减赔偿数额。

If during the dispute over PCT application ownership, the registered PCT applicant fails to perform bona-fide management obligations without justifiable reasons, resulting in termination of the validity of the PCT application, then the PCT applicant should bear the civil liability for compensation of losses to the actual right holder; if the actual right holder is of contributory negligence, the compensation amount may be reduced at discretion.

【关键词】

[Keywords]

PCT 申请　权属争议　诚信原则　善良管理人义务

PCT applications; disputes over ownership; principle of good faith; obligations of bona-fide managers

【案号】

[Case Number]

(2022)最高法知民终 130 号

(2022)SPC IP Civil Final 130

【基本案情】

[Case Facts]

在上诉人古某文、周某荣与被上诉人漳州灿坤实业有限公司(以下简称灿坤公司)、原审被告张某华知识产权损害赔偿纠纷案中,涉及申请号为 PCT/CN2016/071553 的 PCT 申请。该 PCT 申请国际申请日为 2016 年 1 月 21 日、国际公布日为 2017 年 7 月 20 日,其中国优先权专利系专利号为 201620021160.9、名称为“一种自动胶囊面包机”的实用新型专利(以下简称涉案优先权专利)。涉案 PCT 申请的中国优先权专利发明人张某华原系灿坤公司技术人员,其于 2015 年 3 月 10 日自灿坤公司离职后入职辉胜达公司,2016 年 1 月 12 日以辉胜达公司为专利权人申请了涉案优先权专利,2016 年 1 月 21 日以该专利为优先权提交了涉案 PCT 申请,国际检索单位(国家知识产权局)经检索于 2016 年 9 月 21 日出具书面意见认为涉案 PCT 申请全部权利要求(权利要求 1-8)不具有创造性。2016 年 11 月 10 日,辉胜达公司申请清算备案登记,并于 2017 年 5 月 26 日完成注销,清算组成员为其时的股东古某文、周某荣。2017 年 1 月 12 日,灿坤公司起诉涉案优先权专利归其所有,广州知识产权法院作出(2017)粤 73 民初 226 号判决,认定涉案优先权专利归灿坤公司,该判决于 2017 年 11 月 16 日生效,古某文、周某荣此后未对涉案 PCT 申请作出任何处理。2017 年 12 月 8 日,灿坤公司继续就涉案 PCT 申请权属提起诉讼,案件审理期间,涉案 PCT 申请进入国家阶段的期限届满,各方当事人在此过程中均未采取任何措施,2018 年 9 月 13 日广州知识产权法院作出(2017)粤 73 民初 4546 号判决,认定涉案 PCT 申请归灿坤公司。至此,涉案 PCT 申请登记的

申请人为辉胜达公司，实际权利人为灿坤公司。

The case of dispute over intellectual property damages among the Appellants, Gu and Zhou, and the Appellee, Tsann Kuen (Zhangzhou) Enterprise Co., Ltd. (hereinafter referred to as "Tsann Kuen"), and the Defendant of First Instance, Zhang, involves the PCT application with application No. PCT/CN2016/071553. The international filing date of the PCT application is January 21, 2016, and the international publication date is July 20, 2017, and its Chinese priority patent is utility model patent No. 201620021160.9, entitled "a kind of automatic capsule toaster" (hereinafter referred to as the priority patent in question). Zhang, the inventor of the Chinese priority patent of the PCT application in question, was originally a technician of Tsann Kuen, and he joined Huishengda after leaving Tsann Kuen on March 10, 2015, and applied for the priority patent in question on January 12, 2016 with Huishengda as the patentee, and filed the PCT application in question with the priority of the patent on January 21, 2016, which was searched by an international searching authority (China National Intellectual Property Administration) by issuing a written opinion on September 21, 2016 that all the Claims of the PCT application in question (Claims 1-8) were not inventive. On November 10, 2016, Huishengda applied for liquidation filing and registration, and completed the cancellation on May 26, 2017, and the members of the liquidation group were its shareholders at that time, Gu and Zhou. On January 12, 2017, Tsann Kuen sued and claimed that the priority patent in question belonged to it, and the Guangzhou Intellectual Property Court rendered a judgment of (2017) Y73 MC No. 226, finding that the priority patent in question belonged to Tsann Kuen, which came into effect on November 16, 2017, and Gu and Zhou have not made any disposition of the PCT application in question since then. On December 8, 2017, Tsann Kuen continued to file a lawsuit for the ownership of the PCT application in question, and during the trial of the case, the deadline for the PCT application in question to enter the national phase expired, and all parties involved did not take any measures during the process, and on September 13, 2018, the Guangzhou Intellectual Property Court rendered the judgment of (2017) Y73 MC No. 4546, finding that the PCT application in question belonged to Tsann Kuen. So far, the applicant registered in the PCT application in question is Huishengda, and the actual right holder is Tsann Kuen.

灿坤公司认为，古某文、周某荣作为辉胜达公司的股东及清算组成员，在明知涉案 PCT 申请权应归属于灿坤公司的情况下，未给予任何书面通知，其清算行为严重违反清算程序，并导致涉案 PCT 申请失效，给灿坤公司造成无法挽回的损失。故向广东省深圳市中级人民法院（以下简称一审法院）提起诉讼，请求判令古某文、周某荣、张某华连带承担因其未履行义务致使涉案 PCT 申请权利终止造成灿坤公司的经济损失 100 万元。一审法院认为，PCT 申请对应可能存在的外国或其他地区专利局的专利授权，故 PCT 申请人对此享有一定的利益。在辉胜达公司注销前，法院的一审判决已认定涉案 PCT 申请据以登记优先权的涉案优先权专利归灿坤公司所有。古某文、周某荣对此未采取任何措施，主观上存有过错。同时，鉴于国际检索单位对涉案 PCT 申请全部权利要求的创造性持否定意见，亦存在不利于涉案 PCT 申请的较大可能性。酌情确定古某文、周某荣赔偿灿坤公司利益受损及维权支出共计 5 万元。古某文、周某荣不服，向最高人民法院提起上诉。最高人民法院于 2022 年 6 月 22 日判决驳回上诉，维持原判。

Tsann Kuen considered that Gu and Zhou, as the shareholders and members of the liquidation group of Huishengda, did not give any written notice when they knew that the rights of the PCT application in question should be attributed to Tsann Kuen, and their liquidation behaviors seriously violated the

liquidation procedures and led to the invalidation of the PCT application in question, which caused irreparable losses to Tsann Kuen. Therefore, it filed a lawsuit with Shenzhen Intermediate People's Court of Guangdong Province (hereinafter referred to as the Court of First Instance), requesting to order Gu, Zhou, and Zhang to jointly and severally bear the economic loss of CNY 1 million incurred by Tsann Kuen due to the termination of the right of the PCT application because of their failure to fulfill their obligations. The Court of First Instance held that the PCT application corresponds to the patent authorization of foreign countries or other regional patent offices that may exist, so the PCT applicant enjoys certain benefits. Before the cancellation of Huishengda, the court's first instance judgment determined that the priority patent on which the priority of the PCT application is registered belonged to Tsann Kuen. Gu and Zhou did not take any measures in this regard, which was subjectively at fault. At the same time, in view of that the international searching authority held a negative opinion on the inventive step of all the claims of the PCT application, there is also a greater possibility of being unfavorable to the PCT application. It was determined as appropriate that Gu and Zhou compensated a total of CNY 50, 000 for the damage to Tsann Kuen's interests and expenses for the defense of its rights. Unsatisfied, Gu and Zhou filed an appeal to the SPC. The SPC rejected the appeal on June 22, 2022, and upheld the original judgment.

【裁判意见】

[Judge's Opinion]

最高人民法院二审认为，PCT 申请分为国际阶段和国家阶段两个独立的阶段，PCT 申请是否进入国家阶段取决于申请人的意志。灿坤公司提出涉案优先权专利权属纠纷时，涉案 PCT 申请还未进行国际公布，古某文、周某荣应当预见到因涉案优先权专利权属争议，涉案 PCT 申请情况直接影响灿坤公司权益，涉案 PCT 申请是否进入国家阶段，已不属于辉胜达公司可以任意处置的事项。基于辉胜达公司申请涉案优先权专利以及涉案 PCT 申请的在先行为，根据诚信原则，在辉胜达公司进入清算期间，古某文、周某荣作为清算组成员应承担登记的涉案 PCT 申请人负有的善良管理人义务，善意及时履行基于诚信原则所产生的通知、协助、保护等义务，避免涉案 PCT 申请在灿坤公司不知情的情况下效力终止。古某文、周某荣违反诚信原则，未履行善良管理人之义务，未通知灿坤公司涉案 PCT 申请信息，存在过错。

The SPC held in the Second Instance that the PCT application is divided into two independent phases, namely, the international phase and the national phase, and whether the PCT application enters the national stage depends on the will of the applicant. When Tsann Kuen proposed the dispute over the ownership of the priority patent in question, the PCT application in question had not been published internationally, and Gu and Zhou should have foreseen that because of the dispute over the ownership of the priority patent in question, the situation of the PCT application in question had a direct impact on the rights and interests of Tsann Kuen, and the question of whether the PCT application in question had entered into the national phase no longer belonged to the matters that Huishengda could dispose at its discretion. Based on the prior behavior of Huishengda's application for the priority patent and the PCT application, according to the principle of good faith, during the liquidation of Huishengda, Gu and Zhou, as the members of the liquidation group, should undertake the obligations of bona-fide managers to be bound by the registered applicant of the PCT application, and perform the obligations of notification, assistance, and protection based on the principle of good faith in a timely manner, so as to avoid the termination of the effectiveness of the PCT application concerned in the absence of knowledge of Tsann Kuen. Gu and Zhou were

at fault for violating the principle of good faith, failing to fulfill the obligations of bona fide managers, and failing to notify Tsann Kuen of the information of the PCT application in question.

国际初步审查单位对涉案 PCT 申请的全部权利要求无创造性的评价意见，并不必然导致该 PCT 申请进入特定国家的国家阶段后无授权可能性。对于涉案 PCT 申请而言，在该申请的效力终止前，灿坤公司具有合理的尚可期待的授权可能性。由于涉案 PCT 申请的效力终止，致使灿坤公司可期待的授权可能性确定地归于消灭，构成对灿坤公司利益的损害。

The opinion of the international preliminary examination authority that all the Claims of the PCT application in question are not inventive does not necessarily result in the PCT application having no possibility of authorization after it enters the national phase of a particular country. For the PCT application in question, before the termination of the validity of the application, Tsann Kuen had a reasonable possibility of authorization that could still be expected. Due to the termination of the PCT application, the possibility of authorization that Tsann Kuen can expect is definitively eliminated, which constitutes the damage to the interests of Tsann Kuen.

涉案 PCT 申请人为辉胜达公司，在涉案 PCT 申请权未经生效判决确认归属于灿坤公司之前，灿坤公司无法以自己名义决定是否进入国家阶段。古某文、周某荣作为辉胜达公司的清算组成员，应当合理预期涉案 PCT 申请的申请人未依 PCT 行政规程有效变更前，灿坤公司拟推进涉案 PCT 申请进入国家阶段需要以原申请人的名义进行，古某文、周某荣未及时通知灿坤公司涉案 PCT 申请信息，是灿坤公司未能及时推进涉案 PCT 申请进入国家阶段的主要原因。除申请人告知涉案 PCT 申请的信息这一渠道外，灿坤公司也可以从有关公开渠道获得涉案 PCT 申请的信息。灿坤公司因对 PCT 申请的申请人变更的误解，未及时寻求 PCT 规则下直接变更涉案 PCT 申请人的救济方式，是涉案 PCT 申请未能进入国家阶段的次要原因。灿坤公司对涉案 PCT 申请效力终止造成的损失亦负有一定责任，因此可以减轻古某文、周某荣应当承担的责任。

The applicant of the PCT application was Huishengda, and before the PCT application right was confirmed to belong to Tsann Kuen by the effective judgment, Tsann Kuen could not decide whether to enter the national phase in its own name. As members of the liquidation group of Huishengda, Gu and Zhou should have reasonably expected that before the applicant of the PCT application was effectively changed in accordance with the PCT administrative procedures, Tsann Kuen was required to proceed in the name of the original applicant for the purpose of advancing the PCT application into the national phase, and the failure of Gu and Zhou to notify Tsann Kuen of the information of the PCT application in question was the main reason why Tsann Kuen failed to promote the PCT application in question to enter into the national phase. In addition to the channel of the applicant informing the information about the PCT application, Tsann Kuen can also obtain the information about the PCT application from the relevant public channels. Due to the misunderstanding of the change of the applicant of the PCT application, Tsann Kuen did not seek the remedy of direct change of the applicant of the PCT application under the PCT Rules in time, which is the secondary reason for the failure of the PCT application to enter the national phase. Tsann Kuen was also liable for the loss caused by the termination of the validity of the PCT application in question, and therefore, the liabilities borne by Gu and Zhou could be reduced accordingly.

40. 职务发明创造权属纠纷中发明人确认之诉和权属之诉的并案审理

Merged trial of cases on inventor confirmation and patent ownership concerning service invention

【裁判要旨】

[Judgment Digest]

职务发明创造专利权或者专利申请权权属纠纷的原告同时提出确认发明人之诉，有关发明人均参与诉讼的，人民法院可以在一案中一并审理，也可以分立两案但作合并审理。

If the plaintiffs in disputes over the ownership of patents or patent applications concerning service inventions also file a lawsuit for inventor confirmation at the same time, and all the inventors in question happen to participate in the lawsuit, then people's courts may merge these two lawsuits into one case, or alternatively merge the trials while keeping two cases separately filed.

【关键词】

[Keywords]

专利权权属　发明人　职务发明创造　合并审理

Patent ownership; inventor; service invention and creation; joint trial.

【案号】

[Case Number]

(2021) 最高法知民终 2146 号

(2021) SPC IP Civil Final 2146

【基本案情】

[Case Facts]

在上诉人广州万孚生物技术股份有限公司（以下简称万孚公司）、

杨某、赖某强与被上诉人深圳市理邦精密仪器股份有限公司（以下简称理邦公司）、原审被告王某华、朱某华专利权权属纠纷案中，涉及专利号为201620275714.8、名称为“血气分析仪及其血气生化测试卡”的实用新型专利（以下简称涉案专利）。理邦公司认为，涉案专利文件记载的发明人王某华、朱某华均不是涉案专利的实际发明人，涉案专利的发明人为杨某、赖某强，涉案专利系杨某、赖某强与理邦公司终止劳动关系后一年内作出的，与杨某、赖某强在理邦公司的本职工作有关的发明创造，属于职务发明创造，涉案专利权应归属理邦公司。故向广州知识产权法院（以下简称一审法院）提起诉讼，请求确认涉案专利权属于理邦公司，确认杨某、赖某强为涉案专利的发明人。一审法院判决认定，涉案专利发明人是杨某、赖某强，属于职务发明创造，涉案专利权应归属于理邦公司。万孚公司、杨某、赖某强不服，向最高人民法院提起上诉，主张杨某、赖某强不是涉案专利的发明人，该二人在理邦公司的工作与涉案专利不相关。涉案专利的发明人至少应当包括卢某辉、谢某开。因此，涉案专利至少应由万孚公司与理邦公司共有。最高人民法院于2022年12月10日判决驳回上诉，维持原判。

The case of dispute over patent ownership among the Appellants, Guangzhou Wondfo Biotech Co., Ltd. (hereinafter referred to as Wondfo), Yang, and Lai, and the Appellees, Edan Instruments, Inc. (hereinafter referred to as Edan), and the Defendants in the first instance, Wang and Zhu, involves utility model patent No. 201620275714.8, entitled “Blood gas analyzer and its biochemistry test card” (hereinafter referred to as the patent in question). Edan considered that the inventors Wang and Zhu recorded in the documents of the patent in question were not the actual inventors of the patent in question, and the inventors of the patent in question were Yang and Lai, who made the patent in question one year after the termination of the labor relationship with Edan and the inventions related to Yang and Lai's work in Edan be-

longed to the service inventions, and the right of the patent in question should be attributed to Edan. Therefore, they filed a lawsuit with Guangzhou Intellectual Property Court (hereinafter referred to as the Court of First Instance), requesting to confirm that the right of patent in question belonged to Edan, and that Yang and Lai be recognized as the inventors of the patent in question. The judgment of the Court of First Instance held that the inventors of the patent in question were Yang and Lai and that the patent in question should be attributed to Edan as a result of their job-related inventions. Wondfo, Yang, and Lai appealed to the SPC, claiming that Yang and Lai were not the inventors of the patent in question, and that their work in Edan was not related to the patent in question. The inventors of the patent in question should at least include Lu and Xie. Therefore, the patent in question should be jointly owned by at least Wondfo and Edan. The SPC ruled on December 10, 2022 that the appeal was rejected and the original judgment was upheld.

【裁判意见】

[Judge's Opinion]

最高人民法院二审认为，关于理邦公司能否同时提出确认涉案专利发明人的诉讼请求。首先，在职务发明创造专利（申请）权权属纠纷案件中，确认原告是否享有发明创造的专利（申请）权，应首先确认发明创造的发明人，在此基础上，才能对发明创造的权利归属作出认定，发明人的确认直接影响发明创造的权利归属。因此，原告关于发明创造专利权利归属的主张与发明人的确认具有直接关联关系。其次，基于确认发明创造发明人与确认专利（申请）权归属之间的直接关联关系，允许原告同时提出确认发明创造发明人的诉讼请求，有利于查明案件事实，有效解决纠纷，避免分案审理可能出现的裁判冲突。因此，在专利（申请）权权属纠纷案件中，原告可以同时提出确认发明人的诉讼请求。本案中，理邦公司同时提出确认涉案专利发明人的诉讼请求，一审法院将其与涉案专利权属的诉讼请求合并审理，程序并不违法，处理结果正确，应予维持。

The SPC held in the Second Instance that, with regard to whether Edan could simultaneously claim confirmation of the inventor of the patent in question, firstly, in the case of disputes over the patent (application) ownership of service inventions and creations, to confirm whether the Plaintiff enjoys the patent (application) rights of the inventions and creations, the inventor of the inventions and creations should first be confirmed, and only on this basis can a determination be made on the attribution of rights to inventions and creations, and the confirmation of the inventor has a direct impact on the attribution of rights to the inventions and creations. Therefore, the plaintiff's claim on the attribution of patent rights of inventions and creations is directly related to the confirmation of the inventor. Secondly, based on the direct correlation between the confirmation of the inventor of the inventions or creations and the confirmation of the attribution of the patent (application) right, the plaintiff is permitted to simultaneously make a claim for confirmation of the inventor of the inventions or creations, which is conducive to the ascertainment of the facts of the case to effectively resolve the disputes and to avoid possible conflicts of decision in the separate trials. Therefore, in the case of dispute over the patent (application) ownership, the plaintiff can simultaneously make a claim for confirmation of the inventor. In the present case, Edan made a claim for confirmation of the inventor of the patent in question at the same time, and the Court of First Instance consolidated the claim with the claim of the ownership of the patent in question, which was not illegal in the procedure, with correct results, and should be upheld.

41. 职务发明创造发明人奖励报酬支付主体的确定 Determination on who to pay rewards and remunerations to inventors of service invention

【裁判要旨】

[Judgment Digest]

用人单位应当承担支付职务发明创造发明人报酬的义务。职务发明创造发明人请求支付奖励、报酬的权利，不应当因用人单位对职务发明创造的专利申请权或者专利权的处分而受到损害。专利申请权或者专利权的转让不影响用人单位承担支付职务发明创造发明人报酬的义务。

The employer should bear the obligation to pay remuneration to inventors of service invention. The inventor's right to request for such payment should not be impaired by the disposal of the employer's right to file patent application for service invention or the involved patent. The transfer of the right to file the patent application or the involved patent should not affect the employer's obligation to pay remuneration to the inventor of service invention.

【关键词】

[Keywords]

职务发明创造　发明人报酬　被授予专利权的单位　权利转让

Service inventions and creations; inventor's remuneration; employers granted patent rights; transfer of rights

【案号】

[Case Number]

（2021）最高法知民终1172号

（2021）SPC IP Civil Final 1172

【基本案情】

[Case Facts]

在上诉人张某良与上诉人天津狗不理食品股份有限公司（以下简称狗不理食品公司）、被上诉人狗不理集团股份有限公司（以下简称狗不理集团公司）职务发明创造发明人报酬纠纷案中，涉及专利号为200910069864.8、名称为“生物保鲜包馅面食制品的制备方法”的发明专利（以下简称涉案专利）。张某良认为，张某良参与了涉案专利的研发，是涉案专利的发明人，狗不理食品公司、狗不理集团公司实施了涉案专利，应向张某良支付2009年至2016年的发明人报酬，故向天津市第三中级人民法院（以下简称一审法院）提起诉讼，请求判令：狗不理食品公司、狗不理集团公司支付张某良2009年至2016年的研发专利报酬214万元（年利润535万元×5%×8年）。一审法院认为，虽然涉案专利权人为狗不理集团，但是系张某良在狗不理食品公司工作期间，在完成本职工作任务中做出的发明创造，属于职务发明创造。专利法所称的被授予专利权的单位，应理解为本应进行申请并获得专利权的单位。支付职务发明报酬主体的应当是发明人的用人单位，而非是通过受让等其他方式获得专利申请权或专利权的主体。而且，涉案专利的实施者系狗不理食品公司，而非狗不理集团公司。因此，狗不理食品公司应当向张某良支付职务发明创造发明人报酬。张某良关于狗不理集团公司应当支付报酬的主张缺乏事实和法律依据，一审法院不予支持。张某良、狗不理食品公司均不服，向最高人民法院提起上诉，张某良主张狗不理食品公司、狗不理集团公司应支付张某良职务发明创造发明人报酬85.6万元。狗不理食品公司主张，狗不理食品公司不享有涉案专利申请权和专利权，不属于负有支付发明人报酬义务的“被授予专利权的单位”。最高人民法院于2022年9月29日判决驳回上诉，维持原判。

The case of dispute over the remuneration of inventors of service inventions and creations between the Appellants, Zhang and Tianjin Go Believe

Food Co., Ltd. (hereinafter referred to as Go Believe Food), and the Appellee, Go Believe Group Co., Ltd. (hereinafter referred to as Go Believe Food Group), involves a patent for invention, No. 200910069864. 8, entitled "Preparation Method of Bio-preserved Stuffed Flour Products" (hereinafter referred to as the patent in question). Zhang believed that Zhang had participated in the research and development of the patent in question and was the inventor of the patent in question, and that Go Believe Food and Go Believe Group had implemented the patent in question, and should pay Zhang the inventor's remuneration from 2009 to 2016, and therefore filed a lawsuit with the Tianjin No. 3 Intermediate People's Court (hereinafter referred to as the Court of First Instance), requesting that Go Believe Food and Go Believe Group be ordered to pay Zhang's R&D patent remuneration from 2009 to 2016 amounting to CNY 2. 14 million (annual profit of CNY 5. 35 million × 5% × 8 years). The Court of First Instance held that although the patentee of the patent in question was Go Believe Group, it was an invention or creation made by Zhang during his employment with Go Believe Food in the course of fulfilling his job duties, which belonged to the service invention or creation. The entities that were granted patent rights under the Patent Law should be understood as the entities that should have applied for and obtained the patent rights. The subject to pay the remuneration for the service invention should be the employer of the inventor, not the subject who obtains the patent application right or patent right by other means such as assignment. Moreover, the implementer of the patent in question is Go Believe Food, not Go Believe Group Company. Therefore, Go Believe Food should pay Zhang the remuneration of the inventor of the service inventions and creations. Zhang's claim that the Go Believe Group should pay the remuneration lacked factual and legal basis, and was not supported by the Court of First Instance. Unsatisfied, both

Zhang and Go Believe Food appealed to the SPC. Zhang claimed that Go Believe Food and Go Believe Group should pay Zhang CNY 856, 000 as remuneration for his service inventions and creations. Go Believe Food claimed that it did not enjoy the application right and patent right of the patent in question, and did not belong to the "employer granted the patent rights" which had the obligation to pay the remuneration to the inventor. On September 29, 2022, the SPC rejected the appeal and upheld the original judgment.

【裁判意见】

[Judge's Opinion]

最高人民法院二审认为，2008 年修正的专利法第十六条规定："被授予专利权的单位应当对职务发明创造的发明人或者设计人给予奖励；发明创造专利实施后，根据其推广应用的范围和取得的经济效益，对发明人或者设计人给予合理的报酬。"从立法目的来看，该条规定的立法本意是在遵循公平原则的基础上，鼓励发明创造，并推动发明创造的实施。一方面，单位向发明人支付工资薪金，故将发明人在工作中作出的发明创造归属于单位，符合公平原则；同时，在社会化大生产条件下，将发明创造归属于单位亦被认为有利于发明创造的实施应用。另一方面，发明人在原有工资薪金的基础上，可以向单位请求支付奖励，并在单位实施发明创造取得经济效益的基础上还可以向单位进一步请求支付报酬，参与利润分配，这可以极大提高发明人的创造积极性，鼓励发明创造。本案中，根据查明的事实，张某良任职狗不理食品公司期间参与研发"生物保鲜包馅面食制品的制备方法"，该方法后被授予发明专利权，狗不理食品公司在经营过程中实际应用该方法并取得了经济效益，因此，根据 2008 年修正的专利法第十六条的上述规定，狗不理食品公司应当向张某良支付合理的报酬。狗不理食品公司虽非涉案专利的专利权人，从形式上看似不符合 2008 年修正的专利法第十六条关于支付主体为"被授予专利权的单位"这一条件，但实际上涉案专利权是在狗

不理食品公司的控制下才转由其控股股东狗不理集团公司取得。职务发明创造发明人请求支付奖励、报酬的权利，不应当因用人单位对职务发明创造的专利申请权及专利权的处分而受到损害，因此，涉案专利（申请）权的流转不影响狗不理食品公司应向张某良承担支付报酬的义务。

The SPC held in the Second Instance that Article 16 of the Patent Law, as amended in 2008, stipulates: "The employer to which a patent right has been granted shall reward the inventor or designer of the service invention and creation; after the patent for the invention and creation has been implemented, the inventor or designer shall be given a reasonable remuneration in accordance with the scope of the popularization and application of the invention and creation and the economic benefits achieved." From the viewpoint of legislative purpose, the legislative intent of this provision is to encourage inventions and promote their implementation on the basis of following the principle of fairness. On the one hand, the entities pay salaries to the inventors, so the inventors' inventions and creations made in the course of work are attributed to the entities, in line with the principle of fairness; At the same time, under the conditions of socialized mass production, the attribution of inventions to the entities is also considered to be conducive to the implementation and application of inventions. On the other hand, on the basis of the original salaries, the inventors can request the entities to pay the reward, and on the basis of the entities' implementation of the inventions to achieve economic benefits, inventors can further request the entities to pay the remuneration and participate in the distribution of profits, which can greatly enhance the inventors' motivation to create and encourage the inventions and creations. In this case, according to the facts, Zhang participated in the research and development of the "Preparation Method of Bio-preserved Stuffed Flour Products" during his tenure at Go Believe Food, which was later granted a patent for invention, and Go Believe Food made economic benefits by practically applying the method in the course of its operation, so according to the above provisions of Article 16 of the Patent Law amended in 2008, Go Believe Food should pay remuneration to the inventor. Although Go Believe Food was not the patentee of the patent in question, which formally did not meet the condition of Article 16 of the Patent Law as amended in 2008 that the subject to pay was "the employer to which the patent right was granted", as in fact, the right to the patent in question was only acquired by its controlling shareholder, Go Believe Group, under the control of Go Believe Food. The inventor's right to request the payment of rewards and remuneration for service inventions and creations should not be jeopardized by the employer's disposition of the patent application right and patent right for service inventions and creations; therefore, the circulation of the patent (application) right in question does not affect the obligation imposed on Go Believe Food to pay the remuneration to Zhang.

42. 仿制药申请人 4.2 类声明与药品专利权利要求的对应性 Correspondence between Type 4.2 declaration of generic drug applicants and claims of brand-name drug patent

【裁判要旨】

[Judgment Digest]

仿制药申请人依据《药品专利纠纷早期解决机制实施办法(试行)》第六条的规定作出其申请的仿制药技术方案不落入被仿制药品

专利权保护范围的声明的，原则上应当针对被仿制药品所对应的保护范围最大的权利要求作出声明，以保证声明的真实性和准确性。中国上市药品专利信息登记平台公开了被仿制药品所对应的两个或者两个以上的独立权利要求时，仿制药申请人应当针对两个或者两个以上独立权利要求作出声明。

Where an applicant of a generic drug makes a declaration, in accordance with Article 6 of the *Implementation Measures for Early Resolution Mechanism for Drug Patent Disputes (Trial)*, that the technical solution of the generic drug does not fall within the protection scope of the patent of the brand-name drug in question, the applicant should, in principle, make its declaration vis-a-vis the patent claim of the broadest protection scope corresponding to the brand-name drug, so as to ensure the authenticity and accuracy of such declaration. Where two or more independent claims corresponding to the brand-name drug are disclosed on the patent information registration platform for listed drugs in China, the applicant of the generic drug should make its declaration for such two or more independent claims.

【关键词】

[Keywords]

确认是否落入专利权保护范围　药品专利链接　登记　4.2 类声明　独立权利要求

Confirming whether it falls within the protection scope of the patent; drug patent linkage; registration; declaration of Type 4.2; independent claims

【案号】

[Case Number]

(2022) 最高法知民终 905 号

(2022) SPC IP Civil Final 905

【基本案情】

[Case Facts]

在上诉人中外制药株式会社与被上诉人温州海鹤药业有限公司（以下简称海鹤公司）确认是否落入专利权保护范围纠纷案中，“艾地骨化醇软胶囊”是由中外制药株式会社研发的一款治疗骨质疏松的药物，中外制药株式会社拥有相关中国发明专利及上市许可，已在中国上市药品专利信息登记平台（以下简称登记平台）就上述药品和专利进行登记。海鹤公司向国家药品监督管理局申请上述原研药的仿制药上市许可，并作出相关声明，称其仿制药未落入登记平台收录的原研药相关专利权保护范围。中外制药株式会社向北京知识产权法院提起诉讼，请求确认涉案仿制药技术方案落入涉案专利权利要求的保护范围。北京知识产权法院认为，涉案仿制药技术方案未落入涉案专利权保护范围，故驳回中外株式会社的诉讼请求。中外制药株式会社不服，向最高人民法院提起上诉。最高人民法院认为，海鹤公司未针对保护范围最大的权利要求作出声明及未将声明及声明依据通知上市许可持有人即中外制药株式会社的行为有所不当，对此予以指出并作出批评；判断仿制药的技术方案是否落入专利权保护范围时，原则上应以仿制药申请人的申报资料为依据进行比对评判，经比对，涉案仿制药技术方案未落入专利权保护范围，于2022年8月5日判决驳回上诉，维持原判。

In the case of dispute on confirming whether to fall within the protection scope of the patent right between the Appellant, Chugai Pharmaceutical Co., Ltd., and the Appellee, Wenzhou Haihe Pharmaceutical Co. Ltd. (hereinafter referred to as Haihe), “Eldecalcitol Soft Capsules”, a medicine for the treatment of osteoporosis developed by Chugai Pharmaceutical Co., Ltd., who owns the relevant Chinese invention patents and marketing licenses, and has registered the aforesaid medicine and patents on the Chinese Patent Information Registration Platform for Listed Medicines (hereinafter referred to as

the Registration Platform). Haihe applied to the National Medical Products Administration (NMPA) for marketing authorization for the generic version of the abovementioned brand-name drug and made a relevant declaration that its generic drug did not fall within the protection scope of the relevant patent rights of the brand-name drug included on the Registration Platform. Chugai Pharmaceutical Co., Ltd., filed a lawsuit with Beijing Intellectual Property Court, requesting to confirm that the technical solution of the generic drug in question fell within the protection scope of the claims of the patent in question. Beijing Intellectual Property Court held that the technical solution of the generic drug in question did not fall within the protection scope of the patent claims in question, and therefore rejected the claim of Chugai Pharmaceutical Co., Ltd. Unsatisfied, Chugai Pharmaceutical Co., Ltd. appealed to the SPC. The SPC held that Haihe's failure to make a declaration of the claim with the largest scope of protection and failure to notify the marketing licensee, i. e., Chugai Pharmaceutical Co., Ltd., of its declaration and the basis of the declaration was improper and had been pointed and criticized; when judging whether the technical solution of a generic drug falls within the protection scope of the patent, in principle, the comparison and evaluation should be made on the basis of the declaration of the applicant of a generic drug; after the comparison, the technical solution of the generic drug in question did not fall within the protection scope of the patent, and the Court ruled on August 5, 2022, to dismiss the appeal and uphold the original judgment.

【裁判意见】

[Judge's Opinion]

最高人民法院二审认为，根据《药品专利纠纷早期解决机制实施办法（试行）》第六条的规定，化学仿制药申请人提交药品上市许可申请时，应当对照已在登记平台公开的专利信息，针对被仿制药每一件相关的药品专利作出声明。仿制药申请人对相关声明的真实性、准确性负责。该规定仅对仿制药申请人作出声明所针对的专利提出了要求，并未明确声明所应当针对的药品专利的具体权利要求。仿制药申请人作出声明时，通常应该考虑被仿制药品与登记平台公开的专利权利要求的对应关系，即被仿制药品是否实施了登记平台公开的专利权利要求的技术方案。4.2类声明的核心在于申明仿制药申请人申请的仿制药技术方案不落入被仿制药品专利权的保护范围。为保证声明的真实性和准确性，仿制药申请人原则上应该针对被仿制药品所对应的保护范围最大的权利要求作出声明。由于专利独立权利要求的保护范围最大，如果被仿制药品对应着专利独立权利要求，只要仿制药的技术方案不落入独立权利要求的保护范围，必然不落入从属权利要求的保护范围。但是，如果仿制药技术方案不落入药品专利从属权利要求的保护范围，并不能当然得出不落入药品专利权保护范围的结论。因此，对于4.2类不落入专利权保护范围的声明，如果被仿制药品对应着专利独立权利要求，仿制药申请人应当针对独立权利要求作出声明；当被仿制药品所对应的保护范围最大的权利要求存在两个或者两个以上的独立权利要求时，仿制药申请人针对两个或者两个以上独立权利要求作出声明，才能保证声明的真实性和准确性。

The SPC held in the Second Instance that, according to Article 6 of the *Implementation Measures for the Early Settlement Mechanism of Drug Patent Disputes (Trial)*, an applicant for a chemical generic drug, when submitting an application for a marketing authorization for the drug, shall make a declaration in respect of each and every relevant pharmaceutical patent of the brand-name drug, against the patent information that has already been made public on the Registration Platform. The applicant for generic drugs is responsible for the truthfulness and accuracy of the relevant declaration. The provisions only set out the requirements for the patent to which the applicant for a generic

drug should make a declaration, and do not specify the specific claims of the patent of the drug to which the declaration should be made. When the applicant for a generic drug makes a declaration, it should usually consider the correspondence between the brand-name drug and the patent claims disclosed by the Registration Platform, i. e., whether or not the brand-name drug implements the technical solution of the patent claims disclosed by the Registration Platform. For the declaration of Type 4. 2, the core of such declaration is to affirm that the technical solution of the generic drug applied for by the applicant does not fall into the protection scope of the patent right of the brand-name drug. In order to ensure the authenticity and accuracy of the declaration, the applicant for generic drugs should, in principle, make a declaration on the claim corresponding to the brand-name drug with the largest scope of protection. Since the independent claims of the patent have the largest scope of protection, if the brand-name drug corresponds to the independent claims of the patent, as long as the technical solution of the generic drug does not fall into the protection scope of the independent claims, it will certainly not fall into the protection scope of the dependent claims. However, if the technical solution of the generic drug does not fall within the protection scope of the dependent claims of the pharmaceutical patent, it does not, ipso facto, lead to the conclusion that it does not fall within the protection scope of the pharmaceutical patent right. Therefore, for the declaration of not falling into the scope of patent protection of Type 4. 2, if the brand-name drug corresponds to the independent claims of the patent, the applicant for the generic drug shall make a declaration in respect of the independent claims; when there are two or more independent claims corresponding to the claim with the largest scope of protection of the brand-name drug, the applicant for the generic drug shall make a declaration in respect of the two or more independent claims, so that the authenticity and accuracy of the declaration can be guaranteed.

专利权人在登记平台上登记信息之后，有可能在无效宣告程序中修改已登记专利的权利要求，但无论以何种方式修改权利要求，最终被接受的审查文本不得扩大原权利要求的保护范围，故只要仿制药申请人在提出仿制药申请时针对被仿制药品所对应的保护范围最大的权利要求作出4.2类声明，专利权人在无效宣告程序中对权利要求的修改就不会影响声明的真实性和准确性。

After registering the information on the Registration Platform, it is possible for the patentee to amend the claims of the registered patent in the invalidation proceedings, but no matter in what way the claims are amended, the final accepted examination text shall not expand the scope of protection of the original claims, and therefore, as long as the applicant of the generic drug makes a declaration of Type 4.2 in respect of the claim with the widest scope of protection corresponding to the brand-name drug at the time of filing the application for the generic drug, the patentee's modification of the claim in the invalidation proceedings will not affect the authenticity and accuracy of the declaration.

本案的特殊之处在于，仿制药申请人海鹤公司未针对修改前被仿制药品所对应的独立权利要求作出声明，而是仅对修改前的从属权利要求2作出声明。对此，在无效宣告程序中，专利权人对权利要求的修改并不必然导致审查文本的变化，修改后的审查文本被国家知识产权局接受并公开的最早时点系在口头审理过程中。国家药品监督管理局于2021年8月16日受理海鹤公司提出的涉案仿制药注册申请时，国家知识产权局尚未对涉案专利的无效宣告请求进行口头审理。故海鹤公司申请涉案仿制药上市并作出4.2类声明在前，国家知识产权局举行口头审理在后。海鹤公司在作出4.2类声明之时，未对被仿制药品当时所对应的保护范围最大的独立权利要求作出声明，仅对保护范围更小的从属权利要

求作出声明，不具有正当理由，有避重就轻之嫌，其行为难言正当。海鹤公司称其曾向国家药品监督管理局申请修改声明，但该事实发生在中外制药株式会社提起本案诉讼之后，难以证明海鹤公司行为的正当性。

The special feature of this case is that the applicant of the generic drug, Haihe, did not make a declaration on the independent claims corresponding to the brand-name drug before the modification, but only made a declaration on the dependent claim 2 before the modification. In this regard, in an invalidation proceeding, the patentee's amendment of the claims does not necessarily lead to a change in the examination text, and the earliest point at which the amended examination text is accepted and disclosed by the China National Intellectual Property Administration (CNIPA) falls within the oral proceedings. When the National Medical Products Administration accepted Haihe's application for registration of the generic drug in question on August 16, 2021, the China National Intellectual Property Administration (CNIPA) had not yet held an oral hearing on the request for invalidation of the patent in question. Therefore, Haihe applied for the listing of the generic drug in question and made the declaration of Type 4.2 prior to the oral hearing held by the CNIPA. When Haihe made the declaration of Type 4.2, it did not make a declaration of the independent claim with the largest scope of protection corresponding to the brand-name drug at that time, but only made a declaration of the dependent claim with a smaller scope of protection, which was not justified, and it was suspected of keeping silent about the important things while admitting the minor ones, and its behavior could not be said to be justified. Haihe claimed that it had applied to the National Medical Products Administration to revise its declaration, however this fact occurred after Chugai Pharmaceutical Co., Ltd., filed the present lawsuit, and it is difficult to prove the legitimacy of Haihe's behavior.

中外制药株式会社在涉案专利权的无效宣告程序中修改权利要求的方式为，将原权利要求 2 中的部分附加技术特征合并至权利要求 1，删除了权利要求 2，并相应调整了其他权利要求的序号。海鹤公司作出的 4.2 类声明所针对的原权利要求 2 的保护范围大于修改后独立权利要求的保护范围，故海鹤公司的声明所针对的权利要求的保护范围事实上覆盖了修改后涉案专利权的保护范围。考虑到《药品专利纠纷早期解决机制实施办法（试行）》仍处于试行阶段，其仅规定了仿制药申请人针对被仿制药每一件相关的药品专利作出声明，在仿制药申请人的声明所针对的权利要求的保护范围事实上覆盖修改后涉案专利权的保护范围的情况下，人民法院基于修改后的权利要求审理针对该声明提起的诉讼，符合药品专利纠纷早期解决机制的目的。因此，从实际效果来看，海鹤公司作出的 4.2 类声明虽有不当之处，但并未对中外制药株式会社的实体和诉讼权利造成不利影响。

Chugai Pharmaceutical Co., Ltd. amended the claims in the invalidation proceedings of the patent in question by combining some of the additional technical features in the original Claim 2 into Claim 1, deleting Claim 2, and adjusting the serial numbers of the other claims accordingly. The protection scope of the original Claim 2 covered by the declaration of Type 4.2 made by Haihe is larger than the protection scope of the amended independent claim, so the protection scope of the claim covered by the declaration of Haihe in fact covers the protection scope of the amended patent in question. Considering that the *Implementation Measures for the Early Settlement Mechanism of Drug Patent Disputes (Trial)* are still in the trial stage, it only stipulates that the applicant of the generic drug makes a declaration in respect of each and every relevant drug patent of the brand-name drug, and in the event that the protection scope of the claims covered by the declaration of the applicant of the generic drug in fact covers the protection scope of the patent right involved in the

case after the modification, the people's court will hear the litigation filed against the declaration based on the modified claims, which is in line with the purpose of the early resolution mechanism for drug patent disputes. Therefore, in terms of practical effect, the declaration of Type 4.2 made by Haihe, although improper, did not adversely affect the entity and litigation rights of Chugai Pharmaceutical Co., Ltd.

43. 药品专利链接诉讼中确定仿制药技术方案的依据 Basis for determining technical solution of generic drugs in drug patent linkage litigation

【裁判要旨】

[Judgment Digest]

在药品专利链接诉讼中，判断仿制药的技术方案是否落入专利权保护范围时，原则上应当以仿制药申请人的申报资料为依据进行比对评判；仿制药申请人实际实施的技术方案与申报资料是否相同，一般不属于药品专利链接诉讼的审查范围。

In drug patent linkage litigation, when determining whether the technical solution of a generic drug falls within the protection scope of the involved patent, people's courts shall in principle decide according to the comparison on the basis of the application materials submitted by the generic drug applicant; whether the technical solution embodied by the generic drug applicant in fact is the same as that in the application materials generally does not fall within the scope of judicial review in drug patent linkage litigation.

【关键词】

[Keywords]

确认是否落入专利权保护范围　药品专利链接　申报资料　比对

依据

Confirming whether it falls within the protection scope of the patent; drug patent linkage; declaration information; basis of comparison

【案号】

[Case Number]

（2022）最高法知民终 905 号

（2022）SPC IP Civil Final 905

【裁判意见】

[Judge's Opinion]

在上诉人中外制药株式会社与被上诉人温州海鹤药业有限公司（以下简称海鹤公司）确认是否落入专利权保护范围纠纷案中，最高人民法院认为，药品上市审评审批过程中，药品上市许可申请人与有关专利权人或者利害关系人之间因申请注册的药品相关的专利权产生的纠纷仅仅是双方之间关于相关专利权的一种特殊形式的纠纷，通常被称为药品专利链接纠纷。对于化学仿制药而言，国务院药品监督管理部门依据仿制药申请人的申报资料进行药品上市审评审批，并在规定的期限内根据人民法院对该类纠纷作出的生效裁判决定是否暂停批准相关药品上市，故在判断仿制药的技术方案是否落入专利权保护范围时，原则上应以仿制药申请人的申报资料为依据进行比对评判。如果仿制药申请人实际实施的技术方案与申报技术方案不一致，其需要依照药品监督管理相关法律法规承担法律责任；如果专利权人或利害关系人认为仿制药申请人实际实施的技术方案构成侵权，亦可另行提起侵害专利权纠纷之诉。因此，仿制药申请人实际实施的技术方案与申报资料是否相同，一般不属于确认落入专利权保护范围纠纷之诉的审查范围。本案中，海鹤公司将登记为原料药的抗氧化剂作为涉案仿制药的辅料申报是否符合相关规定，属于国务院药品监督管理部门的审查范围，不影响本院对申报资料真实性和本案比对对象的确认。此外，中外制药株式会社亦无其他证据

证明国务院药品监督管理部门审评审批涉案仿制药抗氧化剂的依据发生变化。

In the case of dispute over the confirmation of whether to fall into the protection scope of patent right between the Appellant, Chugai Pharmaceutical Co., Ltd., and the Appellee, Wenzhou Haihe Pharmaceutical Co., Ltd. (hereinafter referred to as Haihe), the SPC held that, during the process of review and approval of the listing of medicines, the disputes between the applicants for the marketing authorization of medicines and the relevant patentee or interested parties arising from the patent rights related to the medicines for which the applicants are applying for registration are only a special form of disputes concerning the relevant patent rights between the two parties, which is usually referred to as a dispute over drug patent linkage. For chemical generic drugs, the National Medical Products Administration under the State Council carries out the review and approval of drugs on the market based on the declarations of the applicants of the generic drugs and decides whether to suspend the approval of the relevant drugs on the market within the prescribed period according to the effective decision of the people's court on such disputes, and therefore, in judging whether the technical solution of a generic drug falls within the protection scope of the patent, the comparison and evaluation should be made on the basis of the declaration of the applicant of the generic drug, in principle. If the technical solutions actually implemented by the applicants for generic drugs are inconsistent with the declared technical solutions, the applicants need to bear the legal responsibility in accordance with the laws and regulations related to drug supervision and management; if the patentee or the interested party believes that the technical solutions actually implemented by the applicants for generic drugs constitutes infringement, it can also file a separate lawsuit of dispute over infringement of patent rights.

Therefore, whether the technical solutions actually implemented by the applicants for generic drugs are the same as the declared information is generally not within the scope of examination of the dispute over the protection scope of the patent right. In this case, whether Haihe's declaration of the antioxidant registered as an API as an excipient of the generic drug in question complied with the relevant regulations belonged to the scope of examination of the National Medical Products Administration under the State Council, and did not affect the Court's confirmation of the authenticity of the declaration information and the object of comparison in this case. In addition, Chugai Pharmaceutical Co., Ltd. has no other evidence to prove that the basis for the review and approval of the antioxidant of the generic drug in question by the State Council's National Medical Products Administration has changed.

44. 药品专利链接诉讼参照适用“先行裁驳、另行起诉” Application of “dismissing patent case for the time being but allowing re-filing later if necessary” on a referential basis in drug patent linkage litigation

【裁判要旨】

[Judgment Digest]

专利权利人提起确认是否落入专利权保护范围纠纷之诉后，涉案专利权被国家知识产权局宣告无效，但宣告专利权无效的审查决定尚未确定发生法律效力的，人民法院可以先行裁定驳回原告的起诉。

After the patentee files a lawsuit to confirm whether the technical solution in question falls within the protection scope of the involved patent, if the involved patent is declared invalid by CNIPA during the litigation, but such administrative decision as made by CNIPA has not been in force and effect with

certainty, then people's courts may rule to dismiss the plaintiff's lawsuit which can be refiled with court if the involved patent ultimately remains valid through judicial review process.

【关键词】

[Keywords]

确认是否落入专利权保护范围　药品专利链接　专利无效　先行裁驳另行起诉

Confirming whether it falls within the protection scope of the patent; drug patent linkage; patent invalidation; dismissing patent case for the time being; allowing re-filing later if necessary

【案号】

[Case Number]

（2022）最高法知民终 2177 号

（2022）SPC IP Civil Final 2177

【基本案情】

[Case Facts]

在上诉人住友制药株式会社与被上诉人浙江华海药业股份有限公司（以下简称华海公司）确认是否落入专利权保护范围纠纷案中，住友制药株式会社系名称为“药物组合物”、专利号为200680018223.4发明专利的专利权人，其拥有相关原研药“盐酸鲁拉西酮片”的上市许可，已在中国上市药品专利信息登记平台（以下简称登记平台）就上述药品和专利进行登记。2020年11月20日，国家知识产权局作出第47048号无效宣告请求审查决定，宣告涉案专利权全部无效。住友制药株式会社不服上述审查决定，提起行政诉讼。一审法院判决驳回住友制药株式会社的诉讼请求，住友制药株式会社对此提起上诉。华海公司向国家药品监督管理局申请上述原研药的仿制药上市许可，并作出相关声明。住友制药株式会社向北京知识产权法院提起诉讼，请求确认涉案仿制药技术方案落入涉案专利权利要求的保护范围。北京知识产权法院认为，由于涉案专利权被宣告无效，应参照《最高人民法院关于审理侵犯专利权纠纷案件应用法律若干问题的解释（二）》第二条的规定，故裁定驳回住友制药株式会社的起诉。住友制药株式会社不服，向最高人民法院提起上诉。针对前述行政诉讼，最高人民法院判决驳回上诉，维持原判。最高人民法院在本案中认为，涉案无效宣告请求审查决定已发生法律效力，涉案专利权应当自始无效，故住友制药株式会社起诉的条件不再具备。鉴于一审法院裁定驳回住友制药株式会社的起诉，未对案件进行实体审理，故原审裁定的结论应予维持，故于 2022 年 12 月 13 日裁定驳回上诉，维持原裁定。

In the case of dispute on confirming whether to fall within the protection scope of the patent right between the Appellant, Sumitomo Pharma Co., Ltd., and the Appellee, Zhejiang Huahai Pharmaceutical Co., Ltd. (hereinafter referred to as Huahai), Sumitomo Pharma Co., Ltd. is the patentee of invention patent No. 200680018223.4 entitled "Pharmaceutical Compositions", and it owns the marketing license of the relevant original drug "Lurasidone Hydrochloride Tablets", and has already registered the said drug and patent in the China Patent Information Registration Platform for Listed Medicines (hereinafter referred to as the Registration Platform). On November 20, 2020, the China National Intellectual Property Administration issued the examination decision of invalidation request No. 47048, declaring that the patent right in question was invalid in its entirety. Unsatisfied, Sumitomo Pharma Co., Ltd. filed an administrative lawsuit against the above decision. The Court of First Instance ruled that the claim of Sumitomo Pharma Co., Ltd. was rejected, and Sumitomo Pharma Co., Ltd. filed an appeal. Huahai applied to the National Medical Products Administration (NMPA) for marketing authorization for the generic version of the abovementioned original drug and

made a declaration in this regard. Sumitomo Pharma Co., Ltd. filed a lawsuit with Beijing Intellectual Property Court, requesting to confirm that the technical solution of the generic drug in question fell within the protection scope of the Claims of the patent in question. Beijing Intellectual Property Court held that since the patent in question had been declared invalid, it should refer to Article 2 of the *Interpretation of the Supreme People's Court on Several Issues concerning the Application of Law in the Trial of Patent Infringement Dispute Cases (II)*, and therefore ruled to dismiss the lawsuit of Sumitomo Pharma Co., Ltd. Unsatisfied, Sumitomo Pharma Co., Ltd. appealed to the SPC. In response to the aforesaid administrative litigation, the SPC ruled that the appeal be dismissed and the original judgment be affirmed. In this case, the SPC held that the examination decision on the invalidation request had become legally effective, and the patent should be invalid ab initio, so the conditions for Sumitomo Pharma Co., Ltd. to file an appeal no longer existed. In view of the fact that the Court of First Instance ruled to dismiss the lawsuit of Sumitomo Pharma Co., Ltd., without conducting a substantive trial of the case, the conclusion of the original ruling should be upheld, and therefore, on December 13, 2022, it ruled that the appeal should be dismissed and the original ruling should be upheld.

【裁判意见】

[Judge's Opinion]

最高人民法院二审认为，专利法第七十六条规定中可以起诉的纠纷是因申请注册的药品相关的专利权产生的，如果不存在合法有效的专利权，则该类纠纷不具备审理的基础。针对住友制药株式会社不服国家知识产权局宣告涉案专利权无效的审查决定提起的行政诉讼，已经二审法院判决确定该审查决定发生法律效力，涉案专利权应当自始无效，故住友制药株式会社起诉的条件不再具备。鉴于一审法院裁定驳回住友制药株式会社的起诉，未对案件进行实体审理，故原审裁定的结论应予维持。

The SPC held in the Second Instance that the disputes that could be sued under Article 76 of the Patent Law arose out of the patent rights related to the medical products for which registration was sought and that such disputes did not have a basis for trial if there were no legally valid patent rights. In response to the administrative litigation filed by Sumitomo Pharma Co., Ltd., against the China National Intellectual Property Administration (CNIPA) for its decision to declare the patent right in question invalid, the Court of Second Instance ruled that the decision had become legally invalid, and the patent right in question should be invalidated ab initio, and therefore, the conditions for Sumitomo Pharma Co., Ltd. to sue no longer existed. In view of the fact that the Court of First Instance ruled to dismiss the lawsuit of Sumitomo Pharma Co., Ltd., without conducting a substantive trial of the case, the conclusion of the original ruling should be upheld.

《最高人民法院关于审理侵犯专利权纠纷案件应用法律若干问题的解释（二）》第二条第一款、第二款规定："权利人在专利侵权诉讼中主张的权利要求被国务院专利行政部门宣告无效的，审理侵犯专利权纠纷案件的人民法院可以裁定驳回权利人基于该无效权利要求的起诉。有证据证明宣告上述权利要求无效的决定被生效的行政判决撤销的，权利人可以另行起诉。"一审法院在涉案专利权被国家知识产权局宣告无效、宣告专利权无效的审查决定尚未确定发生法律效力的情况下，参照适用上述规定，先行裁定驳回住友制药株式会社的起诉，亦无不当，具体理由如下：

Article 2(1) and (2) of the *Interpretation of the Supreme People's Court on Several Issues Concerning the Application of Law in the Trial of Patent Infringement Dispute Cases (II)* stipulate that: "If the claim asserted by the right

holder in a patent infringement litigation has been declared invalid by the patent administrative department under the State Council, the people's court hearing the case of dispute over infringement of patent rights may rule to dismiss the lawsuit filed by the right holder based on the invalid claim. Where there is evidence to prove that the decision to declare the said claim invalid has been revoked by an administrative judgment in force, the right holder may sue separately." It was not improper that the Court of First Instance ruled to reject the lawsuit of Sumitomo Pharma Co., Ltd., with reference to the application of the above provisions when the patent right in question had been declared invalid by the CNIPA, and the examination decision of declaring the patent right invalid had not yet been determined to be legally effective, for the following specific reasons:

首先，在权利人或利害关系人提起的确认是否落入专利权保护范围纠纷之诉中可以参照适用《最高人民法院关于审理侵犯专利权纠纷案件应用法律若干问题的解释（二）》第二条的规定。权利人或利害关系人提起确认是否落入专利权保护范围纠纷与侵害专利权纠纷之诉，其与案件的直接利害关系均在于权利人拥有合法有效的专利权。对于国家知识产权局已宣告专利权无效、宣告专利权无效的审查决定尚未确定发生法律效力时的专利权，其在两类诉讼中应具有相同的地位，即对起诉条件的影响应当相同。因此，人民法院在审理权利人或利害关系人提起的确认是否落入专利权保护范围纠纷之诉时，可以参照适用《最高人民法院关于审理侵犯专利权纠纷案件应用法律若干问题的解释（二）》关于“先行裁驳、另行起诉”的规定。

Firstly, the provisions of Article 2 of the *Interpretation of the Supreme People's Court on Several Issues Concerning the Application of Law in the Trial of Patent Infringement Dispute Cases (II)* can be referred to and applied in the case of a dispute filed by a right holder or an interested party to ascertain whether to fall within the scope of protection of the patent right. For the lawsuits filed by the right holder or the interested party on the dispute of confirming whether to fall into the scope of protection of the patent right and the dispute of infringing the patent right, the direct interest of the case lies in the fact that the right holder owns the lawful and effective patent right. For the patent rights that have been declared invalid by the CNIPA, and when the examination decision of invalidating the patent right has not yet been determined to be legally effective, it should have the same status in the two types of lawsuits, i. e., the impact on the conditions of the prosecution should be the same. Therefore, the people's court may refer to the provisions of the *Interpretation of the Supreme People's Court on Several Issues Concerning the Application of Law in the Trial of Patent Infringement Dispute Cases (II)* on the "dismissing patent case for the time being but allowing re-filing later if necessary" when hearing the case brought by the right holder or the interested party to confirm whether to fall into the scope of the protection of the patent right.

其次，先行裁定驳回起诉符合专利法设立药品专利纠纷早期解决机制的制度定位。药品专利纠纷早期解决机制的作用主要在于，将原研药专利权人或利害关系人与仿制药申请人在药品上市之后可能发生的侵害专利权纠纷提前到药品上市审评审批过程中解决，该制度既保护药品专利权人的合法权益，降低仿制药上市后专利侵权的风险，也保护仿制药企业公平的市场竞争行为，保证符合要求的仿制药的审批程序不会受到不合理影响。若专利权已被国家知识产权局宣告无效，则专利权的状态很不稳定，以该类专利权为基础认定被诉仿制药技术方案是否落入涉案专利权的保护范围，很有可能无法实际达到早期解决药品专利纠纷的效果。

Secondly, dismissing patent case for the time being is in line with the system positioning of the Patent Law to set up a mechanism for early resolution

of drug patent disputes. The role of the early resolution mechanism for drug patent disputes mainly lies in advancing the disputes over infringement of patent rights that may occur between the patentee or interested party of the original drug and the applicant of the generic drug after the drug has been marketed to be resolved during the process of review and approval of the marketing of the drug, and the system not only protects the lawful rights and interests of the patentee of the drug and reduces the risk of patent infringement of the generic drug after the generic drug has been marketed but also protects the fair market competition behaviors of the generic drug enterprises and ensures that the approval process of generic drugs meeting the requirements will not be unreasonably affected. If the patent right has been declared invalid by the CNIPA, the status of the patent right is very unstable, and it is very likely that the effect of early resolution of drug patent disputes will not be achieved by determining whether the technical solution of the sued generic drug falls within the protection scope of the patent right in question on the basis of the patent right of this type.

最后，先行裁定驳回起诉并不会导致双方当事人利益失衡。专利法第七十六条规定的药品专利纠纷早期解决机制并非解决药品专利纠纷的唯一途径。尽管在该类案件中裁定驳回起诉会使得仿制药注册申请可进入行政审批环节，但若有证据证明宣告专利权无效的决定被生效的行政判决撤销，对于仿制药企业实施的制造、销售等行为，专利权人或利害关系人可以另行提起侵权之诉，其合法权益仍可以得到有效维护。相反，若在专利权状态很不稳定的情况下确认落入专利权保护范围，则很有可能导致仿制药上市审批的不当延迟。

Lastly, dismissing patent case for the time being will not lead to the imbalance of interests of both parties. The early resolution mechanism for drug patent disputes under Article 76 of the Patent Law is not the only way to resolve drug patent disputes. Although the decision to dismiss the lawsuit in this type of case will enable the generic drug registration application to enter the administrative approval process, if there is evidence to prove that the decision to declare the patent invalid has been revoked by the effective administrative judgment, the patentee or the interested party can file a separate infringement lawsuit for the manufacturing and sales of the generic drug enterprise, and their legitimate rights and interests can still be effectively safeguarded. In contrast, confirmation of falling within the scope of patent protection when the patent status is very unstable is likely to result in undue delays in the approval of marketing of generic drugs.

三、植物新品种案件

Ⅲ. New Plant Variety Cases

45. 审批机关未保存标准样品的无性繁殖授权品种保护范围的确定

Determination of protection scope of asexually propagated granted variety whose standard sample is not kept by the approval authority

【裁判要旨】

[Judgment Digest]

对于以无性繁殖方式扩繁的果树作物，授予植物新品种权时审批机关并未保存其标准样品的，品种权授权审查过程中作为授权机关现场考察对象的母树，以及该母树以无性繁殖方式扩繁所得的其他个体，均可以作为确定授权品种保护范围的繁殖材料。

For asexually propagated fruit crops, if the approval authority does not keep the standard samples of the fruit crops in granting new plant variety rights, the seed tree that is the subject of on-site inspection by the authority in the course of reviewing and granting variety rights and other individual plants originated from the asexual propagation of the seed tree can both be used as propagation materials to determine the protection scope of granted variety.

【关键词】

[Keywords]

植物新品种　标准样品　无性繁殖　繁殖材料　保护范围确定

New plant varieties; standard samples; asexual reproduction; breeding material; determination of protection scope

【案号】

[Case Number]

(2022) 最高法知民终 782 号

(2022) SPC IP Civil Final 782

【基本案情】

[Case Facts]

在上诉人重庆环霖农业开发有限公司（以下简称环霖公司）与被上诉人重庆奔象果业有限公司（以下简称奔象公司）侵害植物新品种权纠纷案中，涉及柑橘植物新品种“中柑所 5 号”。奔象公司起诉环霖公司侵害其“中柑所 5 号”植物新品种权，要求其承担侵权责任。一审法院经审理认为，奔象公司将公证采样的“中柑所 5 号”样品和涉嫌侵权的“金秋砂糖桔”苗木先后交由农业农村部植物新品种测试中心和河南省依斯特检测技术有限公司检验，所得两份检验报告的结论均为待测样品与“中柑所 5 号”为极近似或相同品种。环霖公司销售“金秋砂糖桔”苗木侵害了“中柑所 5 号”植物新品种权。环霖公司不服，向最高人民法院提起上诉，主要理由为涉案检测报告中的“中柑所 5 号”对照样本来源不明，不能证明环霖公司销售的”金秋砂糖桔”苗木与“中柑所 5 号”是同一品种。最高人民法院于 2022 年 11 月 11 日判决驳回上诉，维持原判。

The case of dispute over the infringement of rights to new plant varieties

between the Appellant, Chongqing Huanlin Agricultural Development Co., Ltd. (hereinafter referred to as Huanlin), and the Appellee, Chongqing Benxiang Fruit Industry Co., Ltd. (hereinafter referred to as Benxiang), involves a new variety of citrus plant, named "CRI 5". Benxiang sued Huanlin for infringement of its rights to the new plant variety of "CRI 5", requiring it to bear the liability for the infringement. The Court of First Instance held from the trial that the samples of "CRI 5" and the seedlings of the alleged infringing "Jinqiu Sugar Tangerine", which were notarized, were successively submitted by Benxiang to the New Plant Variety Testing Center of the Ministry of Agriculture and Rural Affairs of the People's Republic of China and to Henan Yist Testing Technology Co., Ltd. for inspection. Both test reports concluded that the samples to be tested were very similar or identical to "CRI 5". Huanlin's sale of seedlings of "Jinqiu Sugar Tangerine" infringed on the right to new plant varieties of "CRI 5". Unsatisfied, Huanlin appealed to the SPC, arguing that the control samples of "CRI 5" in the test report were of unknown origin, and could not prove that the seedlings of "Jinqiu Sugar Tangerine" sold by Huanlin were the same as "CRI 5". On November 11, 2022, the SPC rejected the appeal and upheld the original judgment.

【裁判意见】

[Judge's Opinion]

最高人民法院二审认为，授权品种的繁殖材料是植物新品种权的保护范围，是品种权人行使排他独占权的基础。一般而言，用来确定授权品种保护范围的繁殖材料是以品种权人向品种权审批机关提交并保存的标准样品为准。未能按照审批机关的要求提供授权品种繁殖材料，或经检测授权品种不再符合授权时的特征和特性的，品种权终止。涉案品种授权后审批机关并未要求品种权的申请人提交标准样品，因授权品种的标准样品并未被审批机关保存，导致在侵权纠纷中无法通过调取审批机关保存的标准样品确定授权品种的性状特征。对于在此情况下确定授权品种的保护范围进而进行同一性认定，第一，从“中柑所5号”的品种权申请以及审查的事实分析，涉案授权品种在进行品种权申请以及授权的审查中，审批机关在申请人的资源圃对申请品种的种植情况进行了现场考察，形成的《农业植物品种DUS测试现场考察报告》记载了申请授权以及进行现场考察的品种种植在重庆市北碚区的资源圃，因此，可以据此确定授权品种母树的所在种植地点。第二，涉案授权品种在申请时是以申请人种植在重庆市北碚区的资源圃的母树作为性状对比的样品，在进行现场考察后认定性状特征具有特异性，并得以授权。因此，资源圃中的母树属于确定涉案授权品种特征特性的样品。第三，从“中柑所5号”的繁殖特性分析，“中柑所5号”作为柑橘属植物品种，通常通过无性繁殖方式，如扦插、嫁接进行扩繁，生产繁殖出与授权品种特征特性相同的繁殖材料，实现授权品种基因的复制和传递，其植株整体和枝条都可以成为繁殖材料，具有与授权审查时的母树相同的性状特征。中柑所资源圃中对母树的繁殖材料通过无性繁殖方式扩繁的其他个体，可以作为授权品种的繁殖材料进而确定其保护范围。因此，考虑授权品种的上述情况，对于审批机关没有保存标准样品，以无性繁殖方式进行扩繁的果树作物而言，在品种权审查中现场考察指向的母树和通过母树的繁殖材料扩繁的其他个体，可以作为确定授权品种保护范围的繁殖材料。

The SPC held in the Second Instance that the propagating material of an authorized variety is the protection scope of the right to new plant varieties, and is the basis for the exercise of exclusive monopoly by the variety right holder. Generally speaking, the propagating materials used to determine the protection scope of authorized varieties are based on the standard samples submitted and kept by the variety right holders to the variety rights approval authorities. Failure to provide propagation materials of the authorized varieties in

accordance with the requirements of the approval authority, or if the authorized varieties are tested to be no longer in conformity with the characteristics and features at the time of authorization, the variety rights shall be terminated. After the authorization of the variety in question, the approval authority did not require the applicant for variety rights to submit standard samples, as the standard samples of the authorized varieties have not been preserved by the approval authority, resulting in no access to the standard samples preserved by the approval authority in infringement disputes to determine the traits and characteristics of the authorized varieties. For the determination of the protection scope of the authorized varieties in this case and then the determination of identity, firstly, from the application for variety rights of "CRI 5" and the review of factual analysis, when conducting the application for variety rights of the authorized varieties in question as well as examining the authorization, the approving authority conducted an on-site examination of the cultivation of the varieties under application in the applicant's resource garden, and the resulting Site Inspection Report of Agricultural Plant Variety DUS Tests documented the varieties applied for authorization and subject to a site inspection were planted in the resource garden in the Beibei District of Chongqing Municipality, and therefore the planting site where the parent trees of the authorized varieties are located can be determined on the basis of the above. Secondly, when applying for the authorized variety in question, the parent tree in the resource garden planted by the applicant in Beibei District, Chongqing Municipality, was used as the sample for trait comparison, and the trait characteristics were determined to be specific after the on-site inspection, and the authorization was granted. Therefore, the parent trees in the resource garden are the samples for determining the characteristics of the authorized variety in question. Thirdly, by analyzing the propagation characteristics of "CRI 5", as a citrus plant variety, "CRI 5" is usually propagated through asexual propagation, such as cuttings and grafting, to produce propagation material with the same characteristics and features as those of the authorized varieties, so as to realize the reproduction and transmission of the genes of the authorized varieties whose plant as a whole and its branches can become propagation material with the same traits as the parent tree at the time of the authorization review. Other individuals propagated by asexual reproduction from the propagation material of the parent tree in the resource garden of the Citrus Research Institute of China can be used as propagation material of the authorized variety to determine the scope of its protection. Therefore, considering the above situation of the authorized varieties, for fruit crops for which no standard samples are kept by the approval authority and which are propagated by asexual reproduction, the parent trees and other individuals propagated through the propagation material of the parent tree pointed out by the on-site inspection during the examination of the variety right can be used as propagation material for determining the scope of protection of the authorized varieties.

46. 杂交玉米品种与其亲本品种的亲子关系认定 Identification of parentage between hybrid maize variety and their parental variety

【裁判要旨】

[Judgment Digest]

在玉米育种生产实践中，使用不同的亲本通过杂交选育相同或者极近似品种的概率通常很小。如果品种权人能够证明被诉侵权的杂交种与使用授权品种作为父本或者母本杂交选育的杂交种构成基因型相同或者极近似品种，可以初步推定被诉侵权的杂交种使用授权品种作为亲本的

可能性较大。

In maize breeding practice, there is usually very low probability of using different parents to select and breed identical or highly similar varieties by crossing. If the variety rights holder can prove that the accused infringing hybrid and the hybrid bred by crossing the granted variety as male or female parent constitute identical or highly similar varieties, it can be preliminarily presumed that the accused infringing hybrid is more likely to use the granted variety as its parent.

【关键词】

[Keywords]

植物新品种　侵权　杂交玉米品种　亲子关系　推定使用

New plant varieties; infringement; hybrid corn varieties; paternity; constructive use

【案号】

[Case Number]

（2022）最高法知民终 13 号

（2022）SPC IP Civil Final 13

【基本案情】

[Case Facts]

在上诉人荆州市恒彩农业科技有限公司（以下简称恒彩公司）与被上诉人甘肃金盛源农业科技有限公司（以下简称金盛源公司）、郑州市华为种业有限公司（以下简称郑州华为种业公司）侵害植物新品种权纠纷案中，涉及“T37”玉米植物新品种（CNA20150367.6）和“WH818”玉米植物新品种（CNA20150368.5）。恒彩公司认为，金盛源公司销售，郑州华为种业公司生产、销售的“彩甜糯 866”是重复使用“T37”“WH818”作为亲本生产的，侵害了授权品种的品种权，故向河南省郑州市中级人民法院（以下简称一审法院）提起诉讼，请求判令两公司停止侵害，共同赔偿经济损失 20 万元及合理费用 2 万元。一审法院认为，恒彩公司提交的证据不足以证明被诉侵权行为侵害了“WH818”“T37”植物新品种权，故驳回了恒彩公司的诉讼请求。恒彩公司不服，向最高人民法院提起上诉，主张一审法院关于被诉侵权玉米种子是否使用“WH818”“T37”作为父、母本生产的事实举证责任分配错误，郑州华为种业公司不能合理解释被诉侵权玉米种子与“彩甜糯 6 号”为同一基因型杂交品种的事实，应该承担对其不利的相应后果。最高人民法院于 2022 年 10 月 20 日判决撤销原判，郑州华为种业公司停止生产销售“彩甜糯 866”，赔偿经济损失 20 万元、维权合理开支 2 万元。

The case of dispute over the infringement of new plant variety rights among the Appellant, Jingzhou Hengcai Agricultural Technology Co., Ltd. (hereinafter referred to as Hengcai), and the Appellees, Gansu Jinshengyuan Agricultural Technology Co., Ltd. (hereinafter referred to as Jinshengyuan), and Zhengzhou Huawei Seed Industry Co., Ltd. (hereinafter referred to as Zhengzhou Huawei Seed Industry), involves the new maize plant variety “T37” (CNA20150367.6) and the new maize plant variety “WH818” (CNA20150368.5). Hengcai believed that “Caitiannuo 866” sold by Jinshengyuan and produced and sold by Zhengzhou Huawei Seed Industry was produced by reusing “T37” and “WH818” as the parents, thus infringing the variety right of the authorized varieties, and it filed a lawsuit with the Intermediate People’s Court of Zhengzhou City, Henan Province (hereinafter referred to as the Court of First Instance), requesting the two companies to stop the infringement and compensate for the loss of CNY 200,000 and reasonable expenses of CNY 20,000. The Court of First Instance held that the exhibits submitted by Hengcai were insufficient to prove that the alleged infringement infringed on the new plant variety rights of “WH818” and “T37”, and therefore

rejected Hengcai's claims. Unsatisfied, Hengcai appealed to the SPC, claiming that the Court of First Instance had wrongly allocated the burden of proof on whether the infringing maize seeds were produced using "WH818" and "T37" as the parents and that Zhengzhou Huawei Seed Industry could not reasonably explain the fact that the infringing corn seed and "Caitiannuo 6" were hybrid varieties of the same genotype, and should bear the corresponding consequences unfavorable to it. The SPC ruled on October 20, 2022 that the original judgment should be reversed and that Zhengzhou Huawei Seed Industry should stop the production and sale of "Caitiannuo 6", and pay compensation of CNY 200, 000 for economic losses and CNY 20, 000 for reasonable expenses for defending its rights.

【裁判意见】

[Judge's Opinion]

最高人民法院二审认为，目前玉米杂交品种与亲本品种的亲子关系鉴定缺少行业标准，杂交玉米品种与其亲本品种的亲子关系这一事实可以结合双方的举证情况来认定。一般而言，在实际玉米育种生产中，使用不同的亲本通过杂交选育得到相同或者极近似品种的概率很小。鉴此，如果品种权人能够证明被诉侵权杂交种与使用授权品种作为父、母本杂交选育的杂交种构成基因型相同或者极近似品种时，可以初步推定被诉侵权杂交种使用了授权品种作为亲本的可能性较大，此时应转由被诉侵权人提供证据证明其实际并未使用品种权人所主张的授权品种作为亲本。在被诉侵权人并未提供证据或者提供的证据不足以推翻上述初步认定的，可以认定被诉侵权杂交种使用了授权品种作为亲本。本案中，由于被诉侵权玉米种子与使用“WH818”“T37”作为亲本获得的杂交品种属于基因型相同或极近似品种，可以初步推定被诉侵权玉米种子使用了与审定品种“彩甜糯 6 号”相同父、母本这一事实具有高度可能性。郑州华为种业公司没有举出被诉侵权玉米种子是通过其他亲本繁育的相反证据，应承担对其不利的后果。

The SPC held in the Second Instance that, at present, there is a lack of industry standards for the identification of the parentage of hybrid maize varieties and their parent varieties, and that the fact of the parentage of hybrid maize varieties and their parent varieties can be determined in conjunction with the evidence adduced by the two parties. In general, in actual maize breeding production, it is highly unlikely that the same or very similar varieties will be obtained through crossbreeding using different parents. In view of this, if the variety right holder can prove that the alleged infringing hybrids and the hybrids produced by using the authorized varieties as the parent crosses constitute the varieties with the same or very similar genotypes, it can be preliminarily presumed that there is a greater likelihood of the alleged infringing hybrids using the authorized varieties as parents, then it shall be turned over to the alleged infringer to provide evidence to prove that it did not actually use the authorized varieties claimed by the variety right holder as the parent, and if the alleged infringer does not provide the evidence or provides evidence insufficient to override the above preliminary determination, it may be determined that the alleged infringing hybrids were made using the authorized varieties as parents. In this case, as the accused infringing corn seed and the hybrid varieties obtained by using “WH818” and “T37” as the parents belong to the variety with the same or very similar genotypes, it can be initially presumed that there is a high possibility that the accused infringing corn seed has used the same parents with the approved variety of “Caitiannuo 6”, and Zhengzhou Huawei Seed Industry does not provide any evidence to the contrary that the accused infringing corn seed has been bred through other parents, and shall bear the adverse consequences for it.

47. 植物新品种特异性判断中已知品种的确定

Determination of known variety in assessing distinctness of new plant variety

【裁判要旨】

[Judgment Digest]

在植物新品种特异性判断中，确定在先的已知品种的目的是固定比对对象，即比较该申请品种与递交申请日以前的已知品种是否存在明显的性状区别。因此，特异性判断中的已知品种，不能是申请授权品种自身。与特异性的判断标准不同，新颖性判断则是以申请植物新品种保护的品种自身作为考察对象，判断其销售推广时间是否已超规定时间。

In assessing the distinctness of a new plant variety, determining the prior known variety aims to fix the comparison object, that is, to confirm whether there is any obvious difference in the characters between the variety to be applied and the known variety before the date of filing. Therefore, the known variety in assessing such distinctness cannot be the variety to be applied for granting of new plant variety. Unlike the criteria in assessing the distinctness, the novelty criterion targets the variety itself which is applied for granting of new plant variety, in which case what needs to be determined is whether its sales and promotion time exceeds the prescribed time limit.

【关键词】

[Keywords]

植物新品种　驳回复审　新颖性　特异性　已知品种　品种审定　申请日

New plant varieties; reexamination of rejection; novelty; specificity; known varieties; variety validation; the date of application

【案号】

[Case Number]

(2021) 最高法知行终 453 号

(2021) SPC IP Civil Final 453

【基本案情】

[Case Facts]

在上诉人黑龙江阳光种业有限公司(以下简称阳光种业公司)与被上诉人农业农村部植物新品种复审委员会(以下简称植物新品种复审委员会)植物新品种申请驳回复审行政纠纷案中,涉及申请号为20150963.4、名称为"哈育189"的玉米植物新品种申请。阳光种业公司认为,"哈育189"是在先已知的植物品种,"利合228"在国内首次申请品种审定或品种权保护的时间均晚于"哈育189",不能作为评价"哈育189"特异性的近似品种。故向北京知识产权法院(以下简称一审法院)提起诉讼,请求判令撤销植物新品种复审委员会于2019年1月17日作出的《关于维持〈哈育189品种实质审查驳回决定〉的决定》(以下简称被诉决定),并判令植物新品种复审委员会重新作出决定。一审法院认为,"哈育189"递交品种权申请时间为2015年6月29日,"利合228"品种权初审合格公告时间为2015年5月1日,"利合228"可以作为本申请递交前已知的植物品种,"哈育189"并未明显区别于在递交申请以前已知的植物品种"利合228",被诉决定关于"哈育189"不具备特异性的认定结论正确,应予确认。据此驳回阳光种业公司的诉讼请求。阳光种业公司不服,向最高人民法院提起上诉,主张"哈育189"通过审定时间为2015年4月8日,"哈育189"与"利合228"相比,"哈育189"系法定在先的"已知的植物品种","哈育189"玉米品种具备特异性。最高人民法院于2021年8月10日判决驳回上诉,维持原判。

The case of administrative dispute concerning the refusal to review the

application for new plant varieties between the Appellant, Heilongjiang Sunshine Seed Industry Co., Ltd. (hereinafter referred to as Sunshine Seed Industry), and the Appellee, the Reexamination Board for New Varieties of Plants of the Ministry of Agriculture and Rural Affairs (hereinafter referred to as the Reexamination Board for New Varieties of Plants), involves the application for corn plant variety of No. 20150963.4 and entitled "Hayu 189". Sunshine Seed Industry argued that "Hayu 189" was a prior known plant variety, and that the time when "Lihe 228" first applied for variety certification or variety right protection in China was later than that of "Hayu 189", and that "Lihe 228" could not be used as a close variety to evaluate the specificity of "Hayu 189". Therefore, a lawsuit was filed with Beijing Intellectual Property Court (hereinafter referred to as the Court of First Instance), requesting an order to revoke the Decision on Maintaining the Decision to Reject the Substantive Examination of the Variety Hayu 189 made by the Reexamination Board for New Varieties of Plants on January 17, 2019 (hereinafter referred to as the Decision under Appeal), and to order the Reexamination Board for New Varieties of Plants to make a new decision. The Court of First Instance held that the application for the variety right of "Hayu 189" was filed on June 29, 2015, and the announcement of the preliminary examination of the variety right of "Lihe 228" was made on May 1, 2015, and that "Lihe 228" could be regarded as a plant variety known prior to the filing of the present application, and that "Hayu 189" did not clearly differentiate itself from the plant variety known prior to the filing of the application, namely "Lihe 228", and that the conclusions contained in the Decision under Appeal regarding the lack of specificity of "Hayu 189" were correct, and should be affirmed. Sunshine Seed Industry's claims were accordingly dismissed. Unsatisfied, Sunshine Seed Industry appealed to the SPC, claiming that "Hayu 189" passed the validation on April 8, 2015, and that "Hayu 189" is a legally pre-existing "Known plant variety" as compared to "Lihe 228", and that "Hayu 189" is a maize variety with specificity. The SPC ruled on August 10, 2021 that the appeal was rejected and the original judgment was upheld.

【裁判意见】

[Judge's Opinion]

最高人民法院二审认为，授予品种权的植物新品种应当具备特异性。植物新品种保护条例第十五条规定，特异性是指申请品种权的植物新品种应当明显区别于在递交申请以前已知的植物品种。在特异性的判定中，确定在先的已知品种的目的是固定比对对象，即比较该申请品种与递交申请日以前的已知品种是否存在明显的性状区别，因此，作为特异性判断的已知品种，不能是申请授权品种自身。与特异性的判断标准不同，对于是否具备新颖性，是以申请植物新品种保护的品种自身作为基准，判断其销售推广的时间是否超过了规定的时间。植物新品种权保护条例第十四条规定，新颖性是指申请品种权的植物新品种在申请日前该品种繁殖材料未被销售，或者经育种者许可，在中国境内销售该品种繁殖材料未超过1年；在中国境外销售藤本植物、林木、果树和观赏树木品种繁殖材料未超过6年，销售其他植物品种繁殖材料未超过4年。因此，申请植物新品种权保护的品种在申请日之前存在的审定、推广的时间，对判断其是否具备新颖性具有重要意义，但与选择确定作为特异性判断的已知品种并无关联。

The SPC held in the Second Instance that new plant varieties for which variety rights are granted should possess specificity. Article 15 of the Regulations for the Protection of New Varieties of Plants stipulates that specificity means that a new variety of plant for which a variety right is applied for should be clearly differentiated from plant varieties known prior to the filing of the application. In the determination of specificity, the purpose of determining the

prior known varieties is to fix the object of comparison, i. e., to compare whether there is any obvious difference in traits between the applied-for variety and the known varieties prior to the date of filing of the application, and therefore, the known varieties used as a basis for the determination of specificity cannot be the varieties themselves for which the application for authorization is filed. Unlike the criteria for determining specificity, for whether there is novelty, the variety itself, which is the subject of the application for plant variety protection, is used as the benchmark for determining whether it has been sold and promoted for more than a specified period of time. Article 14 of the Regulations on the Protection of Rights to New Varieties of Plants stipulates that novelty refers to the fact that the propagating material of a new variety of plant for which a variety right is applied for has not been sold prior to the date of application of the variety, or that the propagating material of the variety has not been sold for more than one year within the territory of China with the permission of the breeder; the sale of propagating materials of vine, forest, fruit, and ornamental tree varieties outside China has not exceeded six years, and the sale of propagating materials of other plant varieties has not exceeded four years. Therefore, the time of validation and promotion of a variety applying for protection of a new plant variety right that existed prior to the date of application is important in determining whether it possesses novelty, but it is not relevant to the selection of the known varieties identified for use as a judgment of specificity.

本案中，阳光种业公司上诉提交的关于“哈育 189”玉米品种参加品种审定预备试验、通过审定初审审核等时间点的证据，是其具备新颖性的重要事实，与选择确定其作为特异性判断的已知品种不具有关联性。否则，以“哈育 189”玉米品种审定提出或通过审定的时间早于申请品种权保护的申请日为由，将其自身作为特异性判断的已知品种，不符合需要两个以上对象比对才有可能判断是否存在区别的逻辑常理，也有悖于品种权保护制度。因此，有关“哈育 189”玉米品种参加品种审定时间的证据与本案中已知品种的认定不具有关联性。

In this case, the exhibits submitted on appeal by Sunshine Seed Industry regarding the point in time when the corn variety “Hayu 189” participated in the variety validation preparatory trial and passed the preliminary examination and approval for validation are important facts of its novelty and are not relevant to the selection of the known varieties that were used to determine it as a specificity. Otherwise, taking the “Hayu 189” itself as a known variety for the judgment of specificity on the grounds that the time when the validation of the maize variety “Hayu 189” was proposed or approved earlier than the date of application for the protection of variety rights does not conform to the logical common sense that requires more than two objects to be compared before it is possible to determine whether there is a difference between them, and is also contrary to the system of protection of variety rights. Therefore, the evidence regarding the time of the participation in variety validation of the “Hayu 189” maize variety is not relevant to the determination of the known varieties in this case.

48. 销售重复使用授权品种繁殖材料生产的另一品种繁殖材料的侵权判定

Infringement identification in case of distributing propagation materials of another variety as produced through repeated use of propagation materials of granted variety

【裁判要旨】

[Judgment Digest]

未经许可重复使用授权品种繁殖材料作为父本或者母本生产其他品种繁殖材料的侵权生产者销售其生产所得繁殖材料的行为，系其侵权生产行为的自然延伸，势必导致侵权生产行为损害结果的进一步扩大。品种权人请求判令侵权生产者停止销售的，人民法院应予支持。

Sales of propagation materials by the infringing producers that produce the propagation materials of other varieties by repeatedly using propagation materials of the granted variety without permission either as male or female parent is a natural extension of the infringing production, which will inevitably result in further expansion of the damages caused by such infringing production. Where the variety right holders claim that the infringing producers cease the aforementioned sales, people's courts shall support such claim.

品种权人能够证明生产者之外的销售者明知所售繁殖材料系由他人未经许可重复使用授权品种繁殖材料作为父本或者母本生产所得，请求判令其停止销售的，人民法院可以认定该销售者构成帮助侵权，判令其停止销售。

If the variety right holders can prove that a seller other than the producer knowingly sells propagation materials that are produced by others by repeatedly using the propagation materials of granted variety either as male or female parent without permission, then people's courts may hold that such seller's act constitutes contributory infringement, and hence may order the seller to cease its sale.

【关键词】

[Keywords]

植物新品种侵权　帮助侵权　杂交玉米品种　亲子关系　侵权责任　停止销售

Infringement of new plant varieties; aiding infringement; hybrid corn varieties; paternity; tort liability; stop selling

【案号】

[Case Number]

(2022) 最高法知民终 13 号

(2022) SPC IP Civil Final 13

【裁判意见】

[Judge's Opinion]

在上诉人荆州市恒彩农业科技有限公司与被上诉人甘肃金盛源农业科技有限公司、郑州市华为种业有限公司侵害植物新品种权纠纷案中，最高人民法院二审认为，种子法第二十八条规定，除另有规定外，未经植物新品种权所有人许可，任何人不得为商业目的将该授权品种的繁殖材料重复使用于生产另一品种的繁殖材料。2006 年制定和 2020 年修正的《最高人民法院关于审理侵害植物新品种权纠纷案件具体应用法律问题的若干规定》第六条第一款均规定，对于侵害植物新品种权纠纷案件，结合案件具体情况，判决侵权人承担停止侵害、赔偿损失等民事责任。按照上述规定，郑州华为种业公司为商业目的，重复使用授权品种的繁殖材料生产被诉侵权玉米种子的行为侵害了“T37”“WH818”的品种权，应承担停止生产行为的侵权责任。郑州华为种业公司还销售

了上述另一品种的繁殖材料。对于销售重复使用授权品种繁殖材料生产的另一品种繁殖材料的行为，虽然种子法并未明确将其规定为侵权行为，但是，如果该另一品种是以同一品种权人的两个授权品种作为父、母本直接杂交繁殖而来，则销售该另一品种繁殖材料的行为系重复使用授权品种生产行为的自然延续，势必导致侵权生产行为造成的损害结果进一步扩大。因此，实施生产行为的侵权行为人不得销售其生产的该另一品种的繁殖材料，是制止生产者侵权行为、防止损失扩大的应有之义。因此，郑州华为种业公司还应承担停止销售行为的责任。

In the case of dispute over the infringement of new plant variety rights between the Appellant, Jingzhou Hengcai Agricultural Technology Co., Ltd. (hereinafter referred to as Hengcai), and the Appellees, Gansu Jinshengyuan Agricultural Technology Co., Ltd. (hereinafter referred to as Jinshengyuan), and Zhengzhou Huawei Seed Industry Co., Ltd. (hereinafter referred to as Zhengzhou Huawei Seed Industry), the SPC held in the Second Instance that Article 28 of the Seed Law stipulates that unless otherwise stipulated, without the permission of the owner of the right to a new variety of plant, no one shall reuse the propagation material of the authorized variety in the production of propagation material of another variety for commercial purposes. Article 6 (1) of the *Several Provisions of the SPC on the Specific Application of Law in the Trial of Cases of Disputes over Infringement of the Rights to New Varieties of Plants*, enacted in 2006 and amended in 2020, stipulates that in cases of disputes over infringement of the rights to new varieties of plants, the infringer shall be adjudged to bear civil liabilities for cessation of infringement and compensation for damages and other civil liabilities, taking into account the specific circumstances of the case. In accordance with the above provisions, Zhengzhou Huawei Seed Industry, for commercial purposes, repeatedly used the propagation materials of the authorized varieties to produce the infringing maize seeds, which infringed the variety rights of "T37" and "WH818", and should bear the liabilities of stopping the production. Zhengzhou Huawei Seed Industry also sold the propagation materials of another variety mentioned above. For the sale and repeated use of propagation materials of authorized varieties to produce propagation materials of another variety, although it is not explicitly stipulated in the Seed Law for infringement, if the other variety is propagated by using two authorized varieties from the same variety right holder as the parents through a direct hybridization, the sale of propagation materials of the other variety is a natural continuation of production by repeated use of the authorized varieties, which will lead to further expansion of the damage caused by the infringing production behavior. Therefore, the infringer who committed the act of production shall not sell the propagation materials of the other variety produced by it, which is necessary to stop the infringing behavior of the producer to prevent the expansion of the loss. Thus, Zhengzhou Huawei Seed Industry shall also bear the liability of stopping the sales behavior.

49. 种植无性繁殖授权品种行为的侵权判定 Infringement determination in case of planting asexually propagated granted variety

【裁判要旨】

[Judgment Digest]

品种权人主张种植无性繁殖授权品种的行为构成生产、繁殖授权品种繁殖材料的，人民法院可以综合考虑被诉侵权人的主体性质、行为目的、规模、是否具有合法来源等因素作出判断。被诉侵权人以育种、育苗为业，种植种苗并实施了许诺销售、销售行为的，可以认定其种植行为系为获取商业利益而非出于私人的非商业目的，该种植行为构成生

产、繁殖行为。

Where the variety right holder claims that the act of planting asexually propagated granted variety constitutes production or reproduction of propagation materials of granted variety, people's courts may make its judgment by comprehensively considering the accused infringer's subject nature, purpose and scale of the accused conduct, availability of legitimate source, etc. Where the alleged infringer's primary business is breeding and seeding, and such infringer plants the seed in question and also conducts the act of selling or offering to sell, then people's courts may deem that such planting is for commercial purpose rather than for private and non-commercial purpose, and hence constitutes act of production or reproduction.

【关键词】

[Keywords]

植物新品种　无性繁殖　种植行为　生产繁殖

New plant varieties; asexual reproduction; planting behavior; production or reproduction

【案号】

[Case Number]

（2022）最高法知民终435号

（2022）SPC IP Civil Final 435

【基本案情】

[Case Facts]

在上诉人河南省郑果红生态农业有限责任公司（以下简称郑果红公司）与被上诉人威海奥孚苗木繁育有限公司（以下简称奥孚苗木公司）侵害植物新品种权纠纷案中，涉及苹果植物新品种。奥孚苗木公司起诉郑果红公司侵害其“鲁丽”植物新品种权，要求其承担侵权责任。一审法院经审理认为，郑果红公司在其网站宣传销售“鲁丽”苹果树苗、收取“鲁丽”苹果树苗预定款以及宣传开挖“鲁丽”苹果树苗的火山小视频，足以证明郑果红公司繁殖“鲁丽”苹果树苗具有高度盖然性，判令郑果红公司停止侵权行为并赔偿奥孚苗木公司经济损失10万元及维权合理开支8500元。郑果红公司不服，向最高人民法院提起上诉，主要理由为种植“鲁丽”苹果树目的是“挂果”而非生产繁殖，奥孚苗木公司仅公证到其种植的“鲁丽”苹果树，并没有实际购买到“鲁丽”种苗，不能证明郑果红公司存在生产繁殖“鲁丽”品种的侵权行为。最高人民法院于2022年9月13日判决驳回上诉，维持原判。

The case of dispute over the infringement of new plant variety rights between the Appellant, Henan Zhengguohong Eco-agriculture Co., Ltd. (hereinafter referred to as Zhengguohong), and the Appellee, Weihai Ofil Seedling Breeding Co., Ltd. (hereinafter referred to as Ofil Seeding), involves the new apple variety, “Luli”. Ofil Seedling sued Zhengguohong for infringement of its plant variety of “Luli”, and demanded it to bear the liability for infringement of the rights. After investigation, the Court of First Instance held that Zhengguohong advertised the sale of “Luli” apple saplings on its website, received booking payments for “Luli” apple saplings, and advertised the excavation of “Luli” apple saplings through Huoshan Video, which was sufficient to prove that it was highly probative for Zhengguohong to propagate the “Luli” apple saplings, and Zhengguohong was ordered to stop the infringement behavior and compensate Ofil Seedling for the economic loss of CNY 100, 000 and for the reasonable expenses of right protection of CNY 8, 500. Unsatisfied, Zhengguohong appealed to the SPC, on the grounds that the planting of “Luli” apple trees was intended to “bear fruit” rather than the production of propagation, and Ofil Seedling only notarized its planting of “Luli” apple trees and did not actually buy the “Luli” seedlings, which cannot prove the existence of

infringement of Zhengguohong to produce and propagate the "Luli" variety. The SPC ruled on September 13, 2022 that the appeal was dismissed and the original judgement was upheld.

【裁判意见】

[Judge's Opinion]

最高人民法院二审认为，被诉侵权的果树叶片是奥孚苗木公司于2021年3月在郑果红公司挂有“鲁丽”的苹果树上公证取得。郑果红公司对于上述叶片来源于“鲁丽”苹果树并无异议，认可其实际种植的果树名称与“鲁丽”品种的名称一致，对于其实际种植的果树与“鲁丽”授权品种具有同一性的认定也未提出异议。关于郑果红公司种植“鲁丽”品种的行为性质，《最高人民法院关于审理侵害植物新品种权纠纷案件具体应用法律问题的若干规定（二）》第五条规定：“种植授权品种的繁殖材料的，人民法院可以根据案件具体情况，以生产、繁殖行为认定处理。”种植无性繁殖授权品种的行为是否属于繁殖授权品种繁殖材料的侵权行为，可以综合考虑被诉侵权人的主体性质、行为目的、规模、是否具有合法来源等因素作出判断。首先，郑果红公司是果树育种和育苗的经营主体，其种植“鲁丽”品种的动机是为获取商业利益，明显不属于私人的非商业目的。其次，郑果红公司主张其种植的“鲁丽”苹果树系来源于山东省果树研究所，但并未提交任何证据予以证明，其持有的“鲁丽”苹果树没有合法的来源。在案证据还显示郑果红公司存在收取“鲁丽”品种树苗预定款、在其网站宣传“鲁丽”品种及视频号、在视频中宣传开挖“鲁丽”树苗的行为。最后，即便郑果红公司种植“鲁丽”苹果树可能是为了获得该品种的果实，但果实来源于适龄的果树，需要对苗木进行管理，增枝扩冠，促使植物体由营养生长转为生殖生长，“鲁丽”品种是无性繁殖作物，在种植过程中可以通过自我复制和自我繁殖直接形成新个体。在郑果红公司无法提供其持有的“鲁丽”苗木存在合法来源的情况下，势必存在未经品种权人许可大量生产、繁殖“鲁丽”品种苗木，从而服务于获得“挂果”目的的行为。结合郑果红公司在网站上展示“鲁丽”品种，在视频中宣传“鲁丽”品种，存在销售授权品种繁殖材料的情节，应当认定其种植行为构成2015年修订的种子法第二十八条规定的繁殖授权品种繁殖材料的侵权行为。

The SPC held in the Second Instance that the leaves of the alleged infringing fruit trees were obtained by Ofil Seeding in March 2021 from Zhengguohong's apple trees bearing the name "Luli" through notarization. Zhengguohong had no objection to the above leaves originating from "Luli" apple trees, recognized that the name of the fruit trees actually planted by it was the same as the name of "Luli" variety, and did not object to the determination that the fruit trees actually planted by it were of the same nature as the authorized varieties of "Luli". With regard to the nature of Zhengguohong's act of planting the "Luli" variety, Article 5 of the *Several Provisions of the SPC on the Specific Application of Law in the Trial of Cases of Disputes over Infringement of the Rights to New Varieties of Plants (II)* stipulates that: "Where the planting of propagation materials of the authorized varieties is concerned, the people's court can determine and deal with it as an act of production and propagation in the light of the specific circumstances of the case." Whether the act of planting asexually propagated authorized varieties is an infringement of the right to propagate the propagation materials of the authorized varieties can be judged by taking into account the nature of the subject of the accused infringer, the purpose of the act, its scale, and whether it has a lawful source and other factors. First of all, Zhengguohong is a business entity of fruit tree breeding and nursery, and its motive for planting "Luli" variety is to obtain commercial benefits, which is obviously not a private non-commercial purpose. Secondly, Zhengguohong claimed that the "Luli" apple trees it planted

originated from the Shandong Province Fruit Tree Research Institute, but it did not submit any evidence to prove it, and thus, its holdings of the "Luli" apple trees have no legitimate source. The exhibits in the case also showed the existence of Zhengguohong to collect the booking payments for "Luli" saplings, advertise the "Luli" variety, and the video account on its website, and advertise the excavation of "Luli" saplings in the video. Lastly, even if "Luli" apple trees may be planted by Zhengguohong in order to obtain the fruit of the variety, but the fruit comes from the appropriate age of the fruit tree, which requires the management of seedlings, addition of branches and expansion of the crown, to promote the plant body from nutrient growth to reproductive growth; as "Luli" varieties are crops that reproduce asexually, and in the process of planting, new individuals can be formed directly through self-replication and self-propagation. Where Zhengguohong cannot prove that its holdings of "Luli" seedlings have a legitimate source, there must be a behavior of large-scale production and propagation of "Luli" varieties of seedlings without the permission of the variety right holder, so as to serve the purpose of obtaining the "fruits". Considering the fact that Zhengguohong displays the "Luli" variety on its website and promotes the "Luli" variety in the video and that there are circumstances of selling the propagation materials of the authorized variety, it should be determined that its planting behavior constitutes the infringement by propagating the propagation materials of the authorized varieties as stipulated in Article 28 of the Seed Law as amended in 2015.

50. 品种权人请求以许可使用费代替停止侵害的处理
Handling of variety rights holder's request for license fee in substitution of the cessation of the infringement

【裁判要旨】

[Judgment Digest]

多年生果树品种权人请求以给付许可使用费代替停止侵害的，既有利于避免资源浪费，又有利于实现果树种植的经济效益，应予肯定和鼓励。在确定许可使用费时，一般可以考虑同时期的可比许可使用费情况，妥善平衡品种权人合法权益和种植者合理预期利益。

Where right holders of perennial fruit tree variety claim license fee in substitution of ceasing the infringement, such claim shall be affirmed and encouraged, because it not only helps to avoid the waste of resources, but also helps to realize economic benefits of fruit tree planting. In determining such license fee, generally, considerations can be given to the comparable license fee for the same period, so as to properly balance the legitimate rights and interests of the variety right holders and the reasonable expected benefits of cultivators.

【关键词】

[Keywords]

植物新品种　侵权　无性繁殖　种植　生产繁殖　农民专业合作社　许可使用费　停止侵害

New plant varieties; infringement; asexual reproduction; cultivation; production or reproduction; farmers' professional cooperatives; royalties; cessation of infringement

【案号】

[Case Number]

(2022) 最高法知民终 211 号

(2022) SPC IP Civil Final 211

【基本案情】

[Case Facts]

在上诉人马边彝族自治县石丈空猕猴桃专业合作社（以下简称石丈空合作社）与被上诉人四川依顿猕猴桃种植有限责任公司（以下简称依顿猕猴桃公司）侵害植物新品种权纠纷案中，涉及品种权号CNA20110642.7、品种名称“杨氏金红1号”的猕猴桃品种（以下简称授权品种）。依顿猕猴桃公司经品种权人授权向四川省成都市中级人民法院（以下简称一审法院）提起诉讼，主张石丈空合作社未经许可，将购买的接穗在砧木上进行嫁接，并从第一次嫁接长成的猕猴桃树上获取接穗进行二次嫁接，构成生产涉案授权品种繁殖材料的行为，侵害了授权品种的植物新品种权。一审法院认定侵权成立，判令石丈空合作社支付从2019年12月18日至2021年7月16日的品种许可使用费110833元；从2021年7月17日起按每株猕猴桃树每年10元的标准按照实际种植株数（目前共计7000株）于每年7月16日前支付品种许可使用费；支付维权合理开支3万元。石丈空合作社不服，向最高人民法院提起上诉。最高人民法院于2022年11月18日判决驳回上诉，维持原判。

The case of dispute over the infringement of new plant variety rights between the Appellant, Shizhangkong Kiwi Professional Cooperative in Mabian Yi Autonomous County (hereinafter referred to as Shizhangkong Cooperative), and the Appellee, Sichuan Yidun Kiwi Planting Co., Ltd. (hereinafter referred to as Yidun Kiwi), involves kiwi variety No. CNA20110642.7 and entitled "Yang's Jinhong 1" (hereinafter referred to as the authorized variety). Yidun Kiwi, with the authorization of the variety right holder, filed a lawsuit with the Chengdu Intermediate People's Court of Sichuan Province (hereinafter referred to as the Court of First Instance), claiming that Shizhangkong Cooperative's behavior of producing propagation materials of the authorized varieties in question by grafting purchased scions on rootstocks and obtaining scions from the kiwifruit trees that had grown from the first grafting to make a second grafting without permission, was infringing on the plant variety right of the authorized varieties. The Court of First Instance found the infringement was established and ordered Shizhangkong Cooperative to pay CNY 110,833 in variety royalties from December 18, 2019 to July 16, 2021; variety royalties will be paid at the rate of CNY 10 per kiwifruit tree per year starting from July 17, 2021, based on the actual number of plants planted (currently totaling 7,000 plants) by July 16 of each year; the payment of CNY 30,000 in reasonable expenses for the defense of rights shall be made. Unsatisfied, Shizhangkong Cooperative appealed to the SPC. The SPC ruled on November 18, 2022, that the appeal should be rejected and the original judgment should be upheld.

【裁判意见】

[Judge's Opinion]

最高人民法院二审认为，涉案授权品种“杨氏金红 1 号”为猕猴桃品种，猕猴桃树为多年生植物，可通过收获猕猴桃果实为种植者持续带来经济效益。依顿猕猴桃公司在本案中请求无须铲除苗木，而要求石丈空合作社向其支付许可使用费，相比于简单地停止侵害和销毁侵权物，品种权人以许可使用费的请求代替停止侵害的请求具有实际可操作性，既符合避免资源浪费、物尽其用的原则，又有利于发挥涉案种植基地的经济效益，对此应予以肯定和鼓励。

The SPC held in the Second Instance that the authorized variety in question, "Yang's Jinhong 1", was a kiwifruit variety and that kiwifruit trees were

perennial plants that could bring continuous economic benefits to growers through harvesting kiwifruit fruits. In this case, Yidun Kiwi requested that the seedlings not be eradicated, and instead requested the Shizhangkong Cooperative to pay royalties to it. Compared with simply stopping the infringement and destroying the infringing materials, it is practical and feasible for the variety right holder to request royalties in lieu of stopping the infringement, which is in line with the principle of avoiding wastage of resources and making full use of the materials, and also helps to give full play to the economic benefit of the planting base involved, and this should be affirmed and encouraged.

二审法院考虑如下因素确定本案许可使用费：第一，尊重涉案授权品种的市场价值，考虑同时期的可比许可使用费情况。从石丈空合作社提交的协议书可以看出授权费存在一定差异。从双方提交的《授权种植与销售协议书》内容可知，品种权人和利害关系人从“杨氏金红 1 号”许可中可以获得的收益不仅包括每年支付的品种权使用费，而且还包括销售繁殖材料的收益、从实施者销售收入中提取的市场管理服务费或者按照固定价格全部买断后自行销售的获利、从代为采购农业生产资料中提取的管理费，以及技术服务费等。在依顿猕猴桃公司请求许可使用费的情况下，虽然免除了其向石丈空合作社提供技术服务、代为进行销售等义务，但石丈空合作社客观上从依顿猕猴桃公司的市场管理行为包括品牌维护中获利，例如石丈空合作社已经在 2019 年选送“杨氏金红 1 号”参加猕猴桃品鉴会并获得金奖。因此，在确定许可使用费时对此也应予以考虑。第二，保障石丈空合作社对于种植行为的合理预期利益。涉案种植基地的经济效益一方面依赖“杨氏金红 1 号”新品种的市场优势，另一方面也需要石丈空合作社付出勤勉劳动和科学管理才能从种植中获取收益。一般而言，猕猴桃树在嫁接、种植后，要经过试挂果期、结果期、盛果期等，一株成熟的猕猴桃树有长达十几年甚至二十多年的盛果期，可以将这一大量结果期的产量作为确定许可使用费考虑的因素。关于生产成本，一审法院考虑每棵树的产值和管理成本、人工成本以及未进入结果期之前的时间成本，同时还考虑了本案存在贫困农民合作入股等特殊情形，确定每株每年许可使用费为 10 元，已经充分保障了贫困农民的合理预期利益，并无不当。并且，一审法院以石丈空合作社主张的从欣耀公司最后一次购买接穗的时间起算许可费的计付时间，已经有利于石丈空合作社。石丈空合作社关于其实际没有盈利，一审判决确定的许可使用费过高的上诉理由，缺乏证据支持，不予支持。

The Court of Second Instance considered the following factors in determining the royalties in the case: first, respecting the market value of the authorized varieties in question, and taking into account comparable royalties over the same period of time. There is some difference in the authorization fee as can be seen by the agreement submitted by the Shizhangkong Cooperative. It can be seen from the content of the Authorized Planting and Sales Agreement submitted by the two parties that the revenues that the variety right holders and interested parties can obtain from the license of "Yang's Jinhong 1" include not only the variety right royalties paid annually, but also the revenues from the sale of propagation materials, the market management service fees extracted from the sales revenues of the implementer, or the profits from the sale of the plant at a fixed price after the total buyout, and the management fees extracted from the procurement of agricultural production materials on their behalf, as well as the technical service fees, and so on. In the case of Yidun Kiwi's request for royalties, although it is relieved of its obligations to provide technical services to the Shizhangkong Cooperative and to conduct sales on its behalf, the Shizhangkong Cooperative objectively benefits from Yidun Kiwi's marketing management practices, including brand maintenance, as, for example, Shizhangkong Cooperative has already selected "Yang's Jinhong 1" to

participate in the kiwifruit tasting in 2019 and won the gold medal. Therefore, this should also be taken into account when determining royalties. Second, the Shizhangkong Cooperative is guaranteed a reasonable expectation of benefit from the act of planting. The economic benefits of the planting base in question depend on the market advantage of the new variety of "Yang's Jinhong 1" on the one hand, and on the other hand, it also requires Shizhangkong Cooperative to put in diligent labor and scientific management in order to obtain income from planting. In general, after grafting and planting, kiwifruit trees go through a trial fruiting period, a fruiting period, a full fruiting period, etc. A mature kiwifruit tree has a full fruiting period of up to a dozen years or even more than 20 years, and the production of this substantial fruiting period can be taken into account as a factor in determining the royalties. Regarding the production cost, the Court of First Instance, taking into account the production value of each tree and the cost of management, labor cost, and the cost of time before entering the fruiting period, and also taking into account the existence of the case of the poor farmers' cooperation in the shares and other special circumstances, determined that the annual license fees for each plant is CNY 10, which has adequately safeguarded the reasonably expected interests of the poor farmers, without any impropriety. Moreover, the Court of First Instance has already favored Shizhangkong Cooperative by calculating the time of payment of the license fee from the time of the last purchase of the scion from Xinyao, as claimed by Shizhangkong Cooperative. The Shizhangkong Cooperative's appeal that it actually did not make a profit and that the royalties determined by the First Instance judgment were too high lacked evidentiary support and could not be upheld.

51. 杂交品种亲本植物新品种权对侵权获利的贡献率 Contribution rate of new variety rights of hybrid parents to profits originating from infringement

【裁判要旨】

[Judgment Digest]

未经许可重复使用授权品种作为亲本生产其他品种繁殖材料的侵权获利计算，应当考虑授权品种对于侵权利润的贡献率。亲本均为授权品种的，贡献率一般可以平均分配；部分亲本为授权品种，其他亲本不受品种权保护的，授权品种的贡献率可以视情酌定为 100%。

The contribution rate of a granted variety to the profits originating from infringement should be taken into account in calculating the profits originating from infringement in the case of producing propagation materials of other varieties by repeatedly using the granted variety as the parent without permission. Where all the parents are granted varieties, the contribution rate may generally be distributed equally; where only the male or female parent is granted variety, and the other is not protected by variety rights, the contribution rate of the granted variety can be set at 100% at discretion, as the case may be.

【关键词】

[Keywords]

植物新品种　杂交品种　亲本　侵权　损害赔偿　侵权获利　贡献率

New plant varieties; hybridization; parentage; infringement; damages; profits from infringement; contribution rate

【案号】

[Case Number]

（2022）最高法知民终 783、789 号

（2022）SPC IP Civil Final 783 & 789

【基本案情】

[Case Facts]

在上诉人四川雅玉科技股份有限公司（以下简称雅玉公司）与上诉人云南金禾种业有限公司（以下简称金禾公司）、被上诉人云南瑞禾种业有限公司（以下简称瑞禾公司）侵害植物新品种权纠纷两案中，涉及"YA8201"玉米植物新品种（CNA20060204.7），品种权人为雅玉公司。雅玉公司认为，金禾公司以商业为目的重复使用"YA8201"生产"金禾玉618""金禾880"玉米种子，瑞禾公司向金禾公司出借农作物种子生产经营许可证，故向云南省昆明市中级人民法院（以下简称一审法院）提起诉讼，请求判令金禾公司、瑞禾公司停止侵害，并承担惩罚性赔偿责任。一审法院认为，金禾公司构成侵权，瑞禾公司构成帮助侵权，适用惩罚性赔偿确定两案中金禾公司分别赔偿104022元、456897元，瑞禾公司承担连带责任。雅玉公司、金禾公司均不服，向最高人民法院提起上诉，雅玉公司主张一审法院确定利润率、贡献率错误，认定赔偿数额过低，金禾公司则主张一审法院确定的赔偿数额过高。最高人民法院于2022年12月7日作出判决，适用惩罚性赔偿，并按照侵权获利作为计算惩罚性赔偿的基数，两案中分别改判金禾公司赔偿雅玉公司经济损失693480元、1522990元，瑞禾公司承担连带责任。

The case of dispute over the infringement of new plant variety rights among the Appellants, Sichuan Yayu Technology Co., Ltd. (hereinafter referred to as Yayu), and Yunnan Jinhe Seed Industry Co., Ltd. (hereinafter referred to as Jinhe), and the Appellee, Yunnan Ruihe Seed Industry Co., Ltd. (hereinafter referred to as Ruihe), involves a new variety of maize, "YA8201"(CNA20060204.7), and the variety right was owned by Yayu. Yayu believed that Jinhe reused "YA8201" to produce maize seeds of "Jinheyu 618" and "Jinhe 880" for commercial purposes, and Ruihe lent crop seed production and operation licenses to Jinhe, so it filed a lawsuit with Kunming Intermediate People's Court of Yunnan Province (hereinafter referred to as the Court of First Instance), requesting to order Jinhe and Ruihe to stop the infringement and bear the liability of punitive damages. The Court of First Instance held that Jinhe constituted an infringement and Ruihe constituted aiding infringement and that punitive damages were applicable to determine that Jinhe compensated CNY 104,022 and CNY 456,897 respectively in the two cases, for which Ruihe was jointly and severally liable. Unsatisfied, both Yayu and Jinhe appealed to the SPC, with Yayu claiming that the Court of First Instance had determined the profit rate and contribution rate incorrectly and found the amount of compensation to be too low, and Jinhe claiming that the amount of compensation determined by the Court of First Instance was too high. The SPC issued a judgment on December 7, 2022, applying punitive damages and using the profit from infringement as the basis for calculating punitive damages, and in the two cases, Jinhe was instead sentenced to compensate Yayu's economic losses of CNY 693,480 and CNY 1,522,990, respectively, and Ruihe was jointly and severally liable.

【裁判意见】

[Judge's Opinion]

最高人民法院二审认为，金禾公司明知“YA8201”为雅玉公司享有品种权的植物新品种，仍然未经品种权人许可为商业目的重复使用“YA8201”的繁殖材料生产“金禾玉 618”“金禾 880”的繁殖材料。瑞禾公司出借其种子生产经营许可证，为金禾公司的侵权行为提供帮助，构成帮助侵权，应承担连带责任。金禾公司租借种子生产经营许可证的行为，构成侵权行为情节严重，依法可以适用惩罚性赔偿。为商业目的故意重复利用他人授权品种作为亲本进行育种的行为，需要父本和母本两个亲本才能完成，本案权利人的授权品种“YA8201”作为“金

禾玉 618”和“金禾 880”的父本只是实施侵权行为的必要因素之一，在以侵权获利计算惩罚性赔偿基数时，需要考虑授权品种对侵权行为的贡献率。在确定贡献率时，两案分别考虑“金禾玉 618”的母本不享有品种权，“金禾 880”的母本同时受品种权保护，从而确定授权品种“YA8201”的贡献率对“金禾玉 618”“金禾 880”的贡献率分别为100%和 50%。

The SPC held in the Second Instance that Jinhe knew that “YA8201” was a new variety of plant for which Yayu enjoyed variety rights, and still reused the propagation material of “YA8201” to produce the propagation material of “Jinheyu 618” and “Jinhe 880” for commercial purposes without the permission of the variety right holder. Ruihe lent its seed production and operation license to provide assistance to Jinhe's infringement, which constituted aiding infringement and should be held jointly and severally liable. Jinhe's act of lending a seed production and operation license constitutes a serious infringement, and punitive damages may be applied in accordance with the law. For breeding behavior with the intent to repeat the use of others' authorized varieties as the parent for commercial purposes, it requires two parents to complete the breeding. The authorized variety “YA8201” of the right holder as the father of “Jinheyu 618” and “Jinhe 880” is only one of the necessary factors to implement the infringing behavior, and when calculating the base of punitive damages in terms of infringing profits, it is necessary to take into account the contribution rate of the authorized varieties to the infringing behavior. In determining the contribution rate, the two cases respectively took into account that the mother of “Jinheyu 618” did not enjoy variety rights, and the mother of “Jinhe 880” was protected by variety rights at the same time, so as to determine that the contribution rate of the authorized variety “YA8201” to “Jinheyu 618” and “Jinhe 880” was 100% and 50%, respectively.

52. 侵权繁殖材料灭活处理后损害赔偿责任的承担

Assumption of liability for damages after devitalization of infringing propagation materials

【裁判要旨】

[Judgment Digest]

责令采取灭活措施与赔偿损失均为侵权责任的具体承担方式，二者并非排斥适用的关系。侵权繁殖材料被灭活处理，在效果上能够减少损失的进一步扩大，但生产侵权繁殖材料的行为本身即已构成对品种权的侵害，势必会挤占品种权人的市场空间，即便侵权繁殖材料因被灭活处理最终没有流入市场，也不意味着品种权人没有因其市场被挤占而遭受损失，侵权人仍然应当承担损害赔偿责任。

Both taking devitalization measures and compensating losses are specific ways to assume tort liabilities, and they can be adopted at the same time. The devitalization of infringing propagation materials can reduce further expansion of losses in effect, but the production of infringing propagation materials in itself has already constituted infringement upon the variety rights, which will inevitably occupy the market space of the variety right holders. Even if infringing propagation materials do not ultimately enter the market because of devitalization, it does not mean that the variety right holders do not suffer any losses as incurred by the aforementioned market space occupation, and hence the infringers should still be liable for damages in such scenario.

【关键词】

[Keywords]

植物新品种　侵权　灭活　赔偿损失

New plant varieties; infringement; devitalization; damages

【案号】

[Case Number]

(2021) 最高法知民终 2105 号

(2021) SPC IP Civil Final 2105

【基本案情】

[Case Facts]

在上诉人北京联创种业有限公司（以下简称联创公司）与被上诉人吴某寿侵害植物新品种权纠纷案中，涉及“裕丰 303”杂交玉米新品种（以下简称涉案品种）。联创公司是涉案品种的品种权人。吴某寿未经许可，自行繁育涉案品种的玉米种子达 207 亩。上述侵权玉米种子成熟后，农业执法部门对种子果穗进行了灭活处理。联创公司认为，吴某寿的行为侵害其涉案品种权，故向甘肃省兰州市中级人民法院（以下简称一审法院）提起诉讼，请求判令吴某寿赔偿经济损失及维权合理开支共计 315500 元。一审法院认为，吴某寿虽实施了侵权行为，但侵权行为已经停止，联创公司无证据证明其因侵权行为遭受的损失，以及吴某寿的侵权获利，结合侵权种子已经灭活、无法作为繁殖材料流入市场的实际情况，涉案侵权行为并未对联创公司造成损害结果，对联创公司赔偿损失的诉讼请求不予支持，酌定吴某寿承担维权合理开支 5000 元。联创公司不服，向最高人民法院提起上诉，主张涉案玉米种子虽然进行了转商灭活处理，但是灭活处理只是制止侵权行为的一种处理方式，吴某寿的侵权行为仍然给联创公司造成了损失，应当承担赔偿责任。最高人民法院于 2022 年 11 月 3 日改判吴某寿赔偿联创公司经济损失 207000 元、维权合理开支 5000 元，共计 212000 元。

The case of dispute over the infringement of new plant variety rights between the Appellant, Beijing Lantron Seed Co., Ltd. (hereinafter referred to as Lantron), and the Appellee, Wu, involves the new hybrid maize variety

"Yufeng 303" (hereinafter referred to as the variety in question). Lantron is the owner of the variety right of the variety in question. Wu bred the corn seed of the variety in question on his own without permission on up to 207 acres. After the above infringing corn seeds matured, the agricultural law enforcement authorities devitalized the seed cobs. Lantron believed that Wu's behavior infringed on its rights to the variety in question, so it filed a lawsuit with Lanzhou Intermediate People's Court of Gansu Province (hereinafter referred to as the Court of First Instance), requesting Wu to compensate for the economic losses and reasonable expenses for defending its rights, totaling CNY 315, 500. The Court of First Instance held that, although Wu had committed the infringement, the infringement had stopped, and Lantron had no evidence to prove that it had suffered losses due to the infringement, as well as Wu's profits from the infringement, and with the fact that the infringing seeds had been devitalized, and could not flow into the market as propagation materials, the infringement did not cause any damages to Lantron, and Lantron's Claims for compensation of damages could not be supported, and Wu was determined to bear CNY 5000 as the reasonable expenditure for defending his rights. Unsatisfied, Lantron appealed to the SPC, claiming that although the corn seeds in question had been devitalized, the devitalization treatment was only a way of stopping the infringement, and that Wu's infringement still caused losses to Lantron and he should bear the liability for the damages. The SPC reversed the judgment on November 3, 2022, and ruled that Wu should compensate Lantron for economic losses of CNY 207, 000 and reasonable expenses of CNY 5, 000 for defending its rights, which amounted to CNY 212, 000 in total.

【裁判意见】

[Judge's Opinion]

最高人民法院二审认为，吴某寿出于商业目的，擅自生产涉案品种的玉米种子，侵害了联创公司的植物新品种权，依法应当承担侵权责任。灭活处理与赔偿损失均为侵权责任的具体承担方式，二者并非排斥适用的关系。责令采取灭活措施既是侵权人因侵权行为应当承担的行政责任，也是民事责任，侵权人承担了采取灭活措施的责任，并不影响其另行承担赔偿损失的民事责任。侵权人承担采取灭活措施的责任，虽然能够产生防止损失进一步扩大的效果，但不能避免损失的发生。吴某寿大规模生产涉案玉米种子的行为本身已经挤占了品种权人的市场空间，包括品种权人自身本来可能实现的种子市场规模和商品粮市场规模。即便作为繁殖材料的被诉侵权玉米种子因被灭活处理最终没有流入种子市场，也不意味着品种权人没有因其市场被挤占而遭受损失，仍会给品种权人造成损失，应当承担赔偿责任。

The SPC held in the Second Instance that Wu produced the corn seeds of the variety in question without authorization for commercial purposes, infringing on Lantron's rights to new varieties of plants, and should be held liable for infringement in accordance with the law. Both devitalization treatment and compensation for damages are specific ways of assuming tort liability, and they are not mutually exclusive. The order to take devitalization measures is both the administrative responsibility and civil liability of the infringer for the infringement, and the infringer's responsibility to take devitalization measures does not affect his civil liability to compensate for damages. The infringer's liability to take measures of devitalization cannot avoid the occurrence of the loss, although it can have the effect of preventing the loss from spreading further. Wu's large-scale production of the corn seed in question has crowded out the variety right holder's market space, including the seed market size and commercial grain market size that the variety right holder itself might have realized. Even if the alleged infringing corn seed as propagation material did not eventually flow into the seed market due to devitalization treatment, it does not mean that the variety right holder did not suffer losses due to its market being crowded out. It will still cause losses to the variety right holder, and Wu should be held liable for compensation.

四、技术秘密案件

Ⅳ. Technical Secrets Cases

53. 杂交种的亲本构成商业秘密保护的对象

Parents of hybrids can be protected as trade secret

【裁判要旨】

[Judgment Digest]

作物育种过程中形成的育种中间材料、自交系亲本等，不同于自然界发现的植物材料，是育种者付出创造性劳动的智力成果，承载有育种者对自然界的植物材料选择驯化或对已有品种的性状进行选择而形成的特定遗传基因，该育种材料具有技术信息和载体实物兼而有之的特点，且二者不可分离。通过育种创新活动获得的具有商业价值的育种材料，在具备不为公众所知悉并采取相应保密措施等条件下，可以作为商业秘密依法获得法律保护。

Different from plant material in the nature, breeding intermediate material and parent variety of the inbred line formed in the process of crop breeding are the intellectual achievements of the breeders’ inventive work and carry specific genetic information formed by the breeders’ cultivation of plant materials in the nature or selection of the properties of existing varieties. The breeding materials are characterized with inseparable technical information and physical objects of the carrier. Breeding materials with commercial value obtained from breeding innovation activities can be protected as trade secrets by law, provided that they are not known to the public and the relevant confidentiality measures are taken.

【关键词】

[Keywords]

商业秘密　技术信息　杂交种自交系亲本

Trade secrets; technical information; hybrid inbred line parents

【案号】

[Case Number]

(2022) 最高法知民终 147 号

(2022) SPC IP Civil Final 147

【基本案情】

[Case Facts]

在上诉人武威市搏盛种业有限责任公司（以下简称搏盛种业公司）与被上诉人河北华穗种业有限公司（以下简称华穗种业公司）侵害技术秘密纠纷案中，涉及玉米植物新品种“万糯 2000”的亲本“W68”。华穗种业公司起诉搏盛种业公司侵害其玉米植物新品种“万糯 2000”的亲本自交系“W68”的技术秘密，要求其承担侵权责任。一审法院经审理认为，搏盛种业公司在其生产经营活动中使用“W68”技术信息，构成侵权，判决搏盛种业公司停止侵害，赔偿经济损失及维权合理开支共计 150.5 万元。搏盛种业公司不服，向最高人民法院提起上诉，主张“W68”作为亲本不属于商业秘密的保护客体。最高人民法院于 2022 年 11 月 2 日判决驳回上诉，维持原判。

The case of dispute over the infringement of technical secrets between the Appellant, Wuwei Bosheng Seed Co., Ltd. (hereinafter referred to as Bosheng Seed), and the Appellee, Hebei Huasui Seed Co., Ltd. (hereinafter re-

ferred to as Huasui Seed), involves the parent "W68" of the new maize variety, "Wannuo 2000". Huasui Seed sued Bosheng Seed for infringement of the technical secret of the parental inbred line "W68" of its new maize plant variety "Wannuo 2000", claiming that it be held liable for the infringement of the technical secret. After hearing the case, the Court of First Instance held that the use of "W68" technical information by Bosheng Seed in its production and business activities constituted infringement, and ruled that Bosheng Seed should stop the infringement, and compensate for the economic loss and reasonable expenses for the protection of rights totaling CNY 1. 505 million. Unsatisfied, Bosheng Seed appealed to the SPC, claiming that "W68" as a parent does not belong to the object of protection of trade secrets. The SPC ruled on November 2, 2022 that the appeal should be dismissed and the original judgement should be upheld.

【裁判意见】

[Judge's Opinion]

最高人民法院二审认为，作物育种过程中形成的育种中间材料、自交系亲本等，不同于自然界发现的植物材料，其是育种者付出创造性劳动的智力成果，承载有育种者对自然界的植物材料选择驯化或对已有品种的性状进行选择而形成的特定遗传基因，该育种材料具有技术信息和载体实物兼而有之的特点，且二者不可分离。通过育种创新活动获得的具有商业价值的育种材料，在具备不为公众所知悉并采取相应保密措施等条件下，可以作为商业秘密依法获得法律保护。本案"W68"作为"万糯2000"亲本的事实已经证明，其在组配具有优良农艺性状、良好制种产量的杂交种中具备商业价值，具有竞争优势。因此，在其符合不为公众所知悉，并经权利人采取相应保密措施的条件下，可以作为商业秘密获得反不正当竞争法的保护。搏盛种业公司关于只有与亲本相关的育种技术信息才能作为商业秘密保护对象的主张，法律依据不足。

The SPC held in the Second Instance that the breeding intermediate materials and inbred line parents formed in the process of crop breeding are different from the plant materials found in nature and are the intellectual achievements of the breeders with creative labors, carrying the specific genetic genes formed by the breeders' selection of domestication of the plant materials in nature or selection of the traits of the existing varieties, and that the breeding materials are characterized by both the technical information and the physical carriers while they are not separable from each other. Breeding materials of commercial value obtained through breeding innovation activities may be legally protected as trade secrets under the conditions that they are not known to the public and that corresponding confidentiality measures are taken. In this case, the fact that "W68" is the parent of "Wannuo 2000" has proved that it has commercial value and competitive advantage in the formulation of hybrids with excellent agronomic traits and good seed yield. Therefore, under the condition that it is not known to the public and the right holder has taken corresponding confidentiality measures, it can be protected as a trade secret by the Anti-Unfair Competition Law. There is insufficient legal basis for the claim of Bosheng Seed that only breeding technology information related to parents can be the object of trade secret protection.

综合运用植物新品种权、专利权、商业秘密等多种知识产权保护手段，构建多元化、立体式的农作物育种成果综合法律保护体系，符合我国种业发展的现状。植物新品种和商业秘密两种制度在权利产生方式、保护条件、保护范围等方面都存在差异，权利人可以根据实际情况选择不同保护方式。在作物育种过程中，符合植物品种权保护条件的育种创新成果，可以受到植物新品种权制度的保护。同时，杂交种的亲本等育种材料符合商业秘密保护要件的，可以受到反不正当竞争法的兜底保护。将未获得植物新品种保护的育种创新成果在符合商业秘密的条件下

给予制止不正当竞争的保护，是鼓励育种创新的必然要求，也是加强知识产权保护的题中应有之义。法律并未限制作物育种材料只能通过植物新品种保护而排除商业秘密等其他知识产权保护，对作物育种材料给予商业秘密等其他知识产权保护不会削弱植物新品种保护法律制度，而是相辅相成、相得益彰的关系。当然，对作物育种材料给予商业秘密保护，并不妨碍他人通过独立研发等合法途径来繁育品种，也并不妨碍科研活动的自由。搏盛种业公司认为一审法院对亲本繁殖材料无限期、无原则的保护会削弱植物新品种保护制度的主张，不予支持。

Comprehensive use of plant variety rights, patents, trade secrets, and other means of intellectual property protection to build a diversified, three-dimensional comprehensive legal protection system for crop breeding achievements is in line with the current situation of the development of China's seed industry. There are differences between the two systems of new plant varieties and trade secrets in terms of the way of generating rights, conditions of protection, scope of protection, etc., and the right holders can choose different ways of protection according to the actual situation. In the course of crop breeding, breeding innovations that meet the conditions for a plant variety right protection may be protected by the system of new plant variety rights. At the same time, breeding materials such as parents of hybrids that meet the elements of trade secret protection can be subject to the protection of the Anti-unfair Competition Law. Giving protection against unfair competition to breeding innovations that are not protected by new plant varieties under the condition of conforming to trade secrets is an inevitable requirement for encouraging breeding innovations, and is also the proper intention of strengthening the protection of intellectual property rights. The Law does not restrict crop breeding materials to be protected only by new plant varieties to the exclusion of other intellectual property rights, such as trade secrets, and giving other intellectual property rights, such as trade secrets, to crop breeding materials will not weaken the legal system of protection of new plant varieties, but rather, they are complementary and mutually reinforcing. Of course, the granting of trade secret protection to crop breeding materials does not prevent others from breeding varieties through independent research and development and other legitimate means, nor does it impede the freedom of scientific research activities. Bosheng Seed Company's claim that the Court of First Instance applied indefinite and unprincipled protection to parental propagation materials, which would weaken the system of protection of new plant varieties, was not supported.

54. 以图纸作为技术秘密载体时技术秘密内容的确定 Determination of the contents of technical secrets when drawings are the carrier of such technical secrets

【裁判要旨】

[Judgment Digest]

图纸可以作为技术秘密的载体，依据图纸可以确定其主张的技术秘密的内容和范围。权利人既可以主张图纸记载的全部技术信息的集合属于技术秘密，也可以主张图纸记载的某个或某些技术信息属于技术秘密。人民法院不能简单以原告未明确图纸中的哪些具体信息属于技术秘密为由而裁定驳回起诉。

As drawings can be the carrier of technical secrets, the content and scope of such technical secrets claimed by the plaintiff can be determined according to such drawings. The technical secrets holder may either claim that the entire technical information as contained in the drawings constitutes technical secrets or claim that one particular piece or several pieces of technical information as

contained in the drawings constitute technical secrets. People's court shall not rule to dismiss the lawsuit simply on the ground that the plaintiff fails to specify which specific information in the drawings is technical secrets at issue.

【关键词】

[Keywords]

技术秘密内容　技术秘密载体　图纸　举证责任

Contents of technical secrets; carrier of technical secrets; drawings; burden of proof

【案号】

[Case Number]

(2021) 最高法知民终 2526 号

(2021) SPC IP Civil Final 2526

【基本案情】

[Case Facts]

在上诉人北京半导体专用设备研究所（中国电子科技集团公司第四十五研究所）（以下简称四十五所）与被上诉人顾某洋、古某、杭州众硅电子科技有限公司（以下简称众硅公司）侵害技术秘密纠纷案中，四十五所向浙江省杭州市中级人民法院（以下简称一审法院）起诉称顾某洋、古某、众硅公司存在侵害其商业秘密的行为。2021 年 6 月 10 日，一审法院组织第一次庭前会议。四十五所提交了秘密点。同年 9 月 26 日，一审法院组织第二次庭前会议。四十五所当庭明确其在本案侵害技术秘密纠纷中所主张的技术信息包括三个部分，第一部分是已经提交的涉及硬件结构的相关的技术信息，包括一些图纸及相应的附件，即《对于相关秘密点说明》中涉及的内容；第二部分是涉案设备相关的计算机软件的技术信息，即《软件秘点说明》中的内容；第三部分是证据保全申请中提及的被诉侵权产品的相关技术资料。同年 9 月 30 日，四十五所向一审法院提交新的图纸，表示这些图纸为其技术信息。一审法院释明，图纸仅是技术信息的载体，要求四十五所对其主张的技术信息进行阐述。同年10月5日，四十五所提交了部分图纸，没有提交这些图纸所涉及的技术信息内容。同年10月12日、13日，一审法院组织第三次庭前会议，四十五所没有提交部分图纸所涉及的技术信息内容。一审法院认为，四十五所主张图纸构成技术秘密的，应当具体指出图纸的哪些内容、技术环节、步骤、数据等构成技术秘密，应当明确该技术秘密的具体构成、具体理由等，并将其与公众所知悉的信息予以区分和说明。图纸仅是固定技术信息的载体，仅凭图纸并不能确定四十五所主张技术秘密的具体内容和范围。故在四十五所主张的技术秘密内容无法确定的情况下，无法确定四十五所诉求的保护范围，一审法院无法就四十五所主张的技术信息是否构成技术秘密进行审理。此外，一审法院多次向四十五所释明并组织庭前会议要求四十五所明确其请求保护技术信息的具体内容，但四十五所始终未予全部明确，也不同意对已明确的部分先行审理。综上，一审法院认为四十五所未明确其所主张权利的客观内容，其起诉不符合法定条件，对其起诉予以驳回。四十五所不服，向最高人民法院提起上诉。最高人民法院于2022年12月26日裁定撤销原裁定，指令一审法院继续审理。

In the case of dispute over the infringement of technical secrets between the Appellant, Beijing Semiconductor Specialized Equipment Research Institute (the 45th Research Institute of China Electronics Technology Group Corporation) (hereinafter referred to as the 45th Institute), and the Appellees, Gu *yang, Gu *, and Hangzhou Sizone Electronic Technology Inc. (hereinafter referred to as Sizone), the 45th Institute filed a lawsuit with Hangzhou Intermediate People's Court of Zhejiang Province (hereinafter referred to as the Court of First Instance), claiming that Gu *yang, Gu *, and Sizone had infringed upon its trade secrets. On June 10, 2021, the Court of First Instance organized the first pre-trial conference. The 45th Institute submitted its

Secret Points. On September 26 of the same year, the Court of First Instance organized a second pre-trial conference. The 45th Institute clarified in court that the technical information it claimed in the dispute over the infringement of technical secrets in this case consisted of three parts, of which the first part was the technical information related to the structure of the hardware that had been submitted, including some drawings and the corresponding annexes, i.e., the content involved in the Description of the Relevant Secret Points; The second part is the technical information of the computer software related to the equipment in question, i. e., the contents in the Description of Secret Points of the Software; The third part is the relevant technical data of the accused infringing products mentioned in the application for evidence preservation. On September 30 of the same year, the 45th Institute submitted new drawings to the Court of First Instance, indicating that they were its technical information. The Court of First Instance explained that the drawings were only a carrier of technical information, and that the 45th Institute was required to elaborate on the technical information it claimed. On October 5 of the same year, the 45th Institute submitted some of the drawings without submitting the content of the technical information to which they relate. On October 12 and 13 of the same year, the Court of First Instance organized the third pre-trial conference, and the 45th Institute did not submit the content of the technical information involved in some of the drawings. The Court of First Instance held that where the 45th Institute claimed that the drawings constituted a technical secret, it should specifically point out which content, technical links, steps, data, etc., of the drawings constituted a technical secret, and it should make clear the specific composition of the technical secret, the specific reasons, etc., and differentiate and explain it from the information known to the public. The drawings were only a carrier of fixed technical information, and the drawings alone could not determine the specific content and scope of the technical secrets claimed by the 45th Institute. Therefore, in the event that the content of the technical secrets claimed by the 45th Institute could not be determined, it was impossible to determine the scope of protection claimed by the 45th Institute, and the Court of First Instance was unable to conduct a trial on whether the technical information claimed by the 45th Institute constituted a technical secret. In addition, the Court of First Instance repeatedly explained to the 45th Institute and organized pre-trial conferences to request the 45th Institute to clarify the specific contents of its request for protection of technical information, but the 45th Institute never clarified all of them, nor did it agree to try the clarified parts first. In summary, the Court of First Instance held that the 45th Institute had not clarified the objective content of the rights it claimed, and that its lawsuit did not meet the statutory conditions, and was dismissed. Unsatisfied, the 45th Institute appealed to the SPC. The SPC ruled on December 26, 2022 to vacate the original ruling and direct the Court of First Instance to continue the trial.

【裁判意见】

[Judge's Opinion]

最高人民法院二审认为，反不正当竞争法第三十二条第一款规定："在侵犯商业秘密的民事审判程序中，商业秘密权利人提供初步证据，证明其已经对所主张的商业秘密采取保密措施，且合理表明商业秘密被侵犯，涉嫌侵权人应当证明权利人所主张的商业秘密不属于本法规定的商业秘密。"第二款规定："商业秘密权利人提供初步证据合理表明商业秘密被侵犯，且提供以下证据之一的，涉嫌侵权人应当证明其不存在侵犯商业秘密的行为：（一）有证据表明涉嫌侵权人有渠道或者机会获取商业秘密，且其使用的信息与该商业秘密实质上相同；（二）有证据表明商业秘密已经被涉嫌侵权人披露、使用或者有被披露、使用的风

险；（三）有其他证据表明商业秘密被涉嫌侵权人侵犯。”据此，商业秘密权利人起诉他人侵害其技术秘密的，应当对其所称技术秘密符合法定条件及被诉侵权人采取不正当手段等事实负初步举证责任。而且，根据上述法律规定，商业秘密权利人在完成该特定初步举证责任后，有关技术秘密的秘密性、侵权行为等事实的举证责任转由被诉侵权人承担。因此，不宜要求商业秘密权利人对其所主张的技术秘密与公知信息的区别作过于严苛的证明。权利人提供了证明技术信息秘密性的初步证据，或对其主张的技术秘密之“不为公众所知悉”作出合理的解释或说明，即可初步认定秘密性成立。权利人初步举证后，即由被诉侵权人承担所涉技术秘密属于公知信息的举证责任，其亦可主张将公知信息从权利人主张范围中剔除，从而在当事人的诉辩对抗中完成涉案技术秘密信息事实认定。

The SPC held in the Second Instance that Article 32(1) of the Anti-Unfair Competition Law provides that "In civil trial proceedings for infringement of trade secrets, the right holder of a trade secret provides prima facie evidence to prove that he or she has taken confidentiality measures in respect of the claimed trade secret and reasonably demonstrates that the trade secret has been infringed upon, then the alleged infringer shall prove that the trade secret claimed by the right holder does not belong to the trade secrets as provided for in this Law." Sub-clause (2) provides: "Where the right holder of a trade secret provides prima facie evidence reasonably suggesting that the trade secret has been infringed and provides one of the following evidence, the alleged infringer shall prove that it has not infringed on the trade secret: (1) there is evidence that the alleged infringer has channels or opportunities to obtain the trade secret and that it has used information that is substantially the same as the trade secret; (2) there is evidence to show that the trade secret has been disclosed or used by the alleged infringer or that there is a risk of disclosure or use; (3) there is other evidence to show that the trade secret has been infringed by the alleged infringer." Accordingly, if a right holder of a trade secret sues another person for infringement of his or her trade secret, he or she shall bear the initial burden of proof of the fact that his or her alleged trade secret complies with the statutory conditions and that the alleged infringer has adopted improper means. Moreover, according to the above legal provisions, after the trade secret right holder has completed that particular initial burden of proof, the burden of proof of facts relating to the secrecy and infringement of the technical secret shifts to the accused infringer. Therefore, it is not appropriate to require the trade secret right holder to make an overly stringent proof of the difference between the technical secret it claims and the information in the public domain. If the right holder provides prima facie evidence to prove the secrecy of the technical information or gives a reasonable explanation or justification for the "Not known to the public" of the technical secret claimed by the right holder, it can be initially recognized that the secrecy has been established. After the initial proof of the right holder, that is, the accused infringer bears the burden of proof that the technical secret belongs to the public knowledge information, and it can also claim that the public knowledge information is excluded from the scope of the right holder's claim, so as to complete the factual determination of the technical secret information involved in the parties' lawsuit and defense confrontation.

《最高人民法院关于审理侵犯商业秘密民事案件适用法律若干问题的规定》第二十七条规定，权利人应当在一审法庭辩论结束前明确所主张的商业秘密具体内容。本案中四十五所主张，其技术秘密（除软件相关的以外）以图纸为载体，根据图纸可进行 CMP 设备的生产，图纸所记载的技术信息具有实用性，亦能为四十五所带来经济利益；图纸所载技术信息需要通过计算、试制才能完成，不是简单的汇编，他人不

经过努力不能形成；图纸并未公开，无法从公开渠道获取图纸。权利人主张图纸记载的技术信息构成技术秘密的，其既可以主张图纸记载的全部技术信息的集合属于技术秘密，也可以主张图纸记载的某个或某些技术信息属于技术秘密。图纸是技术秘密的载体，依据图纸可以确定其主张的技术秘密的内容和范围，因此，本案中四十五所主张保护的技术秘密内容是明确的，其起诉有具体的诉讼请求，一审法院应当审查其主张的技术信息是否具备秘密性、价值性、保密性，并进一步审查对方当事人是否采取不正当手段予以获取、披露、使用等。一审裁定以四十五所主张的技术秘密内容无法确定，无法确定四十五所诉求的保护范围，无法就四十五所主张的技术信息是否构成技术秘密进行审理为由，裁定驳回起诉，系适用法律错误。

Article 27 of the *Provisions of the SPC on Several Issues Concerning the Application of Law in the Trial of Civil Cases Involving Infringement of Trade Secrets* stipulates that the right holder shall specify the specific contents of the trade secrets claimed before the conclusion of the court debate at the First Instance. In this case, the 45th Institute claimed that its technical secrets (except for those related to software) were carried in the form of drawings, according to which the production of CMP equipment could be carried out, and that the technical information contained in the drawings was of practical use, which could also bring economic benefits to the 45th Institute; The technical information contained in the drawings requires calculations and trial production for completion, not a simple compilation that cannot be formed without the efforts of others; The drawings are not publicly available and it is not possible to obtain the drawings from public sources. The right holder claims that the technical information recorded in the drawings constitutes a technical secret, so it can either claim that the collection of all technical information recorded in the drawings belongs to a technical secret or claim that a certain item of or some portion of technical information recorded in the drawings belongs to a technical secret. Drawings are the carrier of technical secrets, and it can be determined based on the drawings that the content and scope of the technical secrets claimed, and therefore, in this case, the content of the technical secrets claimed by the 45th Institute is clear and its prosecution has specific claims; the Court of First Instance shall examine whether the technical information claimed by it is of secrecy, value, and confidentiality, and further review whether the opposing party is taking improper means to obtain, disclose, and use it, and so on. The decision of the First Instance ruled to dismiss the lawsuit on the grounds that the content of the technical secrets claimed by the 45th Institute could not be determined, and that it was impossible to determine the scope of protection claimed by the 45th Institute and to conduct a trial on whether the technical information claimed by the 45th Institute constituted a technical secret, which was an error in the application of the law.

55. 作为技术秘密保护的技术方案的认定 Identification of technical solutions to be protected as technical secrets

【裁判要旨】

[Judgment Digest]

当权利人所主张的技术秘密是技术方案时，其既可以是在一份技术文件中记载的完整技术方案，也可以是在图纸、工艺规程、质量标准、操作指南、实验数据等多份不同技术文件中记载的不为公众所知悉的技术信息的基础上加以合理总结、概括与提炼的技术方案。

When the technical secret claimed by its holder is a technical solution, it

can be either a complete set of technical solution as contained in one particular technical document or a technical solution that can be reasonably summarized, generalized and refined on the basis of the technical information not available to the public as contained in such different technical documents as drawings, process specification, quality standards, operating guidelines and experimental data.

【关键词】

[Keywords]

技术秘密　载体　技术方案

Technical secrets; carriers; technical solutions

【案号】

[Case Number]

（2020）最高法知民终 1889 号

（2020）SPC IP Civil Final 1889

【基本案情】

[Case Facts]

在上诉人程某卓、成都爱兴生物科技有限公司（以下简称爱兴公司）与被上诉人科美博阳诊断技术（上海）有限公司（以下简称博阳公司）侵害技术秘密纠纷案中，博阳公司认为，其研发的用于临床免疫诊断领域的“光激化学发光分析系统通用液（LiCA）”相关技术信息构成不为公众知悉的技术秘密，程某卓原为博阳公司的核心技术开发人员，系统掌握了上述技术秘密，离职后进入爱兴公司并将其掌握的上述技术秘密擅自披露给爱兴公司，爱兴公司生产、销售的体外诊断试剂盒产品中直接使用了其技术秘密，故向上海知识产权法院（以下简称一审法院）提起诉讼。一审法院认为，博阳公司主张的技术信息不为公众所知悉、具有商业价值并且对该技术信息采取了合理保密措施，构成技术秘密，程某卓、爱兴公司实施了侵害技术秘密的行为，故判决程某卓、爱兴公司停止侵害并共同赔偿经济损失 100 万元、维权合理开支 30 万元。程某卓、爱兴公司不服，向最高人民法院提起上诉，主张博阳公司的工艺规程等文件仅反映了其主张的技术秘密方案中的零散、个别要素，没有体现完整的技术方案，涉案技术秘密中技术方案的完整内容与其提交的工艺规程等载体文件不具有对应性，不能证明涉案技术秘密系其自行研发。最高人民法院于 2022 年 12 月 14 日判决驳回上诉，维持原判。

In the case of dispute over the infringement of technical secrets between the Appellants, Cheng and Chengdu Aixing Biotechnology Co., Ltd. (hereinafter referred to as Aixing), and the Appellee, Kemei Boyang Diagnostic Technology (Shanghai) Co., Ltd. (hereinafter referred to as Boyang), Boyang considered that the technical information related to the "Light-activated Chemiluminescent Analysis System Liquid for Clinical Immuno-diagnostic (LiCA)", which was developed by Boyang, constitutes a technical secret that is not known to the general public. Cheng was originally the core technology developer of Boyang, who systematically mastered the above technical secrets, entered Aixing after leaving the company and made unauthorized disclosure of the above technical secrets to Aixing; Aixing directly used such technical secrets in the in vitro diagnostic kit products it produced and sold, so Boyang filed a lawsuit with Shanghai Intellectual Property Court (hereinafter referred to as the Court of First Instance). The Court of First Instance held that the technical information claimed by Boyang is not known to the public and is of commercial value, and it has taken reasonable measures of confidentiality on the technical information, constituting a technical secret; Cheng and Aixing committed the act of infringing on the technical secret, so it ruled that Cheng and Aixing shall stop the infringement and shall jointly compensate for the economic loss of CNY 1 million, and the reasonable expenses of defending the

right of CNY 300, 000. Unsatisfied, Cheng and Aixing appealed to the SPC, claiming that Boyang's process protocols and other documents only reflected the fragmented and individual elements of the technical secret solutions claimed by Boyang and did not embody the complete technical solutions, and the complete contents of the technical solutions in the technical secret in question did not correspond to the process protocols and other carrier documents submitted by Bo Yang, and it could not be proved that the technical secret in question was researched and developed by Bo Yang on its own. The SPC ruled on December 14, 2022 that the appeal was rejected and the original judgment was upheld.

【裁判意见】

[Judge's Opinion]

最高人民法院二审认为，技术秘密通常以图纸、工艺规程、质量标准、操作指南、实验数据的形式来体现，权利人为证明其技术秘密的存在及其内容，通常会在体现上述技术秘密的载体文件基础上，总结、概括、提炼其需要保护的技术信息，其技术秘密既可以是技术方案，也可以是构成技术方案的部分技术信息。权利人在从其技术资料等载体中总结、概括、提炼秘密信息时，应当允许将其具有秘密性的信息结合现有技术及公知常识形成一个完整的技术方案请求保护。权利人从其不为公众所知的工艺规程、质量控制标准等技术文件中合理提炼出的技术方案，只要不为社会公众普遍知悉和容易获得，即可作为技术秘密予以保护。本案中，博阳公司主张的技术秘密为 8 个技术方案，每一技术方案包括若干技术信息，在后技术方案对在前技术方案的技术信息作出进一步限定或增加，从而形成层层递进的技术方案。涉案技术秘密中的微粒 CV 值、粒径等技术信息在博阳公司的技术文件中均有对应记载。博阳公司根据其技术文件，并结合本领域的现有技术、公知常识的合理总结与提炼，能够证明博阳公司实际拥有并掌握上述技术方案，程某卓、爱兴公司关于涉案技术秘密的相应信息没有载体予以对应、不能证明博阳公司为涉案技术秘密权利人的主张不能成立。

The SPC held in the Second Instance that technical secrets are usually embodied in the form of drawings, process protocols, quality standards, operation guidelines, and experimental data, and that the right holders will usually summarize, generalize, and refine the technical information to be protected on the basis of the carrier documents embodying the abovementioned technical secrets to prove the existence and content of the technical secrets, which may be either the technical solutions or some of the technical information constituting the technical solutions. When the right holder summarizes, generalizes, and extracts secret information from his/her technical data and other carriers, he/she shall be allowed to request protection of his/her information of a secret nature in combination with the prior art and common knowledge to form a complete technical solution. Technical solutions reasonably extracted by the right holder from technical documents such as process protocols and quality control standards that are not known to the public can be protected as technical secrets as long as they are not generally known and easily accessible to the public. In this case, the technical secrets claimed by Boyang are 8 technical solutions, each of which includes a number of pieces of technical information, and the latter technical solutions further qualify or increase the technical information of the former technical solutions, thus forming a layer-by-layer technical solution. The technical information such as the CV value and particle size of the particles in the technical secret in question was recorded in the technical documents of Boyang. Boyang was able to prove that Boyang actually owned and mastered the above technical solutions based on its technical documents and reasonable summaries and refinement of prior art and common knowledge in the field, and Cheng's and Aixing's claims that there was no carrier to cor-

respond to the corresponding information of the technical secret in question, which could not prove that Boyang was the rightful owner of the technical secret in question, could not be substantiated.

56. 育种材料保密性的认定 Identification of confidentiality of breeding materials

【裁判要旨】

[Judgment Digest]

育种材料生长依赖土壤、水分、空气和阳光，需要田间管理，权利人对于育种作物材料采取的保密措施难以做到万无一失。有关保密措施是否合理，需要考虑育种材料自身的特点，应当以在正常情况下能够达到防止被泄露的防范程度为宜。制订保密制度、签署保密协议、禁止对外扩散、对繁殖材料以代号称之等，在合适情况下均可构成合理的保密措施。

The growth of breeding material relies on soil, water, air and sunshine, and needs field management, so it is difficult for the technical secret holder to take perfectly safe confidentiality measures to protect breeding crop materials. When determining whether relevant confidentiality measures are reasonable, people's courts shall take into account the characteristics of the breeding material itself, and bear in mind that the measures should reach the extent of preventing any disclosure in normal situations. Establishing a confidentiality system, signing a confidentiality agreement, prohibiting proliferation, and calling propagation materials with codes, etc. may constitute reasonable confidentiality measures under appropriate circumstances.

【关键词】

[Keywords]

商业秘密　技术信息　杂交种自交系亲本　保密措施

Trade secrets; technical information; hybrid inbred line parents; confidentiality measures

【案号】

[Case Number]

（2022）最高法知民终 147 号

（2022）SPC IP Civil Final 147

【裁判意见】

[Judge's Opinion]

在上诉人武威市搏盛种业有限责任公司与被上诉人河北华穗种业有限公司（以下简称华穗种业公司）侵害技术秘密纠纷案中，最高人民法院指出，权利人在被诉侵权行为发生以前采取了合理保密措施，在正常情况下足以防止商业秘密泄露的，人民法院应当认定权利人采取了作为商业秘密法定构成要件的“相应的保密措施”。人民法院认定保密措施时，应当考虑保密措施与商业秘密的对应程度。植物生长依赖土壤、水分、空气和阳光，需要进行光合作用，“W68”作为育种材料自交系亲本，必须施以合理的种植管理，具备一定的制种规模。在进行田间管理中，权利人对于该作物材料采取的保密措施难以做到万无一失。因此，对于育种材料技术信息的保密措施是否合理，需要考虑育种材料自身的特点，对于采取合理保密措施的认定不宜过于严苛，应以在正常情况下能够达到防止被泄露的防范程度为宜。

In the case of dispute over the infringement of technical secrets between the Appellant, Wuwei Bosheng Seed Co., Ltd., and the Appellee, Hebei Huasui Seed Co., Ltd. (hereinafter referred to as Huasui Seed), the SPC pointed out that, where the right holder had taken reasonable confidentiality

measures prior to the alleged infringement, and where such measures were sufficient to prevent leakage of the trade secrets under normal circumstances, the people's court shall determine that the right holder has taken the "appropriate measures of confidentiality" as a statutory component of trade secrets. When the people's court determines the confidentiality measures, it shall consider the degree of correspondence between the confidentiality measures and the trade secrets. Plant growth depends on soil, water, air, and sunlight, and requires photosynthesis. "W68", as an parent variety of the inbred line for breeding material, must be planted with reasonable planting management and a certain scale of seed production. In carrying out field management, it is difficult to ensure that the confidentiality measures taken by the right holder with respect to the crop material are foolproof. Therefore, whether the confidentiality measures for the technical information of breeding materials are reasonable or not needs to take into account the characteristics of the breeding materials themselves, and the determination of the adoption of reasonable confidentiality measures should not be too harsh, which should be able to achieve the degree of precautionary measures to prevent the leakage under normal circumstances.

华穗种业公司在一审中提交了该公司的保密制度以及其与“万糯2000”玉米新品种的育种者、公司高管、委托制种企业签订的保密协议。结合华穗种业公司在二审中提交的证据，经审查，对内而言，华穗种业公司内部有保密制度，规定了公司育种技术资料、育种样品以及育种亲本等繁殖材料属于公司秘密，不得泄露，规定了公司相关人员在任职期间以及离职后的一定期间对种子育种方法、育种亲本以及用于繁育种子的技术资料、繁殖材料等商业秘密进行保密，离职时应当将自己持有的所有商业秘密资料等物品移交指定人员并办妥相关手续，否则承担违约责任；对外而言，华穗种业公司与其有委托制种关系的案外人金源种业公司签订的《委托繁种合同》中约定，繁育品种名称予以代号，金源种业公司按计划生产的合格种子全部交给华穗种业公司，不得截留和自行销售，并对华穗种业公司提供的自交系负责保密，不得向外扩散。在前述金源种业公司委托村民委员会制种的繁育合同中，约定亲本种子不外流、不自留。还需要指出的是，在制种基地，相关行政管理部门要求受委托制种的生产者进行备案，备案内容要求完整，特别是要求委托生产合同齐全，品种权属以及亲本来源清晰，生产品种以及面积与合同约定相一致，上述内容属于生产者在履行合同时应当承担的义务，也是制种散户在履行委托制种合同时应当承担的义务。委托育种合同的受托人擅自扩大委托育种合同的生产繁殖规模，私自截留、私繁滥制、盗取亲本的行为均属于违法违规行为。而且，本案并无证据证明“W68”已被受委托制种单位非法披露、扩散。根据《最高人民法院关于审理侵犯商业秘密民事案件适用法律若干问题的规定》第六条的规定，综合考虑杂交育种的行业惯例、繁育材料以代号称之、制种行为的可获知程度等因素，华穗种业公司采取的上述避免亲本被他人非法盗取、获得及不正当使用的保密措施，符合商业秘密法定构成要件的“相应的保密措施”。

In the First Instance, Huashui Seed submitted its confidentiality system and the confidentiality agreement signed with the breeder of the new maize variety “Wannuo 2000”, its executives, and the commissioned seed-producing enterprises. With the exhibits submitted by Huashui Seed in the Second Instance, after examination, for internal purposes, Huashui Seed has an internal confidentiality system, which stipulates that the Company's breeding technical information, breeding samples, and breeding parents, and other breeding materials are secrets of the Company and shall not be divulged, and stipulates that the relevant personnel of the Company shall keep confidentiality of the seed breeding methods, breeding parents, and technical information used for breeding seeds, breeding materials, and other trade secrets during the period

of their employment as well as for a certain period of time after they leave the Company, and that when they leave their jobs, they should hand over all the items of trade secrets held by them to the designated persons and complete the relevant formalities, or else they shall be held liable for the breach of contract; For external purposes, Huashui Seed and its outsider Jinyuan Seed Company, with whom it has entrusted to produce seeds, signed the Entrusted Seed Breeding Contract, in which it was agreed that the name of the breeding varieties would be coded and that all qualified seeds produced by Jinyuan Seed Company in accordance with the plan would be handed over to Huashui Seed, which shall not be intercepted and sold on its own and Jinyuan Seed Company shall be responsible for the confidentiality of inbred lines provided by Huashui Seed and shall not spread them outward. In the aforementioned Breeding Contract in which the Jinyuan Seed Company entrusted the village committee to produce seeds, it was agreed that the parental seeds would not be exported or retained for their own use. It is also important to point out that, in the seed base, the relevant administrative departments require entrusted seed producers to carry out the record, which requires a complete content of the record, in particular, complete commissioned production contracts, variety ownership and clear source of parentage, and the varieties produced and the area that corresponds to the provisions of the contract, which not only belong to the obligations to be undertaken in the performance of the Contract by the producer, but also the obligations to be undertaken by retailers of the seed production in the performance of the entrusted seed production contract. The unauthorized expansion of the production and breeding scale under the entrusted breeding contract by the trustee of the entrusted breeding contract, and the acts of private interception, private breeding, and the theft of parental material are all violations of the law. Moreover, there is no evidence in this case to prove that

"W68" has been illegally disclosed and proliferated by the commissioned seed-producing organizations. According to the provisions of Article 6 of the *Provisions of the SPC on Several Issues concerning the Application of Law in the Trial of Civil Cases Involving Infringement of Trade Secrets*, taking into account such factors as the industry practice of cross-breeding, the fact that breeding materials are represented by codes, and the degree of accessibility of seed production, the confidentiality measures taken by Huashui Seed to avoid the illegal stealing and acquisition of the parent material by others as well as improper use of the parent material are in line with the "Corresponding confidentiality measures" as a statutory constituent element of a trade secret.

57. 共同实施侵权行为主观过错的三种主要情形 Three main scenarios of subjective fault in cases of joint infringement

【裁判要旨】

[Judgment Digest]

从主观过错角度，共同实施侵权行为主要包括三种情形：其一，共同故意实施的行为；其二，共同过失实施的行为；其三，故意行为与过失行为结合实施的行为，即数个行为人虽主观过错程度不一，但各自行为相结合而实施的行为，造成他人损害的，也可以构成共同侵权行为。以上三种情形，具备其一，即可认定构成共同实施侵权行为。

In terms of subjective fault, joint infringement mainly includes three scenarios as follows: firstly, the act is committed on purpose with joint intent; secondly, the act is committed with joint negligence; and thirdly, the act is committed with combination of intention and negligence, in which case several parties conduct their acts respectively and with different degrees of subjective

fault while the combination of such acts causes damages to other party or parties, and hence such acts may also constitute a joint infringement. Any one of the aforementioned three scenarios shall be deemed as a case of joint infringement.

【关键词】

[Keywords]

技术秘密　侵权　共同侵权　主观过错　故意与过失结合

Technical secrets; infringement; joint infringement; subjective fault; combination of intent and negligence

【案号】

[Case Number]

（2022）最高法知民终 541 号

（2022）SPC IP Civil Final 541

【基本案情】

[Case Facts]

在上诉人四川金象赛瑞化工股份有限公司（以下简称金象公司）与上诉人山东华鲁恒升化工股份有限公司（以下简称华鲁恒升公司）、宁波厚承管理咨询有限公司（原宁波远东化工集团有限公司，以下简称厚承公司）、宁波安泰环境化工工程设计有限公司（原宁波市化工研究设计院有限公司，以下简称设计院公司）、尹某大侵害技术秘密纠纷案中，涉及金象公司的技术秘密即加压气相淬冷法年产 5 万吨三聚氰胺（密胺）生产反应系统（以下简称涉案技术秘密）。金象公司认为，上述四被诉侵权人侵害了涉案技术秘密，构成共同侵权且侵权获利巨大，故向四川省成都市中级人民法院（以下简称一审法院）提起诉讼，请求判令上述四被诉侵权人停止侵权（包括停止披露、使用、允许他人使用涉案技术秘密，销毁承载有涉案技术秘密的资料，华鲁恒升公司销毁承载有涉案技术秘密的生产系统、停止销售使用涉案技术秘密生产的密胺产品)、连带赔偿金象公司经济损失及合理费用9800万元。一审法院认为，尹某大披露涉案技术秘密，华鲁恒升公司、厚承公司、设计院公司共同获取、共同使用涉案技术秘密，共同侵害了金象公司的技术秘密，且一审法院希望通过判令停止使用但不销毁生产设备的方式，鼓励华鲁恒升公司与金象公司达成技术许可，同时，因停止披露、使用、允许他人使用涉案技术秘密足以防止损害后果的扩大，故对金象公司要求华鲁恒升公司停止销售利用涉案技术秘密生产的密胺产品的主张不予支持。一审法院判决，该四者立即停止披露、使用、允许他人使用涉案技术秘密并销毁各自持有的涉案技术秘密的载体资料，华鲁恒升公司赔偿金象公司5000万元，设计院公司、厚承公司对其中的500万元承担连带赔偿责任，尹某大就其中的120万元承担连带赔偿责任。金象公司、华鲁恒升公司、厚承公司、设计院公司、尹某大均不服，分别向最高人民法院提起上诉。金象公司主张，华鲁恒升公司应销毁其持有的侵权生产系统及图纸、技术资料并停止销售使用涉案技术秘密生产的密胺产品，且一审判赔数额过低，不足以弥补金象公司的损失。华鲁恒升公司、厚承公司、设计院公司、尹某大主张未实施侵权行为，四者不构成共同侵权，且一审判决赔偿数额过高。最高人民法院于2022年12月26日判决撤销原判，上述四被诉侵权人停止披露、使用、允许他人使用金象公司的涉案技术秘密，其中华鲁恒升公司的停止使用包括立即停止销售使用涉案技术秘密所生产的密胺产品，厚承公司、设计院公司、尹某大销毁各自所持有的记载有涉案技术秘密的技术资料，华鲁恒升公司销毁其10万吨/年三聚氰胺项目（一期）中涉及涉案技术秘密的设备(销毁的方式包括但不限于拆除有关设备中包含金象公司涉案技术秘密的部分）以及记载有涉案技术秘密的技术资料，华鲁恒升公司、厚承公司、设计院公司、尹某大连带赔偿金象公司经济损失及维权合理开支9800万元。

The case of dispute over the infringement of technical secrets among the

Appellant, Sichuan Golden-Elephant Sincerity Chemical Co., Ltd. (hereinafter referred to as Golden Elephant), and the Appellants, Shandong Hualu Hengsheng Chemical Co., Ltd. (hereinafter referred to as Hualu Hengsheng), Ningbo Houcheng Management Consulting Co., Ltd. (formerly Ningbo Far-East Chemical Industry Group Co., Ltd., hereinafter referred to as Houcheng), Ningbo Antai Environment & Chemical Engineering & Design Co., Ltd. (formerly Ningbo Chemical Industry Research and Design Institute Co., Ltd., hereinafter referred to as Design Institute), and Yin, involves the technical secrets of Golden Elephant, namely, the production reaction system with an annual capacity of 50,000 tons of melamine (i. e., cyanurtriamide) by pressurized gas phase quenching and cooling method (hereinafter referred as the technical secrets in question). Golden Elephant believed that the above four accused infringers infringed the technical secrets in question, which constituted joint infringement and made huge profits from the infringement, so it filed a lawsuit with Chengdu Intermediate People's Court of Sichuan Province (hereinafter referred to as the Court of First Instance), requesting that the above four accused infringers stop the infringement (including stopping disclosing, using, and permitting others to use the technical secrets in question, destroying the materials containing the technical secrets in question, and Hualu Hengsheng destroying the production systems containing the technical secrets in question, and stopping sales of melamine products produced by the use of the technical secrets in question), and compensating the Golden Elephant for the economic losses and reasonable expenses of CNY 98 million jointly and severally. The Court of First Instance held that Yin disclosed the technical secrets in question, and Hualu Hengsheng, Houcheng, and Design Institute jointly obtained and jointly used the technical secrets in question, jointly infringing on the technical secrets of Golden Elephant; and the Court of First Instance hoped to encourage Hualu Hengsheng to reach a technical license agreement with Golden Elephant by ordering to stop the use of the production equipment without destroying the production equipment, and at the same time, as stopping the disclosure of, the use of, and the permitting of the use of the technical secrets in question by other parties was sufficient to prevent the expansion of the consequences of the damages, and therefore, the Court of First Instance did not support the claim of Golden Elephant that Hualu Hengsheng should stop the sales of the melamine products made by using the technical secrets in question. The Court of First Instance ruled that the four parties should immediately stop disclosing, using, or permitting others to use the technical secrets in question and destroy the carrier information of the technical secrets in question held by each of them, and that Hualu Hengsheng should compensate Golden Elephant for CNY 50 million, of which Design Institute and Houcheng should be jointly and severally liable for CNY 5 million, and Yin should be jointly and severally liable for CNY 1.2 million. Unsatisfied, Golden Elephant, Hualu Hengsheng, Houcheng, Design Institute, and Yin all appealed to the SPC, respectively. Golden Elephant claimed that Hualu Hengsheng should destroy the infringing production system, drawings, and technical data in its possession and stop selling melamine products produced by using the technical secrets in question, and that the amount of damages awarded in the First Instance was too low to make up for Golden Elephant's losses. Hualu Hengsheng, Houcheng, Design Institute, and Yin claimed that they did not commit infringement, and the four of them did not constitute joint infringement, and the amount of compensation in the First Instance judgment was too high. The SPC ruled on December 26, 2022 to revoke the original judgment, and that the above four accused infringers shall cease to disclose, use, or permit others to use Golden Elephant's technical secrets in question,

and that such cessation of use by Hualu Hengsheng shall include the immediate cessation of sales of melamine products produced using the technical secrets in question, and that Houcheng, the Design Institute, and Yin shall destroy the technical information held by each of them containing the technical secrets in question, and that Hualu Hengsheng shall destroy the equipment in its melamine project (Phase I) of 100,000 tons per year that contained the technical secrets in question (including, but not limited to, by removing the relevant items of equipment that contained the technical secrets in question), and the technical information containing technical secrets in question, and that Hualu Hengsheng, Houcheng, Design Institute, and Yin shall jointly and severally compensate Golden Elephant for the economic loss and reasonable expenses of CNY 98 million.

【裁判意见】

[Judge's Opinion]

最高人民法院二审认为，共同侵权，是指数人共同不法侵害他人权益造成损害的行为。侵权责任法第八条（民法典第一千一百六十八条）规定："二人以上共同实施侵权行为，造成他人损害的，应当承担连带责任。"根据本条规定，构成共同侵权需要满足以下要件：一是侵权主体的复数性，即共同侵权行为的主体必须是两个以上。二是共同实施侵权行为。从主观过错角度看，这里的共同实施行为主要包括三种情形：其一，共同故意实施的行为，这属于典型的共同侵权行为。其二，共同过失实施的行为，即基于共同的疏忽大意或者过于自信的过失而造成他人的损害，也可以构成共同侵权行为。其三，故意行为与过失行为结合实施的行为，即数个行为人虽主观过错程度不一，但各自行为相结合而实施的行为，造成他人损害的，也可以构成共同侵权行为。以上三种情形，具备其一，即可认定构成共同实施侵权行为。三是造成受害人损害，且损害具有不可分割性。四是各行为人的侵权行为均与损害后果之间具有因果关系。在共同侵权行为中，有时各个行为人的侵权行为对造成损害后果的原因力可以有所不同，但必须存在法律上的因果关系，如果某个行为人的行为与损害后果之间没有因果关系，则不应与其他行为人构成共同侵权。

The SPC held in the Second Instance that joint infringement means the behavior of a group of people who jointly and wrongfully infringe upon the rights and interests of others, causing damage. Article 8 of the Tort Liability Law (i. e., Article 1168 of the Civil Code) provides that: "If two or more persons jointly commit an act of tort and cause damage to another person, they shall be jointly and severally liable." According to this Article, the following elements need to be fulfilled to constitute a joint tort: firstly, the plurality of the subject of the tort, i. e., the subject of the joint tort must be more than two. Secondly, there is a joint commission of infringements. From the subjective fault point of view, the joint implementation of the act here mainly includes three kinds of situations: first of all, the joint intentional implementation of the act, which is a typical joint tort. Second, acts committed with common negligence, i. e., causing damage to others based on common carelessness or overconfident negligence, may also constitute a joint tort. Third, the combination of intentional acts and negligent acts, that is, for several actors, although the degree of subjective fault is not the same, but the combination of their respective acts and the implementation of the act, resulting in damage to others, can also constitute a joint tort. One of the above three situations can be recognized as constituting the joint commission of an act of tort. Thirdly, it causes damage to the victim which is indivisible. Fourthly, there is a causal link between the acts of tort by each actor and the consequences of the damage. In joint torts, sometimes the acts of tort by various actors may differ in their causal force in causing the consequences of the damage, but there must

be a legal causal link, and if there is no causal link between the acts of one actor and the consequences of the damage, he or she should not be considered to be in joint torts with the other actors.

58. 技术秘密侵权案中共同故意侵权的认定及责任承担 Determination of joint intentional infringement and liabilities in technical secrets misappropriation cases

【裁判要旨】

[Judgment Digest]

构成共同故意实施被诉侵权行为不以各参与者事前共谋、事后协同行动为限，各参与者彼此之间心知肚明、心照不宣，先后参与、相互协作，亦可构成共同故意实施被诉侵权行为。各被诉侵权人具有侵害技术秘密的意思联络，主观上彼此明知，各自先后实施相应的侵权行为形成完整的技术秘密侵权行为链，客观上分工协作的，属共同故意实施侵权行为，应当判令各被诉侵权人对全部侵权损害承担连带责任。

Joint intentional infringement is not limited to the scenario of participants' conspiracy beforehand and concerted actions afterwards. If an infringing act is committed when participants are well aware of such act, have a tacit understanding with each other, take a part one after another and coordinate with each other, then such an act can also be deemed as joint intentional infringement. If, with implied association on technical secrets misappropriation and mutual awareness of one another's intent from subjective perspective, the accused infringers conduct their acts of infringement one after another, which form a complete chain of technical secret misappropriation, and objectively they also coordinate with each other, then their respective acts shall constitute joint intentional infringement, and such infringers shall be ordered to be jointly and severally liable for all the damages.

【关键词】

[Keywords]

技术秘密　共同侵权　共同故意　连带责任

Technical secrets; joint infringement; joint intentionality; joint and several liability

【案号】

[Case Number]

(2022) 最高法知民终 541 号

(2022) SPC IP Civil Final 541

【裁判意见】

[Judge's Opinion]

在上诉人四川金象赛瑞化工股份有限公司与上诉人山东华鲁恒升化工股份有限公司、宁波厚承管理咨询有限公司、宁波安泰环境化工工程设计有限公司、尹某大侵害技术秘密纠纷案中，最高人民法院指出，尹某大系涉案技术秘密的主要研发人员之一，能够直接接触到涉案技术秘密。尹某大在未办理离职手续，亦未告知其留存有三聚氰胺生产图纸、资料的情况下，就停止在金象公司工作，其在与厚承公司、设计院公司接触时亦尚在约定的保密期内，亦明知厚承公司、设计院公司与华鲁恒升公司的合作情况，且其作为涉案技术秘密的主要研发人员之一，明知涉案技术信息属于金象公司的技术秘密，仍然将涉案技术秘密披露给华鲁恒升公司、厚承公司、设计院公司使用，收取相应报酬，并使用涉案技术秘密提供后续技术指导。尹某大是涉案技术秘密的提供者，亦是华鲁恒升公司、厚承公司、设计院公司实际使用涉案技术秘密过程中的技术指导者。以上事实足以证明尹某大实施了违反保密义务披露涉案技术秘密给华鲁恒升公司、厚承公司、设计院公司并允许该三者使用涉案技术秘密的行为，其还违反保密义务自己使用涉案技术秘密为他人使用涉

案技术秘密提供技术指导，其行为已构成反不正当竞争法第九条第一款第三项规定的侵犯商业秘密行为。尹某大主观上明知其披露、允许使用和自己使用的行为是在促成华鲁恒升公司、厚承公司、设计院公司后续实施相关侵权行为，系本案共同实施侵权行为中的关键人物和基础环节。

In the case of dispute over the infringement of technical secrets between the Appellant, Sichuan Golden - Elephant Sincerity Chemical Co., Ltd. (hereinafter referred to as Golden Elephant), and the Appellees, Shandong Hualu Hengsheng Chemical Co., Ltd. (hereinafter referred to as Hualu Hengsheng), Ningbo Houcheng Management Consulting Co., Ltd. (hereinafter referred to as Houcheng), Ningbo Antai Environment & Chemical Engineering & Design Co., Ltd. (hereinafter referred to as Design Institute), and Yin, the SPC noted that Yin was one of the main researchers and developers of the technical secrets in question and had direct access to the technical secrets in question. Yin ceased to work at Golden Elephant without completing the formalities for leaving the company or informing the company that he had retained the melamine production drawings and materials, and he was still within the confidentiality period agreed upon when he contacted Houcheng and Design Institute, and was aware of the cooperation between Houcheng and Design Institute and Hualu Hengsheng, and, as one of the main researchers and developers of the technical secrets in question, he knew that the technical information in question belonged to Golden Elephant's technical secrets, but he still disclosed the technical secrets in question to Hualu Hengsheng, Houcheng, and Design Institute for use, by receiving the corresponding remuneration, and used the technical secrets in question to provide subsequent technical guidance. Yin was the provider of the technical secrets in question, and also the technical instructor of Hualu Hengsheng, Houcheng, and Design

Institute in the actual use of the technical secrets in question. The above facts are sufficient to prove that Yin disclosed the technical secrets in question to Hualu Hengsheng, Houcheng, and Design Institute in violation of confidentiality obligation and allowed the three companies to use the technical secrets in question, and he also used the technical secrets in question himself in violation of the obligation of confidentiality to provide technical guidance for the use of the technical secrets in question by others, whose behavior constituted the infringement of trade secrets stipulated in Article 9(1)(c) of the Anti-Unfair Competition Law. Yin subjectively knew that his disclosure, permission to use, and his own use were contributing to the subsequent infringing acts of Hualu Hengsheng, Houcheng, and the Design Institute, and that he was the key person and the basic link in the joint infringing acts in this case.

厚承公司、设计院公司与华鲁恒升公司签订工程设计合同后，在明知尹某大曾是涉案技术秘密主要研发人员之一的情况下，仍以高额利诱的非法手段从尹某大处获取涉案技术秘密，然后由厚承公司作为名义上的技术提供者向华鲁恒升公司转让涉案技术并由设计院公司进行所谓的工程化设计，用于华鲁恒升公司三聚氰胺一期项目并从中获取经济利益，该二者构成非法收买并转卖涉案技术秘密，实施了以不正当手段获取涉案技术秘密并披露、使用、允许他人使用涉案技术秘密的行为，已构成反不正当竞争法第九条第一款第一项、第二项规定的侵犯商业秘密行为，属于本案共同实施被诉侵权行为的始作俑者和中间渠道及名义上的技术提供者。

Houcheng and Design Institute, after signing the engineering design contract with Hualu Hengsheng, knowing that Yin was one of the main researchers and developers of the technical secrets in question, obtained the technical secrets in question from Yin by means of illegal inducement of high profit, which was then transferred by Houcheng as the nominal technology provider to

Hualu Hengsheng and the so-called engineered design was carried out by Design Institute for the purpose of the Melamine Project Phase I of Hualu Hengsheng, thereby obtaining economic benefits. The two parties constituted the illegal purchase and resale of the technical secrets in question and committed the act of obtaining the technical secrets in question by improper means and disclosing, using, and allowing others to use the technical secrets in question, which constituted the infringement of trade secrets as stipulated in Article 9 (1)(a) and (b) of the Anti-Unfair Competition Law, and they were the initiators, the intermediary channels, and the nominal technology providers of the joint infringement in this case.

华鲁恒升公司系涉案三聚氰胺一期项目的最终使用者、最大获益者，其涉案三聚氰胺一期项目的技术图纸、资料来源于厚承公司和设计院公司。原审法院据此认定，华鲁恒升公司获取并使用了涉案技术秘密，具有事实和法律依据。同时，在案证据亦足以证明华鲁恒升公司对其使用的技术实际来源于金象公司是明知的。理由如下：第一，华鲁恒升公司向相关行政管理部门提交备案的设计专篇中明确记载有行业内三聚氰胺生产技术现状以及烨晶公司拥有的相关技术情况，故华鲁恒升公司作为同业竞争者，在被诉侵权生产系统设计、建造过程中，明确了解行业内三聚氰胺生产技术的情况，明知烨晶公司享有加压气相淬冷法三聚氰胺生产技术且已有 5 万吨/年装置成功运行。第二，华鲁恒升公司并未提交证据证明其自身在被诉侵权行为发生前已掌握单一生产线年产 5 万吨三聚氰胺的相应技术。根据原审法院已查明的事实，华鲁恒升公司在 2011 年之前并无制备三聚氰胺的生产技术及设备，其收购的德丰化工公司也只有一套年产 1 万吨三聚氰胺装置，亦无证据显示其有能力自行完成单一生产线年产量增长至 5 万吨的技术改进。第三，华鲁恒升公司作为大型化工企业并计划建设涉及巨额投资的涉案三聚氰胺大型化工工程项目，其在与厚承公司、设计院公司签订工程设计合同前，理应对行业内三聚氰胺生产技术现状进行相应调查、对项目进行可行性研究，理应知晓其拟签订合同的相对方是否拥有合同所涉及的技术、是否具有相应的设计能力，而非按华鲁恒升公司所主张的其只是与厚承公司、设计院公司签订合作协议，由厚承公司提供技术、设计院公司负责工程设计，对其他事项一概不问不知。各被诉侵权人均未提供证据证明厚承公司、设计院公司在与华鲁恒升公司签订合同之前拥有单一生产线年产5万吨三聚氰胺技术的研发或项目设计历史或者已经实际合法掌握了单一生产线年产5万吨三聚氰胺生产技术。据此，可以推定华鲁恒升公司在与厚承公司、设计院公司签订工程设计合同时，对该二公司自身并不掌握相应技术是应知的。最后，由尹某大在相关刑事案件中的供述亦可印证华鲁恒升公司对于厚承公司、设计院公司用于涉案三聚氰胺一期项目的实际技术来源是明知的。基于本案现有证据，即便华鲁恒升公司在与厚承公司、设计院公司签署工程设计合同时并不知晓该二者并不掌握单一生产线年产5万吨三聚氰胺的相应技术或者不知道相应技术的来源，但之后华鲁恒升公司在实际已知悉技术来源于金象公司的情况下，仍予接受且并未停止使用，即已构成明知，并不影响对其主观过错和侵权构成及责任承担的认定。总之，华鲁恒升公司主观上亦明知其使用的技术方案的实际来源，已构成反不正当竞争法第九条第二款规定的视为侵犯商业秘密行为，其虽处于本案共同实施侵权行为的末端环节，但其也是涉案技术秘密的最终使用者和最大获益者。

Hualu Hengsheng was the end-user and the biggest beneficiary of the Melamine Project Phase I, and the technical drawings and information of the Melamine Project Phase I originated from Houcheng and the Design Institute. Accordingly, the Court of First Instance found that Hualu Hengsheng had acquired and used the technical secrets in question, which had factual and legal basis. At the same time, the available exhibits were sufficient to prove that Hualu Hengsheng knew that the technology it used actually originated from

Golden Elephant. The reasons are as follows: First, the design monographs submitted by Hualu Hengsheng to the relevant administrative department for record clearly recorded the current status of melamine production technology in the industry and the relevant technology possessed by Yejing Company, and therefore, Hualu Hengsheng, as a competitor in the same field of business, was clearly aware of the situation of the melamine production technology in the industry in the process of designing and constructing the alleged infringing production system, and knew that Yejing Company was enjoying the melamine production technology by the pressurized gas phase quenching and cooling method, and that the plant, which has a capacity of 50, 000 tons/year, had already been successfully operated. Second, Hualu Hengsheng did not submit evidence to prove that it had mastered the corresponding technology of producing 50, 000 tons of melamine per year from a single production line before the alleged infringement occurred. According to the facts ascertained by the Court of First Instance, Hualu Hengsheng did not have any production technology and equipment for the preparation of melamine before 2011, and the company it acquired, Defeng Chemical Company, only had a melamine plant with an annual production capacity of 10, 000 tons, and there was no evidence to show that it had the ability to complete on its own the technological improvement that would allow the annual output of a single production line to grow to 50, 000 tons. Third, Hualu Hengsheng, as a large-scale chemical enterprise that plans to build a large-scale melamine chemical project involving huge investment, should have investigated the current status of melamine production technology in the industry and conducted a feasibility study of the project before signing the engineering design contract with Houcheng and Design Institute, and should have known whether the counterparty to whom it was going to sign the contract possessed the technology and had the corresponding design capability, rather than just signing a cooperation agreement with Houcheng and Design Institute, as claimed by Hualu Hengsheng, with which Houcheng provided the technology and Design Institute was responsible for the engineering design, without any knowledge of other matters. None of the accused infringers provided evidence to prove that Houcheng and Design Institute had a history of research and development or project design of the technology to produce 50,000 tons of melamine per year in a single production line, or that they had actually and legally mastered the technology to produce 50,000 tons of melamine per year in a single production line prior to signing the contract with Hualu Hengsheng. Accordingly, it can be presumed that Hualu Hengsheng should have known that the Houcheng and Design Institute themselves did not possess the corresponding technology when signing the engineering design contract with them. And last, Yin's statement in the relevant criminal case also proved that Hualu Hengsheng knew the actual source of the technology used by Houcheng and Design Institute for the Melamine Project Phase I in question. Based on the existing evidence in this case, even if Hualu Hengsheng did not know that Houcheng and Design Institute did not possess the corresponding technology of producing 50,000 tons of melamine per year in a single production line or did not know the source of the corresponding technology when signing the engineering design contract with them, Hualu Hengsheng accepted and did not stop the use of the technology despite knowing that the technology originated from the Golden Elephant, which constituted the knowing, and did not affect the subjective fault and the composition of the infringement as well as the determination of the assumption of the liabilities. In short, Hualu Hengsheng subjectively knew the actual source of the technical solutions used by it, which constituted the deemed infringement of trade secrets as stipulated in Article 9(2) of the Anti-Unfair Competition Law, and although

it was at the end link of the joint implementation of infringement in this case, it was also the final user and the biggest beneficiary of the technical secrets in question.

因此，华鲁恒升公司、厚承公司、设计院公司、尹某大之间具有侵害涉案技术秘密的共同意思联络，主观上彼此明知，彼此先后实施相应的侵权行为形成了完整的侵害涉案技术秘密的侵权行为链，客观上已形成分工协作，属于共同故意实施被诉侵权行为。需特别指出的是，构成共同故意实施被诉侵权行为并不以各参与者事前共谋、事后协同行动为限，各参与者彼此之间心知肚明、心照不宣，先后参与、相互协作，亦可构成共同故意实施被诉侵权行为。本案中，华鲁恒升公司等被诉侵权人实施共同侵权行为的过程即属于后者情形，其各自实施的行为均属于实施共同侵权行为的关键环节且为不可或缺的组成部分。

Therefore, there is a link of common intention between Hualu Hengsheng, Houcheng, Design Institute, and Yin to infringe on the technical secrets in question, and subjectively they know each other, and each of them successively implements the corresponding infringing acts which form a complete chain of infringing acts against the technical secrets in question, and objectively they have formed a division of labor, which is a common intentional implementation of the alleged infringing acts. It should be pointed out that, in particular, the common intention to implement the alleged infringement will not be limited to the participants' collusion in advance and coordinated actions afterward, and the participants know each other well and unambiguously, successively engage in, and collaborate with each other, which can also constitute the common intention to implement the alleged infringement. In this case, the process of Hualu Hengsheng and the other accused infringers to implement the joint infringement is the latter situation, and their respective acts are key links in the implementation of the joint infringement and indispensable components.

59. 技术秘密侵权案件中制造者的停止销售责任

Manufacturer's liabilities for cessation of distribution in technical secret misappropriation cases

【裁判要旨】

[Judgment Digest]

当制造者使用的技术秘密为制造特定产品所不可或缺的重要条件且该产品为使用该技术秘密所直接获得的产品时，因其销售该产品的行为显属同一侵权主体实施制造行为的自然延伸和必然结果，权利人主张该制造者停止销售使用该技术秘密所直接获得的产品的，人民法院可予支持。

When the technical secrets used by the manufacturers are indispensable and important conditions for manufacturing specific products that are directly obtained through such usage, if the technical secret holders claims that the manufacturers should cease the distribution of such products on the ground that the aforementioned distribution is obviously the natural extension and inevitable consequence of the manufacturing conduct as carried out by the same infringer, then such claim can be supported by people's courts.

【关键词】

[Keywords]

技术秘密　侵权　停止侵害　制造者停止销售

Technical secrets; infringement; cessation of infringement; cessation of distribution by manufacturers

【案号】

[Case Number]

（2022）最高法知民终 541 号

（2022）SPC IP Civil Final 541

【裁判意见】

[Judge's Opinion]

在上诉人四川金象赛瑞化工股份有限公司与上诉人山东华鲁恒升化工股份有限公司、宁波厚承管理咨询有限公司、宁波安泰环境化工工程设计有限公司、尹某大侵害技术秘密纠纷案中，最高人民法院指出，作为制造者的侵权人在技术秘密侵权案件中的侵权行为通常表现为使用技术秘密制造产品，反不正当竞争法已明确禁止该种行为。当制造者使用的技术秘密为制造该产品所不可或缺的重要条件且该产品为使用该技术秘密所直接获得的产品时，因其销售该产品的行为显属同一侵权主体实施制造行为的自然延伸和必然结果，故此时该禁止使用的范围应当包括禁止该制造者使用该技术秘密制造产品后进行销售。在此情况下，如将不得使用技术秘密狭隘地理解为仅禁止制造者使用技术秘密的制造行为，而不包括禁止其在制造完成后进行销售，不仅于理不通、自相矛盾，而且有销售即有获利，如不禁止制造者继续销售将必然造成侵权损害后果的继续发生或扩大。当然，制造者使用技术秘密制造的产品被其售出后，使用技术秘密的侵权结果即同时发生，且非属制造者的他人的独立的销售行为并不属于反不正当竞争法所列明的侵害技术秘密的行为，因此，在一般情况下，制造者之外的其他人后续销售使用技术秘密制造的产品并不为法律所禁止。但是，如果该后续销售者系因明显过错而依法与产品制造者构成共同侵权或帮助侵权的，则亦应为法律所不许。本案中，华鲁恒升公司使用涉案技术秘密的行为主要表现为使用涉案技术秘密建设被诉侵权生产系统并在被诉侵权生产系统建成后继续使用承载有涉案技术秘密的该侵权生产系统和使用涉案技术秘密中的生产工艺制造密胺产品并进行销售。从涉案技术秘密的内容来看，其所包含的设备选择以及相关设备的结构、尺寸、形状、生产工艺参数等技术信息均是华鲁恒升公司建造和使用被诉侵权生产系统所必需的技术信息，涉案技术秘密中包含的相关技术参数对使用被诉侵权生产系统制造密胺产品亦不可或缺，而且密胺产品是使用涉案技术秘密所直接获得的产品，如不使用涉案技术秘密，则华鲁恒升公司无法建造完成被诉侵权生产系统，更无从使用被诉侵权生产系统得以每年生产 5 万吨的密胺产品。因此，涉案技术秘密既是华鲁恒升公司制造被诉侵权生产系统不可或缺的重要条件，也是其制造涉案密胺产品不可或缺的重要条件，而且其涉案密胺产品为使用涉案技术秘密所直接获得的产品。金象公司所提出的责令华鲁恒升公司停止销售使用涉案技术秘密生产的密胺产品的请求实质上已被涵盖在要求其停止使用涉案技术秘密的范畴内，亦是作为制造者的华鲁恒升公司停止使用涉案技术秘密的题中应有之义，故在一审判决华鲁恒升公司停止使用涉案技术秘密的基础上，进一步明确华鲁恒升公司应当立即停止销售使用涉案技术秘密生产出的密胺产品。

In the case of dispute over the infringement of technical secrets between the Appellant, Sichuan Golden - Elephant Sincerity Chemical Co., Ltd. (hereinafter referred to as Golden Elephant), and the Appellants, Shandong Hualu Hengsheng Chemical Co., Ltd. (hereinafter referred to as Hualu Hengsheng), Ningbo Houcheng Management Consulting Co., Ltd. (hereinafter referred to as Houcheng), Ningbo Antai Environment & Chemical Engineering & Design Co., Ltd. (hereinafter referred to as Design Institute), and Yin, the SPC pointed out that the infringer as a manufacturer usually manifests its infringing behavior in technical secret infringement cases by using technical secrets to manufacture products, which has been explicitly prohibited by the Anti-Unfair Competition Law. When the technical secrets used by the manufacturer are essential for the manufacture of the product and the product is the product obtained directly by using the technical secrets, as the distribution of the product is obviously a natural extension of the same infringing subject to carry out the act of manufacture and the inevitable result, so the scope of the prohibition of use should include the prohibition on the manufac-

turer to use the technical secrets to manufacture the product and then to sell it. In this case, if the prohibition on the use of technical secrets is narrowly understood as only prohibiting the manufacturer to manufacture by using technical secrets, but not including the prohibition on sales after the completion of the manufacture, it is not only unreasonable and self-contradictory, but also sales are profitable, so if not prohibited from continuing to sell, it will certainly result in continued infringement or expansion of the consequences of the damage. Of course, after the product made by the manufacturer using the technical secrets is sold by it, the infringing result of using the technical secrets occurs at the same time, and the independent sales behavior of others who are not the manufacturer does not belong to the infringement of technical secrets listed in the Anti-Unfair Competition Law, and therefore, in general, the subsequent sales of the product made by using the technical secrets by others other than the manufacturer are not prohibited by the law. However, it is not permitted by law if the subsequent seller is clearly at fault and constitutes a joint infringement or contributes to the infringement with the manufacturer of the product according to the law. In this case, Hualu Hengsheng's behavior of using the technical secrets in question is mainly manifested in building the accused infringing production system using the technical secrets in question and continuing to use the infringing production system bearing the technical secrets in question after the accused infringing production system is built and using the production process in the technical secrets in question to manufacture and sell melamine products. From the content of the technical secrets in question, the equipment selection contained therein, as well as the structure, size, shape, production process parameters, and other technical information of the relevant equipment, are all necessary technical information for Hualu Hengsheng to construct and use the infringing production system, and the technical parameters contained in the technical secrets in question are indispensable for manufacturing melamine products by using the infringing production system in question, and the melamine is a product directly obtained by the use of the technical secrets in question; if the technical secrets were not used, Hualu Hengsheng would not be able to construct and complete the alleged infringing production system, let alone be able to use the alleged infringing production system to produce melamine products at an annual capacity of 50, 000 tons. Therefore, possessing the technical secrets in question is not only an important indispensable condition for Hualu Hengsheng to manufacture the alleged infringing production system, but also an important indispensable condition for Hualu Hengsheng to manufacture the melamine products in question, and the melamine product in question is a product directly obtained by using the technical secrets in question. The request made by Golden Elephant to order Hualu Hengsheng to stop selling the melamine products produced by using the technical secrets in question has been covered in the scope of the request to stop using the technical secrets in question, and also the rightful meaning of Hualu Hengsheng as a manufacturer to stop using the technical secrets in question, and therefore, on the basis of the judgment of the First Instance that Hualu Hengsheng stop using the technical secrets in question, it was further clarified that Hualu Hengsheng should stop selling the melamine products produced by using the technical secrets in question at once.

60. 技术秘密侵权人销毁技术秘密载体的责任及其承担方式

Infringer's liability for destroying carriers of technical secrets plus specific ways of such destroying

【裁判要旨】

[Judgment Digest]

在权利人证明相应技术秘密载体存在的情况下，对权利人提出的要求侵权人销毁持有的技术秘密载体的诉讼请求，人民法院一般应予支持。人民法院可以综合考虑载体的性质、技术秘密的内容等情况对侵权人销毁其持有的技术秘密载体的具体方式以及履行期予以指明。被诉侵权生产系统既是承载技术秘密的重要载体，也是侵权人可能继续实施侵权行为的重要工具，销毁承载有该技术秘密的被诉侵权生产系统既是停止侵害的题中应有之义，亦可有效预防侵权人继续使用其上所承载的技术秘密以及在该生产系统上使用该技术秘密中的生产工艺。销毁有关设备的方式包括但不限于拆除。

When the technical secret holders have proved that there does exist the carriers of technical secrets at issue, and also claims that the accused infringer should destroy such carriers as possessed by the infringer, then such claim shall generally be supported by people's courts, in which case the court may take into account the carriers' characteristics and content of the technical secrets at issue, and then specify on how to destroy such carriers plus the deadline. As the accused infringing production system is not only an important carrier of the technical secrets, but also an important tool with which the accused infringer may continue the misappropriation, destroying such production system is not only necessary to cease misappropriation, but also effective to prevent the infringer from continuing to use the technical secrets carried therein plus the corresponding production processes. The way of destroying relevant equipment includes, but is not limited to, dismantling.

【关键词】

[Keywords]

技术秘密　侵权　停止侵害　销毁技术秘密载体

Technical secrets; infringement; cessation of infringement; destruction of technical secret carriers

【案号】

[Case Number]

(2022) 最高法知民终 541 号

(2022) SPC IP Civil Final 541

【裁判意见】

[Judge's Opinion]

在上诉人四川金象赛瑞化工股份有限公司与上诉人山东华鲁恒升化工股份有限公司、宁波厚承管理咨询有限公司、宁波安泰环境化工工程设计有限公司、尹某大侵害技术秘密纠纷案中，最高人民法院认为，华鲁恒升公司持有的记载或包含有涉案技术秘密的载体主要为被诉侵权生产系统以及其向相关行政管理部门备案的图纸或技术资料即本案中的设计专篇，同时，为确保生产设备的正常运行、维护、维修，此类大型生产设备的实际使用者理应持有相应技术资料，故可以推定华鲁恒升公司持有的记载或包含有涉案技术秘密的载体还包括被诉侵权生产系统的相应技术资料。被诉侵权生产系统既是承载涉案技术秘密的重要载体，也是华鲁恒升公司可能继续实施侵权行为的重要工具。销毁承载有涉案技术秘密的被诉侵权生产系统既是停止侵害的应有之义，亦可有效预防华鲁恒升公司继续使用其上所承载的技术秘密以及在该生产系统上使用涉案技术秘密中的生产工艺。华鲁恒升公司所持有的设计专篇等其他记载或包含有涉案技术秘密的相应技术资料也应与被诉侵权生产系统同时销

毁。一审法院基于社会资源的浪费以及生产安全的角度考量，希望通过判令停止使用但不销毁生产设备的方式，鼓励华鲁恒升公司与金象公司达成技术许可。此种处理方式的出发点虽好，在于试图促成技术许可和避免资源浪费，但结合本案华鲁恒升公司等被诉侵权人十分明显的主观过错以及较为严重的侵权情节，该处理方式一方面不当限制了权利人对其知识产权的行使，另一方面，在双方不能达成合意时将形成裁判执行的僵局并可能引发新的争议与诉讼，并不能有效保护金象公司的知识产权，一定程度上也会增加金象公司和华鲁恒升公司的纠纷解决成本。唯有支持金象公司的该诉讼请求，方可既有效制止侵权和保护知识产权，又有利于促使当事人在明了彼此权利和行为边界的基础上开展诚信磋商，就未来有关事宜作出妥善处理。此外，被诉侵权生产系统中还涉及其他未承载涉案技术秘密的设备，涉及华鲁恒升公司的合法财产权利，因此，销毁有关设备的方式包括但不限于以拆除的方式实现。同时，考虑到被诉侵权生产系统涉及大型化工项目，华鲁恒升公司在履行上述销毁该生产系统的责任时需一定的合理履行期间，且该生产系统还涉及相关危险化学品处理，如其进行改建等仍需经相关行政管理部门进行安全条件审查。结合各方当事人在关联案件中关于改造被诉侵权生产系统所需时间的陈述，二审法院给予华鲁恒升公司 90 天的履行宽限期以实现停止侵害的目标。

In the case of dispute over the infringement of technical secrets among the Appellant, Sichuan Golden-Elephant Sincerity Chemical Co., Ltd. (hereinafter referred to as Golden Elephant), and the Appellees, Shandong Hualu Hengsheng Chemical Co., Ltd. (hereinafter referred to as Hualu Hengsheng), Ningbo Houcheng Management Consulting Co., Ltd. (hereinafter referred to as Houcheng), Ningbo Antai Environment & Chemical Engineering & Design Co., Ltd. (hereinafter referred to as Design Institute), and Yin, the SPC held that the carrier which records or contains the technical secrets in question held by Hualu Hengsheng is mainly the alleged infringing production system as well as the drawings or technical information filed with the relevant administrative departments, i. e., the design monographs in this case, and at the same time, in order to ensure the normal operation, maintenance, and repair of the production equipment, the actual users of this kind of large-scale production equipment should hold the corresponding technical information, so that it can be presumed that the carrier which records or contains the technical secrets in question held by Hualu Hengsheng also includes the corresponding technical information of the alleged infringing production system. The alleged infringing production system is not only an important carrier of the technical secrets in question, but also an important tool for Hualu Hengsheng to continue to carry out the infringement behavior. Destroying the alleged infringing production system which carries the technical secrets in question is not only the proper obligation to stop the infringement, but also can effectively prevent Hualu Hengsheng from continuing to use the technical secrets carried thereon as well as using the production process of the technical secrets in question on the production system. The design monographs and other corresponding technical information held by Hualu Hengsheng that records or contains the technical secrets in question should also be simultaneously destroyed with the alleged infringing production system. The Court of First Instance, based on the consideration of waste of social resources and production safety, hoped to encourage Hualu Hengsheng to reach a technology license agreement with Golden Elephant by ordering the cessation of use but not the destruction of the production equipment. Despite the good intention of such treatment, which was to try to promote technology licensing and avoid the waste of resources, such treatment, in combination with the obvious subjective fault of the accused infringers such as Hualu Hengsheng and the more serious infringement circum-

stances, on the one hand, unduly restricted the right holders' exercise of intellectual property rights; on the other hand, when both parties failed to reach a consensus, it would form a deadlock in the implementation of the decision and may lead to new disputes and litigation, which could not protect the intellectual property rights of Golden Elephant, and, to some extent, would increase the cost of the dispute settlement between Golden Elephant and Hualu Hengsheng. The only way to effectively stop the infringement and protect the intellectual property rights was to support the Golden Elephant's Claim, which was also conducive to prompting the parties to negotiate in good faith on the basis of understanding the boundaries of each other's rights and behaviors and to make appropriate arrangements for the future. In addition, the alleged infringing production system also involved other equipment that does not carry the technical secrets in question, which involved the lawful property rights of Hualu Hengsheng, and therefore, the destruction of the relevant equipment would be realized in a manner including, but not limited to, dismantling. At the same time, considering that the alleged infringing production system involves a large-scale chemical project, Hualu Hengsheng will need a certain reasonable period of time to fulfill its responsibility of destroying the production system, and the production system also involved the handling of related hazardous chemicals, which would still need to be examined by the relevant administrative departments for the review of safety conditions in case of reconstruction. Taking into account the parties' statements in the connected cases about the time needed to transform the alleged infringing production system, the Court of Second Instance granted Hualu Hengsheng a 90-day grace period for performance to achieve the goal of cessation of infringement.

61. 侵害技术秘密赔偿约定的认定与处理
Determination and handling of agreement on compensation for damages caused by technical secrets misappropriation

【裁判要旨】

[Judgment Digest]

技术秘密权利人与职工经协商在保守商业秘密条款中就侵权责任的方式、侵权损害赔偿数额计算作出的约定，属于双方就未来可能发生的侵权损害赔偿达成的事前约定，人民法院在确定侵害技术秘密赔偿数额时可以将之作为重要参考。

The provision on the way of assuming liabilities and calculating damages as contained in the confidentiality clause agreed upon by the technical secret holders and their employees is the agreement reached by the two sides on damages for possible misappropriation in the future. Such provisions can be taken as important references by people's courts in determining the amount of damages for technical secret misappropriation.

【关键词】

[Keywords]

技术秘密　侵权　赔偿数额　约定

Technical secrets; infringement; amount of compensation; agreement

【案号】

[Case Number]

(2021) 最高法知民终 1687 号

(2021) SPC IP Civil Final 1687

【基本案情】

[Case Facts]

在上诉人大连倍通数据平台管理中心（以下简称倍通数据）与上诉人崔某吉侵害技术秘密纠纷案中，涉及爬虫平台数据信息（以下简称涉案技术秘密）。倍通数据认为，崔某吉在离职前违反倍通数据关于保密协议的约定及公司信息安全规章制度，将该公司具有保密要求的爬虫平台数据信息，擅自通过公司邮件系统发送至个人邮箱，使涉案技术秘密脱离公司控制，造成信息严重泄露，故向辽宁省大连市中级人民法院（以下简称一审法院）提起诉讼，请求判令崔某吉立即停止侵害、赔偿倍通数据经济损失 50 万元及律师费 1.5 万元。一审法院认为，崔某吉的行为构成反不正当竞争法第九条禁止的“以其他不正当手段获取权利人的商业秘密”的侵害商业秘密行为，应当停止侵权。故判决崔某吉立即停止侵害，并赔偿倍通数据经济损失及合理开支共计 5 万元。倍通数据及崔某吉均不服，向最高人民法院提起上诉。倍通数据主张，一审法院判赔金额远低于因侵权行为给倍通数据带来的实际损失及潜在损失，应依据《保密协议书》约定的侵害绝密信息的赔偿金额 50 万元至 100 万元确定本案赔偿数额。崔某吉主张，其与倍通数据已就被诉侵权行为达成和解，且其并未实施其他侵权行为，一审法院判决停止侵害及赔偿损失，没有事实基础。最高人民法院于 2022 年 3 月 14 日判决禁止崔某吉披露、使用或者允许他人使用倍通数据的涉案技术秘密，并赔偿倍通数据经济损失 25 万元及维权合理开支 1.5 万元。

The case of dispute over the infringement of technical secrets between the Appellant, Dalian Beitong Data Platform Management Center (hereinafter referred to as Beitong Data), and Appellant, Cui, involves data information of the crawler platform (hereinafter referred to as the technical secret in question). Beitong Data believed that Cui violated the confidentiality agreement of Beitong Data and the Company's information security rules and regulations before he left the Company, and sent the information on the Company's crawler platform data with confidentiality requirements to his personal mailbox through the Company's mail system without authorization, so that the technical secret in question was taken out of the Company's control, resulting in serious leakage of the information, and therefore filed a lawsuit to Dalian Intermediate People's Court of Liaoning Province (hereinafter referred to as the Court of First Instance), requesting to order Cui to immediately stop the infringement, and compensate Beitong Data for the economic loss of CNY 500,000 and attorney's fee of CNY 15,000. The Court of First Instance held that Cui's behavior constituted the infringement of trade secrets prohibited by Article 9 of the Anti-Unfair Competition Law, which was "Obtaining the trade secrets of the right holder by other improper means", and he shall stop the infringement. Therefore, it was judged that Cui immediately stopped the infringement and compensated Beitong Data for economic losses and reasonable expenses totaling CNY 50,000. Unsatisfied, both Beitong Data and Cui appealed to the SPC, respectively. Beitong Data claimed that the amount of damages awarded by the Court of First Instance was far lower than the actual and potential damages caused to Beitong Data due to the infringement and that the amount of damages in this case should be determined on the basis of the amount of damages for infringement of top-secret information between CNY 500,000 and CNY 1,000,000 as stipulated in the Non-disclosure Agreement. Cui claimed that he and Beitong Data had reached a settlement on the alleged infringement, and that he had not committed any other infringing acts, and that there was no factual basis for the judgment of the Court of First Instance to stop the infringement and to compensate for the damages. The SPC ruled on March 14, 2022 that Cui shall be prohibited from disclosing, using, or permitting others to use the technical secret in question of Beitong Data, and shall compensate

Beitong Data with CNY 250,000 for economic loss and CNY 15,000 for reasonable expenses in defending its rights.

【裁判意见】

[Judge's Opinion]

最高人民法院二审认为，在确定崔某吉应承担的侵权损害赔偿数额时，应重点考量下列因素：第一，涉案技术秘密的开发情况。涉案技术秘密是倍通数据针对医药行业的特定要求而开发的特定计算机程序，倍通数据为开发涉案技术秘密，专门组建开发团队，并在短短4个月就投入开发成本25.2万元。但目前涉案技术秘密仍处于开发过程中，并未投入使用。第二，侵权人的侵权情节。崔某吉作为爬虫平台项目的负责人，在入职和离职时，均与倍通数据签订严格的保密协议，约定崔某吉不得泄露公司商业秘密；离职时不得私自带走任职期间完成的文案和模板等内容，需要带走的文件均须向倍通数据备案并经倍通数据同意。但是崔某吉无视公司的保密要求和保密协议约定，仍然实施了盗窃涉案技术秘密的行为，主观上具有恶意。但在案证据证明崔某吉目前仅有盗窃技术秘密的侵权行为，并无实施其他侵害技术秘密的行为。第三，权利人与侵权人关于违反保密协议的侵权损害赔偿数额约定。倍通数据与崔某吉在《保密协议书》中约定，公司数据库、系统源代码及内含资料等文件资料属于公司的绝密级秘密，并约定倍通数据每月向崔某吉支付保密工资作为其保守公司商业秘密的补偿金。该协议还约定，若崔某吉违反以上协议，侵害倍通数据绝密级秘密的，应当向倍通数据赔偿50万元至100万元。本案为侵害技术秘密纠纷，倍通数据与崔某吉的约定属于双方就侵权损害赔偿达成的事前约定，且崔某吉根据这一约定在工作期间每月可以获得相应的保密工资，故在崔某吉违反相关约定时，可以将双方约定的侵权赔偿数额作为确定本案侵权损害赔偿的重要参考因素。综合考虑上述因素，酌情改判崔某吉赔偿倍通数据经济损失25万元及合理开支1.5万元。

The SPC held in the Second Instance that, in determining the amount of damages for infringement to be borne by Cui, it should focus on the following factors: firstly, the development of the technical secret in question. The technical secret in question was a specific computer program developed by Beitong Data for the specific requirements of the pharmaceutical industry, and Beitong Data set up a special development team for the development of the technical secrets in question and invested CNY 252, 000 in development costs in just four months. However, the technical secret in question is still in the process of development and has not been put into use. Secondly, the circumstances of the infringement by the infringer. Cui, as the person in charge of the crawler platform project, signed a strict confidentiality agreement with Beitong Data at the time of joining and leaving the Company, agreeing that Cui shall not disclose the Company's trade secrets; When you leave the Company, you are not allowed to take away the contents of the paperwork and templates that you have completed during your term of office, and any documents that you need to take away must be filed with and agreed to by Beitong Data. But Cui, disregarding the Company's confidentiality requirements and confidentiality agreement, still implemented the theft of the technical secrets, with subjective malicious intent. However, the available exhibits prove that Cui has only committed the infringement by stealing technical secrets, without committing other acts of infringing on technical secrets. Thirdly, the right holder and the infringer agree on the amount of infringement damages for breach of the confidentiality agreement. Beitong Data and Cui agreed in the Non-Disclosure Agreement that the Company's database, system source code, and internal information and other documents and materials belonged to the Company's top-secret secrets, and agreed that Beitong Data would pay Cui a monthly confidentiality salary as the compensation for keeping the Company's commercial secrets. In the Agree-

ment, it was also agreed that if Cui violated the above agreement and infringed on the top secret of Beitong Data, he should compensate Beitong Data an amount of CNY 500,000 to CNY 1,000,000. This case is a dispute over infringement of technical secrets, the arrangement between Beitong Data and Cui belongs to the prior understanding between the two parties on the infringement damages, and Cui can get the corresponding confidentiality salary every month during the working period according to such arrangement, so the amount of infringement damages agreed between the two parties can be taken as an important reference factor for determining the infringement damages in this case when Cui violates the relevant agreement. Taking the above factors into consideration, Cui was ordered to compensate Beitong Data for CNY 250,000 in economic loss and CNY 15,000 in reasonable expenses, as appropriate.

62. 技术秘密侵权损害赔偿确定中的商业机会因素考量 Consideration on business opportunity in determining damages for technical secrets misappropriation

【裁判要旨】

[Judgment Digest]

对于侵权人存在明显过错且根据在案证据能够认定或者根据具体案情可以推定侵害技术秘密行为直接决定了侵权人商业机会的获得或者权利人商业机会的丧失的，原则上可以将侵权人的全部获利作为侵权获利。

If the infringer is obviously at fault, and it can be ascertained with documented evidence that, or it can be presumed based on specific circumstances of the case that the technical secret misappropriation directly leads to the infringer's acquisition or the technical secret holder's loss of business opportunity, then all the profits obtained by the infringer on the basis of such misappropriation can in principle be regarded as the profits originating from technical secret misappropriation.

【关键词】

[Keywords]

技术秘密　侵权　赔偿数额　商业机会

Technical secrets; infringement; amount of compensation; business opportunity

【案号】

[Case Number]

（2021）最高法知民终 1363 号

（2021）SPC IP Civil Final 1363

【基本案情】

[Case Facts]

在上诉人盎亿泰地质微生物技术（北京）有限公司（以下简称盎亿泰公司）、英索油能源科技（北京）有限责任公司（以下简称英索油公司）、罗某平、李某与被上诉人胡某宇、张某梦侵害技术秘密纠纷案中，盎亿泰公司认为，罗某平、李某、胡某宇、张某梦违反保密义务，向英索油公司披露涉案技术信息，英索油公司明知罗某平等人不当获取涉案技术信息仍使用涉案技术信息，均构成侵权，故向北京知识产权法院（以下简称一审法院）提起诉讼，请求判令英索油公司等立即停止涉案侵权行为，连带赔偿经济损失 588 万元及维权合理开支 50.7 万元，张某梦在 638.7 万元的 10%范围内承担连带责任。一审法院认为，被诉技术秘密侵权成立，酌定英索油公司、李某连带赔偿经济损失 50 万元、维权合理开支 25 万元。盎亿泰公司和英索油公司、罗某平、李某均不服，向最高人民法院提起上诉，其中盎亿泰公司主张胡某宇、张某梦亦构成侵权，且一审判赔金额过低，请求判令英索油公司等立即停止涉案

侵权行为，连带赔偿经济损失 200 万元及维权合理开支 50.7 万元。最高人民法院二审查明涉案技术信息应用的领域为油气微生物勘探领域，并非市场竞争充分的普通商业领域，推定英索油公司不当攫取了原本属于盎亿泰公司的交易机会，于 2022 年 10 月 26 日判决撤销原判，英索油公司、罗某平、李某、胡某宇立即停止侵权，并连带赔偿盎亿泰公司经济损失 200 万元、维权合理开支 50.7 万元。

In the case of dispute over the infringement of technical secrets among the Appellant, AE&E Geomicrobial Technologies Inc. (hereinafter referred to as AE&E), and the Appellees InSoil Energy Technologies Co., Ltd. (hereinafter referred to as InSoil), Luo, and Li, and the Appellees, Hu and Zhang, AE&E believed that Luo, Li, Hu, and Zhang had violated the duty of confidentiality by disclosing the technical information in question to InSoil, and InSoil knew that Luo and others had improperly accessed the technical information in question but still used it, which constituted the infringement, and therefore, filed a lawsuit with Beijing Intellectual Property Court (hereinafter referred to as the Court of First Instance), requesting that InSoil and others be ordered to immediately cease the alleged infringing acts, and jointly and severally compensate CNY 5.88 million of economic losses and CNY 507,000 of reasonable expenses, and Zhang bear joint liability to the extent of 10% of CNY 6.387 million. The Court of First Instance held that the alleged infringement of technical secrets was established, and decided that InSoil and Li shall jointly and severally compensate CNY 500,000 of economic losses and CNY 250,000 of reasonable expenses for safeguarding rights. Unsatisfied, AE&E and InSoil, Luo, and Li appealed to the SPC, respectively, in which AE&E claimed that Hu and Zhang also constituted the infringement and that the amount of compensation in the First Instance was too low, and requested that InSoil be ordered to immediately stop the alleged infringing acts and to jointly and severally compensate CNY 2 million in economic losses and CNY 507,000 in reasonable expenses for safeguarding rights. The SPC found in the Second Instance that the field of application of the technical information in question was the field of oil and gas microbial exploration, not an ordinary commercial field with sufficient market competition, and presumed that InSoil had improperly seized the trading opportunities that originally belonged to AE&E, and decided on October 26, 2022 to set aside the original judgment, and that InSoil, Luo, Li, and Hu shall cease the infringement immediately, and jointly and severally compensate AE&E for CNY 2 million of economic losses and CNY 507,000 of reasonable expenses for safeguarding rights.

【裁判意见】

[Judge's Opinion]

最高人民法院二审认为，英索油公司明知系盎亿泰公司的技术秘密而获取并使用；罗某平、胡某宇违反其与盎亿泰公司的保密协议约定，将包含盎亿泰公司技术秘密的“微生物油气勘探采集技术规程”直接用于制定英索油公司的《地质微生物勘探野外采集技术规程》；李某作为盎亿泰公司研发部的研究员，违反其与盎亿泰公司保密协议的约定，未在离职时交还其在盎亿泰公司任职期间所接触并掌握的包含有盎亿泰公司涉案技术秘密信息的资料，且将上述技术秘密用于英索油公司中标的洛克项目，故英索油公司、罗某平、李某、胡某宇均构成侵权，应承担停止侵权及赔偿责任。

The SPC held in the Second Instance that InSoil had obtained and used the technical secrets as it knew they were the technical secrets of AE&E; Luo and Hu violated the confidentiality agreement with AE&E by using the "Technical Procedures for Microbial Oil and Gas Exploration and Collection", which contained the technical secrets of AE&E, to directly formulate the Technical Procedures for Geological Microbial Exploration and Collection in

the Field of InSoil; Li, as a researcher in the R&D Department of AE&E, violated the confidentiality agreement with AE&E and failed to return the information containing the technical secrets involved of AE&E that she had contacted and mastered during her tenure in AE&E, and used the said technical secrets in the Luoke Project that was awarded to InSoil, and therefore, InSoil, Luo, Li, and Hu constituted infringement of the rights of AE&E, and they shall be liable for the cessation of infringement and the compensation to AE&E.

鉴于本案系因前员工组建新公司并侵害原任职公司技术秘密引发的案件，英索油公司在实际经营中使用盎亿泰公司的技术秘密，具有明显的主观恶意，且考虑涉案技术信息应用的领域为油气微生物勘探领域，并非市场竞争充分的普通商业领域，可推定英索油公司不当攫取了原本属于盎亿泰公司的交易机会。在此情况下，英索油公司是否存在恶意低价竞标行为、是否在洛克项目中还使用了其他自有技术，以及所使用技术秘密的技术贡献率大小，均不影响赔偿金额的计算。

Given that this case was triggered by the fact that the former employees had formed a new company and infringed on the technical secrets of the former employer, InSoil's use of AE&E' s technical secrets in its actual business operations has obvious subjective malice; considering that the field of application of the technical information in question is the field of microbial exploration of oil and gas and not an ordinary business field with sufficient market competition, it can be assumed that InSoil improperly seized the trading opportunities that originally belonged to AE&E. In this context, whether InSoil had acted in bad faith in underbidding, whether it had also used other own technologies in the Luoke Project, and the size of the technical contribution of the technical secrets used did not affect the calculation of the amount of compensation.

根据盎亿泰公司所提交的海域项目审计报告所反映的盈利情况，两个项目的平均营业利润率约为 43. 85%，以盎亿泰公司在洛克项目中的最终报价 775 万元计算，营业利润约为 339 万余元，远超出盎亿泰公司的诉请金额 200 万元。即便依据英索油公司在洛克项目中的获利情况计算，英索油公司因洛克项目实际收到项目款项 735 万元，洛克项目利润率为 27. 91%，英索油公司在洛克项目中的营业利润为 205 万余元（735 万元×27. 91%），亦超出盎亿泰公司在本案中诉请赔偿的金额。考虑本案的具体侵权情节，故对盎亿泰公司的诉请金额予以全额支持。

According to the profitability reflected in the audit reports of the Sea Area Projects submitted by AE&E, the average operating profit margin of the two projects was about 43. 85%, and based on AE&E' s final offer of CNY 7. 75 million in the Luoke Project, the operating profit was about CNY 3. 39 million, far exceeding the amount of CNY 2 million claimed by AE&E. Even if the calculation was based on the profitability of InSoil in the Luoke Project, InSoil actually received CNY 7. 35 million for the Rock Project, and the profit margin of the Luoke Project was 27. 91%, InSoil's operating profit in the Luoke Project was more than CNY 2. 05 million (CNY 7. 35 million × 27. 91%), which exceeded the amount of damages claimed by AE&E in the present case. In view of the specific infringing circumstances in this case, the amount claimed by AE&E was therefore supported in full.

五、垄断案件

V. Anti-monopoly Cases

63. 因专利侵权纠纷达成的和解协议的反垄断审查 Anti-monopoly review of settlement agreements on patent infringement disputes

【裁判要旨】

[Judgment Digest]

因专利侵权纠纷达成的和解协议，如与涉案专利保护范围缺乏实质关联，所涉产品超出涉嫌侵权的产品范围，其核心并不在于保护和行使专利权，而是以行使专利权为掩护，实际上追求分割销售市场、限制商品生产和销售数量、固定价格等效果的，可以认定为横向垄断协议。

If a settlement agreement on patent infringement dispute has no substantive connection with the protection scope of the involved patent, the involved products exceed the scope of suspected infringing products, and its core purpose is not to protect and exercise patent rights, but to seek for dividing sales market, restricting quantity of production and distribution and fixing price, under the cloak of exercising patent rights, then such agreement may be identified as horizontal monopoly agreement.

【关键词】

[Keywords]

横向垄断协议　专利侵权　和解协议　专利权保护范围　涉嫌侵权产品

Horizontal monopoly agreement; patent infringement; settlement agreement; protection scope of patent; suspected infringing product

【案号】

[Case Number]

(2021) 最高法知民终 1298 号

(2021) SPC IP Civil Final 1298

【基本案情】

[Case Facts]

在上诉人上海华明电力设备制造有限公司（以下简称华明公司）与被上诉人武汉泰普变压器开关有限公司（以下简称泰普公司）垄断协议纠纷案中，涉及专利号为 200610019247.3、名称为“一种带有屏蔽装置的无励磁分接开关”的发明专利（以下简称涉案专利）。2015 年 10 月，泰普公司起诉华明公司侵害涉案专利权（该案以下简称 2015 年专利侵权纠纷），2016 年 1 月，双方经协商自行签署《调解协议》（实为和解协议），泰普公司向法院申请撤回 2015 年专利侵权纠纷案的起诉，并获得准许。2019 年 6 月，华明公司向湖北省武汉市中级人民法院（以下简称一审法院）提起本案诉讼，主张涉案调解协议违反反垄断法，请求确认涉案调解协议无效，判令泰普公司赔偿华明公司经济损失 798626 元、维权合理开支 10 万元。一审法院认为，涉案调解协议不属于垄断协议，判决驳回华明公司的全部诉讼请求。华明公司不服，向最高人民法院提起上诉。最高人民法院于 2022 年 2 月 22 日判决撤销原判，确认涉案调解协议全部无效，泰普公司赔偿华明公司合理开支 10 万元。

In the dispute over the monopoly agreement between Shanghai Huaming Power Equipment Co., Ltd. (the appellant, hereinafter referred to as "HM") and Wuhan Taipu Transformer Switch Co., Ltd. (the appellee, hereinafter referred to as "Taipu"), the name of the invention patent involved (patent No. 200610019247.3) is "An Off-circuit Tap-changer with a Shielding Device" (hereinafter referred to as "The patent involved"). In October 2015, Taipu sued HM for infringement of the patent involved (the case is hereinafter referred to as the 2015 dispute over patent infringement); in January 2016, the two parties signed a mediation agreement after negotiation (which is in fact a settlement agreement), under which Taipu requested withdrawal of the 2015 dispute over patent infringement, which was granted by the court. In June 2019, HM filed a lawsuit with the Hubei Wuhan Intermediate People's Court (hereinafter referred to as the "Court of First Instance"), claiming that the mediation agreement involved violates the Anti-monopoly Law and requesting the court to confirm that the mediation agreement involved is invalid and order Taipu to compensate HM for CNY 798,626 in economic losses and CNY 100,000 in reasonable expenses on safeguarding the latter's rights. The Court of First Instance held that the mediation agreement involved is not a monopoly agreement, so it rejected the claims of HM. HM then appealed to the SPC. On February 22, 2022, the SPC ruled to revoke the original judgment, confirming that the mediation agreement involved is invalid and ordering Taipu to compensate HM for CNY 100,000 in reasonable expenses.

【裁判意见】

[Judge's Opinion]

最高人民法院二审认为，关于泰普公司拥有并行使涉案专利权这一事实是否能够排除涉案调解协议的违法性这一问题。首先，关于知识产权权利行使与垄断行为之间的关系，反垄断法第五十五条规定：“经营者依照有关知识产权的法律、行政法规规定行使知识产权的行为，不适用本法；但是，经营者滥用知识产权，排除、限制竞争的行为，适用本法。”根据上述规定，权利人依照知识产权法律、行政法规规定行使知识产权的行为原则上并不违反反垄断法；但是，权利人逾越其享有的专有权，滥用知识产权排除、限制竞争的，则涉嫌违反反垄断法。其次，关于泰普公司行使涉案专利权的行为是否构成滥用知识产权。本案中，双方 2015 年专利侵权纠纷涉及泰普公司所有的“一种带有屏蔽装置的无励磁分接开关”的发明专利权，其技术效果主要在于降低开关制造成本，增强开关使用的稳定性、可靠性，属于对无励磁分接开关的改进，并非无励磁分接开关领域无法回避的基础性专利。涉案专利的权利要求保护的是一种带有特定结构的屏蔽装置的无励磁分接开关，不涉及特定类型或形状的无励磁分接开关，而涉案调解协议以无励磁分接开关的形式划分产品，将其分为笼形、非笼形（包括鼓形、条形、筒形、鼠笼形等）；在海外市场，又以无励磁分接开关的生产企业划分产品，将其分为泰普公司所参股的泰普联合公司生产的开关和其他企业生产的开关，并以上述划分为基础对华明公司生产和销售某些特定类型的无励磁分接开关加以限制，但这种限制与涉案专利的权利保护范围并无实质关联。泰普公司在原审答辩中也自称，涉案调解协议约定内容已经超出专利侵权纠纷，合同条款也与泰普公司涉案专利权脱钩。此外，华明公司与泰普公司在无载分接开关市场存在竞争关系，涉案调解协议对无载分接开关市场进行划分，并以此对协议所涉及产品，即无励磁分接开关的销售价格、生产数量、销售数量、销售种类、销售地域等加以限制，排除、限制了经营者之间的正常竞争。可见，涉案调解协议与涉案专利权的保护范围缺乏实质关联性，其核心并不在于保护专利权，而是以行使专利权为掩护，实际上追求分割销售市场、限制商品生产和销售数量、固定价格的效果，属于滥用专利权，构成排除、限制竞争的行为，违反了反垄断法的规定。最后，关于涉案调解协议所涉及产品是否包括

涉嫌侵犯专利权的产品。前已述及，由于涉案调解协议对于所限制生产和销售的产品种类及相关的销售市场的划分并非以涉案专利权的保护范围为划分依据，且调解协议的内容已经超出了 2015 年专利侵权纠纷案件中的争议内容，因此涉案调解协议所涉及的产品是否包含涉嫌侵犯专利权的产品与本案并无直接关联性。华明公司主张一审漏查，缺乏法律依据，不予支持。综上所述，泰普公司拥有并行使涉案专利权这一事实并不能够排除涉案调解协议的违法性。

The SPC held that the question is whether Taipu's ownership and exercise of the patent rights involved could preclude the illegality of the mediation agreement involved. First of all, regarding the relationship between the exercise of intellectual property rights and the act of monopoly, Article 55 of the Anti-monopoly Law provides that: "This Law shall not apply to the exercise of intellectual property rights by business operators in accordance with the provisions of laws and administrative regulations concerning intellectual property rights. However, this Law shall apply to business operators' abuse of intellectual property rights to exclude or restrict competition." In other words, the right holder's exercise of intellectual property rights in accordance with relevant laws and administrative regulations will not violate the Anti-monopoly Law in principle. However, the right holder shall be considered to be violating the Anti-monopoly Law if he goes beyond the exclusive right he enjoys and abuses intellectual property rights to exclude or restrict competition. Secondly, regarding whether the exercise of the patent rights involved by Taipu constitutes an abuse of intellectual property rights, in this case, the dispute in 2015 over patent infringement involves the invention patent "An Off-circuit Tap-changer with a Shielding Device" owned by Taipu. The technical effect of the patent is mainly to reduce the manufacturing cost of the tap-changer and increase its stability and reliability. It should be seen as an improvement of the off-circuit tap-changer, not a basic patent that cannot be avoided in the field of off-circuit tap-changers. The claim of the patent involved protects off-circuit tap-changers with a specific structured shielding device, not the off-circuit tap-changers of a specific type or shape; and the mediation agreement involved divides the products into cage and non-cage types (including drum, bar, barrel, squirrel-cage, etc.) according to the type of off-circuit tap-changers. In the overseas market, the products are divided according to off-circuit tap-changer makers into those produced by Taipu and those by other companies, on the basis of which HM is restricted to produce and sell certain types of off-circuit tap-changers. However, such restriction has nothing to do with the protection scope of the patent involved. Taipu also claimed in the original trial that the content of the mediation agreement involved covers more than a patent infringement dispute, and the contractual terms are also detached from the patent rights involved owned by Taipu. In addition, HM and Taipu are rivals in no-load tap-changers; the mediation agreement involved divides the no-load tap-changer market and restricts the product involved in the agreement (i. e., the off-circuit tap-changer) in terms of its sales price, production quantity, sales quantity, sales type, and sales region, which excludes and restricts the normal competition between operators. It can be seen that there is no substantial correlation between the mediation agreement involved and the protection scope of the patent involved. It is not about protecting the patent right, but about using the exercise of the patent right to divide the market, restrict the production and sales quantity of products, and fix price. It is an abuse of the patent right to exclude and restrict competition, which violates the provisions of the Anti-monopoly Law. Lastly, regarding whether the products involved in the mediation agreement include the products suspected of patent infringement, as mentioned above, because 1) the media-

tion agreement involved does not divide the types of products whose production and sales are restricted by it and the relevant sales market based on the protection scope of the patent right involved, and 2) the content of the mediation agreement involved covers more than the dispute in 2015 over patent infringement, whether the products involved in the mediation agreement include the products suspected of patent infringement has no direct relevance to the case. There is a lack of legal basis in HM's claim that relevant inspection was missed in the first instance, so it is not supported. In summary, the fact that Taipu owns and exercises the patent rights involved does not preclude the illegality of the mediation agreement involved.

64. 反垄断行政处罚决定在后继民事赔偿诉讼中的证明力 Probetive force of anti-monopoly administrative penalty decisions in subsequent civil lawsuits

【裁判要旨】

[Judgment Digest]

反垄断执法机构认定构成垄断行为的处罚决定在法定期限内未被提起行政诉讼或者已为人民法院生效裁判所确认，原告在相关垄断民事纠纷案件中据此主张该垄断行为成立的，无须再行举证证明，但有相反证据足以推翻的除外。

If there is no action brought within the statutory period against the penalty decisions made by anti-monopoly authorities, or such decisions have been confirmed by the judiciary, and the plaintiff thereby claims in the associated civil anti-monopoly case that the practice constitutes monopoly, then it is unnecessary for the plaintiff to prove the same monopolistic act, except there is sufficient evidence to the contrary.

【关键词】

[Keywords]

纵向垄断协议　行政处罚决定　垄断行为成立　举证责任

Vertical monopoly agreement; decision on administrative penalty; constitution of monopoly; burden of proof

【案号】

[Case Number]

(2020) 最高法知民终1137号

(2020) SPC IP Civil Final 1137

【基本案情】

[Case Facts]

在上诉人缪某与被上诉人上汽通用汽车销售有限公司（以下简称通用公司）、上海逸隆汽车销售服务有限公司（以下简称逸隆公司）纵向垄断协议纠纷案中，2014年，缪某从逸隆公司处购买涉案车辆。2016年，上海市物价局作出涉案处罚决定书，认定通用公司2014年在分销汽车过程中，相关营销部门存在与上海地区经销商达成并实施限定向第三人转售商品最低价格垄断协议的事实，决定责令当事人立即停止违法行为，处以上一年度相关销售额百分之四的罚款。缪某认为，其购买涉案车辆时正是通用公司在上海地区普遍实施垄断价格期间，故向上海知识产权法院（以下简称一审法院）提起诉讼，请求判令通用公司赔偿缪某购车损失10000元及维权合理支出7500元，逸隆公司对缪某上述购车损失承担补充赔偿责任。一审法院认为，在案证据尚不能认定逸隆公司实施了限定向第三人转售商品最低价格的垄断协议行为，判决驳回缪某的诉讼请求。缪某不服，向最高人民法院提起上诉。最高人民法院于2022年12月15日判决撤销原判，改判支持缪某的全部诉讼请求。

In the dispute over the vertical monopoly agreement between Miao (the appellant) and SAIC Motor Corporation Limited (the appellee, hereinafter referred to as "SAIC Motor") and Shanghai Yilong Automobile Sales Co., Ltd. (the appellee, hereinafter referred to as "Yilong"), Miao Chong purchased the car involved from Yilong in 2014. In 2016, the Shanghai Price Bureau found that when distributing cars in 2014, the Marketing Department of SAIC Motor reached and implemented a monopoly agreement with dealers in Shanghai to offer a minimum resale price to a third party. The Bureau ordered the parties concerned to immediately stop the illegal acts and imposed a fine of 4% of the relevant sales in the previous year. Miao Chong believed that he bought his car involved when SAIC Motor was offering a monopoly price in Shanghai, so he filed a lawsuit with the Shanghai Intellectual Property Court (hereinafter referred to as the Court of First Instance), requesting SAIC Motor to compensate him CNY 10,000 for his loss in car purchase and CNY 7,500 for other reasonable expenditure, and Yilong to bear supplementary compensation liability for his loss in car purchase. The Court of First Instance held that the evidence on the record could not prove that Yilong performed a monopoly agreement by offering a minimum resale price to a third party, so it rejected Miao Chong's requests. Miao Chong then appealed to the SPC. On December 15, 2022, the SPC decided to revoke the original judgment and support all of Miao Chong's claims.

【裁判意见】

[Judge's Opinion]

最高人民法院二审认为，反垄断执法机构认定构成垄断行为的处理决定在法定期限内未被提起行政诉讼或者已为人民法院生效裁判所确认，原告在相关垄断民事纠纷案件中据此主张该垄断行为成立的，无须再行举证证明，但有相反证据足以推翻的除外。据此，在缪某提交了已经发生法律效力的涉案处罚决定书后，其仅需要证明通用公司与逸隆公司系涉案处罚决定书认定的垄断行为实施者，且缪某因通用公司与逸隆公司达成并实施了涉案处罚决定书认定的垄断行为而受到损害。根据一审法院调取的作出涉案处罚决定书所依据的相关证据，其中涉及的品牌授权经销商合同与通用公司二审时提交的《雪佛兰品牌授权经销商合同（销售售后）》（品牌授权经销商合同 201303-Ver. 1. 2）约定的授权经销商相关权利义务均一致，且逸隆公司属于被调查的上海地区经销商之一。据此，可以认定通用公司与逸隆公司系涉案处罚决定书认定的垄断行为实施者。缪某为证明其因通用公司与逸隆公司达成并实施了涉案处罚决定书认定的垄断行为而受到损害，提交了缪某与逸隆公司于 2014 年 7 月 5 日签订的涉案销售合同以及完成交易后的发票。经与涉案处罚决定书依据的处罚事实相比较，该销售合同的签订时间、所涉车型、执行的购买价格 131900 元，均属于上海市物价局作出涉案处罚决定书所依据的通用公司与包括逸隆公司在内的上海地区经销商达成并实施限定向第三人转售商品最低价格垄断协议的相关事实。特别是，通用公司在涉案车型上市时限定向第三人转售商品最低价格即为缪某购买涉案车辆的价格 131900 元。综上所述，基于本案证据可以认定缪某购买涉案车辆所执行的价格是通用公司与逸隆公司达成并实施涉案处罚决定书认定的限定向第三人转售商品的最低价格的纵向垄断协议行为的具体表现，缪某已经完成了其因通用公司与逸隆公司实施垄断行为而造成损害的举证责任。

In the second instance, the SPC held that if the decision made by the Anti-monopoly Law enforcement agency on the establishment of monopoly has not caused an administrative action or been confirmed by the effective judgment of the people's court within the statutory time limit, the appellant does not need to provide evidence to prove the establishment of monopoly on that basis in the relevant civil case over monopoly, except that there is contrary evidence suffi-

cient to overturn it. So, after he submitted the legally effective penalty decision, all Miao Chong needed to prove is that SAIC Motor and Yilong are the perpetrators of the monopoly identified in the penalty decision, and that he suffered damage because SAIC Motor and Yilong had agreed on and carried out the monopoly identified in the decision. According to the evidence obtained by the Court of First Instance to make the penalty decision, the authorized dealer contract involved is consistent with the *Chevrolet Authorized Dealer Contract (Sales and After-sales)* submitted by SAIC Motor in the second instance (Authorized Dealer Contract 201303-Ver. 1. 2) in terms of the rights and obligations of authorized dealers; and Yilong is one of the dealers based in Shanghai that have been investigated. It can thus be found that SAIC Motor and Yilong are perpetrators of the monopoly identified in the penalty decision. In order to prove that he suffered from that monopoly, Miao Chong submitted the sales contract involved signed by him and Yilong on July 5, 2014 and the invoice after the completion of the transaction. After comparing it with the facts listed in the penalty decision, it is found that the signing date of the sales contract, the model involved, and the price paid by Miao (CNY 131, 900) are all considered the facts related to the penalty decision made by the Shanghai Price Bureau on the basis of the monopoly agreement between SAIC Motor and Yilong and other Shanghai-based dealers to offer a minimum resale price to a third party. In particular, the minimum price that SAIC Motor offered to a third party when the model involved came out is CNY 131, 900, the exact amount of money that Miao Chong paid for the car involved. To sum up, as the evidence can prove that the price of the car involved purchased by Miao Chong is a manifestation of the vertical monopoly agreement as identified by the penalty decision between SAIC Motor and Yilong to offer a minimum resale price to a third party, Miao Chong has fulfilled the burden of proof that he suffered damage due to the monopoly of SAIC Motor and Yilong.

65. 存量住房买卖经纪服务相关市场的认定 Identification of the relevant market of brokerage services for inventory housing transactions

【裁判要旨】

[Judgment Digest]

基于在竞争主体、服务对象和内容、佣金收取方式、行业规范要求等方面存在明显不同，无论从需求替代还是从供给替代的角度分析，对于存量住房买卖经纪服务相关市场而言，存量住房租赁经纪服务、存量非住房买卖经纪服务、新建住房买卖经纪服务、存量房买卖自行成交等，一般对其不构成紧密替代。

Due to the obvious differences in competitors, service object and content, methods of charging commissions and norms in their respective sectors, either from demand substitution perspective or from supply substitution one, brokerage services for inventory housing leasing, non-residential real estate purchasing and newly-built housing purchasing, as well as transactions of inventory housing without engaging brokers generally do not constitute close substitution for the relevant market of brokerage services for inventory housing transaction.

【关键词】

[Keywords]

滥用市场支配地位　存量房买卖经纪服务　相关市场

Abuse of dominant market position; brokerage service for the purchase and sale of inventory housing; relevant market

【案号】

[Case Number]

（2020）最高法知民终 1463 号

（2020）SPC IP Civil Final 1463

【基本案情】

[Case Facts]

在上诉人王某林与被上诉人北京链家房地产经纪有限公司（以下简称链家公司）、北京中融信融资担保有限公司（以下简称中融信公司）滥用市场支配地位纠纷案中，2016 年 2 月，王某林、链家公司、案外人苗某某共同签订涉案房屋买卖合同。同月，三方共同签订涉案居间合同，约定按照房屋交易总额的 2.2%收取居间代理费，由王某林承担；还约定本次交易的后续手续由中融信公司办理，并另行签署相关合同。同月，王某林、中融信公司、案外人苗某某共同签订涉案交易保障合同，约定中融信公司提供保管与交易相关的产权资料等十三项交易保障服务，保障服务费的收费标准为按房屋交易总额的 0.5%收取，由王某林承担。交易完成后，王某林认为链家公司存在滥用市场支配地位的行为，故向北京知识产权法院（以下简称一审法院）提起诉讼，请求判令链家公司退还王某林支付的居间代理费 2250 元、保障服务费 9750 元及合理支出 8000 元。一审法院认为，链家公司在本案相关市场范围内不具备市场支配地位，判决驳回王某林的诉讼请求。王某林不服，向最高人民法院提起上诉。最高人民法院认为，本案相关市场应为北京市全域存量住房买卖经纪服务市场，2016 年链家公司在本案相关市场范围内具有市场支配地位，王某林提交的现有证据不能证明链家公司实施了滥用市场支配地位行为，于 2022 年 12 月 14 日判决驳回上诉，维持原判。

In the dispute over the abuse of market dominance between Wang and Beijing Lianjia Real Estate Brokerage Co., Ltd. (the appellee, hereinafter referred to as "Lianjia") and Beijing ZRX Financing Guarantee Co., Ltd. (the appellee, hereinafter referred to as "ZRX"), Wang, Lianjia, and Miao, an outsider, signed the housing transaction contract involved in February 2016. On that day, the three parties also signed the intermediary contract involved, under which Wang should be charged 2.2% of the total housing price for the intermediary agency fee; and a separate contract will be signed for ZRX to handle the follow-up procedures of the transaction. Also on that day, Wang, ZRX, and Miao signed a security contract, under which ZRX should provide 13 security services such as keeping the property documents related to the transaction; and the service fee would be charged at 0.5% of the total housing price and paid by Wang. After the transaction was completed, Wang believed that Lianjia had abused its dominant market position, so he filed a lawsuit with the Beijing Intellectual Property Court (hereinafter referred to as the Court of First Instance), requesting that Lianjia refund the intermediary agency fee of CNY 2,250, the security service fee of CNY 9,750, and the reasonable expenditure of CNY 8,000. The Court of First Instance held that Lianjia does not enjoy a dominant position in the relevant market in this case, so it rejected Wang's request. Wang then appealed to the Supreme People's Court. The Supreme People's Court held that the relevant market in this case should be the brokerage service market for sale of inventory housing in Beijing; in 2016, Lianjia did enjoy a dominant position in the relevant market, yet the existing evidence submitted by Wang could not prove that Lianjia had abused its dominant market position. Therefore, it rejected the appeal and upheld the original judgment on December 14, 2022.

【裁判意见】

[Judge's Opinion]

最高人民法院二审认为，关于本案相关商品市场的界定，从需求替

代的角度分析界定相关商品市场时，一般根据需求者对于商品特性、功能和用途的需求、质量的认可、价格的接受以及获取的难易程度等因素，确定由需求者认为具有较为紧密替代关系的一组或者一类商品所构成的市场为相关商品市场。从供给替代的角度分析界定相关商品市场时，可以综合考虑其他经营者进入市场的意图和能力、承担的成本与风险、克服的市场障碍、需要的时间等因素。

According to the Supreme People's Court, the relevant market in this case can be defined from two perspectives: 1) From the perspective of demand substitution: generally considering factors such as the demand for the characteristics, functions, and purposes of the commodity, the recognition of commodity quality, the acceptance of commodity price, and the difficulty of obtaining it, the relevant market shall be defined as a market composed of a group or a type of commodities that the needer considers to have a close substituting relationship; 2) From the perspective of supply substitution: factors such as the intention and ability of other operators to enter the market, the cost and risk to bear, the market obstacles to overcome, and the time required are considered.

本案中，王某林主张本案的相关服务市场应当界定为存量住房买卖经纪服务市场；链家公司认为应当界定为新建房、存量房的买卖、租赁经纪服务及存量房买卖自行成交市场。对此具体分析如下：

In this case, Wang maintains that the relevant market should be the brokerage service market for sale of inventory housing; and Lianjia believes that it should be the brokerage service market for the sales and leasing of newly-builting housing and inventory housing, as well as an open market for the sales of inventory housing. The analysis is listed as below:

（1）关于本案被诉垄断行为直接影响的商品及其特点

(1) The commodity directly affected by the alleged monopoly in this case

and its characteristics

本案中，王某林主张链家公司在提供存量住房买卖经纪服务过程中实施了反垄断法第十七条第一款禁止的滥用市场支配地位行为主要包括：以交易房价2.2%的比率收取居间服务费的行为属于以不公平的高价销售商品或者提供服务；要求王某林同时签订涉案居间合同和交易保障合同属于搭售行为；涉案交易保障合同同时提供十三项交易保障服务属于搭售行为；交易完成后才提供发票给王某林属于附加不合理交易条件行为等。显然，本案被诉垄断行为直接涉及的系链家公司提供的存量住房买卖经纪服务。《房地产经纪管理办法》第三条规定："本办法所称房地产经纪，是指房地产经纪机构和房地产经纪人员为促成房地产交易，向委托人提供房地产居间、代理等服务并收取佣金的行为。"第七条第一款规定："本办法所称房地产经纪机构，是指依法设立，从事房地产经纪活动的中介服务机构。"第十五条第一款规定："房地产经纪机构及其分支机构应当在其经营场所醒目位置公示下列内容：（一）营业执照和备案证明文件；（二）服务项目、内容、标准；（三）业务流程；（四）收费项目、依据、标准；（五）交易资金监管方式；（六）信用档案查询方式、投诉电话及12358价格举报电话；（七）政府主管部门或者行业组织制定的房地产经纪服务合同、房屋买卖合同、房屋租赁合同示范文本；（八）法律、法规、规章规定的其他事项。"第三款规定："房地产经纪机构代理销售商品房项目的，还应当在销售现场明显位置明示商品房销售委托书和批准销售商品房的有关证明文件。"依据上述规定，结合本案证据，本案所直接涉及的存量住房买卖经纪服务具有如下特点：第一，竞争主体为依法设立的房地产经纪机构。第二，服务对象为存量住房的出售人和买受人，服务内容系为存量住房买卖提供居间服务，因此，交易规模与房地产经纪服务机构所拥有的房源和客源的数量直接相关。第三，价格竞争主要体现在收费比率，即按照房屋买卖交易价格多少比率收取佣金。第四，行业规范要求与房地产经纪机构

代理销售商品房项目明显不同，具体要求主要包括：公示服务项目、内容、标准，收费项目、依据、标准，交易资金监管方式等；且需要按照政府主管部门或者行业组织制定的房地产经纪服务合同、房屋买卖合同示范文本，与委托人签订合同。

In this case, Wang claims that Lianjia abused its dominant market position, which is prohibited by Paragraph 1 of Article 17 of the Anti-monopoly Law, when providing brokerage services for the sale of inventory housing. Specifically, Lianjia charged an intermediary service fee at 2.2% of the transaction price, which is to sell goods or provide services at an unfairly high price; it asked Wang to sign both the intermediary contract and the security contract, which is a tying act; the security contract involved provides 13 security services, which is a tying act; it only provided the invoice to Wang after the transaction was completed, which is an extra unreasonable condition. Obviously, it is the brokerage service provided by Lianjia for the sale of inventory housing that is directly involved in the monopoly in this case. In the Measures for the Administration of Real Estate Brokerage, Article 3 says: "The 'real estate brokerage' mentioned here refers to the behavior of real estate brokerage agencies and personnel providing real estate services such as intermediary and agency to the client and receiving commission from that in order to complete real estate transactions." Paragraph 1 of Article 7 says: "The real estate brokerage agencies mentioned here refer to the intermediary service institutions established according to law and engaged in real estate brokerage activities." Paragraph 1 of Article 15 says: "Real estate brokerage agencies and their branches shall publish in prominent positions on their business premises: (1) business license and record certification document; (2) service items, contents, and standards; (3) business process; (4) items, bases, and standards of charges; (5) supervision methods of transaction funds; (6) credit file inquiry, complaint telephone, and 12358 (to report price issues); (7) model texts of real estate brokerage service contracts, housing sale contracts, and housing leasing contracts formulated by competent government departments or industry organizations; (8) other matters stipulated by laws, rules, and regulations." Paragraph 3 says: "Where a real estate brokerage agency sells commercial housing, it shall also show in prominent positions on the sales site the power of attorney for the sale of commercial housing and the documents approving the sale of commercial housing." According to the above provisions, combined with the evidence of this case, the brokerage service for the sale of inventory housing directly involved in this case has the following characteristics: 1) The competition subject is a real estate brokerage agency established by law; 2) The service object is the seller and buyer of inventory housing, and the service content is to provide intermediary services for the sale of inventory housing. Therefore, the transaction scale is directly related to the number of houses and customers owned by the real estate brokerage agency; 3) Price competition is mainly reflected in the rate charged, that is, the commission is charged at a certain proportion of the transaction price; 4) The industry standards are obviously different from those for the agency and sale of commercial housing by real estate brokerage agencies. The brokerage agency is required to publish service items, content, and standards; charging items, bases, and standards; supervision methods of transaction funds; and sign a contract with the client in accordance with the model text of real estate brokerage service contract and housing sale contract formulated by competent government departments or industry organizations.

(2) 关于存量住房租赁经纪服务应否纳入本案相关服务市场范围

(2) Whether the brokerage service for the leasing of inventory housing should be included in the relevant market in this case

第一，从服务性质而言，存量住房租赁经纪服务与存量住房买卖经纪服务虽然均为向委托人提供中介服务，但是服务对象和服务内容显然不同，前者系向有出租房屋需求的出租人和有租赁房屋需求的租房人提供中介服务，而后者系向有卖房需求的出卖人和有买房需求的买受人提供中介服务，如涉案居间合同载明服务对象为出卖人苗某某、买受人王某林，服务内容包括链家公司提供房屋买卖市场行情咨询，寻找、提供并发布房源、客源信息，促成交易双方签署合法有效的买卖合同等，无论服务对象还是服务内容均明显不同于房屋租赁经纪服务。第二，两者行业规范要求并不相同，《房地产经纪管理办法》第十五条第一款第七项规定，政府主管部门或者行业组织分别制定房屋买卖合同、房屋租赁合同以及相应的房地产经纪服务示范文本。第三，从服务价格而言，根据在案证据，房屋买卖经纪服务佣金系根据房屋买卖合同的价款按照一定比率收取，而房屋租赁经纪服务佣金一般按照房屋租赁合同 1 个月租金收取，两者服务价格相差悬殊。因此，从需求者角度，无论从服务内容还是从服务价格等方面，存量住房租赁经纪服务与存量住房买卖经纪服务都不构成需求替代。第四，虽然链家公司提交证据证明中原地产、我爱我家、麦田房产等房地产经纪服务机构均存在经纪人同时提供房屋租赁和买卖经纪服务情况，但是，由于存量住房租赁市场和存量住房买卖市场的房源和客源信息均不相同，对于存量住房买卖市场经纪服务需求而言，存量住房租赁市场经纪服务显然难以与存量住房租赁市场经纪服务形成紧密替代关系。综上所述，存量住房租赁经纪服务不应当纳入本案相关服务市场。

First of all, on the nature of services, although the brokerage service for the leasing of inventory housing and the brokerage service for the sale of inventory housing are both intermediary services provided to the client, they are different in terms of service object and service content. The former is provided to those who want to rent out their houses and those who want to rent one; the latter is provided to those who want to sell their houses and those who want to buy one. For example, the intermediary contract involved specifies that the service objects are Miao, the seller, and Wang, the buyer, and the service contents include Lianjia providing consultation on the housing sale market, searching, providing, and publishing information on housing and buyers, and facilitating a legal and effective sales contract to be signed between the buyer and the seller. Both the service object and the service content are different from that of the brokerage service of housing leasing. Secondly, the two services are different in terms of industry norms. In the *Measures for the Administration of Real Estate Brokerage*, Paragraph 1 (7) of Article 15 stipulates that the competent government departments or industry organizations shall formulate the housing sales contract, housing leasing contract, and the corresponding model text of real estate brokerage service. Thirdly, in terms of service price, according to the documented evidence, the commission for housing sale brokerage service is charged a certain rate of the price of the housing sale contract, and that for housing lease brokerage service is normally charged one-month rent of the housing lease contract, so the service prices are greatly different. Therefore, from the perspective of demanders, whether it being service content or service price, demand substitution does not exist in the brokerage service for the leasing of inventory housing or the brokerage service for the sale of inventory housing. Fourth, although Lianjia has submitted evidence to prove that real estate brokerage service agencies like Centaline Property, 5I5J, and Maitian Real Estate provide services for both housing lease and sale, the inventory housing lease market and the inventory housing sale market have different sources of houses and customers; in terms of the demand for brokerage service in the inventory housing sale market, it is unlikely to form a close substituting relationship with the brokerage service in the inventory hous-

ing lease market. To sum up, the brokerage service for the lease of inventory housing should not be included in the market of this case.

(3) 关于存量非住房买卖经纪服务应否纳入本案相关服务市场范围

(3) Whether the brokerage service for the sale of inventory non-housing should be included in the relevant market of this case

第一，从房地产买卖经纪服务所涉及的房屋性质和用途而言，一般区分为用于居住使用的房屋，简称住房；用于工业、商业等非居住使用的房屋，简称非住房。如王某林提交的中介协会出具的成交情况载明，按照规划用途划分，存量房可分为存量住房、公寓、商业写字楼、工业厂房等，其中，存量住房包括商品住房、自住型商品房、经济适用住房、两限房、公共租赁住房等保障性住房。第二，由于住房的性能和用途在于满足普通人的生活居住，而非满足商业生产经营使用，因此，从需求替代角度分析，对于住房购买者而言，不会由于住房买卖经纪服务费用上涨等因素转换为非住房购买者；同理，对于住房销售者而言，亦不会由于住房买卖经纪服务费用下降等因素转换为非住房销售者。第三，从供给替代的角度分析，由于住房与非住房的商品性能和用途完全不同，住房供给与商业写字楼、工业厂房等的非住房供给，从土地使用权的获得、建筑许可证的取得、上市交易条件等方面均不具有紧密替代关系。第四，即使房产经纪服务提供者从市场准入的角度，既可以提供住房买卖经纪服务，又可以提供非住房买卖经纪服务，但是，由于存量住房和存量非住房的买方、卖方从需求角度和供给角度均不具有紧密替代关系，相应地，存量住房和存量非住房买卖经纪服务亦不具有可替代性。因此，本案相关服务市场应当不包括存量非住房买卖经纪服务。

First of all, there are two types of housing involved in the real estate brokerage services: one is for residential use and thus referred to as housing; the other is for industrial, commercial, and other non-residential use and thus referred to as non–housing. As stated in the transaction, which is issued by the intermediary association and submitted by Wang, from the perspective of planning purposes, inventory housing is divided into inventory houses, apartments, commercial office buildings, industrial plants, etc., and inventory housing includes commodity houses, owner–occupied commercial houses, affordable houses, houses with a limited price and area, public rental houses, etc. Secondly, since housing is designed for people to live in, and non–housing is designed for commercial production and operation, from the perspective of demand substitution, housing buyers will not switch to non–housing due to factors such as an increase in the cost of housing brokerage service. Similarly, housing sellers will not switch to non–housing sellers due to factors such as a decline in the cost of housing brokerage service. Thirdly, from the perspective of supply substitution, since housing and non–housing are completely different in terms of commodity performance and use, there is no substituting relationship between the supply of housing and the supply of non–housing like commercial office buildings and industrial plants in terms of land use rights, construction permits, listing conditions, etc. Fourthly, even if real estate brokers can provide, from the perspective of market access, brokerage services for the sale of both housing and non–housing, as there is no substituting relationship between the buyers and sellers of inventory housing and inventory non–housing from the perspective of demand and supply, the brokerage services for the sale of inventory housing and inventory non–housing are accordingly not fungible. Therefore, the relevant market in this case should not include the brokerage service for the sale of inventory non–housing.

(4) 关于新建住房买卖经纪服务应否纳入本案相关服务市场范围

(4) Whether the brokerage service for the sale of new housing should be included in the relevant market of this case

首先，新建住房、存量住房的商品来源、交易方式、交易价格、居住体验等都不相同，从房屋的购买者角度，链家公司并没有提交证据证明存量住房的购买者由于存量住房买卖经纪服务价格的上涨会转而购买新建住房，并且成为新建住房买卖经纪服务的需求者；从房屋出售者的角度，由于新建住房提供者为房地产开发商，而存量住房提供者为已经取得房地产登记证书的房屋产权人，两者之间不可能由于存量住房买卖经纪服务价格的变动而发生转换。其次，新建住房买卖经纪服务与存量住房买卖经纪服务的服务方式、收费价格和收费方式明显不同，新建住房买卖经纪服务的服务方式系经纪服务公司接受房地产开发商的单方面委托，且价格及收费计算方式均系由双方约定；而存量住房买卖经纪服务的服务方式系经纪服务公司接受房屋买方和卖方的委托，提供中介服务，收费方式系由购房人向经纪服务机构交付，收费计算方式必须向社会公示，显然，从收费价格和收费方式角度，新建住房买卖经纪服务与存量住房买卖经纪服务不构成需求替代。最后，即使房产经纪服务提供者从市场准入的角度，既可以提供新建住房销售代理经纪服务，又可以提供存量住房买卖经纪服务，但是，由于新建住房和存量住房的买方、卖方从需求角度和供给角度均不具有紧密替代关系，相应地，新建住房和存量住房买卖经纪服务亦不具有可替代性。因此，本案相关服务市场应当不包括新建住房买卖经纪服务。

First of all, new housing and inventory housing are different in terms of source, transaction method, transaction price, and living experience. From the perspective of buyers, Lianjia does not submit evidence to prove that buyers of inventory housing will switch to new housing and become needers of brokerage service for new housing due to a rise in the price of brokerage service for inventory housing. From the perspective of sellers, new housing is provided by real estate developers, and inventory housing is provided by house owners who have obtained the property registration certificate; it is impossible to switch between them due to any changes in the price of brokerage service for inventory housing. Secondly, the brokerage service for new housing and the brokerage service for inventory housing is obviously different in terms of service mode, charging price, and charging method. In the former, the brokerage agency is entrusted by the real estate developer, and the calculation method of price and fees is agreed on by both parties. In the latter, the brokerage agency is entrusted by both the buyer and the seller to provide intermediary services, the buyer shall pay the brokerage agency, and the calculation method of fees must be publicized to the public. Obviously, there is no substituting demand between the brokerage service for new housing and the brokerage service for inventory housing in terms of charging price and charging method. Thirdly, even if, from the perspective of market access, real estate brokers can provide brokerage services for both new housing and inventory housing, there is no substituting relationship between the brokerage service for new housing and the brokerage service for inventory housing since there is no substituting relationship between the buyers and the sellers of new housing and inventory housing from the perspective of demand and supply. Therefore, the relevant market in this case should not include the brokerage service for the sale of new housing.

(5) 关于存量房买卖自行成交市场应否纳入本案相关服务市场范围

(5) Whether the open market for the sale of inventory homes should be included in the relevant market of this case

相关市场界定的目的是明确经营者所面对的竞争约束，合理认定经营者的市场地位，并正确判断其行为对市场竞争的影响。判断存量房买卖自行成交市场是否纳入本案相关服务市场范围，关键在于自行成交市场是否对存量房经纪服务市场构成竞争约束。第一，从交易性质而言，本案所涉及的系存量房买卖经纪服务，存在三方交易主体，出卖人、买

受人和房地产经纪机构，而存量房买卖自行成交市场仅有两方主体，出卖人和买受人。第二，从需求者的角度而言，存量房出卖人和买受人选择自行交易，就必然不会选择通过房地产经纪机构完成交易。第三，根据链家公司提供的相关证据，首都之窗网站上提供了《北京市存量房屋买卖合同（自行成交版）》的合同模板，与本案所涉及的通过房地产经纪机构完成交易的存量住房房屋买卖合同模板并不相同。第四，链家公司提供的相关证据还显示，百度贴吧、北京论坛、首都之窗等网站上均可以查询到个人发布的二手房源信息，知乎、房天下、水木社区、简书创作社区、凤凰网等网站可以查询到二手房自行成交的经验总结及优势介绍，在存量房买卖自行成交市场存在大量实践的情况下，由于选择自行成交的买受人并不需要支付中介服务费用，交易价格的差异，使得存量房买卖自行成交市场对存量住房买卖经纪服务市场不会构成竞争约束。故本案相关服务市场应当不包括存量房买卖自行成交市场。

The relevant market is defined to clarify the competition constraints faced by operators, identify the market position of operators, and reckon the impact of their behavior on market competition. The key to deciding whether the open market for the sale of inventory housing is included in the relevant market of this case is to decide whether the open market imposes competitive constraints on the brokerage service market for inventory housing. First of all, in terms of the nature of the transaction, the brokerage service concerned involves three parties: the seller, the buyer, and the real estate brokerage agency, while the open market involves two parties: the seller and the buyer. Secondly, from the perspective of needers, the seller and the buyer of an inventory house will not choose a broker if they want to deal on their own. Thirdly, according to the evidence provided by Lianjia, the template of the *Beijing Inventory Housing Sales Contract (For Open Market)* provided on beijing. gov. cn is different from that of the inventory housing sales contract involved in this case, under which the transaction is completed through a brokerage agency. Fourthly, the evidence provided by Lianjia also shows that the second-hand housing information posted by individuals can be found on websites like tieba. baidu. com, Beijing Forum, and beijing. gov. cn; experience and benefits of second-hand housing transactions can be found on websites like Zhihu, Fang. com, NewSMTH, jianshu. com, and ifeng. com. With such a large number of practices in the open market for the sale of inventory housing, the buyer does not need to pay a broker, plus the difference in transaction prices, that causes the open market not to have a competitive constraint on the brokerage service market for the sale of inventory housing. Therefore, the relevant market in this case should not include the open market for the sale of inventory housing.

综上所述，本案相关服务市场应当界定为存量住房买卖经纪服务市场。链家公司认为本案相关服务市场应当包括新建住房、存量住房的买卖、租赁经纪服务及存量房买卖自行成交市场，无事实和法律依据。

To sum up, the relevant market in this case should be defined as the brokerage service market for the sale of inventory housing. There is no factual or legal basis for Lianjia to assume that the relevant market in this case should include the brokerage service market for the sale and lease of new housing and inventory housing and the open market for the sale of inventory housing.

66. 中介服务市场份额的评价指标

Evaluation indicators for market share of intermediary service markets

【裁判要旨】

[Judgment Digest]

经营者在相关市场的市场份额，可以根据被诉垄断行为发生时经营者一定时期内的相关商品或者服务的交易金额、交易数量、生产能力或者其他指标在相关市场中所占的比例确定。就中介服务市场而言，经营者实际撮合交易的数量，以及其所掌握的潜在交易者信息，一般是评价其市场力量的恰当指标。经营者本身的机构规模、雇员数量等仅仅能够反映其服务规模，可以作为经营者财力和技术条件等的考量指标，但原则上不宜直接作为市场份额的评价指标。

The market share of an operator in the relevant market can be determined based on the ratios of transaction amount, number of transactions, production capacity or other indicators in the relevant markets of goods or services within the period when the accused monopoly occurs and endures. As to the intermediary service market, generally, the number of transactions actually matched by the operator and the information on potential traders in the possession of the operator are the appropriate indicators for assessing the operator's market power. An operator's institutional size and number of employees can only reflect its service scale and can be taken into consideration for assessing its financial capacity and technical conditions, but in principle, it is not appropriate to directly view them as indicators for assessing the market share.

【关键词】

[Keywords]

滥用市场支配地位　相关市场　中介服务市场　市场份额

Abuse of dominant market position; relevant market; intermediary service market; market share

【案号】

[Case Number]

(2020) 最高法知民终 1463 号

(2020) SPC IP Civil Final 1463

【裁判意见】

[Judge's Opinion]

在上诉人王某林与被上诉人北京链家房地产经纪有限公司、北京中融信融资担保有限公司滥用市场支配地位纠纷案中，最高人民法院指出，市场份额是指特定企业的总产量、销售量或者生产能力在相关市场中所占的比例，又称为市场占有率。市场份额是判定一个企业是否具有市场支配地位的一个重要因素。因此，经营者市场份额的确定以合理划分相关市场为前提。经营者在相关市场的市场份额，可以根据被诉垄断行为发生时经营者一定时期内的相关商品交易金额、交易数量、生产能力或者其他指标在相关市场中所占的比例确定。2008 年施行的反垄断法第十九条规定了根据经营者的市场份额可以推定经营者具有市场支配地位的情形，其中第一款第一项规定，“一个经营者在相关市场的市场份额达到二分之一的”，可以推定该经营者具有市场支配地位；第三款规定：“被推定具有市场支配地位的经营者，有证据证明不具有市场支配地位的，不应当认定其具有市场支配地位”。依据上述规定，如果原告能够证明经营者的市场份额达到二分之一，则可以推定经营者具有市场支配地位，除非经营者具有相反证据。

In the dispute between Wang (the Appellant), and Beijing Lianjia Real Estate Brokerage Co., Ltd. (the Appellee), Beijing ZRX Financing Guarantee Co., Ltd. (the Appellee), the Supreme People's Court says that market share, also known as market occupancy, refers to the proportion of the total

production, sales, or production capacity of a specific enterprise in a given market. Market share is an important factor to determine whether an enterprise leads a dominant market position. Therefore, the market share of an operator is determined based on a reasonable division of the given market. And it can be determined according to the proportion of the transaction amount, transaction quantity, or production capacity of the operator in the relevant market at a given time when the alleged monopoly occurred or according to the proportion of other indicators in the relevant market. Article 19 of the Anti-Monopoly Law, implemented in 2008, provides for the circumstances in which an operator can be presumed to have a dominant market position based on its market share: Article 19 (1) (i) stipulates that "Where an operator's relevant market share reaches half", the operator can be presumed to lead a dominant market position; Article 19 (3) stipulates that "An operator presumed to lead a dominant market position shall not be deemed as such if there is evidence to prove the contrary." According to those provisions, if the plaintiff can prove that the operator's market share reaches half, the operator can be presumed to lead a dominant market position, unless the operator has evidence to the contrary.

首先，本案相关市场应当为 2016 年北京市存量住房买卖经纪服务市场。2016 年，链家公司、我爱我家、麦田房产等主要的房地产经纪公司对于存量住房买卖经纪服务的收费比例均为房屋总价款的 2.2%，显然服务价格竞争对于经营者市场支配力的影响不明显。其次，由于房产经纪服务市场的竞争一方面体现为房源的竞争，即争夺卖方市场的竞争；另一方面体现为客源的竞争，即争夺买方市场的竞争，而无论房源还是客源的竞争最终能够体现市场主体竞争能力的系实际成交量。因此，在本案所涉及的存量住房买卖经纪服务市场，市场成交量、房源、客源等是考量经营者是否具有市场支配力较为恰当的指标。房地产经纪机构的分支机构数量、经纪人人数等指标仅仅能够反映经营者自身的服务规模，不能直接反映经营者房源、客源以及市场成交量，可作为经营者财力和技术条件等的考量指标。根据在案证据，链家公司在 2016 年北京市存量住房买卖经纪服务中按照成交量计算所占的市场份额为 54.76%，且链家公司未能提交证据证明其不具有市场支配地位，应当认定链家公司在本案相关市场具有市场支配地位。一审法院由于相关市场判断错误，导致认定链家公司在本案相关市场不具有市场支配地位，属于事实认定错误。

First of all, the relevant market in this case should be the brokerage service market for the sale of inventory housing in Beijing in 2016, when major real estate brokerage companies like Lianjia, 5I5J, and Maitian Real Estate all charged 2.2% of the total housing price for their service. Obviously the service price competition has no significant impact on the operators' dominance over the market. Secondly, the competition in the real estate brokerage market lies in two aspects: One, the competition for housing, that is, for the seller's market; Two, the competition for customers, that is, for the buyer's market, and whether it is for housing or customers, a broker's competitiveness is ultimately reflected in the actual turnover. Therefore, in the inventory housing brokerage market involved in this case, the actual turnover and the quantity of houses and customers are more appropriate indicators to consider whether the operator has dominance over the market. The number of branches and brokers can only reflect the scale of a real estate brokerage institution; they cannot directly reflect how many houses and customers an operator has or how many transactions it has concluded. They can be used as indicators to measure the financial status and technical conditions of the operator. According to the documented evidence, the share of Lianjia in the inventory housing brokerage market in Beijing in 2016 was 54.76% in terms of turnover, and the company failed to provide evidence to prove that it does not lead a market dominant po-

sition, so it should be determined that Lianjia leads a dominant position in the relevant market of this case. The Court of First Instance wrongly determined that Lianjia does not lead a dominant market position in the relevant market of the case, which is a factual error.

67. 其他协同行为的认定
Identification of so-called other concerted acts

【裁判要旨】

[Judgment Digest]

具有竞争关系的经营者之间存在一致性市场行为，且存在排除、限制竞争共谋的，可以推定其实施了反垄断法所禁止的协同行为，但经营者能够对一致性市场行为作出合理解释，证明其系根据市场和竞争状况独立作出有关市场行为的除外。

Where the operators in competition carried out market acts in concert and also with conspiracy on excluding or restricting competition, people's court may presume that these operators have committed the so-called other concerted act as prohibited in the Anti-monopoly Law, unless they can present a reasonable explanation for their market acts seemingly in concert, proving that they independently conducted such acts according to market and competition conditions.

【关键词】

[Keywords]

垄断协议　协同行为　行政处罚

Monopoly agreement; concerted act; administrative penalty

【案号】

[Case Number]

（2022）最高法知行终 29 号

（2022）SPC IP Admin. Final 29

【基本案情】

[Case Facts]

在上诉人茂名市电白区建科混凝土有限公司（以下简称建科公司）与被上诉人广东省市场监督管理局反垄断行政处罚案中，2016 年 9 月至 12 月期间，包括建科公司在内的 19 家广东省茂名市城区及高州市预拌混凝土企业通过聚会、微信群等形式就统一上调混凝土销售价格交流协商，并各自同期不同幅度地上调了价格。2020 年 6 月，广东省市场监督管理局对该 19 家企业达成并实施“固定或者变更商品价格”横向垄断协议的行为进行查处，均以 2016 年度销售额为基数，对 3 家牵头企业处以 2%的罚款，对建科公司等其他 16 家企业处以 1%的罚款。建科公司不服行政处罚决定，分别向广州知识产权法院（以下简称一审法院）提起行政诉讼，请求撤销被诉处罚决定。一审法院判决驳回建科公司的诉讼请求。建科公司不服，向最高人民法院提起上诉。最高人民法院于 2022 年 6 月 23 日判决驳回上诉，维持原判。

In the anti-monopoly administrative penalty case of Maoming Dianbai District Jianke Concrete Co., Ltd. (the appellant, hereinafter referred to as “Jianke”) v. Guangdong Market Supervision Administration (the appellee), from September to December 2016, Jianke and 18 other companies trading in ready-mixed concrete in Maoming and Gaozhou, Guangdong Province, negotiated on the increase of concrete prices through meetings and WeChat, and raised various concrete prices in that period. In June 2020, the Guangdong Market Supervision Administration investigated the 19 companies for creating and implementing the horizontal monopoly agreement of “Fixing or changing

commodity prices", and imposed, based on their sales for 2016, a 2% fine on three leading companies and a 1% fine on 16 other enterprises including Jianke. Refusing to accept the administrative penalty decision, Jianke filed a lawsuit with the Guangzhou Intellectual Property Court (hereinafter referred to as the Court of First Instance) to request the cancellation of the penalty decision. The Court of First Instance rejected Jianke's claim. Jianke then appealed to the Supreme People's Court. On June 23, 2022, the Supreme People's Court rejected the appeal and upheld the original judgment.

【裁判意见】

[Judge's Opinion]

最高人民法院二审认为，2008 年实施的反垄断法第十三条第二款规定："本法所称垄断协议，是指排除、限制竞争的协议、决定或者其他协同行为。"该款所规定的"其他协同行为"，属于垄断协议的一种表现形式，是指具有竞争关系的经营者没有订立书面或口头协议或者决定，但是相互进行了沟通，心照不宣地实施了协同一致的排除、限制竞争行为。认定其他协同行为，需要具备以下两个条件：首先，具有竞争关系的经营者之间存在一致性市场行为，即经营者同时或相继作出协调的、共同的市场行为；其次，具有竞争关系的经营者之间存在排除、限制竞争的共谋，即经营者之间进行过相关意思联络或信息交流，比如交流经营信息、商业计划等。认定其他协同行为，还需要考虑相关市场的市场结构、竞争状况、市场变化等情况，排除各个经营者根据市场和竞争状况独立作出的相同市场行为的情形。对此，国家市场监督管理总局《禁止垄断协议暂行规定》第六条具体规定了认定其他协同行为应当考虑的四项因素，该规定符合反垄断法的规定，人民法院可参照该规定进行具体分析认定。其中，判断是否存在共谋，关键在于判断经营者之间存在限制或者排除竞争的意思联络或信息交流，而并不要求经营者之间就具体商品价格、数量等达成清晰或具体的一致意见。在具有竞争关系的经营者之间存在意思联络或信息交流，且在意思联络或信息交流之后采取了一致性市场行为的情况下，除非经营者能够合理说明并提供证据证明该行为系其根据市场和竞争状况独立作出的市场行为，包括跟随、仿效其他竞争者而采取的相同市场行为，或者符合反垄断法第十五条规定的豁免事由，原则上即可以认定经营者以协同行为的方式达成并实施了横向垄断协议。而且，前已述及，反垄断法第十三条第一款明文列举的横向垄断协议在所有垄断行为类型中对竞争的影响相对较为严重，一般可以推定其具有限制或者排除竞争的效果，即所谓的反竞争效果。

According to the Supreme People's Court, Article 13 (2) of the Anti-monopoly Law implemented in 2008 stipulates that "monopoly agreements as mentioned in this Law refer to agreements, decisions, or other concerted acts that exclude or restrict competition." The "other concerted acts" mentioned here are a form of monopoly agreement, in which competing operators do not conclude a written or oral agreement or decision, but they have communicated with each other and tacitly undertaken a concerted act to exclude or restrict competition. Two conditions should be met to identify "other concerted acts": first, competing operators should have consistent market behaviors, that is, they should have coordinated and common market behaviors simultaneously or successively; second, competing operators should conspire to exclude or restrict competition, that is, they should communicate or exchange with each other on relevant matters such as business information, business plans, etc. To identify "other concerted acts", it is also necessary to consider the market structure, the competition status, market changes, and other conditions of the relevant market, excluding the scenario in which each operator independently undertakes the same market behavior according to the market and competition situations. In this regard, Article 6 of the Interim Provisions on the Prohibition of Monopoly Agreement promulgated by the State Administration for Mar-

ket Regulation specifically provides four factors that should be considered in determining "other concerted acts", which is in line with the provisions of the Anti-monopoly Law and could be used by the people's court for specific analysis and identification. The key to deciding the existence of collusion is to discover the existence of intentional communication or information exchange between operators that restricts or excludes competition; it does not require operators to reach a clear or specific agreement on the price and quantity of specific commodities. In the case where there is intentional communication or information exchange between the competing operators who, after such communication or exchange, undertake a consistent market behavior, unless the operators can reasonably explain and provide evidence that they have undertaken the behavior independently according to the market and competition situations, or that they have undertaken the same market behavior by following or imitating their rivals, or that their behavior is in compliance with the exemption stipulated in Article 15 of the Anti-monopoly Law, it can be determined in principle that the operators have reached and performed a horizontal monopoly agreement by undertaking a concerted act. Moreover, as mentioned above, among all types of monopolies, the horizontal monopoly agreement expressly listed in Article 13 (1) of the Anti-monopoly Law has a relatively serious impact on competition, and it can generally be presumed that it has the effect of restricting or excluding competition, i. e., an anti-competitive effect.

本案中，涉案 19 家混凝土企业均系从事预拌混凝土生产和销售的经营者，且其产品主要在同一区域销售，彼此之间具有竞争关系，属于反垄断法上的具有竞争关系的经营者。根据本案查明的事实，可以认定涉案 19 家混凝土企业的被诉行为构成反垄断第十三条第二款规定“其他协同行为”。对此，本院具体分析如下：第一，涉案 19 家混凝土企业的被诉行为具有一致性。该 19 家企业从 2016 年 9 月 25 日起开始对预拌混凝土销售价格进行上调，调价时间主要集中于 2016 年 9 月底至 10 月，其中各家企业针对具体客户实际供货价格有所不同，但是从总的价格趋势看均存在一定程度的上调，较为明显地体现出各自行为的一致性，被诉行为构成一致性市场行为。第二，涉案 19 家混凝土企业之间进行了意思联络、信息交流，明显具有限制、排除相互间价格竞争的共谋。该 19 家企业围绕预拌混凝土变更价格、价格变动幅度，专门建立微信群并通过聚餐等线下方式进行一系列的信息交流、涨价提议与互相督促。其中，虽有部分企业在微信群内没有明确披露其实际交易中的具体提价情况，但是其参与微信群就足以了解群内其他企业的价格调整情况，且没有对价格调整提出异议，群内其他企业也有理由相信没有披露具体提价情况的企业已经采取或将要采取同样的提价行为，相关交流信息让加入微信群的企业之间形成了某种心照不宣的默契，便于其实施相关调价策略。而且，上述参与微信群的企业事实上均在同一时期不同程度地调高了各自的供货价格，反映出其实施合谋涨价的行为过程。第三，涉案 19 家混凝土企业对其行为的一致性并不能作出合理解释。经营者因经营成本增加可以单独自主合理调整销售价格，但不能与其他具有竞争关系的经营者共谋以垄断行为的方式提高价格。建科公司以交通运输管理部门治理超载导致运输成本增加为由对其提价行为进行辩解，但其并没有提供证据证明该 19 家企业之前均存在超载运输情况以及其提价幅度与其恢复正常未超载运输而增加的平均运输成本幅度相当，故其该项辩解不能成立。而且，多达 19 家企业通过微信群持续讨论调价信息、交流执行提价情况，并提出针对客户的应对措施，事后相关企业纷纷提高价格，极可能是共谋的结果。建科公司主张其系根据市场因素变化而相应独立作出的市场行为，明显缺乏说服力。第四，审查相关市场的市场结构、竞争状况、市场变化等情况，可以看出涉案 19 家混凝土企业的被诉行为产生了反竞争效果。对于涉案预拌混凝土市场，在特定区域内的产能规划和搅拌站站点布局相对稳定，新的经营者较难在短

期内进入相关市场；同时，预拌混凝土初凝时间等因素制约着预拌混凝土供应的辐射范围（通常在距搅拌站 50 公里范围内），在该特定区域内预拌混凝土企业向外开拓新市场受到限制，下游企业挑选预拌混凝土供应商的范围也受到限制。一旦相关市场内全部或者大部分混凝土企业联络一致涨价，则其下游企业（混凝土购买方）基本上没有多少可协商或者另行选择的余地而只能被动接受涨价。涉案 19 家混凝土企业中绝大多数的年营业额超过 1000 万元，在相关市场上具有较高的市场份额，对相关市场内的预拌混凝土供应有较强的控制能力。本案事实已经表明，涉案 19 家混凝土企业共谋集中上调预拌混凝土单价，已经损害下游企业及终端消费者的利益，客观上产生了排除、限制竞争的实际效果。综合上述分析，可以认定涉案 19 家混凝土企业达成并实施了反垄断法第十三条第一款第一项规定的“固定或者变更商品价格”的横向垄断协议。

In this case, the 19 companies involved are all engaged in the production and sales of ready-mixed concrete, and their products are mainly sold in the same area, which makes them the competing operators under the Anti-Monopoly Law. According to the facts ascertained, it can be determined that the alleged behavior of the 19 concrete companies involved constitutes the "other concerted acts" as stipulated in Article 13 (2) of the Anti-Monopoly Law. The Supreme People's Court offers its analysis as below: first, the 19 concrete companies involved are consistent in terms of the alleged behavior. From September 25, 2016, the 19 companies started talking about increasing the sales price of ready-mixed concrete and did so from late September to October 2016. Each company increased their price differently for different customers, but there is a general rise in the price, which obviously reflects the consistency of the companies' behavior. The alleged behavior thus constitutes a consistent market behavior. Second, the intentional communication and information exchange among the 19 companies involved is an obvious conspiracy to restrict and exclude price competition among them. The 19 companies set up a WeChat group and held dinner parties offline to exchange information, make proposals on price increase, and supervise each other over the range of price changes. Although some of the companies did not explicitly disclose in the WeChat group their actual price increase, their membership in the group enables them to know the price change of other members, and they did not raise objections to the price change; the other companies in the group are reasonable to believe that the companies that did not disclose have also increased their price or will do so. The exchange of information has formed a tacit understanding between the companies that have joined the WeChat group, and made it easier for them to increase their price. Moreover, the companies that have joined the WeChat group did increase their respective price to varying degrees during the same period, showing the process of their conspiracy to increase the price. Third, the 19 companies involved could not make a reasonable explanation for the consistency of their behavior. A business operator may independently and reasonably increase the price due to a rise in the operating cost, but it should not do so by conspiring with its competitors through monopoly. Jianke defended its price increase on the grounds that the transportation department's handling of overloading caused an increase in its transportation cost, but it did not provide evidence to prove that all the 19 enterprises had overloading problems before and that the increase in price is equivalent to the increase in average transportation cost caused by non-overloading, so its defense could not be established. Moreover, it is highly likely a process of conspiracy that as many as 19 companies kept discussing price change, talking about the outcome of it, and proposing measures for customers in a WeChat group and did increase their price offline. Jianke's claim that it has undertak-

en the market behavior independently based on the changes in market factors is quite unconvincing. Fourth, after reviewing the structure, competition, and changes of the relevant market, it shows that the accused behavior of the 19 companies involved has produced an anti-competitive effect. As for the ready-mixed concrete market involved in the case, the stable capacity planning and layout of mixing stations in a specific area makes it difficult for new operators to enter the market within a short time. Factors such as the initial setting time of ready-mixed concrete also restrict the coverage of ready-mixed concrete supply (usually within a 50-km-radius from the mixing station). Ready-mixed concrete enterprises in the specific area are thus limited to open up new markets, as are the downstream enterprises to select from ready-mixed concrete suppliers. Once all or most of the concrete enterprises in the relevant market increase their price unanimously, little room for negotiation or alternatives is left for the downstream enterprises (concrete buyers), who have no choice but to accept the price increase. Most of the 19 companies involved have an annual turnover of more than CNY 10 million; they have a big market share and a strong control over the supply of ready-mixed concrete in the relevant market. The facts of this case have shown that the 19 companies involved have conspired to increase the unit price of ready-mixed concrete, which has damaged the interests of downstream enterprises and end consumers, and objectively produced the effect of excluding and restricting competition. Based on the above analysis, it can be concluded that the 19 companies involved undertook and performed the horizontal monopoly agreement of "Fixing or changing commodity prices" as stipulated in Article 13 (1) (i) of the Anti-Monopoly Law.

68. 共同市场支配地位认定中行为一致性的考量

Assessment on behavioral consistency in determination of collect market dominance

【裁判要旨】

[Judgment Digest]

认定共同市场支配地位时，除考察市场份额外，还应当考察多个经营者是否就相关商品或者服务采取相同行为，体现出行为一致性。

When determining collect market dominance, people's courts shall consider, in addition to market shares, whether multiple operators at issue conducted the same acts for relevant products or services, which may reflect behavioral consistency.

【关键词】

[Keywords]

滥用市场支配地位　市场支配地位　共同市场支配地位　市场份额　行为一致性

Abuse of dominant market position; dominant market position; collect market dominance; market share; consistency in behavior

【案号】

[Case Number]

（2021）最高法知民终 1977 号

（2021）SPC IP Civil Final 1977

【基本案情】

[Case Facts]

在上诉人马某杰与被上诉人中国移动通信集团河南有限公司（以下简称河南移动通信公司）滥用市场支配地位纠纷案中，马某杰是河南移动通信公司的“特需号码”客户，马某杰认为，河南移动通信公

司滥用市场支配地位，不为其办理携号转网等业务，造成其经济损失，故向河南省郑州市中级人民法院（以下简称一审法院）提起本案诉讼，请求确认河南移动通信公司制定的《“特需号码”客户协议》部分条款违反反垄断法第十七条第一款，判令河南移动通信公司赔偿其经济损失870元。一审法院认为，马某杰没有提供证据证明河南移动通信公司具有市场支配地位，且马某杰在签订《“特需号码”客户协议》时已自愿放弃“过户、携号转网、停机保号”，判决驳回马某杰的全部诉讼请求。马某杰不服，向最高人民法院提起上诉。最高人民法院认定河南移动通信公司在相关市场内具有市场支配地位，但马某杰关于河南移动通信公司实施滥用市场支配地位的行为的上诉主张缺乏事实和法律依据，于2022年6月23日判决驳回上诉，维持原判。

In the dispute between Ma (the appellant, hereinafter referred to as “Ma”) and China Mobile Communications Group Co., Ltd. (Henan) (the appellee, hereinafter referred to as “China Mobile Henan”), over abuse of dominant market position, Ma was a “special number” client of China Mobile Henan and he claimed that the company had abused its dominant market position and refused to handle business such as “operator change, number retained” for him, resulting in his economic losses. So he filed a lawsuit with the Henan Zhengzhou Intermediate People's Court (hereinafter referred to as the Court of First Instance), requesting the Court to confirm that part of the provisions of the Special Number Client Agreement formulated by China Mobile Henan has violated Article 17 (1) of the Anti-monopoly Law, and to order China Mobile Henan to compensate for his economic losses of CNY 870. The Court of First Instance held that Ma did not provide evidence to prove that China Mobile Henan enjoys a dominant market position, and that he had voluntarily given up services such as the transfer of account, “operator change, number retained”, and “no service, number kept” when signing the *Special*

Number Client Agreement, so it rejected all of Ma's requests. Ma then appealed to the Supreme People's Court. The Supreme People's Court found that China Mobile Henan does enjoy a dominant position in the relevant market, but there is a lack of factual and legal bases for Ma to claim that China Mobile Henan abused its dominant market position, so it rejected the appeal and upheld the original judgment on June 23, 2022.

【裁判意见】

[Judge's Opinion]

最高人民法院二审认为，关于河南移动通信公司在相关市场是否具有市场支配地位，根据反垄断法第十九条第一款第三项的规定，三个经营者在相关市场的市场份额合计达到四分之三的，可以推定经营者具有市场支配地位。同时，根据市场经营的一般经验，如果相关市场内多个经营者就同类业务分别采取不同行为，则往往是经营者之间开展市场竞争的正常表现，此时并无考虑共同市场支配地位的必要。因此，只有相关市场内多个经营者就同类业务均采取相同行为，体现出行为一致性，才有考虑共同市场支配地位的必要性。正因如此，认定多个经营者形成共同市场支配地位，除了审查其市场份额外，还应当考虑经营者行为一致性等因素。在涉案被诉行为发生前后，国内移动通信服务市场只有中国移动通信集团有限公司、中国联合网络通信集团有限公司、中国电信集团有限公司三家运营商，相应地在本案相关市场内只有河南移动通信公司、河南联通公司和河南电信公司这三家经营者，本案符合反垄断法第十九条第一款第三项规定的情形。河南移动通信公司在二审中自认其与河南省内另外两家移动通信服务商在2019年工业和信息化部启动携号转网仪式前对于服务期内的普通号码和特需号码均不提供携号转网服务。而且，河南移动通信公司还提供了该三家移动通信服务商针对特需号码的移动通信服务格式合同，该三份格式合同显示河南省内三家移动通信服务商对在协议期内携号转网采用基本相同的格式条款约定。工业

和信息化部《携号转网服务管理规定》自 2019 年 12 月 1 日施行后，河南省内三家移动通信服务商也相应同时提供携号转网服务。上述事实初步表明，河南省内三家移动通信服务商长期以来在相关市场内存在一致性经营行为。在没有相反证据表明该三家服务商相关经营存在差异性的前提下，可以认为河南移动通信公司与河南省内另外两家移动通信服务商在相关市场内具有市场行动的一致性。

According to the Supreme People's Court, as to whether China Mobile Henan enjoys a dominant position in the relevant market, according to Article 19 (1) (iii) of the Anti-Monopoly Law, an operator shall be deemed as enjoying a dominant market position if the joint market share of three operators accounts for three-quarters of the relevant market. And in light of the general experience of market management, if several operators in the relevant market exhibit different behaviors on the same business, it should be seen as normal market competition among the operators, and there is no need to consider dominant position of the common market. It is necessary to consider dominant position of the common market only when consistency is reflected in the behavior undertaken by multiple operators in the relevant market in respect of the same business. Therefore, when determining the dominant position of multiple operators in the common market, apart from the market share, the consistency of the operators' behavior should also be considered. Before and after the occurrence of the accused act, there were and are only three operators in China's mobile communication service market: China Mobile Communications Group Co., Ltd., China United Network Communications Group Co., Ltd., and China Telecommunications Corporation. Correspondingly, there are only three operators in the relevant market of this case: China Mobile Henan, China Unicom Henan, and China Telecom Henan, which is in compliance with Article 19 (1) (iii) of the Anti-Monopoly Law. China Mobile Henan admitted in the Second Instance that it and the other two mobile communication operators in Henan province did not provide "operator change, number retained" service for ordinary numbers and special numbers during the service period before the Ministry of Industry and Information Technology launched the "operator change, number retained" ceremony in 2019. China Mobile Henan also provided three format contracts of the three operators for special numbers. The three format contracts show that the three operators in Henan province follow basically the same format terms for the "operator change, number retained" service in the agreement period. After the Ministry of Industry and Information Technology introduced the Regulations on the "*Operator Change, Number Retained" Service* on December 1, 2019, the three operators in Henan province also provided the service accordingly. The above facts preliminarily show that the three mobile communication operators in Henan province have exhibited a consistent business behavior in the relevant market for some time. On the premise that there is no contrary evidence to show that there are differences in the relevant operations of the three operators, it can be considered that China Mobile Henan and the other two mobile communication operators in Henan province take consistent actions in the relevant market.

本案中，马某杰提供了关于河南省的移动电话用户数量、河南省4G用户中河南移动通信公司的用户数量以及对河南省洛阳市手机号段的查询信息等证据，可以初步证明河南移动通信公司在相关市场具有一定的影响力。而河南移动通信公司并未根据反垄断法第十九条第二款、第三款的规定，举证证明其市场份额不足十分之一或者其并不具有市场支配地位。综合考虑上述因素，可以认定河南移动通信公司在相关市场内具有市场支配地位。

In this case, the evidence provided by Ma, which includes the number of mobile service users in Henan province, the number of 4G users in Henan

province who are clients of China Mobile Henan, and the query of phone numbers with the area code for Luoyang, Henan province, can preliminarily prove that China Mobile Henan has a certain influence in the relevant market. China Mobile Henan did not provide evidence to prove that its market share is less than one-tenth or that it does not lead a dominant market position in accordance with the provisions of Article 19 (2) and (3) of the Anti-monopoly Law. To sum up, China Mobile Henan has a dominant position in the relevant market.

69. 体育赛事商业权利独家授权的反垄断审查 Anti-monopoly review of exclusive authorization of commercial rights in association with sporting events

【裁判要旨】

[Judgment Digest]

体育赛事组织者基于其组织赛事、依据法律法规规定取得的独家经营赛事资源的民事权利所呈现的独家性和排他性属于权利自身的内在属性。由该权利内在的排他属性所形成的“垄断状态”本身，并非反垄断法预防和制止的对象。体育赛事组织者行使其独家经营赛事资源的权利时进行公开招标投标，其他经营者据此取得该独家经营的授权，实质上是公平竞争的结果，原则上不宜认定该经营权的独家授予属于滥用市场支配地位的行为。

The exclusivity of the sporting event organizers' civil rights obtained in accordance with laws and regulations through the events they organized is the intrinsic nature of such rights. The "monopoly status" itself formed by the intrinsic exclusive nature of such rights is not the object as prevented and prohibited in the Anti-monopoly law. The authorization of exclusive operation obtained by other operators through the bidding initiated by the sporting event organizer in exercising its rights to exclusively operate sporting event resources is substantially the result of fair competition, and therefore in principle should not be viewed as abuse of market dominance.

【关键词】

[Keywords]

中超联赛　经营权授予　市场支配地位　滥用

Chinese Super League (CSL); grant of management right; dominant market position; abuse

【案号】

[Case Number]

（2021）最高法知民终 1790 号

（2021）SPC IP Civil Final 1790

【基本案情】

[Case Facts]

在上诉人体娱（北京）文化传媒股份有限公司（以下简称体娱公司）与被上诉人中超联赛有限责任公司（以下简称中超公司）、上海映脉文化传播有限公司（以下简称映脉公司）滥用市场支配地位纠纷案中，经中国足协授权，中超公司取得中超联赛资源代理开发经营权；中超公司于 2016 年网上公开招标 2017—2019 年中超联赛官方图片合作机构，映脉公司以相应报价中标，由此取得独家经营中超联赛图片资源的权利，而体娱公司未中标。但体娱公司仍于 2017 年、2018 年派人进入中超联赛现场拍摄图片并销售传播，其间中国足协出面发布声明予以制止以维护映脉公司的独家经营权。体娱公司故以中超公司、映脉公司滥用市场支配地位限定交易相对人只能与映脉公司进行交易为由，向上海知识产权法院（以下简称一审法院）起诉，请求判令中超公司、映脉

公司停止垄断行为、消除影响、赔偿经济损失及维权合理开支。一审法院认为，现有证据不能证明中超公司、映脉公司具有市场支配地位，且两公司从事被诉行为具有正当理由，判决驳回体娱公司全部诉讼请求。体娱公司不服，向最高人民法院提起上诉，主张中超公司与映脉公司存在滥用市场支配地位的行为。最高人民法院于2022年6月23日判决驳回上诉，维持原判。

In the dispute between Osports Beijing Culture Media Co., Ltd. (the appellant, hereinafter referred to as "Osports"), Chinese Football Association Super League Co., Ltd. (the appellee, hereinafter referred to as "CSL"), and Shanghai ImagineChina Culture Communication Co., Ltd. (the appellee, hereinafter referred to as "ImagineChina"), over abuse of dominant market position, CSL obtained, with the authorization of the Chinese Football Association (the "CFA"), the right to resource agent, development, and management of the Chinese Football Association Super League (the "Chinese Super League"); in 2016, CSL called online for bids for taking pictures of the 2017–2019 Chinese Super League, ImagineChina won the bid and obtained the exclusive right to manage the CSL resources, while Osports failed to win the bid. However, Osports still sent people to the Chinese Super League in 2017 and 2018 to take pictures, and sold and distributed them; the CFA issued a statement to stop it from doing that in order to protect ImagineChina's exclusive right. Osports filed a lawsuit with the Shanghai Intellectual Property Court (hereinafter referred to as the Court of First Instance) on the grounds that CSL and ImagineChina abused their dominant market position and limited the transaction parties to only transact with ImagineChina, requesting that CSL and ImagineChina stop their monopolistic behavior, eliminate the impact, and compensate for its economic losses and reasonable expenses. The Court of First Instance held that the existing evidence could not prove that CSL and

ImagineChina had a dominant market position, and that the alleged behaviors of the two companies are justified, so it rejected all the claims of Osports. Osports then appealed to the Supreme People's Court, claiming that CSL and ImagineChina had abused their dominant market position. On June 23, 2022, the Supreme People's Court rejected the appeal and upheld the original judgment.

【裁判意见】

[Judge's Opinion]

最高人民法院二审认为，中国足球协会根据体育法（2016年修正）第三十一条、第三十九条规定的授权和政府的委托管理全国足球事务，其享有的赛事商业权利主要是基于其组织赛事而产生的以财产利益为主要内容的民事权益。该类赛事商业权利的取得符合本案赛事发生当时（2017—2019年）所施行的民法总则第一百二十九条（现民法典同条）关于“民事权利可以依据民事法律行为、事实行为、法律规定的事件或者法律规定的其他方式取得”的规定。由于赛事商业权利属于一种民事权利，也是一种独家排他性权利，其原始权利人可以选择由本人自己行使、授权他人行使、与他人合作行使。中国足球协会独家授权中超公司行使足球赛事商业权利，中超公司又部分转授映脉公司独家行使其中赛事图片经营权，均是中国足球协会和中超公司行使民事权利的体现。中国足球协会对足球赛事商业权利的独家排他性属于财产权的排他性，是其组织赛事并依法取得的一种垄断权利，反垄断法预防和制止垄断行为，但不预防和制止垄断状态和垄断权利，预防和制止的是利用垄断状态和垄断权利进行某些作为或者不作为以排除、限制竞争的行为，即滥用行为。权利的排他属性与滥用行为属于不同概念，权利的排他性或者排他性权利本身并不是反垄断法预防和制止的对象，排他性权利的行使可能成为反垄断法预防和制止的对象。

According to the SPC, the CFA manages national football affairs in ac-

cordance with the authorization provided in Articles 31 and 39 of the Sports Law(amended in 2016) and the delegation of the government, and the commercial right enjoyed by the CFA to the football games is a civil right, which is mainly property interest arising from its organization of the games. The commercial right to the games is obtained in accordance with the General Provisions of the Civil Law in force at the time when the games involved took place (2017—2019), of which Article 129 (the same article of the Civil Code) stipulates that "civil rights may be obtained based on civil legal acts, factual acts, events provided by law, or through other ways provided by law". Since the commercial right to the games is a civil right and an exclusive right, the original right holder can choose to exercise the right by itself, or authorize others to exercise it, or co-exercise it with others. The CFA was exercising its civil right by exclusively authorizing CSL to exercise the commercial right to the football games, and CSL was exercising its right by partially authorizing ImagineChina to exercise the exclusive right to manage the pictures of the games. The exclusivity of the CFA's commercial right to football games belongs to the exclusivity of property right, which is a monopoly right obtained by the CFA in organizing the matches according to law. The Anti-monopoly Law prevents and prohibits the monopoly behavior, not the monopoly state and monopoly right; it prevents and prohibits the use of the monopoly state and monopoly right to exclude and restrict competition by doing things or not doing any, or, in other words, abusing the monopoly state and monopoly right. The exclusivity of a right and the abuse of it are two different things. The Anti-monopoly Law does not prevent or prohibit the exclusivity of a right or the exclusive right itself, but it may prevent and prohibit the exercise of the exclusive right.

在特定地域内独家授权经营是商业实践中一种常见的授权经营模

式。经营权独家授予是经营者独立行使民事权利的体现，在经济效果上被授权的经营者只不过是授权经营者具体经营的替代，一般不会对外额外产生反竞争效果，故原则上不为反垄断法所禁止，除非存在经营者通谋损害消费者利益等特殊情形。中超公司、映脉公司在中超联赛图片经营市场具有市场支配地位，但中超公司通过公开招标方式选择授权映脉公司独家经营 2017—2019 年中超联赛图片资源，在程序上体现了竞争；该经营权独家授予是竞争的应然结果，且有其合理理由，不具有反竞争效果。同时，中超联赛图片用户（需求方）只能向映脉公司购买该赛事图片，系基于原始经营权人中国足协依法享有的经营权并通过授权形成的结果，符合法律规定且有合理性，该限定交易情形有正当理由。

Exclusive grant of right to management in a specific region is commonly seen in business practice. It shows how an operator exercises its civil rights independently. In terms of economic effect, the grant-receiving operator is only a substitute operator, and generally it will not produce additional anti-competitive effect, so it is not prohibited by the Anti-monopoly Law in principle, unless there are special circumstances such as operators collude to harm the interests of consumers. CSL and ImagineChina lead a dominant position in the Chinese Super League picture market, but CSL chose to authorize, through open bidding, ImagineChina to exclusively manage the picture resources of the Chinese Super League from 2017 to 2019, which can be seen as procedural competition. An expected result of the competition, the exclusive grant of the right to management is reasonable and has no anti-competitive effect. Also, users (the demand side) can only purchase pictures of the Chinese Super League from ImagineChina, which is based on the right of operation enjoyed by the CFA, the original right holder, and results from the act of grant. It is lawful and reasonable; the restrictive transaction is justified.

70. 公用事业经营者隐性限定交易行为的认定 Identification of implicit restrictions on transactions by public utility operators

【裁判要旨】

[Judgment Digest]

反垄断法上的限定交易行为可以是明示的、直接的，也可以是隐含的、间接的。具有市场支配地位的经营者为供水、供电、供气等公用事业经营者或者其他依法具有独占地位的经营者，对于市场竞争可以施加更大的影响，其在相关交易中只推荐特定交易对象或者只公开特定交易对象的信息，交易相对人基于上述情势难以自由选择其他经营者进行交易的，通常可以初步认定其实质上实施了限定交易行为。

Restrictive trade practices under the Anti-monopoly Law not only refer to those express and direct practices, but also to implied and indirect ones. If the operators with market dominance are public utility operators engaging in supply of water, power and gas etc, or such other operators as having an exclusive position by law and thus can exert more influence on market competition, and they only recommend specific transaction parties or only publicize the information on the same in the relevant transactions, which scenario makes it difficult for their counter parties to freely choose other operators for transaction, then generally speaking, it may preliminarily be viewed that such operators have conducted restrictive trade practices.

【关键词】

[Keywords]

滥用市场支配地位　限定交易行为　隐性限定　公用企业　损害赔偿

Abuse of dominant market position; restrictive trade practices; implicit restriction; public enterprises; damages

【案号】

[Case Number]

（2022）最高法知民终395号

（2022）SPC IP Civil Final 395

【基本案情】

[Case Facts]

在上诉人威海宏福置业有限公司（以下简称宏福置业公司）与被上诉人威海市水务集团有限公司（以下简称威海水务集团）滥用市场支配地位纠纷案中，宏福置业公司是一家位于山东省威海市的房地产开发公司，其向山东省青岛市中级人民法院（以下简称一审法院）提起本案诉讼，请求判令威海水务集团赔偿因其实施滥用市场支配地位的行为给宏福置业公司造成的经济损失230余万元及合理开支15万元。一审法院认定，威海水务集团在威海市区供水、污水设施建设和管理中处于市场支配地位，但现有证据不能证明威海水务集团存在限定交易行为，判决驳回宏福置业公司诉讼请求。宏福置业公司不服，向最高人民法院提起上诉。最高人民法院认定威海水务集团实施了限定交易行为，于2022年6月23日判决撤销原判，改判威海水务集团赔偿宏福置业公司为调查、制止垄断行为所支付的合理开支15万元。

In the dispute between Weihai Hongfu Real Estate Co., Ltd. (the appellant, hereinafter referred to as "Hongfu"), and Weihai Water Group Co., Ltd. (the appellee, hereinafter referred to as "Weihai Water"), over abuse of dominant market position, Hongfu, a real estate development company based in Weihai, Shandong province, filed a lawsuit with the Shandong Qingdao Intermediate People's Court (hereinafter referred to as the Court of First Instance), accusing Weihai Water of abusing its dominant market position and requesting it to compensate for the economic loss of more than CNY 2. 3 mil-

lion and reasonable expenses of CNY 150, 000. The Court of First Instance found that Weihai Water is in a dominant market position in the construction and management of water supply and sewage facilities in Weihai, but the existing evidence could not prove that Weihai Water had implemented restrictive trade practices, so it rejected the requests of Hongfu. Hongfu then appealed to the SPC. The SPC found that Weihai Water had implemented restrictive trade practices, so it revoked the original judgment on June 23, 2022, ordering Weihai Water to compensate Hongfu for the reasonable expenses of CNY 150, 000 on investigating and stopping the monopoly concerned.

【裁判意见】

[Judge's Opinion]

最高人民法院二审认为，反垄断法第十七条第一款第四项所禁止的限定交易行为，是指具有市场支配地位的经营者直接限定或者以设定交易条件等方式变相限定交易相对人只能与其进行交易，或者只能与其指定的经营者进行交易。限定交易行为损害了交易相对人的合法权益，破坏了正常的市场秩序和竞争机制。本案中，威海水务集团实施了限定交易的垄断行为，具体分析如下：

According to the Supreme People's Court, the restrictive trade practice prohibited by Article 17 (1) (iv) of the Anti-monopoly Law means that an operator with a dominant market position directly restricts or in a disguised way sets certain conditions to restrict the counterparty of the transaction to transact only with itself or with its designated operator. Restrictive trade practices would damage the legitimate rights and interests of the counterparty and destroy the normal market order and competition mechanism. In this case, Weihai Water has implemented the monopolistic act to restrict transaction. The analysis is listed as below:

首先，威海水务集团提供《市水务集团供排水业务办理服务指南》

具有限定交易的意图与内容。在判断经营者是否限定交易相对人只能与其进行交易或者只能与其指定的经营者进行交易时，重点在于考察经营者是否实质上限制了交易相对人的自由选择权。限定交易行为可以是明示的、直接的，也可以是隐含的、间接的。如果具有市场支配地位的经营者为公用事业经营者，如供水、供电、供气等公用企业，或者其他依法具有独占地位的经营者，其兼具市场经营和行业管理的双重特点，对于市场竞争可以施加的影响更大，其在相关交易中只推荐特定交易对象或者只公开特定交易对象的信息，交易相对人基于上述情势难以自由选择其他经营者进行交易的，则通常可以初步认定该经营者实施了限定交易行为。本案中，威海水务集团在山东省威海市市区的供水设施建设市场具有市场支配地位，同时，其在威海市市区不仅独家提供城市公共供水服务，而且承担着供水设施审核、验收等公用事业管理职责，其在受理供排水业务时，在业务办理服务流程清单中仅注明其公司及其下属企业的联系方式等信息，而没有告知、提示交易相对人可以选择其他具有相关资质的给排水施工企业，属于隐性限定了只能由其指定的设计、施工单位办理新建项目的供排水设计和施工，或者说，由此给交易相对人带来如果不选择其指定的设计、施工单位则在办理供水设施审核、验收等管理手续时可能出现种种不便的隐忧。因此，可以认定威海水务集团具有限定交易的主观意图与客观内容。

First of all, the *Service Guide for Water Supply and Drainage Business of Weihai Water Group*(the “Service Guide”) provided by Weihai Water has the intention and content of restricting transaction. When deciding whether an operator restricts the counterparty to transact only with itself or with its designated operator, the key point is to examine whether the operator essentially restricts the free choice of the counterparty. Restrictive transactions can be explicit and direct, or implied and indirect. If the operator with a dominant market position is a public utility operator, such as water supply, power supply,

and gas supply, or an operator with an exclusive position according to law, it has the dual characteristics of market operation and industry management, and can exert a greater influence on market competition. If it only recommends specific traders or only discloses information about specific traders in transactions, which makes it difficult for the counterparty to freely choose a different operator for the transaction, it can be preliminarily determined that the operator has implemented restrictive trade practices. In this case, apart from leading a dominant position in the water supply facilities construction market of Weihai, Weihai Water also exclusively specializes in urban public water supply services in the city, and is responsible for public utility management such as the review and inspection of water supply facilities. In terms of the water supply and drainage business, Weihai Water only lists information about its own group and its subordinate enterprises, without informing the counterparty of a transaction that they can choose other water supply and drainage construction enterprises with relevant qualifications. It indicates that only the enterprises designated by Weihai Water can handle the water supply and drainage design and construction of new projects. Or, it worries the counterparty that if they do not choose its designated enterprise, there might be trouble in the review and inspection of water supply facilities. Therefore, it can be concluded that Weihai Water has the intention and content of restricting transactions.

其次，威海水务集团的被诉垄断行为实际上具有相应的排除、限制竞争的效果。根据在案证据，可以认定威海水务集团不仅在威海市市区的供水设施建设市场具有市场支配地位，也是威海市市区城市公共供水服务市场的独家经营者，其在城市公共供水服务市场的市场支配力不可避免地影响到供水设施建设市场，其在受理供排水市政业务时仅公开其公司及其下属企业信息的行为不仅排除、限制了其他具有相关资质的设计、施工企业同等参与威海市市区供水设施建设市场竞争的机会，也剥夺了对新建项目存在供排水业务需求的房地产开发企业的自主选择权，造成了其在威海市市区的供水设施建设市场内集中、大量承揽供排水设计和施工的后果，产生了更加明显的反竞争效果。

Secondly, Weihai Water's alleged monopolistic behavior actually has the effect of excluding and restricting competition. The documented evidence shows that Weihai Water not only leads a dominant position in the water supply facilities construction market in Weihai, but also is an exclusive operator in the city's public water supply market. Its dominance in the urban public water supply market inevitably affects the water supply facilities construction market. In terms of the municipal water supply and drainage business, Weihai Water discloses the information of its group and its subordinate enterprises only, which not only excludes and restricts other design and construction enterprises with relevant qualifications to participate in the market competition, but also deprives real estate developers of the right to independently choose water supply and drainage services for their new projects. The result is that Weihai Water gets to undertake a centrally large number of water supply and drainage design and construction projects in the relevant market, which produces a more obvious anti-competitive effect.

最后，威海水务集团缺乏正当理据。城市公共供水服务具有公用事业属性，一方面对质量、安全存在更高的要求，另一方面因其通常由政府指定的独家企业经营而具有自然垄断属性。但是，与供水服务密切相关的供水设施建设市场是开放竞争的，满足相关资质要求、遵守国家有关技术标准和规范的企业原则上均应能够进入市场公平竞争。威海水务集团不仅在威海市市区的供水设施建设市场具有市场支配地位，同时，作为公用企业，威海水务集团是威海市市区城市公共供水服务市场的独家经营者，其还承担着威海市市区供水设施审核、验收等供排水市政业务管理职责，在其自身及下属企业参与威海市市区供水设施建设市场竞

争时，其负有更高的不得排除、限制竞争的特别注意义务。威海水务集团在其服务指南中列明其公司及其下属企业信息的同时，应当一并以同等方式列明其他具有相应资质的企业信息或者以其他明确、合理的方式表明办理供排水业务的用户可以充分自由地选择其他经营者。威海水务集团主张其在服务指南中提供其公司及其下属企业的信息是提供便民服务并非限定交易，但如上分析，其有关行为已实质上排除、限制了其他经营者参与威海市市区供水设施建设市场的竞争，威海水务集团的该项主张难以成立，故不予支持。

Lastly, Weihai Water lacks justification. Urban public water supply is a public utility: on the one hand, it has higher requirement for water quality and safety; on the other hand, it is a natural monopoly as it is often managed exclusively by an enterprise designated by the government. However, the water supply facilities construction market, which is closely related to water supply, is open to competition, and enterprises that meet the requirements for qualification and comply with the relevant technical standards and norms of the country should in principle be able to enter the market for fair competition. Weihai Water leads a dominant position in the water supply facilities construction market of Weihai, and as a public utility, it is the exclusive operator in the city's public water supply service market, and is responsible for the municipal water supply and drainage services such as the review and inspection of water supply facilities. When it and its subordinate enterprises participate in the competition of water supply facilities construction in Weihai, Weihai Water has a greater duty of care not to exclude or restrict the competition. When listing its group and subordinate enterprises in the Service Guide, Weihai Water should also include in the same manner the information of other qualified enterprises or indicate in other clear and reasonable ways that users can fully and freely choose other operators for water supply and drainage business.

Weihai Water argued that it only listed the group and its subordinate enterprises in the Service Guide for convenience, not to restrict transactions. However, according to the above analysis, its behavior has essentially excluded and restricted other operators from participating in the competition in the water supply facilities construction market in Weihai. Its defense cannot be established and shall not be supported by the court.

71. 限定转售商品最低价格纵向垄断协议的损害赔偿 Damages caused by vertical monopoly agreements on minimum resale price maintenance

【裁判要旨】

[Judgment Digest]

消费者因经营者达成并实施限定向第三人转售商品最低价格的纵向垄断协议提起民事赔偿诉讼，赔偿金额一般可以以经营者之间限定的最低转售价格与竞争价格之间的差额为依据计算。

Where a consumer files a civil lawsuit for compensation against operators for their entering and performing vertical monopoly agreement that sets the minimum price for the commodities resold to any third party, the amount of damages can generally be calculated on the basis of the price margin between the minimum resale price fixed by the operators and the reasonable price in fair competition.

【关键词】

[Keywords]

纵向垄断协议　限定转售价格　行政处罚决定　民事赔偿

Vertical monopoly agreement; minimum resale price; administrative penalty decision; civil compensation

【案号】

[Case Number]

(2020) 最高法知民终 1137 号

(2020) SPC IP Civil Final 1137

【裁判意见】

[Judge's Opinion]

在上诉人缪某与被上诉人上汽通用汽车销售有限公司、上海逸隆汽车销售服务有限公司纵向垄断协议纠纷案中，最高人民法院指出，本案属于经营者之间达成并实施纵向垄断协议被行政机关处罚后，消费者作为受害人提起的后续民事赔偿诉讼。根据被诉行政处罚决定书及在案事实，通用公司与逸隆公司达成并实施了反垄断法所禁止的限定向第三人转售商品最低价格的垄断协议行为，使得缪某依据垄断价格购买了涉案车辆，应当认定通用公司与逸隆公司共同实施了侵权行为，支持缪某提出的通用公司承担赔偿责任，逸隆公司承担补充责任的主张。

In the dispute over a vertical monopoly agreement between Miao (the appellant), and SAIC Motor Co., Ltd. (the appellee), and Shanghai Yilong Automobile Sales Co., Ltd. (the appellee), the SPC says that this case is a civil compensation lawsuit filed by the consumer as the victim after the operators got punished by the administrative organ for reaching and performing a vertical monopoly agreement. According to the administrative penalty decision and the facts on the record, SAIC Motor and Yilong reached and performed a monopoly agreement, which offers a minimum resale price to a third party and is prohibited by the Anti-monopoly Law; and Miao purchased the vehicle involved at the monopoly price. It should be determined that SAIC Motor and Yilong jointly committed the infringement. Miao should be supported for requesting that SAIC Motor should bear the liability for compensation and Yilong bear the supplementary liability.

由于本案系经营者之间达成并实施纵向垄断协议被行政机关处罚后，消费者作为受害人提起的后续民事赔偿诉讼，赔偿金额应当为经营者之间限定的最低转售非竞争价格与竞争价格之间的差额。缪某已经举证证明涉案车辆在 2014 年其购买时的垄断价格为 131900 元，涉案车辆在 2016 年涉案行政处罚决定作出后的市场价格为 119900 元，两者差额为 12000 元，其已经对所受损害完成了初步证明责任。缪某据此主张其因被诉垄断行为造成的损害应当大于其诉请的 10000 元。此时，举证责任应当转移给通用公司与逸隆公司。通用公司与逸隆公司均未能证明缪某购买涉案车辆时执行的非竞争价格与竞争价格之间不存在差额。而且，根据逸隆公司一审程序中提供的 2014 年 7 月至 12 月销售涉案车型车辆的 32 张发票，在涉案车型指导价 2014 年 7 月为 131900 元，2014 年 9 月调整为 128900 元和 2014 年 10 月调整为 121900 元期间，逸隆公司销售涉案车辆的平均价格为 115956.25 元，基于此，缪某要求赔偿 10000 元经济损失具有一定合理性，应予支持。

Since this case is a civil compensation lawsuit filed by the consumer as the victim after the operators got punished by the administrative organ for reaching and performing a vertical monopoly agreement, the compensation amount should be the difference between the minimum resale non-competitive price and the competitive price. Miao has proved that the monopoly price of the vehicle that he purchased in 2014 was CNY 131, 900, and after the administrative penalty decision was made in 2016, the market price of the vehicle involved was CNY 119, 900, so the difference is CNY 12, 000. Miao has completed the preliminary burden of proof for damages. Miao thus argued that the damages caused by the alleged monopolistic behavior should be greater than the CNY 10, 000 that he claimed. The burden of proof now should be transferred to SAIC Motor and Yilong. Neither SAIC Motor nor Yilong was able to prove that there was no difference between the non-competitive price when

Miao purchased the vehicle involved and the competitive price. And according to the 32 invoices of vehicles of the model involved sold between July 2014 and December 2014, which were provided by Yilong in the First Instance, during the period when the guidance price of the model involved was CNY 131,900 in July 2014, adjusted to CNY 128,900 in September 2014 and CNY 121,900 in October 2014, the average price of the vehicles involved sold by Yilong was CNY 115,956.25. Therefore, it is reasonable of Miao to claim CNY 10,000 of economic losses, which should be supported by the court.

72. 限定交易行为造成损失的认定
Identification of damages caused by restrictive trade practices

【裁判要旨】

[Judgment Digest]

当事人主张因滥用市场支配地位的限定交易行为而遭受的损失的，应当证明限定交易情形下的实际价格高于正常竞争条件下的合理交易价格的差额。当事人未能举证证明上述差额，亦未能提出具体差额计算方法，或者不存在或难以确定可供对比的合理交易价格，导致具体损失数额难以确定的，人民法院可以根据案件具体情况合理酌定赔偿数额。

Where the involved party claims for damages arising out of restrictive trade practices which constitute abuse of market dominance, such party should present evidence to prove the margin between the actual price under the circumstance of restrictive trade practices and the reasonable price under normal competition conditions. If it is difficult to determine the amount of damages because such party fails to present evidence to prove such margin, or put forward a specific way to calculate such margin, or there is no reasonable price for reference, or it is difficult to determine such price reference, then people's courts may determine a reasonable amount of damages at its discretion according to the case circumstances.

【关键词】

[Keywords]

限定交易行为　损害赔偿　合理开支

Restrictive trade practices; damages; reasonable expenses

【案号】

[Case Number]

(2022) 最高法知民终 395 号

(2022) SPC IP Civil Final 395

【裁判意见】

[Judge's Opinion]

在上诉人威海宏福置业有限公司与被上诉人威海市水务集团有限公司滥用市场支配地位纠纷案中，最高人民法院认为，反垄断法第五十条规定："经营者实施垄断行为，给他人造成损失的，依法承担民事责任。"《最高人民法院关于审理因垄断行为引发的民事纠纷案件应用法律若干问题的规定》第十四条第一款规定："被告实施垄断行为，给原告造成损失的，根据原告的诉讼请求和查明的事实，人民法院可以依法判令被告承担停止侵害、赔偿损失等民事责任。"根据上述法律和司法解释的规定，宏福置业公司主张损害赔偿，应当举证证明其损失以及损失与垄断行为之间的因果关系。

In the dispute between Weihai Hongfu Real Estate Co., Ltd. (the Appellant), and Weihai Water Group Co., Ltd. (the Appellee), over abuse of dominant market position, the SPC cites Article 50 of the Anti-monopoly Law, which stipulates that "a business operator shall bear civil liability according to law for committing monopoly and causing losses to others"; and Ar-

ticle 14 of the *Provisions of the Supreme People's Court on Several Issues Concerning the Application of Law in the Trial of Civil Disputes Arising from Monopoly*, which provides that: "where the defendant commits monopoly and causes losses to the plaintiff, the people's court may, according to the plaintiff's claim and the facts ascertained, order the defendant to bear civil liabilities such as ceasing the infringement and compensating for the losses". According to the provisions of law and judicial interpretation, Hongfu should prove its losses and the causality between its losses and the accused monopoly for its claim for damages.

宏福置业公司主张的损失包括直接损失 2064749. 22 元（包括拆除旧给排水设施损失 30 万元和给排水设施重新设计施工损失 1764749. 22 元）和间接损失 241219. 55 元（包括实际损失发生之日起至宏福置业公司起诉之日的利息）。

The losses claimed by Hongfu include direct losses of CNY 2, 064, 749. 22 (CNY 300, 000 for the demolition of the old water supply and drainage facilities and CNY 1, 764, 749. 22 for the redesign and construction of the water supply and drainage facilities) and indirect losses of CNY 241, 219. 55 (including the interest from the date of the actual loss to the date on which Hongfu sued).

首先，威海水务集团要求昌鸿小区 K 区住宅楼拆除原有“二区”给水管道、按“三区”改建，不属于附加不合理的交易条件的垄断行为，且工程拆除也是宏福置业公司自行安排的，故宏福置业公司基于原已建成的“二区”给排水设施拆除所提出的直接损失和间接损失赔偿请求，缺乏事实和法律依据，不予支持。

First of all, Weihai Water requires the residential buildings in District K of Changhong Residential Quarter to demolish the original water supply pipelines of "Area No. 2" and rebuild them based on those in "Area No. 3" -

there is no extra unreasonable trading condition and should not be deemed as a monopoly; and the demolition is arranged by Hongfu on its own. Therefore, there is no factual or legal basis for Hongfu's request for compensation for direct losses and indirect losses caused by the demolition of the water supply and drainage facilities in "Area No. 2", and the request should not be supported.

其次，就原已建成的“二区”给排水设施拆除后的重建而言，虽然威海水务集团要求该给排水设施拆除重建具有正当理由，但其存在指定设计、施工单位的限定交易行为，宏福置业公司可能因该限定交易的垄断行为遭受损失，但其全部重建费用并不能想当然地认为全部是因垄断行为而遭受的损失。一般情况下，因限定交易行为而遭受的损失，应当以限定交易的实际支出高于正常竞争条件下的合理交易价格的差额来计算，当事人主张这部分损失的，对此负有举证责任。如果当事人未举证证明上述差额或提出具体差额计算方法，或者不存在或难以确定可供对比的合理交易价格，导致具体损失数额难以确定的，人民法院在特定条件情况下也可以合理酌定赔偿数额。

Secondly, although Weihai Water has legitimate reasons to require the demolition and reconstruction of the water supply and drainage facilities in "Area No. 2", its designation of the design and construction enterprise should be regarded as a restrictive trade practice, and Hongfu may suffer losses due to that restrictive trade practice. But the entire cost of reconstruction does not necessarily equal all the losses suffered as a result of the monopoly. Normally, the loss caused by a restrictive transaction practice should be calculated as the difference between the actual expenditure of the restrictive transaction and the reasonable transaction price under normal competition conditions, and the party claiming loss of this kind shall bear the burden of proof. If said party fails to prove the difference or propose a specific calculation method for the difference, or if there is not a reasonable trade price for comparison or it is difficult

to determine such a price, which makes it hard to determine the specific amount of loss, the people's court may determine, under certain conditions, a reasonable amount of compensation.

本案中，宏福置业公司在正常竞争（非垄断）市场条件下所应支出的重建费用，属于其本应支出的合理费用，原则上不应纳入其损失范围。如果宏福置业公司在限定交易情况下超出正常竞争条件下的合理交易价格而多支出了额外费用，该额外费用则属于其因垄断行为而遭受的损失，应当纳入赔偿范围。即在宏福置业公司支出的全部重建费用中，原则上其仅可请求威海水务集团赔偿其中限定交易情况下的额外费用部分。对此，宏福置业公司应当举证证明其实际支出的重建费用高于正常竞争条件下的合理交易价格（包括由此计算的差额）。但是，宏福置业公司没有提供证据证明威海水务集团所限定的单位实际设计和施工价格高于其他具有同等资质的设计、施工单位的正常市场价格，宏福置业公司本身对涉案给排水设施的拆除重建负有主要责任，其也没有提供证据证明可供酌定损失的相关因素，本案缺乏酌定损失的必要条件，故对于宏福置业公司要求赔偿经济损失的上诉请求不予支持。

In this case, the reconstruction expenses incurred by Hongfu under normal competition (not monopoly) are reasonable expenses it should have incurred, and should not be included in its losses in principle. If Hongfu paid more than the reasonable transaction price under normal competition due to the restrictive transaction, the extra it paid should be seen as a loss caused by monopoly and included in the scope of compensation. That is, in principle, Hongfu can only ask Weihai Water to compensate for the additional costs caused by restrictive transactions. In this regard, Hongfu should prove that its actual reconstruction costs are higher than the reasonable transaction price under normal competition (including the difference thus calculated). However, Hongfu does not provide evidence to prove that the actual design and construction price of the enterprise designated by Weihai Water is higher than the normal market price of other equally qualified design and construction enterprises, nor does it provides evidence to prove the relevant factors that could be used to determine the loss as it is primarily responsible for the demolition and reconstruction of the water supply and drainage facilities involved. Therefore, Hongfu's request for compensation for economic losses is not supported for a lack of necessary conditions to determine the losses.

73. 反垄断法对消费者权益的保护 Protection of consumer's rights and interests by the Anti-monopoly Law

【裁判要旨】

[Judgment Digest]

反垄断法的立法目的主要在于维护市场竞争机制，有效配置资源，保护和促进竞争。其对消费者的保护着眼于竞争行为是否损害了保障消费者福利的竞争机制，既不以某一行为是否为消费者所满意作为判断标准，也不刻意保护某一具体消费者的利益。消费者认为因经营者销售相关商品违反价格法等相关规定，损害其消费者权益的，原则上应当依据消费者权益保护法等其他法律保护自己的权益。

The main legislative purpose of the Anti-monopoly Law is to safeguard market competition mechanism and allocate resources effectively, so as to protect and promote competition. Its protection on consumers focuses on whether the competitive practices will harm the competition mechanism which ultimately protects consumers' welfare. In doing so, it neither takes whether consumers are satisfied with certain acts as the judgment criteria, nor deliberately protects the interests of some specific consumers. If a consumer believes that

the operator has harmed his rights and interests by selling relevant commodities in violation of the Price Law and other related regulations, then in principle he or she should seek protection over his rights and interests in accordance with such other applicable law as the Law on the Protection of Consumer Rights and Interests.

【关键词】

[Keywords]

横向垄断协议　反垄断法　价格法　消费者权益保护法　立法目的　消费者权益

Horizontal monopoly agreement; Anti-monopoly Law; Price Law; protection of consumer rights and interests; legislative purpose; consumer rights and interests

【案号】

[Case Number]

(2021) 最高法知民终1020号

(2021) SPC IP Civil Final 1020

【基本案情】

[Case Facts]

在上诉人李某全与被上诉人湖南湘品堂工贸有限责任公司（以下简称湘品堂公司）、长沙凯源珊珊商贸连锁管理有限公司（以下简称珊珊公司）、湖南佳宜企业管理有限公司（以下简称佳宜公司）、北京泰和瑞通云商科技有限公司（以下简称泰和瑞通公司）、北京泰和瑞通云商科技有限公司长沙分公司（以下简称泰和瑞通长沙分公司）垄断纠纷案中，李某全发现湘品堂公司等五被诉经营者在中国铁路广州局集团有限公司长沙南车站（以下简称长沙南站）二层候车厅以每瓶3元的价格销售555ml怡宝饮用纯净水，且长沙南站二层候车厅公共区域内只免费供应开水，没有免费供应凉水或温水。李某全还发现湘品堂公司、珊珊公司、佳宜公司在长沙市内贺龙体育商圈周边以及距离长沙南站较近的住宅小区开设的超市所出售 555ml 怡宝饮用纯净水为每瓶 2 元。李某全主张，湘品堂公司等五被诉经营者利用垄断长沙南站二层候车厅区域饮用水消费市场的优势，相互串通抬高价格，违反了 2008 年施行的反垄断法、价格法的相关规定，向湖南省长沙市中级人民法院（以下简称一审法院）提起诉讼，请求判令湘品堂公司向李某全返还 1 元，湘品堂公司等五被诉经营者共同赔偿李某全 3017 元并公开道歉。一审法院认定，长沙南站二层候车厅为本案的相关市场，湘品堂公司等五被诉经营者价格行为具有一致性，但根据本案现有证据无法认定湘品堂公司等五被诉经营者之间具有固定价格的意思联络。据此，一审法院判决驳回李某全的诉讼请求。李某全不服，向最高人民法院提起上诉。最高人民法院于 2022 年 6 月 24 日判决驳回上诉，维持原判。

In the dispute over monopoly between the Appellant, Li, and the Appellees, Hunan SHXPT Industry and Trade Co., Ltd. (hereinafter referred to as "SHXPT"), Changsha KY SHAN SHAN Trade Chain Management Co., Ltd. (hereinafter referred to as "SHAN SHAN"), Hunan NEWJOY Business Management Co., Ltd. (hereinafter referred to as "NEWJOY"), Beijing TAHO Technology Co., Ltd. (hereinafter referred to as "TAHO"), and Beijing TAHO Technology Co., Ltd. (Changsha Branch) (hereinafter referred to as "TAHO Changsha"), Li found that SHXPT and the other four operators were selling C' estbon purified drinking water at the price of CNY 3 per (555 ml) bottle at the second-floor waiting hall of the Changsha South Railway Station, which is run by China Railway Guangzhou Group Co., Ltd. (hereinafter referred to as the "Railway Station"); in the public area of the second-floor waiting hall of the Railway Station, only boiled water was provided free of charge; there was no free supply of cool or warm water. Li also found that SHXPT, SHAN SHAN, and NEWJOY sold the same water at CNY 2 per (555

ml) bottle in the vicinity of the Helong Sports Business District in Changsha and in the residential quarters close to the Railway Station. Li claimed that SHXPT and the other four operators listed above monopolized the drinking water market of the second-floor waiting hall of the Railway Station, and colluded with each other to increase the price, which violated the relevant provisions of the Anti-monopoly Law and Price Law implemented in 2008. He filed a lawsuit with the Hunan Changsha Intermediate People's Court (hereinafter referred to as the Court of First Instance), requesting SHXPT to return him CNY 1, and SHXPT and the other four operators to jointly compensate him CNY 3017 and apologize publicly. The Court of First Instance found that the second-floor waiting hall of the Railway Station is the relevant market of the case, and the five accused operators are consistent in terms of the price involved; but the existing evidence could not prove that there was intentional communication among the five accused operators of a fixed price. Accordingly, it ruled to reject Li's requests. Li then appealed to the SPC. On June 24, 2022, the SPC rejected the appeal and upheld the original judgment.

【裁判意见】

[Judge's Opinion]

最高人民法院二审认为，关于湘品堂公司等五被诉经营者将长沙南站二层候车厅所售 555ml 怡宝饮用纯净水价格确定为每瓶 3 元是否违反价格法相关规定，是否损害了李某全消费者权益的问题。消费者权益保护法与反垄断法（2008 年施行，下同）均系维护社会经济秩序，促进社会主义市场经济健康发展的重要法律，对于规范市场主体的经营行为，维护消费者利益和社会公共利益，促进高质量发展等发挥着重要作用。但是，消费者权益保护法和反垄断法的立法目的并不相同。消费者权益保护法作为保护市场交易中处于弱势地位的消费者的法律，立法目的主要在于对消费者提供特殊保护。反垄断法的立法目的主要在于维护市场竞争机制，有效配置资源，保护和促进竞争。反垄断法虽然不排除对消费者直接和具体的保护，但其目的侧重于维护统一、开放、竞争、有序的市场秩序，从而最终使消费者获得福利。可见，反垄断法对消费者的保护着眼于竞争行为是否损害了保障消费者福利的竞争机制，既不以某一行为是否为消费者满意作为判断标准，也不刻意保护某一具体消费者的利益。因此，如果个别消费者认为因经营者销售相关商品违反价格法等相关规定，损害了其消费者权益，原则上应当依据消费者权益保护法等法律及时有效保护自己的权益。本案中，李某全认为湘品堂公司等五被诉经营者将长沙南站二层候车厅所售 555ml 怡宝饮用纯净水价格确定为每瓶 3 元违反价格法相关规定，损害了其作为普通消费者的合法权益，其应当依据消费者权益保护法主张权利。本案系垄断纠纷，湘品堂公司等五被诉经营者是否违反消费者权益保护法对于本案审理并无直接关联性，不再予以评述。

According to the SPC, the focus of the case is whether the five accused operators have violated the price law by selling C' estbon purified drinking water at CNY 3 per (555 ml) bottle at the second-floor waiting hall of the Railway Station and whether it has harmed the rights and interests of Li as a consumer. The Law on the Protection of Consumer Rights and Interests and the Anti-monopoly Law (implemented in 2008) are important laws for maintaining social and economic order and promoting the healthy development of the socialist market economy. They play an important role in regulating market players, protecting the interests of consumers and public interests, and promoting high-quality development. However, the Law on the Protection of Consumer Rights and Interests and the Anti-monopoly Law serve different purposes. The former serves to protect consumers who are in a vulnerable position in market transactions; and the latter serves to maintain the market competition mechanism, allocate resources effectively, and protect and promote competi-

tion. Although the Anti-monopoly Law does not exclude the direct and specific protection of consumers, it mainly focuses on maintaining a unified, open, competitive, and orderly market order, so as to ultimately benefit the consumers. So in terms of protecting consumers, the Anti-monopoly Law will see if a competitive behavior has damaged the competition mechanism that protects the benefit of consumers; it will not consider if a certain behavior has satisfied consumers, nor will it deliberately protect the interests of a specific consumer. Therefore, if a consumer believes that the operator's sale of a commodity has violated the Price Law and other relevant provisions and damaged their rights and interests, they should promptly and effectively protect their rights and interests in accordance with laws such as the Law on the Protection of Consumer Rights and Interests. In this case, Li believes that the accused five operators have violated the relevant provisions of the price law and damaged his legitimate rights and interests as a consumer by selling the water at CNY 3 per (555 ml) bottle at the Railway Station, then he should claim in accordance with the Law on the Protection of Consumer Rights and Interests. This case is about monopoly, and whether the accused five operators have violated the Law on the Protection of Consumer Rights and Interests has no direct relevance to the trial of this case, so there will be no comment.

74. 反垄断法罚款规定中“上一年度销售额”中“上一年度”的确定

Definition of “preceding year” as a term in“sales volume of the preceding year” under the provisions for fines in Anti-monopoly Law

【裁判要旨】

[Judgment Digest]

反垄断法罚款规定中“上一年度销售额”中的“上一年度”，通常指反垄断执法机构启动调查时的上一个会计年度；垄断行为在启动调查时已经停止的，“上一年度”则通常为垄断行为停止时的上一个会计年度；如果垄断行为实施后于当年内停止，则垄断行为实施的会计年度可以作为该“上一年度”。即，原则上“上一年度”应当确定为与作出处罚时在时间上最接近、事实上最关联的违法行为存在年度。

The term “preceding year” in the “sales in the preceding year” as stated in the provisions for fines in the Anti-monopoly Law usually refers to the fiscal year preceding to the date on which the Anti-monopoly Law enforcement agency initiates its investigation. If the monopoly act has halted before such investigation is initiated, the term “preceding year” usually refers to the fiscal year preceding to date on which the monopoly act ceases. If the monopoly act ceases within the same year as it starts, the fiscal year within which the monopoly act is conducted can be deemed as the “preceding year”. In principle, the “preceding year” shall refer to the year in which the closest and most relevant illegal act exists at the time of imposing the penalty.

【关键词】

[Keywords]

垄断协议　行政处罚　上一年度销售额

Monopoly agreement; administrative penalty; sales of previous year

【案号】

[Case Number]

(2022) 最高法知行终 29 号

(2022) SPC IP Admin. Final 29

【裁判意见】

[Judge's Opinion]

在上诉人茂名市电白区建科混凝土有限公司与被上诉人广东省市场监督管理局反垄断行政处罚案中，最高人民法院指出，2008 年施行的反垄断法第四十六条第一款规定："经营者违反本法规定，达成并实施垄断协议的，由反垄断执法机构责令停止违法行为，没收违法所得，并处上一年度销售额百分之一以上百分之十以下的罚款"。"上一年度销售额"是计算罚款的基数，其中"上一年度"通常指启动调查时的上一个会计年度；对于垄断行为在反垄断执法机构启动调查时已经停止的，"上一年度"则通常为垄断行为停止时的上一个会计年度；如果垄断行为实施后于当年内停止，则垄断行为实施的会计年度也可以作为反垄断法第四十六条第一款规定"上一年度销售额"中"上一年度"，即原则上"上一年度"应确定为与作出处罚时在时间上最接近、事实上最关联的违法行为存在年度。执法实践中，之所以绝大多数垄断案件处罚所采纳的"上一年度"是立案调查的上一年度，是因为一旦反垄断执法机构启动立案调查，有关经营者一般会停止涉嫌垄断行为，以立案调查为基准确定"上一年度"主要目的是选择距离垄断行为较近的年度，以经营者在该年度的销售额为基数计算罚款，由此体现行政处罚对垄断行为的震慑性。

In the anti – monopoly administrative penalty case of the Appellant, Jianke Concrete Co., Ltd., in Dianbai District, Maoming, v. the Appellee, Guangdong Market Supervision Administration, the Supreme People's Court cites Article 46 (1) of the Anti–monopoly Law, implemented in 2008, which stipulates that "where a business operator, in violation of the provisions of this law, reaches and performs a monopoly agreement, the anti–monopoly law enforcement agency shall order the operator to cease its illegal act, confiscate its illegal income, and impose a fine of not less than one percent but not more than ten percent of the previous year's sales. ""Previous year's sales" is the basis for calculating the penalty, and the "Previous year" usually means the previous fiscal year at the time of initiation of the investigation. Where the monopoly has ceased at the time when the anti–monopoly law enforcement agency starts the investigation, the "Previous year" is usually the previous fiscal year when the monopoly ceases; where the monopoly ceases within the year after the implementation of it, the fiscal year in which the monopoly is implemented may be regarded as the "Previous year" as stipulated in Article 46 (1) of the Anti–Monopoly Law. In principle, the "Previous year" shall be determined as the year which is closest in time and most related in fact to the illegal conduct when the penalty is imposed. In law enforcement practice, most monopoly cases will see the "Previous year" as the previous year of investigation because once the anti–monopoly law enforcement agency starts the investigation, the operator will usually cease the suspected monopoly. The aim of seeing "Previous year" based on the investigation is to choose the year closer to the monopoly and to calculate the penalty based on the sales of the operator in the year, which may increase the deterrent effect of administrative penalty on monopoly.

本案中，涉案垄断行为发生于 2016 年且在 2016 年底已经停止，原

广东省发改委反垄断局于 2017 年 7 月启动对涉案垄断行为的调查。如果以反垄断执法机构启动调查时的上一个会计年度计算，本案应以 2016 年销售额计算罚款并作出处罚。而且，本案中以 2016 年销售额作为计算罚款的基准，更接近违法行为发生时涉案企业的实际经营情况，与执法实践中通常以垄断行为停止时的上一个会计年度来计算经营者销售额的基本精神保持一致，也同样符合行政处罚法第四条第二款及反垄断法第四十九条的规定所体现的过罚相当原则。广东省市场监督管理局作出被诉处罚决定时，考虑了建科公司等 16 家企业具有积极配合调查、违法行为持续时间短、对市场竞争损害程度较轻、影响范围较小等因素，因而处以上一年度销售额 1%的罚款处罚，而仅对化州大道公司等 3 家牵头企业处以 2%的罚款处罚，以达到警示效果。被诉处罚决定与涉案企业违法行为的事实、性质、情节以及社会危害程度相适应，符合过罚相当原则。广东省市场监督管理局在本案中以建科公司 2016 年销售额为基数按 1%的比例计算罚款并作出处罚，并无不当。

In this case, the monopoly involved occurred in 2016 and ceased at the end of 2016; and the former Anti-monopoly Bureau of the Guangdong Development and Reform Commission launched an investigation into the monopoly involved in July 2017. If the calculation is based on the previous fiscal year when the investigation is started, the penalty in this case should then be calculated on the basis of sales in 2016. Moreover, in this case, the sales volume in 2016 was used as the basis for calculating fines, which is closer to the actual operating status of the enterprise involved when the illegal act occurred, consistent with the law enforcement practice in which the sales of an operator are calculated based on the previous fiscal year when the monopoly ceases, and in compliance with Article 4 (2) of the Administrative Penalty Law of the People's Republic of China and Article 49 of the Anti-Monopoly Law on appropriate punishment. In making the penalty decision, given that Jianke and the 15 other companies were cooperative in the investigation and the illegal behavior had not lasted long, had not caused so much damage to market competition, and had not influenced a very large scope, the Guangdong Market Supervision Administration decided to impose a fine of 1% of the sales of the previous year, and a fine of 2% on the three leading companies only, including Huazhou Dadao, so as to warn the market players. The penalty decision involved is made based on the fact, nature, and circumstance of the illegal act of the companies involved and the harm it has caused to society, and conforms to the principle of appropriate punishment. Therefore, the Guangdong Market Supervision Administration is justified in calculating a fine of 1% of Jianke's sales in 2016 and imposing it as such.

六、诉讼程序
Ⅵ. Proceedings

75. 诉讼过程中对专门性问题是否需要进行鉴定的考量 Consideration on whether to authenticate specialized matters in litigation

【裁判要旨】

[Judgment Digest]

诉讼过程中当事人申请司法鉴定并不必然启动鉴定程序，人民法院仍应当根据对相关事实的认定需要作出是否启动鉴定程序的决定。对此一般应当着重从以下四方面予以审查：一是关联性，即申请鉴定的事项与案件有待查明的事实是否具有关联；二是必要性，即是否必须通过特殊技术手段或者专门方法才能查明相应的专门性问题，是否已经通过其他的举证、质证手段仍然对专门性问题无法查明；三是可行性，即对于待鉴定的专门性问题，是否有较为权威的鉴定方法和相应有资质的鉴定人，是否有明确充分的鉴定材料；四是正当性，即鉴定申请的提出是否遵循了相应的民事诉讼规则，在启动鉴定之前是否已充分听取各方当事人的意见，以确保程序上的正当性。

In proceedings of litigation, an involved party's application for judicial authentication does not necessarily trigger the procedure on the same, in which case people's court shall decide whether to initiate such procedure based on the necessity of the relevant facts finding. Generally, considerations should be mainly given to the following four aspects. The first aspect is relevance. In other words, whether the matter to be authenticated is relevant to the facts finding for the case. The second aspect is necessity. In other words, whether people's court has to rely on special technical means or particular methods for ascertaining specialized matters, and whether the court is still unable to ascertain such matters after exhausting such other means as presenting evidence and cross-examining evidence. The third aspect is feasibility. In other words, whether there are relatively authoritative authentication methods, qualified authentication institute plus specific and sufficient materials for authentication. The fourth aspect is due process. In other words, whether the application for authentication complies with the corresponding civil procedure rules and whether all the involved parties' views have been fully heard before initiation of the judicial authentication procedure, so as to ensure due process.

【关键词】

[Keywords]

技术秘密　侵权　专门性问题　司法鉴定

Technical secrets; infringement; specialized issues; judicial authentication

【案号】

[Case Number]

(2022) 最高法知民终 541 号

(2022) SPC IP Civil Final 541

【裁判意见】

[Judge's Opinion]

在上诉人四川金象赛瑞化工股份有限公司与上诉人山东华鲁恒升化

工股份有限公司、宁波厚承管理咨询有限公司、宁波安泰环境化工工程设计有限公司、尹某大侵害技术秘密纠纷案中，最高人民法院指出，根据 2021 年修正的民事诉讼法第六十七条第一款的规定，当事人对自己提出的主张，有责任提供证据。司法鉴定是指在诉讼活动中鉴定人运用科学技术或者专门知识对诉讼涉及的专门性问题进行鉴别和判断并提供鉴定意见的活动。而鉴定意见属于民事诉讼证据的一种，需经各方当事人质证后，再由人民法院决定是否予以采纳。当事人申请鉴定并不必然启动鉴定程序，人民法院仍需根据对相关事实的认定需要作出是否启动鉴定程序的决定。鉴定程序启动与否的关键在于法官在审理案件过程中对相关专门性问题缺乏判断认定能力，而需要委托相关鉴定机构通过科学的方法和手段来查明该专门性问题的相关事实。对于当事人提出的鉴定申请，既要避免当事人滥用申请鉴定的权利，也要避免不当剥夺其相关的诉讼权利，一般应着重从以下四方面予以审查：一是关联性，申请鉴定的事项与案件有待查明的事实是否具有关联；二是必要性，即是否必须通过特殊技术手段或者专门方法才能确定相应的专门性问题，是否已经通过其他的举证、质证手段仍然对专门性问题无法查明；三是可行性，对于待鉴定的专门性问题，是否有较为权威的鉴定方法和相应有资质的鉴定机构，是否有明确充分的鉴定材料；四是正当性，鉴定申请的提出是否遵循了相应的民事诉讼规则，在启动鉴定之前是否已充分听取各方当事人的意见，以确保程序上的正当性。

In the dispute over infringement of technical secrets between the Appellant, Sichuan Golden-Elephant Sincerity Chemical Co., Ltd., and the Appellees, Shandong Hualu-Hengsheng Chemical Co., Ltd., Ningbo Houcheng Management Consulting Co., Ltd., Ningbo AT&M Environmental & Chemical Engineering Design Co., Ltd., and Yin, the Supreme People's Court points out that according to Article 67 (1) of the Civil Procedure Law, amended in 2021, the parties involved have the duty to provide evidence for their claims. Judicial authentication refers to the activities in which the expert uses science and technology or specialized knowledge to identify and judge the specialized issues involved in litigation and provides expert opinion. The expert opinion is a kind of evidence in civil proceedings, which needs to be cross-examined by the parties involved before the people's court decides to accept it or not. A party's request for judicial authentication does not necessarily initiate the authentication procedure; the people's court still needs to decide whether to start the procedure according to the facts ascertained. The authentication procedure will be initiated when the judge is incapable of deciding the specialized issues in the process of trial and has to entrust an authentication institution to find out the truth about the specialized issues through scientific methods and means. As for the request for judicial authentication, four things should be considered so that the parties will not abuse their right to it, nor will they be deprived of relevant litigation rights: The first aspect is relevance. In other words, whether the matter to be authenticated is relevant to the facts finding for the case. The second aspect is necessity. In other words, whether people's court has to rely on special technical means or particular methods for ascertaining specialized matters, and whether the court is still unable to ascertain such matters after exhausting such other means as presenting evidence and cross-examining evidence. The third aspect is feasibility. In other words, whether there are relatively authoritative authentication methods, qualified authentication institute plus specific and sufficient materials for authentication. The fourth aspect is due process. In other words, whether the application for authentication complies with the corresponding civil procedure rules and whether all the involved parties' views have been fully heard before initiation of the judicial authentication procedure, so as to ensure due process.

（1）关于华鲁恒升公司提出的技术秘密鉴定申请

(1) About Hualu-Hengsheng's request for authentication of technical secret

分别于2020年、2022年修正的《最高人民法院关于适用〈中华人民共和国民事诉讼法〉的解释》第一百二十一条第一款均规定："当事人申请鉴定，可以在举证期限届满前提出。申请鉴定的事项与待证事实无关联，或者对证明待证事实无意义的，人民法院不予准许。"本案于2017年8月28日由原审法院立案，金象赛瑞公司提交了其主张作为技术秘密保护的技术信息证据，至原审判决作出时止，在四年的审理过程中，原审法院分别于2019年2月18日至20日、2019年3月20日至22日、2020年1月14日至15日、2020年7月28日至29日、2021年3月2日至4日、2021年5月27日至28日、2021年9月22日至24日组织了七次庭前会议，组织各方当事人在签署保密协议的前提下进行举证、质证，并于2021年10月20日、21日开庭审理本案，在此期间原审法院亦多次询问华鲁恒升公司、宁波厚承公司是否查阅本案保密证据，但华鲁恒升公司均明确拒绝查阅金象赛瑞公司提交的保密证据并无故中途退出七次庭前会议及两次庭审。直至2021年9月28日，华鲁恒升公司向原审法院提出书面《司法鉴定申请书》，载明："鉴定事项：1. 原告主张作为商业秘密保护的技术信息是否不为公众所知悉；2. 原告主张作为商业秘密保护的技术信息是否具有经济性、实用性"，其提出该鉴定申请已明显超过举证期限。二审期间，在原审法院已经对涉案技术信息的秘密性、价值性作出认定的情况下，华鲁恒升公司虽然坚持提出鉴定申请，但是仍拒绝查阅金象赛瑞公司提交的载有其技术信息的保密证据或发表质证意见，也未就原审判决的有关认定提出有针对性的反驳意见。换言之，华鲁恒升公司因其自身原因，实质上已放弃了对金象赛瑞公司提交的载有金象赛瑞公司主张的技术信息的保密证据进行质证的诉讼权利，其在原审所提鉴定申请既无准许之必要，也因过于迟延提出而缺少鉴定申请提出的程序正当性。同理，二审法院对其二审提出的鉴定申请亦不予准许。

The first Paragraph of Article 121 of the *Interpretation of the Supreme People's Court on the Application of the Civil Procedure Law of the People's Republic of China*, which was amended in 2020 and 2022, stipulates that: "A party may request for judicial authentication before the expiration of the time limit for providing evidence. The people's court shall not allow it if it has no connection with or means nothing to the facts to be identified." The case was filed by the Court of First Instance on August 28, 2017, and Golden-Elephant Sincerity submitted evidence for claiming itself as protector of the technical secret involved. Before the original judgment was made, the Court of First Instance organized seven pre-trial conferences on February 18 to 20, 2019, March 20 to 22, 2019, January 14 to 15, 2020, July 28 to 29, 2020, March 2 to 4, 2021, May 27 to 28, 2021, and September 22 to 24, 2021, to have all parties concerned present and cross-examine evidence after signing a confidentiality agreement. The case was heard on October 20 and 21, 2021. During the period, the Court of First Instance asked more than once if Hualu-Hengsheng and Houcheng would like to check the confidential evidence of the case. Hualu-Hengsheng explicitly refused to check the confidential evidence submitted by Golden-Elephant Sincerity and withdrew without reason from the seven pre-trial conferences and the two hearings. On September 28, 2021, Hualu-Hengsheng submitted a written Request for Judicial Authentication to the Court of First Instance, which states: "Items for authentication: 1. If the technical information that the plaintiff claims to protect as a trade secret is not known to the public; 2. If the technical information that the plaintiff claims to protect as a trade secret is economical and practical." The request has obviously exceeded the time limit for presenting evidence. In the Second Instance,

with the determination of the confidentiality and value of the technical information involved by the Court of First Instance, Hualu-Hengsheng insisted on requesting for authentication, and still refused to check the confidential evidence submitted by Golden-Elephant Sincerity that contains its technical information or express cross-examination opinions, and it raised no objection to the relevant determination in the original judgment. In other words, due to its own reasons, Hualu-Hengsheng has in fact given up its right to cross-examine the confidential evidence submitted by Golden-Elephant Sincerity. There is no need to allow for its request in the First Instance; and it also lacks procedural legitimacy as the request is delayed. For the same reason, the Court of Second Instance refused to allow the request for judicial authentication.

（2）关于华鲁恒升公司、宁波厚承公司提出的对电脑操作痕迹的鉴定申请

(2) About Hualu-Hengsheng and Houcheng's request for authentication of computer operation trace

华鲁恒升公司、宁波厚承公司上诉均主张原审法院未准许其提出的此项鉴定申请，损害了其诉讼权利。原审期间，华鲁恒升公司、宁波厚承公司、宁波设计院公司申请对存储金象赛瑞公司原审证据 30 的笔记本电脑的操作痕迹进行鉴定。原审法院经审查认为，在案证据可以认定该证据是在正常业务活动中形成、传输和存储的电子数据，且与网易邮箱储存的电子数据互相印证，在没有反驳或相反证据的情况下，可以确认其真实性，故未准许鉴定申请。对此，二审法院认为，原审中金象赛瑞公司提供了存储有证据 30 电子图纸的载体，原审法院通过随机抽取对相应文件夹内的若干文档、逐一查看证据 30 中所有电子图纸的文档属性，并结合与在案其他证据的关联性已可确定其所记载的创建时间与修改时间的真实性。华鲁恒升公司、宁波厚承公司虽然对真实性提出异议但并未提供反驳证据，宁波厚承公司提出的可以通过修改操作系统时

间的方式来修改文档创建时间、修改时间的意见亦不足以推翻原审法院通过上述方式的验证对相关证据真实性所作的判定。因此，通过金象赛瑞公司的举证、组织现场勘验的方式已足以对该证据的真实性作出判断，在华鲁恒升公司、宁波厚承公司、宁波设计院公司未提供证据支持其质疑的情况下，并无启动鉴定程序之必要，故原审法院对该鉴定申请不予准许，并无不当。基于相同的理由，二审法院对华鲁恒升公司、宁波厚承公司二审再次提出的该项鉴定申请亦不予准许。

In their appeal, Hualu-Hengsheng and Houcheng both claimed that the Court of First Instance had damaged their litigation right by not allowing their request for judicial authentication. In the First Instance, Hualu-Hengsheng, Houcheng, and AT&M requested for authentication of the operation trace of the laptop computer that stored First Instance Evidence 30 of Golden-Elephant Sincerity. The Court of First Instance held that the evidence on the record could be identified as electronic data formed, transmitted, and stored in normal business activities, and it is verified with the electronic data stored in NetEase Mail. With no refutation or contrary evidence, its authenticity could be confirmed, so the court did not allow the request for authentication. In this regard, the Court of Second Instance held that in the First Instance, Golden-Elephant Sincerity provided the carrier that stored electronic drawings of Evidence 30, and the Court of First Instance could determine the authenticity of the creation time and modification time recorded by randomly selecting the files in the relevant folder and checking one by one the property of all electronic drawings in Evidence 30, and combining it with the correlation with other evidence on the record. Although Hualu-Hengsheng and Houcheng raised objection to the authenticity of the files, they did not provide refuting evidence. The proposal made by Houcheng that it is possible to change the file creation time and modification time by modifying the operating system time is

not enough to overturn the judgment made by the Court of First Instance on the authenticity of relevant evidence through verification mentioned above. Therefore, it is enough to decide the authenticity of the evidence through the evidence presented by Golden-Elephant Sincerity and the way of on-site inspection. As Hualu-Hengsheng, Houcheng, and AT&M did not provide evidence to support their doubts, there was no need to start the authentication procedure, so the Court of First Instance is justified in not approving the request. For the same reason, the Court of Second Instance refused to allow Hualu-Hengsheng and Houcheng's second request for the authentication.

（3）关于华鲁恒升公司、宁波厚承公司提出的对眉山市公安局扣押的笔记本电脑、调取的电子数据载体以及眉山中院保全的电子数据载体等进行痕迹鉴定的申请

(3) About Hualu-Hengsheng and Houcheng's request for authentication of the laptop computer seized and the electronic data carrier retrieved by Meishan Public Security Bureau and of the electronic data carrier preserved by Meishan Intermediate People's Court

原审中，经金象赛瑞公司申请，原审法院分别向眉山中院、眉山市公安局调取了（2016）川 14 民初 8 号案全部案卷材料及尹某大涉嫌犯侵犯商业秘密罪的侦查阶段部分案卷材料，其中包括了眉山市公安局扣押的笔记本电脑、眉山中院在宁波设计院公司保全的电子数据、眉山市公安局在宁波设计院公司调取的电子数据。上述证据材料均系相关部门依照法定程序调取或保全，华鲁恒升公司、宁波厚承公司主张上述证据材料被篡改、不具有真实性，但并未提供任何证据支持其提出的该质疑，未能对鉴定的必要性提供相应证据佐证，故二审法院对华鲁恒升公司、宁波厚承公司提出的上述鉴定申请不予准许。

In the First Instance, at the request of Golden-Elephant Sincerity, the court obtained from the Meishan Intermediate People's Court and the Meishan

Public Security Bureau all the files of (2016) Chuan 14 Min Chu Case No. 8 and some files of the investigation stage of Yin's suspected crime of violating business secrets, which include the laptop computer seized by the Meishan Public Security Bureau, the electronic data preserved by the Meishan Intermediate People's Court at AT&M, and the electronic data obtained by the Meishan Public Security Bureau at AT&M. The above evidence materials were obtained or preserved by relevant departments in accordance with legal procedures. Hualu-Hengsheng and Houcheng claimed that those materials had been tampered with and were not authentic, but they did not provide any evidence to support their claim, nor did they provide evidence for the necessity of identification. Therefore, the Court of Second Instance did not approve their request for judicial authentication of the materials.